3D AutoCAD 2007

One Step at a Time

Timothy Sean Sykes

Forager Publications
Spring, Texas
ForagerPub.com

Everyone involved in the publication of this text has used his or her best efforts in preparing it. These efforts include the development, research, and testing of the theories and programs to determine their effectiveness. The author and publisher make no warranty of any kind, expressed or implied, with regard to these programs or the documentation contained in this book. The author and publisher shall not be liable in any event for incidental or consequential damages in connection with, or arising out of, the furnishing, performance, or use of these programs.

ISBN 0-9778938-0-4 (ebook)

ISBN 0-9765888-8-9 (print)

Forager Publications

2043 Cherry Laurel

Spring, TX 77386

www.foragerpub.com

AUTHOR'S NOTES

Where to Find the Required Files (and Review Questions) for Using This Text:

All of the files required to complete the lessons in this text can be downloaded free of charge from this site:

http://www.uneedcad.com/2007/Files/

Select on the file called *3D2007Files.zip* and save it to your computer. (Windows XP will open a zipped file. If you need a zip utility, however, I suggest the free WinZip download at: http://www.winzip.com/. The evaluation version will do to get your files. You'll have to follow WinZip procedures to unzip the files.)

Once you've downloaded the zip file, follow these instructions to unzip it with Windows XP.

1. Double-click on the file. Windows XP will display a window with the Step folder listed.

2. Right click on the Step folder and select **Copy** from the menu that appears.

3. Using Windows Explorer, navigate to the C-drive.

4. Select **Paste** from the Edit pull down menu.

To get the review questions, go to the website indicated at the end of each lesson. A PDF file will open in your Internet browser. These files are fully printable, or you can save them to your disk if you wish. The last page of each file contains the answers to the questions in that file.

eBook Printing

We're trying an experiment with this release – eBook readers may print one copy of the text. *Be cautious how you print – you are limited to the number of pages of the text, one time. If you print something twice, you won't be able to print something else!*

eBook Graphics & The Best Resolution for Reading This Text:

A tremendous amount of effort went into creating the thousands of graphics associated with this text. We worked hard to make the right compromises between image quality and file size. Hopefully, we achieved our goal.

You may notice that I took some occasional liberties in terms of cropping graphics to get them to fit better on the page. I ask your indulgence for these indiscretions – I believe I managed to avoid obscuring the purpose of the dialog boxes in question.

On my laptop (a Compaq with a widescreen), I find it best to view the final file at a page size of 100% in Adobe Reader 6.0. This proves adequate for both text and image viewing. If I'm just viewing the text, I can opt for a *page width* viewing size without sacrificing anything.

On my 17" desktop monitor (as well the 15" monitor on the family computer), I can view the file at anywhere from 100% to 150% and the quality of both text and graphics is quite pleasing.

Regardless of the monitor, however, I still need my "readers" to see anything clearly. Ah, the trials of hitting 50 before my time! (Can you do that?)

Contacting the Author/Publisher:

Although we tried awfully hard to avoid errors, typos, and the occasional boo boos, I admit to complete fallibility. Should you find it necessary to let me know of my blunders, or to ask just about anything about the text – or even to make suggestions as to how to better the next edition, please feel free to contact me at: comments@foragerpub.com. I can't promise a fast response (although I'm usually pretty good about answering my email), but I can promise to read (almost) everything that comes my way.

An after thought for that email address: this particular address suffers heavy spam traffic. As a result, it is severely filtered. For best results: don't try to contact me from a hotmail or yahoo address, don't use html, don't attach anything, and don't include RE or FW in the header.

Frequently Asked Questions (and responses to less-frequently-asked but more annoying questions):

I went to the web site but got a Page cannot be found *error. What gives?*

This is the most common complaint I get. The fix is simple: make sure you capitalize the "Files" in the address. The web is case-sensitive.

Why don't my graphics work? (I can't see my grips when I'm using certain visual styles.)

Turn your hardware accelerator off – enter **3dconfig** at the command line, pick the **Manual Tune** button, and remove the check next to **Enable hardware acceleration** in the **Hardware settings** frame.

Hardware acceleration makes a really good graphic, but it can interfere with the function of some basic stuff like viewing grips.

Contents

Chapter 7: Solid Modeling Creation Tools - Basics

Chapter 8: Composite Solids

Chapter 9: Editing 3D Solids

Chapter 10: Three-Dimensional Blocks & Three-Dimensional Plotting Tools

Chapter 11: Presentation Tools

Appendices

Lesson 1

Following this lesson, you will:

✓ *Know how to maneuver in three-dimensional space*

- o *Understand the **VPoint** command*
- o *Understand the Right-Hand Rule*
- o *Know how to use the **Plan** command*

✓ *Know how to draw simple three-dimensional objects*

- o *Know how to use **Elevation** and **Thickness** in your drawings*

✓ *Know some of the basic tricks used to view a three-dimensional drawing*

✓ *Know how to use Visual Styles*

"Z" Basics

Thanks, Mr. Woopie! You're the greatest.

Tennessee Tuxedo

Does anyone not remember Mr. Woopie's coveted 3D BB? How many times did he pull that tiny block from his closet, stretch it into a full-size blackboard, and help Tennessee Tuxedo devise yet another wonderful scheme?

Who would have thought – way back in those simple cartoon days – that one day you'd be learning to use your very own 3D BB?!

You're about to go where no board draftsman has gone before. You are about to enter Z-Space. (Hear that cool science fiction music playing in the background? Keep your eyes open for Dr. Who.) Z-Space is that area defined by the Z-axis. Remember the X- and Y-axes? They travel left to right and top to bottom on a sheet of paper (or drafting board). The Z-axis rises and falls into the space above and below the paper. It takes all three axes to create a three-dimensional object. (Later in this text, you'll even see where AutoCAD has taken its first tentative steps into that fourth dimension of which Einstein spoke ... that's right, AutoCAD has finally given you the rudiments of animation! (Well, walk-thru capability anyway.) We'll have to leave those other dimensions Stephen Hawking explains so well (at least to other PHDs) for a later time. But for now, three dimensions are quite enough to keep me confused.)

1.1	The 3D Look – AutoCAD's 3D Modeling Workspace

You'll notice when opening AutoCAD 2007 for the first time that you're facing a whole new world. For experienced AutoCAD users (one of which you must be or you wouldn't be reading a 3D text!), this can be unnerving. It's the first time since we went to a Windows format that the user interface has changed!

Your screen doesn't look any different? That's easily fixed. Enter this command sequence:

Command: *wscurrent*

Enter new value for WSCURRENT <"AutoCAD Classic">: *3D Modeling*

AutoCAD normally defaults to the **3D Modeling** workspace, but if someone has been working on 2-dimensional drawings, yours may have been reset to **AutoCAD Classic**. We'll work in the **3D Modeling** workspace for this text.

We'll spend the next few minutes getting familiar with some of the changes.

First, you notice the three-dimensional layout of the work area (Figure 1.001).

You have a fancier grid to use now – but you can still toggle it on or off with the F7 key or ^g. In Z-space, you may find it more helpful to leave it on.

Your crosshairs now include an up/down line to guide you. Use these as you will the 3D UCS Icon to help keep yourself oriented within the drawing. Remember: Red = East/West, Green = North/South, and Blue = Up/Down. You'll also benefit from the Right-Hand Rule.

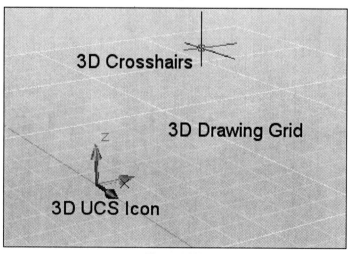

Figure 1.001

1.1.1	The UCS Icon and the Right-Hand Rule

Before entering Z-Space (the third dimension), you must learn how to keep your bearings. That is, you must learn to tell up from down, top from bottom, and left from right, regardless of your orientation within the drawing (feel like an astronaut?). It's not as easy as it sounds. Place your hand over Figure 1.003 and look carefully at Figure 1.002. Are you looking at the top or bottom of the object? Now look at Figure 1.003. How did you do?

I've removed the hidden lines in Figure 1.002 (more on how I did that in Section 1.4.1). However, it isn't always practical to do that, so AutoCAD has provided a method to determine your orientation at any time and at any place in the drawing. We'll use the UCS icon (Figure 1.003).

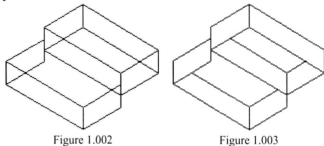

Figure 1.002   Figure 1.003

1.1.1a	The UCS Icon

In our basic text, I told you how to turn off the UCS icon. In two-dimensional space, it has little use. However, to operate in three-dimensional space, you must activate the UCS icon or risk being forever lost. (The icon acts like a lighthouse on a dark and stormy night – giving the mariner a reference point from which to navigate.) Use the *UCSIcon* command to control the UCS icon. It works like this:

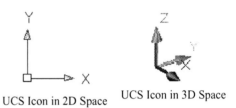

UCS Icon in 2D Space   UCS Icon in 3D Space

> **Command:** *ucsicon*
> **Enter an option [ON/OFF/All/Noorigin/ORigin/Properties] <ON>:**

The simple command provides options that will prove indispensable in a three-dimensional drawing:

- The **ON/OFF** options are self-explanatory. They turn the icon **On** or **Off**. They work only in the current viewport in Model Space or on the Paper Space icon in Paper Space.
- The **All** option prompts as follows:
  > **Enter an option [ON/OFF/Noorigin/ORigin/Properties] <OFF>:**

  These options perform the same function as the first tier of options, but operate on *all* the viewports.
- The UCS icon remains in the lower-left part of the graphics screen by default. Normal display manipulations (zooms and pans) won't affect it.

  With the **ORigin** option, however, you can attach the UCS icon to the 0,0,0 coordinate where it will remain regardless of the display (as long as the 0,0,0 coordinate is on the screen). This will provide a fixed point in space (a lighthouse) from which you can navigate. If the 0,0,0 coordinate leaves the graphics area through zooming or panning, the UCS icon returns to the lower-left corner of the screen.
- **Noorigin** disables the **ORigin** setting.
- The **Properties** option calls the UCS icon dialog box shown in Figure 1.004 (next page). Here you can set up the icon's physical properties to suit your preferences.
  - In the **UCS icon style** frame, you can tell AutoCAD to use a two-dimensional (**2D**) or three-dimensional (**3D**) icon. AutoCAD will use the 3D icon by default. (We used the

2D icon in earlier releases of AutoCAD. It's considerably more complicated to understand, so we'll welcome the 3D icon and ignore its honorable ancestor.)

You can use conical pointers at the ends of the icon arrows (the default setting) or remove them in favor of simple arrowheads by removing the check next to **Cone**. You can also control the **Line width** of the icon using the selection box in the lower right corner of the frame.

o The **UCS icon size** frame presents two tools – a text box and a slider bar – which allow you to control the size of the icon. The default works well, but some operators prefer something a bit smaller and less obtrusive. Three-dimensional novices might prefer something larger until they become accustomed to Z-Space.

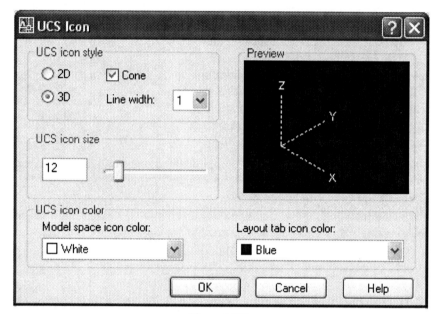

Figure 1.004

o The UCS icon color frame allows you more control over the color of the icon. Most people leave this at its default, although an occasional change in color does tend to relieve the monotony.

Let's experiment a bit with the UCS icon.

> You can access some of the options of the *UCSIcon* command using the View pull-down menu. Follow this path:
>
> *View – Display – UCS Icon – [option]*

Do This: 1.1.1.1	**Manipulating the UCS Icon**

I. Open the *ucs practice.dwg* file in the C:\Steps3D\Lesson01 folder. The drawing looks like Figure 1.005. (Don't let the funny angle of the crosshairs or UCS icon bother you – you're viewing the model from an angle in Z-Space. More on this setup in Section 1.2.)

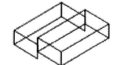

Figure 1.005

II. Pan to center the object on the screen.

III. Follow these steps.

1. Enter the *UCSIcon* command. [Note: There are two UCS toolbars but neither will help in this exercise. We'll look at those tools in our next lesson.]

Command: *ucsicon*

2. Use the **ORigin** option ORigin (enter *or* at the prompt or select **ORigin** from the cursor menu).

      Enter an option [ON/OFF/All/ Noorigin/ORigin/Properties] <ON>: *or*

Notice that the icon moves to the **0,0,0** coordinate.

3. Now disable the **ORigin** option Noorigin as indicated.

      Command: *ucsicon*

      Enter an option [ON/OFF/All/ Noorigin/ORigin/Properties] <ON>: *n*

The icon returns to the lower-left quadrant of the screen.

4. Use the *View* command to change the view to **negative z space** (already created for you – look under **Model Views**).

      Command: *v*

The view changes to that shown. Notice the UCS icon.

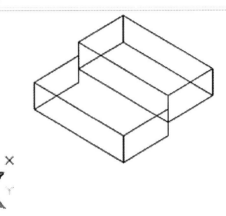

5. Use the *Vports* command to set up **Four: Equal** viewports. Notice (below) that each viewport has a UCS icon.

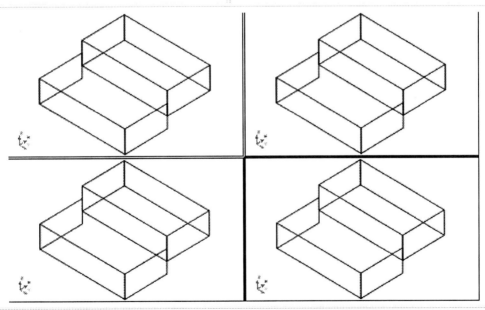

6. Use the *UCSIcon* command to turn **OFF** the icon 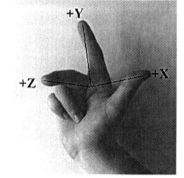. Notice that only the icon in the currently active viewport (lower right) disappears.

> **Command:** *ucsicon*
>
> **Enter an option [ON/OFF/All/ Noorigin/ ORigin/Properties] <ON>:** *OFF*

7. Now use the *UCSIcon* command to turn **OFF** the icon in **All** the viewports.

> **Command:** *[enter]*
>
> **Enter an option [ON/OFF/All/Noorigin/ORigin/Properties] <OFF>:** *a*
>
> **Enter an option [ON/OFF/Noorigin/ORigin/Properties] <OFF>:** *off*

8. Save and exit the drawing.

> **Command:** *qsave*

These simple tricks to manipulate and read the UCS icon will become second nature with experience. But there is another tool you can use to ease the learning curve – the Right-Hand Rule.

1.1.1b	The Right-Hand Rule

The Right-Hand Rule provides another means of navigating Z-space. It works very much like the UCS icon but is a bit more "handy." It works like this (refer to Figure 1.006):

1. Make a fist with your right hand.
2. Extend the index finger upward (no no – the *index* finger!).
3. Extend the thumb at a right angle to the index finger.
4. Extend the middle finger at a right angle to the index finger (pointing outward).

How's that for feeling really awkward?

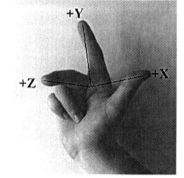

Figure 1.006

Each finger serves a purpose; each indicates the positive direction of one of the XYZ axes as indicated in the picture. See how it correlates with the UCS icon? Using the right hand in this fashion, you'll always be able to determine the third axis if you know the other two. Simply orient your right hand with the appropriate fingers pointing along the known axes and the location of the unknown axis becomes clear!

1.1.2	The Dashboard

Did you notice the new screen contains none (that's right! – *0*) toolbars!? Did you panic and seriously consider just going back to the drawing board? (It was *so* much simpler!)

Well, for those of you who made it this far despite the terror, take heart. AutoCAD is introducing a new tool called the *Dashboard* (Figure 1.008 – next page), which you'll use in place of the toolbars. It makes use of the best aspects of both tool palettes and toolbars. When you learn to use it correctly, it can even free up a lot of the space the toolbars use to occupy (even that place in your heart!).

We'll use the dashboard throughout this text, and I'll explain more as we go, but let's take a quick look at it now.

The first thing I'd recommend would be to take advantage of the dashboard's ability to hide (just as the tool palettes can hide). If yours is docked, pick the dash on the left side of the top (Figure

Figure 1.007

1.007). This frees the dashboard so that you can anchor it to the side of your screen as you would a palette. Be sure you put a check next to **Auto-Hide** on the menu that pops up when you pick the **Properties** button at the bottom of the title bar. Now look at all the screen area you have to work in!

- The dashboard contains six *control panels* by default. (A seventh – the 2D Draw Control Panel was too limited to discuss the dashboard in the 2D text. You're just as well off not displaying it.) Selecting the symbol in the upper left corner of the control panel tells AutoCAD to expand the panel to display more tools. Additionally, AutoCAD will open a tool palette specific to that panel with tools appropriate to what you're doing. I recommend docking the dashboard on one side of your screen and the tool palettes on the other to avoid confusion. Then again, others dock them both to the same side to avoid having to jump back and forth. It's up to you. Let's take a quick look. Refer to the figures below. (We'll look at specific tools over the course of this text.)

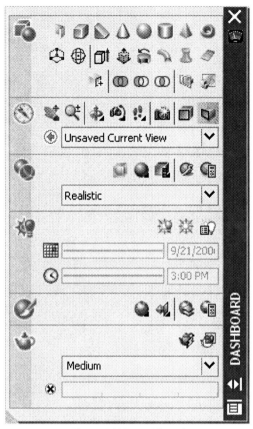

Figure 1.008: Dashboard

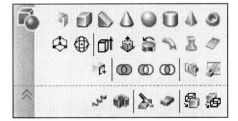

3D Make Control Panel

The 3D Make tool palettes contain these palettes: Draw, Modify, and Modeling. You're familiar with Draw and Modify from your basic studies. Modeling contains tools for creating and manipulating 3-dimensional objects.

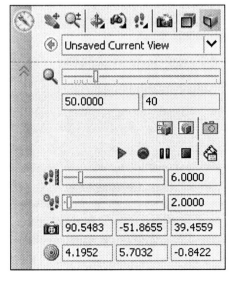

3D Navigate Control Panel

This panel offers some of your more familiar tools – *Zoom* and *Pan* – as well as some new ones for your 3D work. You'll also find a convenient selection box for views and viewports.

AutoCAD dedicates most of this panel to its new walk thru tools. We'll look at those in more detail in Lesson 11.

The 3D Navigate control panel opens a Camera tool palette which will come in handy when we discuss the walk thru tools later.

Visual Styles Control Panel

Here AutoCAD has placed its display tools. The upper control box contains a list of predefined visual styles. We'll discuss visual styles later in this lesson.

AutoCAD also provides a Visual Styles tool palette when you select this control panel. This particular tool palette isn't as useful as the control panel.

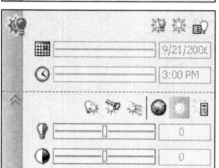

Light Control Panel

We'll tackle this one in Lesson 11 as well. Here you'll find tools and a tool palette to help you define lighting for your renderings.

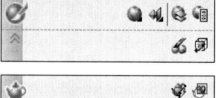

Materials Control Panel

We'll discuss materials and how to assign them to your objects prior to rendering in Lesson 11. Man, that's going to be a busy lesson!

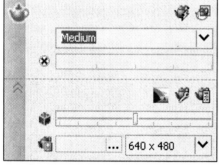

Render Control Panel

Another Lesson 11 tool – Rendering is the coup de grace in the 3D world. It's where you take a drawing and make it look like a photograph! You'll find the tools you'll need for that one the Render control panel.

If you still wish to use toolbars, AutoCAD provides quite a few of those, too, to help you with your 3D work. But the concentration of tools (and for future releases) will focus on the dashboard and tool palettes.

1.2 Maneuvering Through Z-Space with the *VPoint* Command

Okay. Now you know how to determine your orientation in Z-Space, but how do you reorient the model itself? In other words, how do you turn the model this way and that in order to work on all sides of it?

Not to worry; AutoCAD has provided a simple but powerful tool to help you – the *VPoint* command.

It might help your understanding if I begin by telling you that the model will not actually move or rotate. Using the *VPoint* command, the model holds still while you change position.

Let's use an airplane as an example. The airplane is a three-dimensional object (it has length, width, and height or thickness). To draw the top of the airplane, we'll climb into a helicopter and hover above it for a better view. To draw the front, we must fly to the front of the airplane. Side and bottom views will also require us to fly to a better vantage point.

AutoCAD's helicopter is the *VPoint* command (perhaps better defined as *Vantage* Point).

There are three approaches to using the *VPoint* command: coordinate input, compass, and dialog box. Let's look at each.

1.2.1	Using Coordinates to Assign a Viewpoint

The *VPoint* command prompt looks like this:

> **Command:** *vpoint* (or *–vp*)
>
> **Current view direction: VIEWDIR=1.0000,-1.0000,-1.0000**
>
> **Specify a view point or [Rotate] <display compass and tripod>:** *[enter a coordinate]*

- The default response to this prompt requires you to enter the coordinates from which you wish to view the model. Does that sound simple? Only if you know the coordinates, you say? Well, it's actually easier than that! AutoCAD won't read the XYZ coordinates entered as actual coordinates but rather as a ratio. That is (keeping it simple), a coordinate of 1,-1,1 tells AutoCAD that you wish to stand – in relation to the model – a step to the right (+1 on the X-axis), back a step (-1 on the Y-axis), and up a step (+1 on the Z-axis).

> The default viewpoint two-dimensional drawings is **0,0,1**. This means that you view the drawing from above (+1 on the Z-axis). Draftsmen generally refer to this as the *Plan* view.

Remembering the simple ratio approach, what do you think a coordinate of 4,-2,1 will mean?[*]

> When the *absolute* value of all three axis entries is the same (as in 1,1,1 or 1,-1,1), you have an isometric view of the drawing. (*Iso* means one – you're using the same absolute *value* on each axis).
>
> When only two of the absolute values are the same (as in 2,2,1 or –2,2,1), you have a *dimetric* view. (*Di* means two.)
>
> What do you suppose you have when all three of the absolute values are different? Of course, it's a *trimetric* view.

Why the ratio approach? When you change your vantage or viewpoint (your *VPoint*), AutoCAD will automatically zoom to the drawing's extents (move as close as possible while showing you everything on the model)!

- The **Rotate** option of the *VPoint* command allows you to specify your vantage point by the angle at which you wish to see the model. The prompts look like this:

> **Command:** *vpoint*
>
> **Current view direction: VIEWDIR=0.0000,-1.0000,0.0000**
>
> **Specify a view point or [Rotate] <display compass and tripod>:** *r [tell AutoCAD you wish to use the Rotate option]*

---

[*] It means: I want to stand twice as far to the right as I'm standing back, and twice as far back as I'm standing above the model.

Enter angle in XY plane from X axis: *[indicate the two-dimensional angle (the angle along the ground) at which you wish to see the model]*

Enter angle from XY plane: *[indicate the three-dimensional angle (the upward angle – like the angle of the sun in the sky) at which you wish to see the model]*

This will become clearer in our next exercise.

> You already know that a plan view is achieved when the VPoint coordinates are 0,0,1. These coordinates allow you to view the model from a step up (+Z). What do you suppose happens when you set the coordinates to 1,0,0 or 0,-1,0?
>
> These coordinates provide elevations of the model – 1,0,0 provides a right elevation (a step to the right or +X) and 0,-1,0 provides a front elevation (a step back or –Y). Which coordinates would provide a back or left elevation?**

We'll look at the compass and tripod in Section 1.2.2, but first let's try the coordinate approach to the *VPoint* command.

> You can access several preset viewpoints using buttons on the View toolbar or by selecting the view from the View pull-down menu. Follow this path:
>
> *View – 3D Views – [selection]*

Do This: 1.2.1.1	**The Coordinate Approach to Setting the Viewpoint**

    I.   Open the *VPoint practice.dwg* file in the C:\Steps3D\Lesson01 folder. The drawing looks like Figure 1.008. It's currently in the plan view

    II.   Follow these steps.

Figure 1.008

1.2.1.1: THE COORDINATE APPROACH

1. Enter the *VPoint* command.

    Command: *-vp*

2. AutoCAD tells you the current coordinate setting and prompts you to either **Specify a view point** or to **Rotate**. Let's use the first option. Tell AutoCAD to move to the right, back, and up as indicated (the SE Isometric View).

    Command: *-vp*

    Current view direction: VIEWDIR=0.0000,0.0000,1.0000

    Specify a view point or [Rotate] <display compass and tripod>: *1,-1,1*

Your drawing looks like this. You can achieve the same results as Steps 1 and 2 using the **Southeast Isometric View**

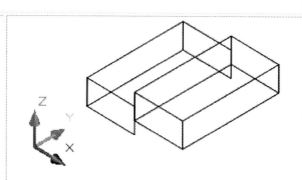

** Back elevation coordinates = 0,1,0; left elevation coordinates = -1,0,0

option. Select it in the control box of the 3D Navigate control panel (on the dashboard).

3. Let's try the **Rotate** option [Rotate]. Repeat the *VPoint* command and select it.

>**Command:** *[enter]*
>**Current view direction: VIEWDIR=1.0000,-.0000,1.0000**
>**Specify a view point or [Rotate] <display compass and tripod>:** *r*

4. AutoCAD asks for a two-dimensional angle. We'll stand in the –X,-Y quadrant of the XY plane. Enter the angle indicated.

>**Enter angle in XY plane from X axis <315>:** *225*

5. Now AutoCAD asks for a three-dimensional angle (the angle up or down in Z-space). We'll stand above the model. Enter the angle indicated.

>**Enter angle from XY plane <35>:** *45*

Your drawing now looks like this.

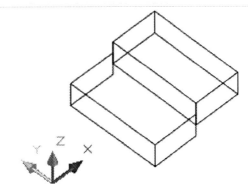

6. Repeat the *VPoint* command. This time, enter coordinates for a front elevation as indicated.

>**Command:** *[enter]*
>**Current view direction: VIEWDIR=-0.8660,-0.866,1.2247**
>**Specify a view point or [Rotate] <display compass and tripod>:** *0,-1,0*

Your drawing looks like this. Notice the UCS icon. (*Caution:* Do *not* use the **Front View** button on the 3D Navigate control panel as it will also change the UCS.)

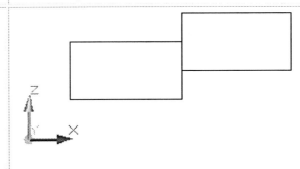

7. Experiment with different coordinate and angular entries. Use different combinations of positive and negative numbers, and watch the UCS icon (and use the Right-Hand Rule) to keep track of your orientation.

8. Save the drawing [💾] but don't exit.

>**Command:** *qsave*

1.2.2	Using the Compass to Assign a Viewpoint

Often the precise coordinate or angle from which you view the model won't be all that important. You'll be in a hurry, know the general area in which you wish to stand, and want to go there quickly. For these times, AutoCAD provides the **compass and tripod** option of the *VPoint* command.

Access the compass and tripod by hitting enter at the **Specify a view point or [Rotate]<display compass and tripod>** prompt. AutoCAD presents the tripod and compass screen (Figure 1.009).

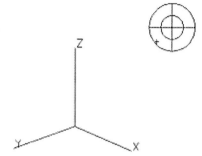

Figure 1.009

- Although it's fast, the tripod is difficult to use. Imagine your drawing resting at the vertex (center) of the tripod. Use the mouse to maneuver the XYZ-axes as desired. When you're happy with the orientation, left-click to return to the graphics screen.

- The compass in the upper-right quadrant of the screen is much easier to use than the tripod. This ingenious tool represents the positive and negative regions of a model. Refer to Figure 1.010.

  Imagine that your model exists at the core of a globe. Where you stand on the globe determines your view of the model. The VPoint compass is a two-dimensional representation of that globe. Use it to show AutoCAD where you wish to stand.

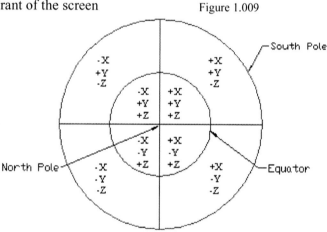

Figure 1.010

The inside of the compass's inner circle represents the upper (or northern) hemisphere of the globe. Since this is the upper part of the globe, we see the model from the top – so the area inside the inner circle is on the +Z-axis. The four quadrants of the inner circle represent the positive and negative X- and Y-axes as shown.

Between the inner and outer circles of the compass is the lower (or southern) hemisphere of the globe. Since this is the lower part of the globe, we see the model from the bottom – so this area is on the –Z-axis. The four outer quadrants represent the positive and negative X- and Y-axes as shown.

The compass may seem confusing at first, but (except for the toolbar) it's considerably faster than any other method of VPoint selection once you get used to it.

> You can create a series of viewpoints by saving each, using the same *View* command that was so beneficial in two-dimensional AutoCAD.

Let's try the compass approach to the *VPoint* command.

Do This: 1.2.2.1	Using the VPoint Compass

    I.   Reopen the *vpoint practice.dwg* file in the C:\Steps3D\Lesson01 folder. If not, please open it now.

II.   Follow these steps.

1.2.2.1: USING THE VPOINT COMPASS

1. Begin the *VPoint* command.

   Command: -vp

2. Hit *enter* at the first prompt to access the tripod and compass.

   Current view direction: VIEWDIR=0.0000,-1.0000,0.0000

   Specify a view point or [Rotate] <display compass and tripod>: [enter]

3. Place the compass cursor in the +X+Y+Z coordinates area as indicated, and then pick once with the left mouse button to return to the graphics screen. Your drawing looks something like the figure below.

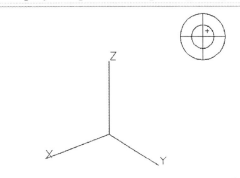

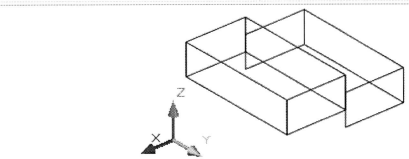

4. Experiment using different quadrants (and locations within quadrants) of the compass. Try using the tripod instead of the compass. Which is easier?

5. Save the drawing ⊞ but don't exit.

   Command: qsave

1.2.3	Setting Viewpoints Using a Dialog Box

Setting viewpoints using a dialog box is very similar to setting viewpoints using the **Rotate** option of the *VPoint* command.

Access the Viewpoint Presets dialog box (Figure 1.011 – next page) with the *VPoint* command or the *VP* hotkey. [You can also access the dialog box using the View pull down menu. Follow this path: *View – 3dViews – Viewpoint Presets.*]

The first things you'll notice on the dialog box are the two large drawings in the center. The first (on the left) looks something like a compass, and the second looks like half a compass. Use the compass on the left to set the two-dimensional angle (*in* the XY-plane); use the compass on the right to set the three-dimensional angle (up or down *from* the XY plane).

You can set the angles in two ways – by keyboard entry in the text boxes below the compasses or by mouse selection on the compasses themselves.

At the top of the dialog box, AutoCAD asks you to identify the angle in **Absolute to WCS** or **Relative to UCS** terms. We'll learn more about the WCS (World Coordinate System) and UCS (User Coordinate System) in Lesson 2. For now, leave the viewing angles set to **Absolute to WCS**.

The long button across the bottom of the dialog box is our first "Hail Mary" button for this text. If you read the basic text, you know to use a Hail Mary button in an emergency. AutoCAD designed this button to return the drawing to the plan view from anywhere. Set the **Absolute to WCS** option at the top of the dialog box and then pick the **Set to Plan View** button to return to a "normal" two-dimensional view of your model. This is quite handy when you become lost in Z-space.

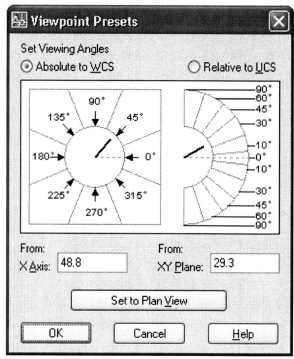

Figure 1.011

The keyboard equivalent of the **Set to Plan View** "Hail Mary" button is the *Plan* command. It looks like this:

> **Command:** *plan*
>
> **Enter an option [Current ucs/Ucs/World] <Current>:**

Again, we'll look at the WCS and UCS in Lesson 2. Enter *w* for the **World** option and hit *enter* to do what the **Set to Plan View** button does – return to a normal two-dimensional view of your model.

Let's try the dialog box.

Do This: 1.2.3.1	Using the Viewpoint Presets Dialog Box

    I.   Be sure you're still in the *vpoint practice.dwg* file in the C:\Steps3D\Lesson01 folder. If not, please open it now.

    II.   Follow these steps.

1.2.3.1: USING THE VIEWPOINT PRESETS DIALOG BOX

1. Enter the *VPoint* command.

> **Command:** *vp*

AutoCAD presents the Viewpoint Presets dialog box (Figure 1.011).

2. Set the viewpoint to **315°** on the left compass. Set the viewpoint to **-30°** on the right compass. (You can do this by typing the numbers into their respective text boxes or by picking on the numbers on the compasses themselves.)

Pick the **OK** button [OK] to complete the command. Your drawing looks like the figure below. Notice the UCS icon.

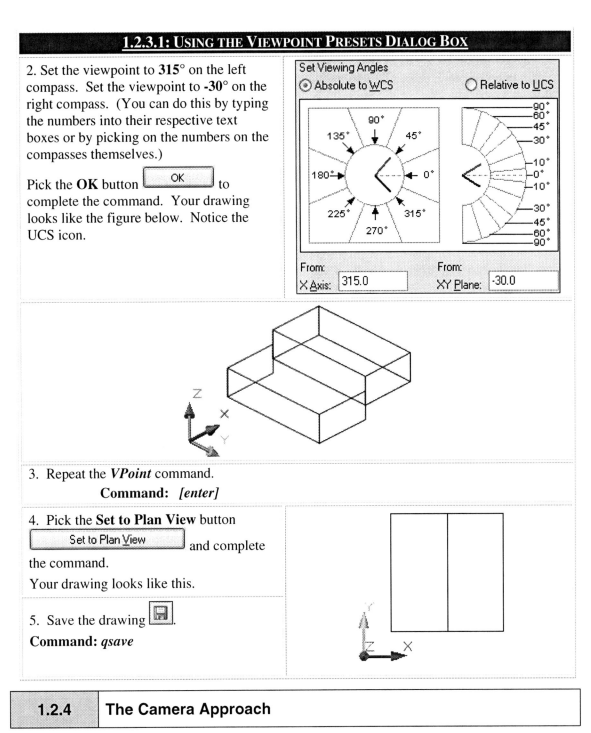

3. Repeat the *VPoint* command.
   Command: *[enter]*

4. Pick the **Set to Plan View** button [Set to Plan View] and complete the command.
   Your drawing looks like this.

5. Save the drawing.
   Command: *qsave*

1.2.4   The Camera Approach

At first glance, the camera approach seems like the best approach to adjusting how you view objects in a three-dimensional drawing. It works by locating the camera (your vantage point) and then

identifying the position of its target. AutoCAD will automatically place a camera icon at your vantage point. You can set up more than one camera at a time. Name it, and AutoCAD automatically creates a corresponding named view.

AutoCAD uses a fairly straightforward command sequence for its camera:
   Command: *camera* (**or** *cam*)
   Current camera settings: Height=0.0000 Lens Length=50.0000 mm

16

Specify camera location: *[locate the camera – your vantage point]*
Specify target location: *[locate the camera's target – what you want to see]*
Enter an option [?/Name/LOcation/Height/Target/LEns/Clipping/View/eXit]<eXit>:

Let's look at the options.

- The question mark (**?**) tells AutoCAD to display a list of camera currently defined in your drawing.
- The **LOcation** option gives you the opportunity to set the location by coordinate rather than just picking a point on the screen.
- **Height** let's you manually set the height of the camera.
- **Target** lets you select the target.
- The **LEns** option allows you to define the lens of your camera (35mm, 120mm, etc.) Not being a photographer, I tend to let the default ride on this one.
- Clipping lets you define a clipping plane for your view. Using this, you can remove background (or even foreground) clutter. Don't you wish you could do that with a real camera?!
- **View** conveniently allows you to set the current view to the camera's settings.

Let me show you some of these cool options.

Do This: 1.2.4.1	Working with the Camera

I. Open the *CameraPositionExercise* drawing file in the C:\Steps3D\Lesson01 folder. The drawing looks like Figure 1.012.
II. Follow these steps.

Figure 1.012

1.2.4.1: WORKING WITH THE CAMERA

1. Enter the *Camera* command. Alternately, you can pick the **Create Camera** button [camera icon] on the 3D Navigate control panel.

    Command: *cam*

2. Select the center [icon] of the red sphere as your vantage point. (Use the center OSNAP.)

    Current camera settings: Height=0.0000 Lens Length=50.0000 mm
    Specify camera location: _cen of

3. Select the insertion point [icon] of the larger sphere block as your target.

    Specify target location: _ins of

4. Tell AutoCAD to adjust to the camera view [View].

> **Enter an option [?/Name/LOcation/Height/ Target/LEns/Clipping/View/ eXit]<eXit>:** *V*
>
> **Switch to camera view? [Yes/No] <No>:** *Y*

AutoCAD adjusts the view.

5. From the control box on the Navigation control panel, select the side view [SIDE]. Notice the difference? AutoCAD has even adjusted the visual style to accommodate the predefined view.

6. Take a few minutes to experiment with the different options of the *Camera* command.

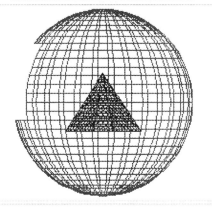

7. Exit the drawing without saving.

> **Command:** *quit*

You'll create the nifty pyramid-in-a-sphere in later lessons.

We've spent a great deal of time in this lesson on a single concept – viewpoints. I can't overemphasize the importance of being comfortable with viewpoints.

Consider the astronaut floating in space. A basic understanding of geography will tell him where he is in terms of continent, nation, or even city (XY-space). But if he doesn't understand his altitude (his Z-space position), he can't know if he's coming or going. He might wind up on the wrong planet altogether!

If necessary, repeat this lesson to this point to get comfortable with viewpoints and the VPoint command (the astronaut's navigator). Experiment with viewpoints in different viewports (each viewport can have its own viewpoint). Then proceed to the next section where we'll take our first tender steps in creating three-dimensional objects.

> Okay, I didn't cover two of the most important (although less precise) navigational tools – the *3DOrbit* and *3DCOrbit* commands. Don't fret – this just gives you something really cool to look forward to. (We'll look at these in Lesson 2.)

1.3   Drawing with the Z-Axis

I wish I could begin this section by saying that three-dimensional drafting is no different from two-dimensional drafting. However, that simply isn't the case. (I could lie if you'd prefer.) You've already seen that you'll have to master more navigation tools. Additionally, you must consider a couple things that have no meaning in a two-dimensional drawing – the Z-coordinate (or *elevation*) and the *thickness* of the object you're drawing.

Let's take a look at these.

1.3.1	Three-Dimensional Coordinate Entry

We must begin our study of three-dimensional drafting as we began our basic text – with a look at the Cartesian Coordinate System. This time, we need to understand how it works with the Z-axis. Consider the following table.

SYSTEM	ABSOLUTE	RELATIVE	POLAR/SPHERICAL/CYLINDRICAL
2D Entry	X,Y	@X,Y	@Dist<Angle
3D Entry	X,Y,Z	@X,Y,Z	@truedist<Xyangle<Zangle or @dist<2Dangle,Z-dist

The Absolute and Relative systems are easy enough to understand. Simply add the location on the Z-axis to the X and Y locations to have an XYZ-coordinate. But Polar Coordinate entry might need some explaining. (Refer to Figures 1.013 and 1.014.)

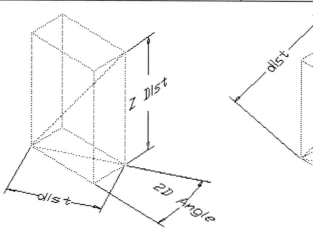

Figure 1.013: Spherical Coordinate Entry   Figure 1.014: Cylindrical Coordinate Entry

The first formula for 3D entry of polar coordinates looks like this:

@truedist<XYangle<Zangle

(Read this line as: *at a true distance of ___ ... at an XY angle of ___ ... and a Z angle of ___.*)
We call this type of coordinate entry *Spherical* (Figure 1.013). Begin Spherical coordinate entry with the true three-dimensional length of the line (or other object). Follow with the same two-dimensional (XY) angle you've always used for Polar Coordinates. Follow that with the three-dimensional angle (above or below the XY-plane).

The other formula for 3D entry of polar coordinates looks like this:

@dist<XYangle,Z-dist

(Read this line as: *at a distance of ___ ... and an XY angle of ___ ... at a Z distance of ___.*)
We call this type of coordinate entry *Cylindrical* (Figure 1.014). Like the spherical coordinate entry method, begin cylindrical coordinate entry with the distance of the line *but this time, use only the XY distance*. Follow with the two-dimensional angle, but conclude with the distance *along the Z-axis* (perpendicular to the XY-plane).

We'll use these methods to draw the stick figure of a house in our next exercise.

Do This: 1.3.1.1	Three-Dimensional Coordinate Entry

I. Open the *1-3D-1.dwg* file in the C:\Steps3D\Lesson01 folder. This drawing has been set up with a viewpoint of 1,-2,1, and layers have been created for you.

II. Be sure that layer **obj1** is current. (Toggle dynamic input on or off as needed.)

III. Follow these steps.

1.3.1.1: THREE-DIMENSIONAL COORDINATE ENTRY

1. We'll begin using absolute coordinates. Draw a line as indicated. Don't exit the command.

      Command: *l*
      Specify first point: *1,1*
      Specify next point or [Undo]: *4,1*

Notice that a Z-coordinate entry isn't required if the value is **0**.

2. Now draw a line straight up into Z-Space.
      Specify next point or [Undo]: *4,1,2*

3. Continue the line to complete the first side of the house.
      Specify next point or [Close/ Undo]: *1,1,2*
      Specify next point or [Close/ Undo]: *c*

4. We'll use relative coordinates as indicated to draw the other side.
      Command: *[enter]*
      Specify first point: *1,3*
      Specify next point or [Undo]: *@3,0*
      Specify next point or [Undo]: *@0,0,2*
      Specify next point or [Close/ Undo]: *@-3,0,0*
      Specify next point or [Close/ Undo]: *c*

5. Using the Endpoint OSNAP , draw lines to connect the two walls as shown.

6. Remember to save occasionally. Save the drawing as My Stick House in the C:\Steps3D\Lesson01 folder.
      Command: *saveas*

7. Now use spherical coordinates as indicated to locate the peak of the roof. Begin at the midpoint of the upper line marking the west side of the house.
      Command: *l*
      Specify first point: *mid*

8. We'll want a **1.5"** line at **0°** on the XY-plane and **60°** upward.
      Specify next point or [Undo]: *@1.5<0<60*
      Specify next point or [Undo]: *[enter]*

9. Repeat Steps 7 and 8 to locate the roof peak on the opposite wall. **Command:** *[enter]* **Specify first point:** *mid* **Specify next point or [Undo]:** *@1.5<180<60* **Specify next point or [Undo]:** *[enter]* Your drawing looks like this.	
10. Using the Endpoint OSNAP ⬚, draw the roof as shown here. Erase the roof peak locators.	
11. Save the drawing ⬚ but don't exit. **Command:** *qsave*	
12. Take a few moments and examine the model using different viewpoints. Return to a location of 1,-2,1 when you've finished. **Command:** *vp*	

Congratulations! You've created your first three-dimensional drawing.

You may have noticed some three-dimensional idiosyncrasies. If not, let me list a few.

- Ortho works on all planes (X, Y, and Z). (This wasn't true in earlier releases.)
- Object and Polar Tracking work on all planes (X, Y, and Z). (This, also, wasn't true in earlier releases.)
- OSNAPs work on most objects regardless of their XYZ-coordinates.
- It's impossible to locate a point in a three-dimensional drawing by arbitrarily picking a point on the screen. Remember that your screen is two-dimensional. An arbitrary point lacks a definition on one of the X-, Y-, or Z-axes, so there's no guarantee where it may actually be. *Always identify a three-dimensional point using a coordinate entry method or an OSNAP!* (Now you see why we put so much emphasis on coordinates and OSNAPs in the basic book!)
- Use three-dimensional coordinates just as you did two-dimensional coordinates when modifying the drawing (copying, moving, etc).
- Only very rarely will you want to create a three-dimensional object using a simple *Line* command. (After all, how often does your boss request stick figure drawings?)

Let's look next at adding a new dimension to our objects. We'll call our new dimension *thickness* and do marvelous things with it.

1.3.2	**Using the Thickness and Elevation System Variables**

Thickness is that property of an object that takes it from a stick figure to a true three-dimensional object. Until now, all the objects you've drawn have been stick figures. That is, they've all existed on a single two-dimensional plane. Even the lines we used to create our stick house in the last exercise existed in two-dimensional planes (although they crossed three-dimensional space).

> Point filters are also very useful in Z-Space. Refer to Section 3.5.1 in the basic *One Step at a Time* text for details on the use of point filters.

Clear as milk? Let me help.

Consider each line created in our stick house. (Consider each line individually – not as it relates to other lines or coordinates.) Describe each in terms of length, width, and height. In each case, you can describe the line using two of the three terms mentioned. In no case can you use all three terms. Consider the first line you drew. It has a length of 3 units and a width (or lineweight) of 0.01" (AutoCAD's default). But it has no height – no *thickness*.

Drawing with thickness is as easy as setting the system variable, like this:

> **Command: *thickness* (or *th*)**
>
> **Enter new value for THICKNESS <0.0000>: *.25***

All objects drawn while the **Thickness** system variable is set to **.25** will have a thickness of .25. This brings up another very important point: *Always remember to reset the **Thickness** system variable to **0** when you've finished drawing an object.*

Let's redraw our walls using **Thickness**.

You can access the ***Thickness*** command from the Format pull-down menu. Follow this path:
Format – Thickness

Do This: 1.3.2.1	**Drawing with Thickness**

   I.   Be sure you're still in the *My Stick House.dwg* file in the C:\Steps3D\Lesson01 folder. If not, please open it now.

   II. Follow these steps.

1.3.2.1: DRAWING WITH THICKNESS

1. Set the **Thickness** system variable to 2.

   Command: *th*

   Enter new value for THICKNESS <0.0000>: *2*

2. Draw ⬜ the walls as indicated.

   Command: *l*

   Specify first point: *6,1*

   Specify next point or [Undo]: *@3<0*

   Specify next point or [Undo]: *@2<90*

   Specify next point or [Close/Undo]: *@3<180*

   Specify next point or [Close/Undo]: *c*

3. Reset the **Thickness** to *0*.

   Command: *th*

   Enter new value for THICKNESS <2.0000>: *0*

Notice that we used simple two-dimensional coordinate entry. The **Thickness** system variable took care of the Z requirements.

Another very useful tool to employ in three-dimensional drafting is the **Elevation** system variable. When we drew our original house, we had to enter a location on the Z-axis as part of the coordinate whenever the value of Z wasn't zero (whenever it was above or below zero-Z). The **Elevation** system variable is designed to minimize the need for entering that third number.

The command looks like this:

Command: *elevation*

Enter new value for ELEVATION <0.0000>: *[enter the desired elevation]*

Once set, AutoCAD draws all objects at the identified elevation.

> Use the ***Elev*** command to set both the **Elevation** and **Thickness** system variables at once. The command looks like this:
>
>   **Command:** *elev*
>
>   **Specify new default elevation <0.0000>:** *[enter the elevation]*
>
>   **Specify new default thickness <0.0000>:** *[enter the thickness]*

Let's try using elevation.

Do This: 1.3.2.2	Drawing with Thickness and Elevation

    I.   Be sure you're still in the *My Stick House.dwg* file in the C:\Steps3D\Lesson01 folder. If not, please open it now.

    II.   Follow these steps.

1.3.2.2: DRAWING WITH THICKNESS AND ELEVATION

1. Set the **Elevation** to *2* and the **Thickness** to *1.299*.

   Command: *elev*

   Specify new default elevation <0.0000>: *2*

   Specify new default thickness <0.0000>: *1.299*

2. Draw a line ⬜ as indicated. Notice that, although no Z-axis location is given, AutoCAD assumes an elevation of 2.

   Command: *l*

   Specify first point: *6.75,2*

   Specify next point or [Undo]: *8.25,2*

   Specify next point or [Undo]: *[enter]*

3. Reset the **Thickness** to *0*.

   Command: *th*

   Enter new value for THICKNESS <1.2990>: *0*

4. Draw ⬜ the roof as shown.

   Command: *l*

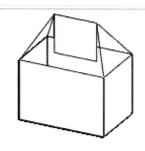

5. And now let's use the Properties Palette to modify the roof. Select the roof locator line and then enter the ***Properties*** command ⬜.

   Command: *props*

6. In the Geometry section of the Properties Palette, pick on **Start Z**. Notice that a **Select objects** button appears to the right.

Geometry	
Start X	6.7500
Start Y	2.0000
Start Z	2.0000
End X	8.2500
End Y	2.0000
End Z	2.0000
Delta X	1.5000
Delta Y	0.0000
Delta Z	0.0000
Length	1.5000
Angle	0

7. Pick on the **Select objects** button. AutoCAD highlights that location and allows you to redefine it by picking another point on the screen. Using the Endpoint OSNAP, pick the upper point of that same line (the western point of the roof peak).

8. Repeat Steps 6 and 7 to relocate the **End Z** point. Your drawing looks like this.

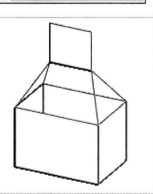

9. Now change the thickness of the line to *0*. The **Thickness** property is located in the General section of the Properties Palette.

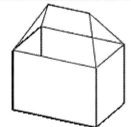

General	
Color	■ ByLayer
Layer	obj1
Linetype	——— ByLayer
Linetyp...	1.0000
Plot style	ByColor
Linewei...	——— ByLayer
Hyperlink	
Thickness	0.0000

Clear the grips.
Your drawing now looks like this.

10. Save the drawing .

Command: *qsave*

Of course, it would've been a lot easier to simply erase the roof peak line and redraw it without thickness. But I wanted to give you some experience working with the Properties Palette and 3-dimensional objects.

Do the two houses look the same? They should. But don't let that fool you. There are subtle (and remarkable) differences. We'll look at those in a few moments. First, let me list some things to remember about drawing with thickness and elevation (don't you just love my lists?).

- Always remember to reset **Thickness** and **Elevation** to zero when you've finished drawing an object. Otherwise, you may have to redo the next object when it's drawn with incorrect properties.
- Use the Properties Palette to change the thickness and elevation of drawn objects.
- You can enter positive or negative values for **Elevation** and **Thickness**.
- Closed objects behave differently from opened objects when drawn with thickness. We'll see examples of this in our next section.

1.4   Three-Dimensional Viewing Made Easy – Visual Styles

A visual style controls how AutoCAD produces the display you see. You define the visual styles you'll use, and you can even define different styles for different viewports.

In this section, we'll look at tools designed to help us to see our drawings more clearly. Earlier commands – *Hide* and *Shademode* –are being phased out in favor of the newer Visual Styles. I'll post the older information on *Hide* and *Shademode* at http://www.uneedcad.com/Files for those who wish to see how they worked.

Let's take a look at what's available and how you'll use it. We'll begin with the Visual Style control panel (Figure 1.015) in the dashboard.

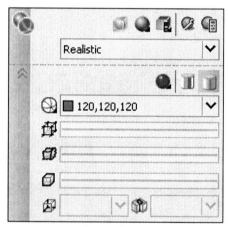

Figure 1.015

- The **Visual Styles** control box (which reads **Realistic** in our figure) offers selections of predefined visual style configurations. These include: 2D Wireframe, 3D Hidden, 3D Wireframe, Conceptual, and Realistic. The table below provides examples of each.

(Don't let it bother you that **Realistic** doesn't look realistic – I'll show you how to fix that shortly.)

2D Wireframe

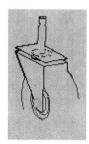

3D Hidden

3D Wireframe

Conceptual

Realistic

- Across the top of the Visual Styles control panel, you'll find several buttons (some with flyouts attached). These include:

X-Ray Mode

This button toggles the **VSFaceOpacity** system variable between 60 and -60. (The range is actually between 100 and -100.) Positive numbers indicate that objects on the screen will be opaque.

Visual Styles Manager

This button calls the Visual Styles Manager – a tool palette used to create or modify visual styles. We'll see more on this in a few minutes.

Shadows

These buttons work with the **VSShadows** system variable to control shadows. From the top, this flyout includes:

- **Shadows off** – (setting of **0**) turns shadows off to avoid the distraction and improve system performance.
- **Ground shadows** – (**1**) Helpful for a more realistic look. Works with default lights or user-defined lights.
- **Full shadows** – (**2**) These are shadows cast by one object onto another. Full shadows only work with user-defined lights.

These buttons work with the **VSFaceColorMode** system variable to control how AutoCAD displays color. From the top, this flyout includes:

- **Regular Face Mode** – (setting of 0) uses default face colors based on layer/color settings
- **Monochrome Mode** – (**1**) displays all objects in different shades of one color (determined by the **VSMonoColor** system variable)
- **Tint Mode** – (**2**) Displays all objects in one color but changes hue and saturation values of the color (also bases color on **VSMonoColor** system variable)
- **Desaturate Mode** – (3) Displays all objects with a softened saturation (about 30% less)

Tuning Dialog

Calls the Adaptive Degradation and Performance Tuning dialog box. In this dialog box, you can adjust how the AutoCAD display degrades when you reach the limit of your system's resources. My best advice here is that, if your system consistently runs short of resources – spend the money to upgrade it. AutoCAD won't get any less demanding of your system in the future!

Well, that was a lot of buttons. But we still have to look at the bottom frame of the Visual Styles control panel!

- The lower frame includes three buttons across the top, four down the side, and another one on the bottom. These include:

Facets & Smooth

These two buttons act as **On** (Facets) and **Off** (Smooth) toggles for the **VSLightingQuality** system variable. Facets show sharper edges on your model; smooth presents a more realistic image.

These buttons toggle the **VSFaceStyle** system variable to control how your object's faces will appear as follows:

- **No Face Style** – (setting of 0) turns faces off and leaves you with a wireframe. (You can't have both **VSFaceStyle** and **VSEdges** off at once.)
- **Realistic Face Style** – (1) when you turn isolines off (see below), this presents a fairly realistic view of the objects in your drawing.
- **Gooch Face Style** – (2) uses warm/cool tones to soften the contrast.

These three buttons toggle the **VSEdges** system variable to control the lines on your objects.

- **No Edges** – (setting of **0**) turns off display of lines in objects. This creates the most realistic view of an object.
- **Isolines** – (1) displays isolines. We'll spend some time with isolines in Lesson 7.
- **Faceted Edges** – (2) displays faceted (sharper) edges in your objects

You can control the color of your edges using the control box next to these buttons.

Edge Overhang

Makes the drawing look semi-hand-drawn. Toggles the **VSEdgeOverhang** system variable between -6 and 6 pixels to control how much of an overhang you get. (You can manually go as high as 100 – but don't.) You can also use the slider bar to adjust the setting.

Edge Jitter

Also makes the drawing look semi-hand-drawn. Toggles the **VSEdgeJitter** system variable between -2 and 2 pixels. Settings include: 1 - Low jitter, 2 - Medium jitter and 3 - High jitter. Any number preceded by a negative sign turns jitter off. You can also use the slider bar to adjust the setting.

Silhouette Edges

Toggles the **VSSilhEdges** system variable between **0** (off) and **1** (on) to determine whether or not silhouette edges will appear. Again, you can use the slider bar to adjust the settings.

Obscured Edges

Works when you're using faceted edges to allow you to see hidden edges. Toggles the **VSObscuredEdges** system variable between **0** (off) and **1** (on). Use the control box next to the button to control the color of the faceted edges.

Intersection Edges

Toggles the **VSIntersectionEdges** system variable on (**1**) or off (**2**) to control whether or no you will see intersecting edges. Use the control box next to the button to control the color of the faceted intersection edges.

Once you've set things up the way you like them, you can save your style with the *VSSave* command. AutoCAD will prompt you for a name like this:

> **Command:** *vssave*
>
> **Save current visual style as or [?]:** *[give your new style a name]*

AutoCAD will save the style and place a visual representation in the **Visual Styles** control box (on the Visual Styles control panel) for you to select it whenever you wish.

- I know, you've sure looked at a lot of buttons, but we have one more thing to consider before we try an exercise. Consider the Visual Styles Manager (Figure 1.016 – next page). This appears when you pick the **Visual Styles Manager** button at the top of the Visual Styles control panel, or when you enter *VisualStyles* at the command prompt.

o In the Available Visual Styles in Drawing frame at the top, you'll find a panel of visual representations of those styles already defined. When you create your own styles, they, too, will appear here.

o Below the Available Visual Styles in Drawing panel, you'll see four buttons:

- Use the **Create Visual Style** button ![icon] to create your own style from the current setup.

- Use the **Apply Selected Visual Style to Current Viewport** button ![icon] to do just that. (Isn't that simple?)

- **Export the Selected Visual Style to the Tool Palette** ![icon] will place a shortcut pick for the selected style on the Visual Styles tool palette.

- Of course, **Delete the Selected Visual Style** ![icon] removes the selected style. You can't remove the five AutoCAD-provided styles.

o You'll find a few expandable frames below the button. These may include one or some of the following depending upon which style you've selected in the panel above.

- **Face Settings** – includes options to help you control how faces appear in your drawing.

- **Materials and Color** – includes options to help you control how AutoCAD displays materials and color.

- **Environment Settings** – options for background and shadow display.

- **Edge Settings** – options to control how edges are displayed.

- Several 2D frames available only when you've selected the **2D Wireframe** setup in the upper panel. Since this is a 3D text, we won't concern ourselves with these.

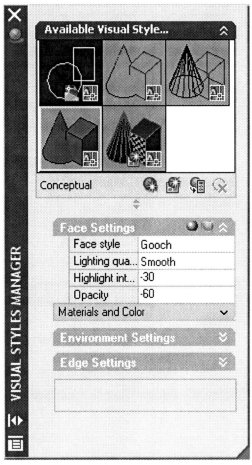

Figure 1.016

We've gone too long without an exercise! Let's take a look at how some of this stuff works.

You can also find the default Visual Styles options on the View pull down menu. Follow this path:

View – Visual Styles – [option]

Do This: 1.4.1	Working with Visual Styles

I. Open the *caster-01.dwg* file in the C:\Steps3D\Lesson01 folder. It looks like Figure 1.017.

II. Follow these steps.

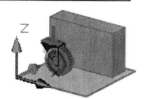

Figure 1.017

1.4.1: WORKING WITH VISUAL STYLES

1. Let's start with the easy stuff. Pick each of the options on the **Visual Styles** control box for comparison. The results appear on p. X.

2. Toggle the **X-Ray mode** (**VSFaceOpacity** system variable) to *60*.

> **Command:** *vsfaceopacity*
> **Enter new value for VSFACEOPACITY <-60>:** *60*

Your drawing looks like this.
Toggle back to *-60*.

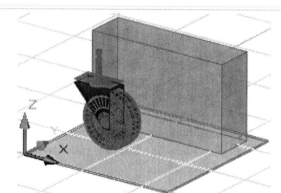

3. Toggle the **Ground Shadows** on. (You'll find the button under the shadows flyout.)

> **Command:** *vsshadows*
> **Enter new value for VSSHADOWS <0>:** *1*

Notice the shadow beneath the caster.

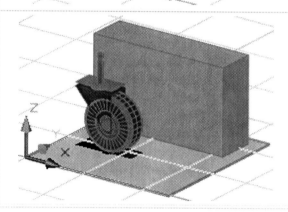

4. For the Full Shadows to work properly, you must first toggle the Sun and Viewport Lighting mode on. You'll find toggles for these in the Light control panel (just below the Visual Styles control panel. (They'll appear yellow when on.)

5. Now toggle Full Shadows 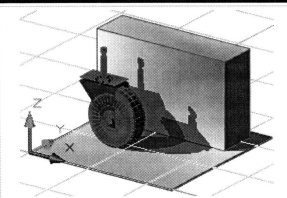 on.

   Command: *vsshadows*

   Enter new value for VSSHADOWS <1>: *2*

   Notice the shadows now. You're viewing shadows from a user-defined spotlight. (More on those in Lesson 11.)

6. Freeze everything except the **Obj5** layer. This just leaves the box.

7. Experiment with the first three edge toggles – **Edge Overhang** , **Edge Jitter** , **Silhouette Edges** . They'll produce the results shown atop the following page.

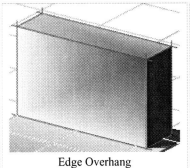

Edge Overhang

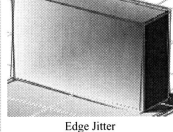

Edge Jitter

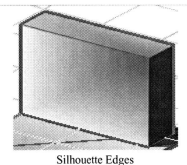

Silhouette Edges

8. Thaw all the layers.

9. Toggle the edge type buttons – No Edges , Isolines , and Facet Edges . The results appear below.

No Edges

Isolines

Facet Edges

10. Let's set up a Visual Style of our own and save it for future use.

    - Turn the Sun and Viewport Lighting modes off

    - Use no edges and only Ground Shadows

    - Use a Smooth , Realistic face style.

11. Now let's save our Visual Style for later recall. Pick the Visual Style Manager button 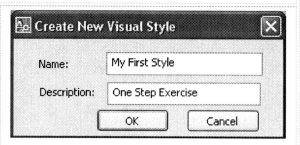 to call the manager (Figure 1.016).

12. In the Visual Style Manger, pick the Create New Visual Style button ![icon]. AutoCAD asks you for a name for your new style. Call it *My First Style* as shown.

Notice (atop the next page) that AutoCAD now displays your style in the Visual Style panel (at the top of the manager).

Create New Visual Style

Name: My First Style

Description: One Step Exercise

[OK]   [Cancel]

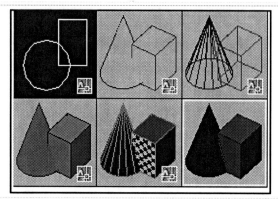

13. Save and exit the drawing.

1.5	**Extra Steps**

- Open some of the three-dimensional sample files that ship with AutoCAD (look in the \Sample subfolder of the AutoCAD folder). Practice your viewpoint manipulation options and visual styles.
- Print/Plot a drawing or two using Paper Space and Visual Styles.

1.6	**What Have We Learned?**

Items covered in this lesson include:
- *The UCS icon and the Right-Hand Rule*
- *Adjusting your view of the model*
    - *Isometric view*
    - *Dimetric view*
    - *Trimetric view*
    - *Plan view*
    - *Coordinate approach*
    - *Compass and tripod approaches*
    - *Dialog box approach*
- *Coordinates in a three-dimensional drawing*
    - *Cartesian Coordinate entry*

o   *Spherical and Cylindrical Coordinate entry*
- Visual Styles
- *Commands*

o **Ucsicon**	o **VSShadows**	o **VSEdges**
o **VPoint**	o **VSFaceOpacity**	o **VSFaceStyle**
o **VPoint**	o **VSIntersectionEdges**	o **VSLightningQuality**
o **Thickness**	o **VSObscuredEdges**	o **VSMoveColor**
o **Elevation**	o **VSSilhEdges**	o **VSFaceColor**
o **Elev**	o **VSEdgeJitter**	
o **VSSave**	o **VSEdgeOverhang**	

What a list! Stop and catch your breath!

We covered a tremendous amount of new material in this lesson. But it's all fundamental to three-dimensional drafting. After some practice, you'll find this material as easy as two-dimensional work.

I must caution you, however, about just how *fundamental* this material is. You must achieve at least a small degree of expertise with these methods and those in Lesson 2 to be able to function effectively in Z-space. But that's the benefit of a good textbook! You can repeat the lesson(s) until you're comfortable.

We've seen how to maneuver around a three-dimensional model, how to improve our view for better navigation (and aesthetics), and some fundamentals of creating three-dimensional objects. But there's much more to consider! How do you draw a three-dimensional object at an angle – such as creating a solid roof instead of the stick figure outline on your stick house? Is there an easier way to rotate your viewpoint in Z-space for a better view?

We'll continue our study of Z-Basics in Lesson 2 where we'll answer some of these questions (and present some others). But first, we should practice what we've learned so far.

1.7   Exercises

1. through 8. Create the "w" drawings in Appendix B (Refer to the "su" drawings for a clearer image.) Follow these guidelines.

   1.1. Don't try to create the dimensions yet.

   1.2. Start each drawing from scratch and use the default settings.

   1.3. Adjust the viewpoint as needed to help your drawing.

   1.4. Save each drawing as *My [title].dwg* (as in *MyB-1w.dwg*) in the C:\Steps3D\Lesson01 folder.

9. Create the drawing in Figure 1.018 according to the following parameters:

   9.1. Start the drawing from scratch and use the default settings.

   9.2. Set the viewpoint to 8.5,11,5.75.

   9.3. Don't attempt to draw the dimensions yet.

   9.4. Use a thickness setting of 0.

   9.5. The depth of the piece is ½".

   9.6. Save the drawing as *My Twisted Y.dwg* in the C:\Steps3D\Lesson01 folder.

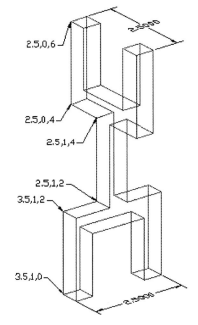

Figure 1.018

10. Create the 3-Dimensional Block drawing in Figure 1.019 (next page), according to the following parameters:
    10.1. Start the drawing from scratch and use the default settings.
    10.2. Don't attempt to draw the dimensions yet.
    10.3. Text is in Paper Space and is 3/16" and 1/8".
    10.4. Title block text is ¼", 3/16", and 1/8".
    10.5. The viewpoint for each viewport is indicated.
    10.6. Use lines with thickness.
    10.7. Use the 3D Wireframe visual style for all views except the diametric; use the 3D Hidden visual style to achieve the diametric view.
    10.8. Save the drawing as *My Block.dwg* in the C:\Steps3D\Lesson01 folder.

11. Create the Grill drawing in Figure 1.020 (next page) according to the following parameters.
    11.1. Start the drawing from scratch and use the default settings.
    11.2. Use polylines with 1/16" width for everything except the handle.
    11.3. Use a thickness of 1/16" for all objects.
    11.4. I used a scale of 1:4 in the plan and elevation views but no scale in the isometric.
    11.5. Don't attempt to draw the dimensions yet.
    11.6. Use the 3D Wireframe visual style for all views.
    11.7. Text is in Paper Space and is 3/16" and 1/8".
    11.8. Title block text is ¼", 3/16", and 1/8".
    11.9. Save the drawing as *MyGrill.dwg* in the C:\Steps3D\Lesson01 folder.

12. Create the Bookend drawing in Figure 1.021 (2nd page following) according to the following parameters:
    12.1. Start the drawing from scratch and use the default settings.
    12.2. I used a scale of 1:2 for all views.
    12.3. Don't attempt to draw the dimensions yet.
    12.4. Text is in Paper Space and is 3/16" and 1/8"
    12.5. Title block text is ¼", 3/16", and 1/8".
    12.6. You'll find it easier to fillet the corners rather than drawing arcs.
    12.7. Use the 3D Wireframe visual style for all views.
    12.8. Save the drawing as *MyBookEnd.dwg* in the C:\Steps3D\Lesson01 folder.

13. Create the drawing in Figure 1.022 according to the following parameters:
    13.1. Start the drawing from scratch and use the default settings.
    13.2. Use 0.6mm lineweights for all lines.
    13.3. Don't attempt to draw the dimensions yet.
    13.4. Use the 3D Wireframe visual style for all views.
    13.5. Text is in Paper Space and is 3/16" and 1/8"
    13.6. Title block text is ¼", 3/16", and 1/8".
    13.7. I used ½" diameter circles with ½" thickness for the legs.
    13.8. Save the drawing as *MyMagRack.dwg* in the C:\Steps3D\Lesson01 folder.

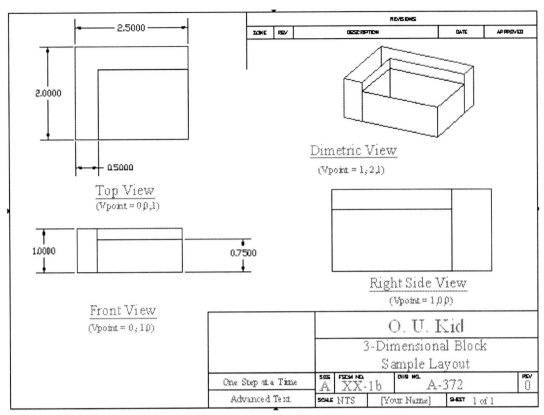

Figure 1.019

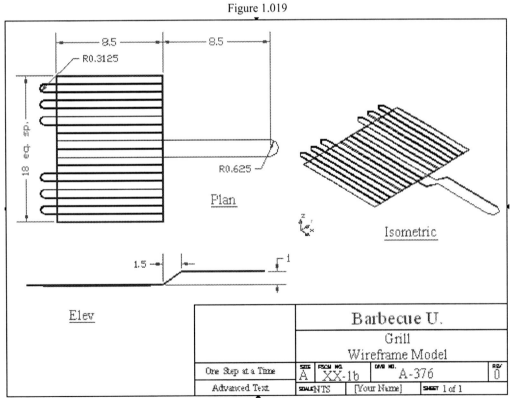

Figure 1.020

34

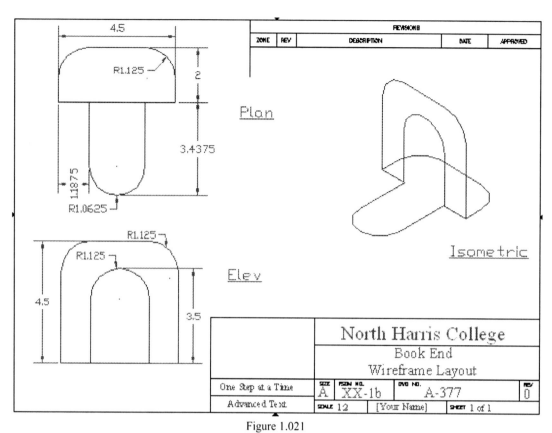

Figure 1.021

Plan

R1.125

4.5

2

3.4375

1.1875

R1.0625

Elev

R1.125

R1.125

4.5

3.5

Isometric

Figure 1.021

Side Elevation

12

6.3507

0.9327

0.5

Isometric

7.1459

140°

95°

1

8.5

9.6748

3.25

4.25

End Elevation

Figure 1.022

14. Create the Anchor Stop drawing in Figure 1.023 (next page) according to the following parameters:
    14.1. Start the drawing from scratch and use the default settings.
    14.2. Don't attempt to draw the dimensions yet.
    14.3. Text is in Paper Space and is 3/16" and 1/8"
    14.4. Title block text is ¼", 3/16", and 1/8".
    14.5. The viewpoint for each viewport is indicated. Use the 3D Wireframe visual style for all views.
    14.6. Use lines without thickness except when drawing the slot.
    14.7. Save the drawing as *MyBookEnd.dwg* in the C:\Steps3D\Lesson01 folder.

15. Here's a challenge. Create the drawing in Figure 1.024 (next page) according to the following parameters:
    15.1. Start the drawing using *template #1* found in the C:\Steps3D\Lesson01 folder.
    15.2. Don't attempt to draw the dimensions yet.
    15.3. Text is in Paper Space and is 3/16" and 1/8".
    15.4. Title block text is ¼", 3/16", and 1/8".
    15.5. The crown is made up of solids drawn with thickness.
    15.6. The round pieces are donuts drawn with thickness.
    15.7. Use the 3D Wireframe visual style for all views except the diametric; use the Realistic visual style for the diametric.
    15.8. Save the drawing as *MyQueen.dwg* in the C:\Steps3D\Lesson01 folder.

16. Here's another challenge. Create the drawing in Figure 1.025 (2nd page following) according to the following parameters:
    16.1. Start the drawing using *template #1* found in the C:\Steps3D\Lesson01 folder.
    16.2. Don't attempt to draw the dimensions yet.
    16.3. Text is in Paper Space and is 3/16" and 1/8"
    16.4. Title block text is ¼", 3/16", and 1/8".
    16.5. Polylines have a width of 1/16".
    16.6. Anchors are donuts with an outer diameter of 9/16" and an inner diameter of 3/16".
    16.7. The nut is a six-sided polygon inscribed in a radius of ¼"; its width is 1/16".
    16.8. Use the 3D Wireframe visual style for all views except the diametric; use the Realistic visual style for the diametric.
    16.9. Save the drawing as *MyRingStand.dwg* in the C:\Steps3D\Lesson01 folder.

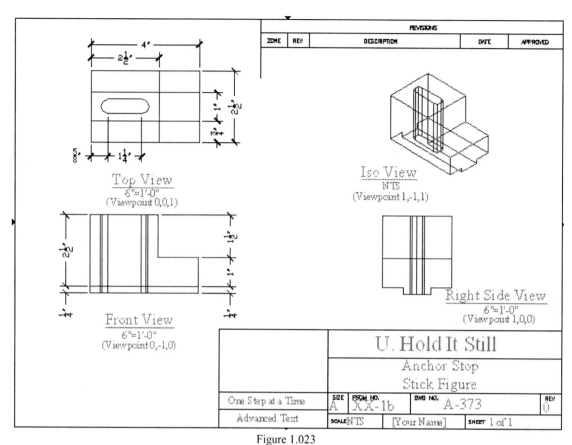

Top View
6"=1'-0"
(Viewpoint 0,0,1)

Iso View
NTS
(Viewpoint 1,-1,1)

Front View
6"=1'-0"
(Viewpoint 0,-1,0)

Right Side View
6"=1'-0"
(Viewpoint 1,0,0)

REVISIONS				
ZONE	REV	DESCRIPTION	DATE	APPROVED

U. Hold It Still

Anchor Stop
Stick Figure

One Step at a Time	SIZE A	FSCM NO. XX-1b	DWG NO. A-373		REV 0
Advanced Text	SCALE NTS		[Your Name]	SHEET 1 of 1	

Figure 1.023

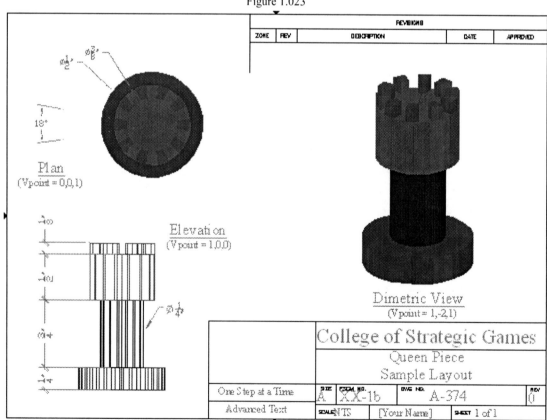

Plan
(Vpoint = 0,0,1)

Elevation
(Vpoint = 1,0,0)

Dimetric View
(Vpoint = 1,-2,1)

REVISIONS				
ZONE	REV	DESCRIPTION	DATE	APPROVED

College of Strategic Games

Queen Piece
Sample Layout

One Step at a Time	SIZE A	FSCM NO. XX-1b	DWG NO. A-374		REV 0
Advanced Text	SCALE NTS		[Your Name]	SHEET 1 of 1	

Figure 1.024

37

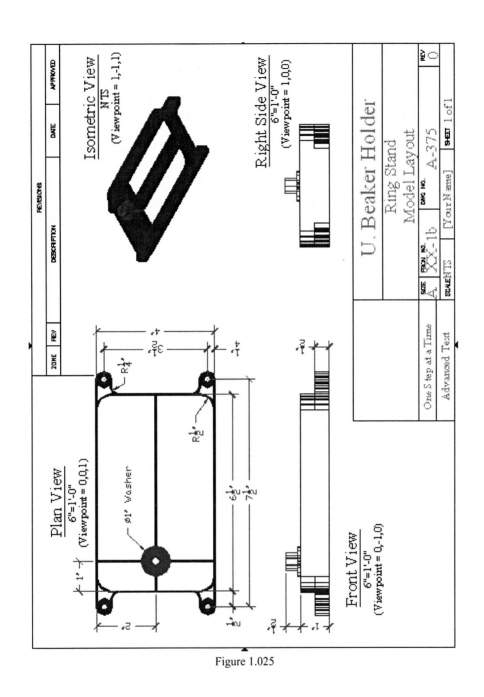

Figure 1.025

1.8 For Web-Based Review Questions, visit:
http://www.uneedcad.com/2007/Files/07R1-3D.pdf

38

Lesson

2

Following this lesson, you will:

- ✓ *Understand the differences between the UCS and the WCS*
  - ○ *Know how to use the **UCS** command to create working planes*
  - ○ *Understand dynamic UCS*
  - ○ *Know how to use the UCS Dialog Box (Manager)*
  - ○ *Know how to dimension a three-dimensional drawing*
- ✓ *Be familiar with some advanced viewing techniques*
  - ○ *Be able to use the **3DOrbit**, **3DCOrbit**, and **3DFOrbit** commands*
  - ○ *Be able to use the **3DDistance** and **3DSwivel** commands*
- ✓ *Be able to use the **3DClip** command*

More of Z Basics

When we first drew our three-dimensional stick figure house, it had no walls and only sticks for a roof. Later we saw that, by using the Thickness and Elevation system variables, we could make our walls solid. But what about the roof? There must be an AutoCAD tool for making it solid as well.

We also discussed the need for point entry precision in Z-space. What about text and dimensions? Must we use coordinates to place them? (Have you tried to dimension a three-dimensional drawing yet?) And what if you want to place text along a slope (like the roof)?

Believe it or not, all of these questions have the same answer! The answer lies in a tool called the User Coordinate System – the UCS.

In Lesson 1, you learned how to create simple three-dimensional objects and how to view those objects from different angles. In this lesson, we'll discuss the tools with which you'll work on the different faces of your three-dimensional objects. Then we'll look at some more advanced viewing tools.

Let's start with the UCS.

2.1	WCS vs. UCS

Although you may not be aware of it, you're already familiar with the UCS. You've been using it since you began your study of AutoCAD. However, it's always been aligned with the World Coordinate System – the WCS – so you never noticed it. So what's the difference? You need to understand a little about how AutoCAD works to really understand the UCS.

> To avoid any chance of damage to the WCS, AutoCAD placed it out of your reach.

In the basic text, you learned that all objects in an AutoCAD drawing are defined by information stored in that drawing's database. When you regenerate a drawing, AutoCAD reads this information and restores the drawing accordingly. When you create an attributed block, the attribute information is also stored in the database.

Part of the information stored in a drawing's database is the location and orientation of each object. For consistency (and to avoid a programming nightmare), AutoCAD developed a coordinate system that remains the same throughout the life of the drawing. Thus, the definition of point 0,0,0 will remain the same, and the point will always be in the same place. The X, Y, and Z directions will never change.

This coordinate system is the WCS.

AutoCAD uses the WCS point 0,0,0 much as a mariner uses the North Star. Unchanging in the night sky, Polaris shows the sailor the way home. Unchanging in the WCS, point 0,0,0 shows AutoCAD how to orient any object in the drawing.

The User Coordinate System – or UCS – is what the CAD operator uses to determine up from down and left from right for the immediate task at hand. Until now, the UCS has always been aligned with the WCS – our mariner's ship has always been pointed toward the North Star. Until now, the front of our ship has always been north; the masts have always pointed upward. With a compass, our sailor could find anything on the ship. Until now, we had only two dimensions with which to create a drawing – our sailor had only a single deck on which to work. Until now, the CAD operator had no need to know about the UCS or WCS. Until now...

Sigh. It used to be so easy ...

Now our ship has changed directions and acquired new decks. Our sailor with the compass is completely lost. To make it easier for him to understand where things are on the ship, he must change his reference point from the North Star to something on the ship itself. This way, he can always find his way regardless of the direction in which the ship is sailing.

He'll use the mainsail as his reference point (0,0,0). His compass directions will now reference points on the ship – the bow becomes north, the stern becomes south, starboard and port become east and west. The mainsail will always point upward from the main deck (regardless of how violently the sea rocks the ship). So now, using the North Star, our mariner's ship will never be lost, and using his new Mariners Coordinate System, he'll never be lost on the ship.

CAD operators must adjust for Z-space as our mariner adjusted for a change in the ship's direction. Using the 0,0,0 coordinate of the WCS as our North Star, we can always find our way home. And using the User Coordinate System as our sailor uses his Mariner's Coordinate System, we can work on any surface – or working plane – of a three-dimensional model (as our mariner could work on any deck of his ship).

So how do you use the UCS? Where do you begin?

> Beginning with the 2007 release of AutoCAD, the UCS has become dynamic – that is, it will change automatically when you pass over a face of a 3-dimensional solid object. Unfortunately, not all objects are solid, so we'll spend some time learning to manually change the UCS.

Let's begin by accessing the *UCS* command. What do you suppose the command would be?

To keep it simple, AutoCAD calls the command *UCS*! The command line approach looks like this:

> **Command:** *ucs*
>
> **Current ucs name: *WORLD***
>
> **Specify origin of UCS or [Face/NAmed/OBject/Previous/View/World/X/Y/Z/ZAxis]**
> **<World>:** *[enter an option]*

If you accept the default (**Specify origin**) option, AutoCAD prompts

> **Current ucs name: *WORLD***
>
> **Specify origin of UCS or [Face/NAmed/OBject/Previous/View/World/X/Y/Z/ZAxis]**
> **<World>:** *[locate the origin]*
>
> **Specify point on X-axis or <Accept>:** *[tell AutoCAD in which direction you want the X-axis to go]*
>
> **Specify point on the XY plane or <Accept>:** *[tell AutoCAD in which direction you want the y-axis to go]*

With this procedure, AutoCAD will determine the direction for Z from the locations of the X & Y axes.

Let's look at the other options. We'll begin with the options listed at the command prompt, then look at some which don't show up with the other prompts.

> AutoCAD provides several methods of accessing the *UCS* command and its options. Easiest, perhaps, is the UCS toolbar. If you'll look at this (and the UCS II toolbar), you'll notice that the *UCS* command has some options which don't show up on the command line. We'll look at these as well. But you can also access the *UCS* command's options by cursor or dynamic input menu, or by selecting from the Tools pull down menu.

- The **Face** option allows you to define the new UCS by selecting a face on an existing three-dimensional solid object.
- The **NAmed** option allows you to **Save** a new UCS (define a new 0,0,0 and new orientations for the X-, Y-, and Z-axes), **Restore** a named UCS, or **Delete** a named UCS. You can even have AutoCAD list the named UCSs with the question mark (**?**).

   It prompts

   > **Enter an option [Restore/Save/Delete/?]:**

- The **OBject** option allows you to define the new UCS by selecting an existing three-dimensional object. (Remember, a line without thickness is two-dimensional regardless of its orientation.) AutoCAD aligns the new UCS with that object.

- **Previous** restores the previous UCS.
- **View** sets the UCS flat against the screen (the X-axis parallel to the bottom of the screen and the Y axis parallel to the left side of the screen). The 0,0,0 coordinate remains where it is currently located.
- The **World** option is the most important (so important, in fact, it deserves "Hail Mary" status). It tells AutoCAD to restore the UCS to match the WCS's orientation. In other words, when you're lost, use the World option to reorient yourself.
- The **X/Y/Z** options allow you to rotate the UCS around the selected axis. They prompt

    Specify rotation angle about X *[or Y or Z]* axis <90>:

- Using the **ZAxis** option, you'll define the new UCS by identifying a location for 0,0,0, and then a point on the Z-axis.

Some options appear on the toolbar that don't appear on the command prompt, but they're well worth examination.

- The **3point** option is the same as the default **Specify origin** option.
- The **Origin** button provides the opportunity to change the UCS origin without changing the XYZ planes. If you accept the defaults at the **Specify origin** option of the command line, you'll accomplish the same thing.

Some other options include:

- **Move** (entering *M* at the UCS prompt) allows you to move the UCS without changing its orientation. It prompts

    Specify new origin point or [Zdepth]<0,0,0>:

    Respond by picking a new origin point or by selecting the **Zdepth** option. The **Zdepth** option allows you to move the origin along the Z-axis.

- The **orthoGraphic** option (entering *G* at the UCS prompt) offers a quick way to change the UCS to one of the standard orthographic projections without moving 0,0,0 from the WCS location. It prompts

    Enter an option [Top/Bottom/Front/BAck/Left/Right]<Top>:

Most of this will become clearer with practice. Let's try a get-acquainted exercise.

Some knowledge of the UCS Icon will help in this exercise. You can access the various options of the *UCSIcon* command using right-click cursor menus or the View pull-down menu. Follow this path:

View – Display – UCS Icon – [option]

Do This: 2.1.1	Manipulating the UCS

I. Open the *ucs practice2.dwg* file in the C:\Steps3D\Lesson02 folder. The drawing looks like Figure 2.001.

II. Follow these steps.

Figure 2.001

2.1.1: MANIPULATING THE UCS

1. Our first step is one of the most important steps to remember when manipulating the UCS. Set the UCS icon to **ORigin**. This way, you'll always know where 0,0,0 is.

    Command: *ucsicon*

    Enter an option [ON/OFF/All/Noorigin/ORigin Properties] <ON>: *or*

2. Now we'll tell AutoCAD to use the UCS (our mariner must navigate within the ship).

Enter the *UCS* command. Alternately, you can pick the **UCS** button  on the UCS toolbar.

> **Command:** *ucs*

3. Our first UCS will simply relocate 0,0,0. We'll use the **ZAxis** option [ZAxis].

> **Current ucs name: *WORLD***
>
> **Specify origin of UCS or [Face/NAmed/OBject/Previous/View/World/X/Y/Z/ZAxis] <World>:** *za*

4. Specify the bottom-left corner of the object …

> **Specify new origin point or [Object] <0,0,0>:**

… and accept the default **Z-axis point**.

> **Specify point on positive portion of Z-axis <1.0000, 1.0000,1.0000>:** *[enter]*

Notice that the UCS icon moves. It's locating 0,0,0 as we told it to do in Step 1.

5. Now we'll save this UCS for later retrieval. Repeat the *UCS* command.

> **Command:** *[enter]*

6. AutoCAD responds by asking what you would like to do. Select the **NAmed** option [NAmed].

> **Current ucs name: *WORLD***
>
> **Specify origin of UCS or [Face/NAmed/OBject/Previous/View/World/X/Y/Z/ZAxis] <World>:** *na*

7. Tell AutoCAD you wish to save [Save] the UCS …

> **Enter an option [Restore/Save/Delete/?]:** *s*

8. … and call it something appropriate.

> **Enter name to save current UCS or [?]:** *lower left base*

9. Let's create another UCS. Repeat the command. (Alternately, the **3 Point UCS** button will work.)

> **Command:** *ucs*

10. Select the points indicated.

> **Current ucs name: lower left base**
>
> **Specify origin of UCS or [Face/NAmed/OBject/ Previous/ View/World/X/ Y/Z/ZAxis] <World>:**
>
> **Specify point on X-axis or <Accept>:**
>
> **Specify point on the XY plane or <Accept>:**

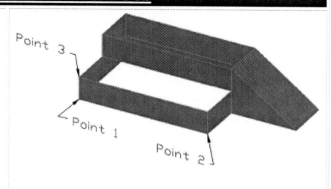

12. The UCS icon now looks like this.

Before continuing, stop and ask yourself where the X-, Y-, and Z-axes are located. Use the UCS icon and the Right-Hand Rule to help answer that question.[*]

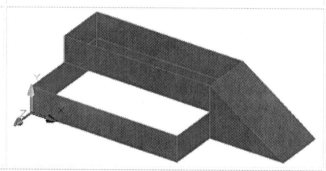

13. Repeat Steps 6 through 8 to save this UCS as **MyFront**.

14. Now let's look at some other ways to set the UCS. You can select the option of the *UCS* command for the next several steps, or you can simply pick the button indicated.

Let's begin with the **Object** option. Enter the sequence shown or pick the **Object UCS** button on the UCS toolbar.

> **Command:** *ucs*
>
> **Current ucs name: MyFront**
>
> **Specify origin of UCS or [Face/NAmed/OBject/Previous/View/World/X/Y/Z/ ZAxis] <World>:** *ob*

15. Select the "Z" line closest to the lower-left corner of the screen.

> **Select object to align UCS:**

The UCS icon now looks like this. The 0,0,0 coordinate of the UCS matches the line's end point closest to where you picked. The Y- and Z-axes also line up according to the line's definition.

16. Restore the **Previous** UCS.

> **Command:** *ucs*
>
> **Current ucs name: *NO NAME***
>
> **Specify origin of UCS or [Face/NAmed/OBject/Previous/View/World/X/Y/Z/ ZAxis] <World>:** *p*

---

[*] The UCS icon indicates the X-, and Y-, and Z-axes.

17. Now we'll use the **Face** option. (The wedge piece is a three-dimensional solid – an item we'll discuss in Lesson 7. It was necessary to include it here for demonstration purposes.)

Enter the ***Line*** command 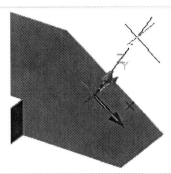 and move your cursor over the angled face of the solid to see how the new dynamic UCS works. (Be sure the DUCS toggle on the status bar is depressed.) Notice that the crosshairs change to indicate the dynamic UCS.

18. Begin the line around the center of the angled face. Notice that the UCS icon moves and changes to reflect the UCS of the face.

19. Cancel the command.

20. Now set the UCS according to the current view. Enter the sequence shown or pick the **View UCS** button ⬛. Notice the new orientation of the UCS icon. Notice also that, although it changes orientation, it doesn't change position.

> **Command:** *ucs*
>
> **Current ucs name: MyFront**
>
> **Specify origin of UCS or [Face/NAmed/OBject/Previous/View/World/X/Y/Z/ ZAxis] <World>:** *v*

21. Let's experiment with the X/Y/Z options. Watch the UCS icon as we rotate the UCS. Select the **X** button ⬛.

22. Accept the **90°** default and watch the UCS icon.
> **Specify rotation angle about X axis <90>:**

It can be difficult to follow axial rotations, but that's where the Right-Hand Rule comes in handy. Here's how it works:

Point the finger that represents the axis about which you're rotating (in this case, the thumb) directly at your nose. Now rotate your hand 90° (or the desired angle of rotation) counterclockwise. This configuration will match the UCS icon and show you the orientation of your UCS.

23. Repeat Steps 21 and 22 for the **Y** and **Z** options.

24. Using any of the tools just discussed, create the new UCS setups identified in the following. Save the setups as indicated.

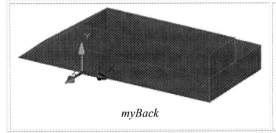

myBack

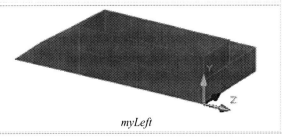

myLeft

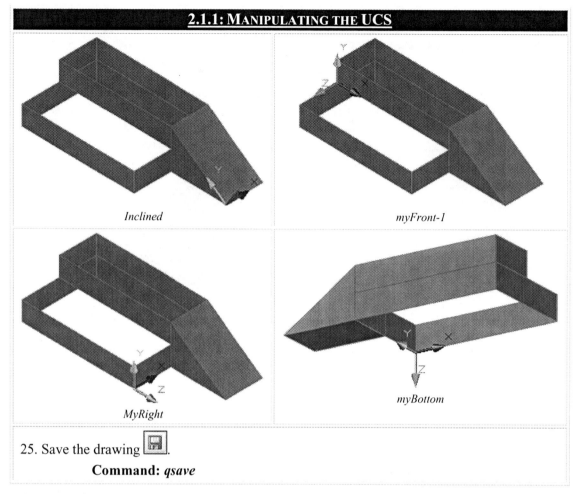

Inclined

myFront-1

MyRight

myBottom

25. Save the drawing 🖫.

       Command: *qsave*

You've created several UCS setups using a variety of methods. It's okay to be a bit confused at this point. Let's pause for a moment, catch our breath, and review what we've learned. Here are some important things to remember.

- Despite their similarities, viewpoints, viewports and the UCS are three different things. Remember:
  - Viewpoints are *points* (where you stand) *from which you view* the model.
  - Viewports are like *port*holes in a ship *through which you view* the model.
  - The UCS orients you *on* the model itself.
- Points used to define viewpoints will always reference the WCS (*not* the UCS). This will make it easier for you to get your bearings.

COOL STUFF

- The *View* command will save viewpoints.
- Each viewport can have a unique viewpoint and/or UCS assigned to it.
- Each – viewpoint, viewport, and UCS – works independently of the other two, but all should be considered as a team to assist you when you work on a three-dimensional model.

Let's take a moment to look at a tool that might make UCS management easier. Then we'll use the working planes to create some lines, text, and dimensions on our stick house.

Over the course of creating a drawing – particularly a larger drawing – you may find it necessary to create several UCSs. You have already seen how to save these setups for later retrieval, but where do you keep the list of names you've assigned the UCSs?

AutoCAD makes it simple with the UCS Manager (Figure 2.002). This provides a dialog box approach to keeping track of the various setups as well as some additional tools. Access the UCS Manager by entering the **UCSMan** command. Let's take a look.

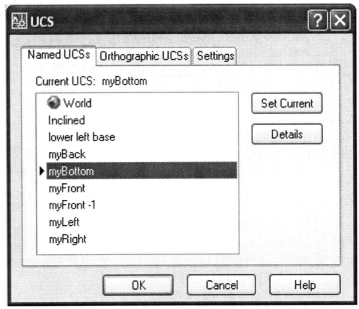

Figure 2.002

- The first tab presents a list of **Named UCSs** as well as **World** and **Previous**

options. To set a UCS current, either double click on its name or select the name and pick the **Set Current** button. Then pick the **OK** button to complete the procedure. It's that simple – no need to remember or to store a list of names! (But it's always a good idea when assigning the names to make them self-explanatory.)

The **Details** button presents a dialog box (Figure 2.003) that indicates the origin location, as well as the orientation of the X-, Y-, and Z-axes for the currently selected UCS. You view the data in relation to the WCS or any other existing UCS by selecting the coordinate system from the **Relative to** control box.

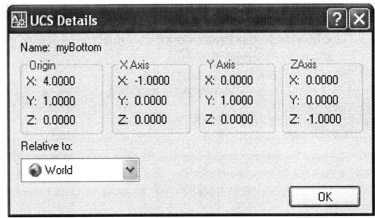

Figure 2.003

- The middle tab (Figure 2.004 – next page) – **Orthographic UCSs** – lists several standard UCSs (the same ones available using the **orthoGraphic** option of the *UCS* command). Use the same procedure you used on the **Named UCSs** to set one current.

Notice the **Relative to** control box on this tab. You can set one of the orthographic UCSs relative to the WCS or relative to one of the user-defined UCSs. I suggest leaving this control set relative to the WCS at least for now. Any other setting might make it difficult to orient yourself.

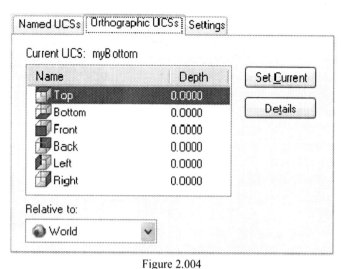

Figure 2.004

- The **UCS icon settings** frame of the **Settings** tab (Figure 2.005) is a dialog box interface for the *UCSIcon* command.

  Use the **UCS settings** frame to **Save UCS with viewport** (the default). This means that each viewport can have its own UCS setting. Clear this check and each viewport will reflect the UCS settings of the current viewport.

  A check next to **Update view to Plan when UCS is changed** will regenerate the viewport in a plan view of the current UCS whenever the UCS settings are changed. I suggest leaving this box clear since you're more likely to want to keep the view even if you change the UCS.

Figure 2.005

We'll use the UCS dialog box in our next exercise to help us see how using different UCS settings can benefit us.

2.3	Using Working Planes

We've spent many pages learning to set up User Coordinate Systems. But as yet, we haven't seen how to use the UCS once it's set up. We haven't seen the answers to the questions that began our lesson – How do we make a solid roof? How do we place text and dimensions in a three-dimensional drawing.

Let's do an exercise to put UCSs to practical use.

Do This: 2.3.1	Manipulating the UCS

I. Open the *Stick House 2.dwg* file in the C:\Steps3D\Lesson02 folder. The drawing looks like Figure 2.006.

This drawing has already been set up for you with several UCSs and Paper Space viewports. The house is a stick figure (wireframe) structure with thickness assigned to the lower lines. We'll create a solid roof. Then we'll add a few dimensions.

II. Be sure **Obj2** is the current layer.

Figure 2.006

III. Follow these steps.

1. Try drawing a solid using the points indicated. **Command: *so***	
2. Notice (right) that the solid was drawn two-dimensionally in the current UCS. To use a solid to form the roof, the UCS must be aligned to the side of the roof you wish to draw. Erase ✐ the solid. **Command: *e***	
3. Call the UCS Manager. The button 🔲 is on the UCS II toolbar. **Command: *ucsman***	
4. Double-click on the south roof UCS to make it current. Then pick the **OK** button [OK]. Notice that the UCS icon moves to align itself with the face of the south roof.	
5. Now that the UCS has been properly set, repeat Step 1.	
6. Using the techniques seen in this exercise, complete the roof using solids (adjust the viewpoint as necessary, then return to the current setting of 1,-2,1). Your drawing looks like this.	
7. Set the current UCS to **south west floor**.	

49

8. Now we'll add some dimensions, but we need to use viewports to this properly. Activate the **Layout1** tab 🔲.

9. Open Model Space within one of the viewports. (Refer to the figure following Step 14 for the next few steps.)

10. Activate the upper-left viewport and do the following:
   - Create a WCS plan view (set the viewpoint to 0,0,1).
   - Set the scale for this viewport to 1:8.

11. Activate the lower-left viewport and do the following:
   - Create a WCS front view (set the viewpoint to 0,-1,0).
   - Set the scale for this viewport to 1:8.
   - Adjust the size of the viewport and the position of the house as necessary to see the entire house.

12. Activate the lower-right viewport and do the following:
   - Create a WCS right side view (set the viewpoint to 1,0,0).
   - Set the scale for this viewport to 1:8.
   - Adjust the size of the viewport and the position of the house as necessary to see the entire house.

13. Activate the upper-right viewport and do the following:
   - Set the scale to 1:8.
   - Adjust the size of the viewport and the position of the house as necessary to see the entire house.

14. Using the *MVSetup* command to align the plan, front, and side views. Adjust the position of the viewports as necessary for aesthetics.

   Command: *mvsetup*

Your drawing looks something like the following figure.

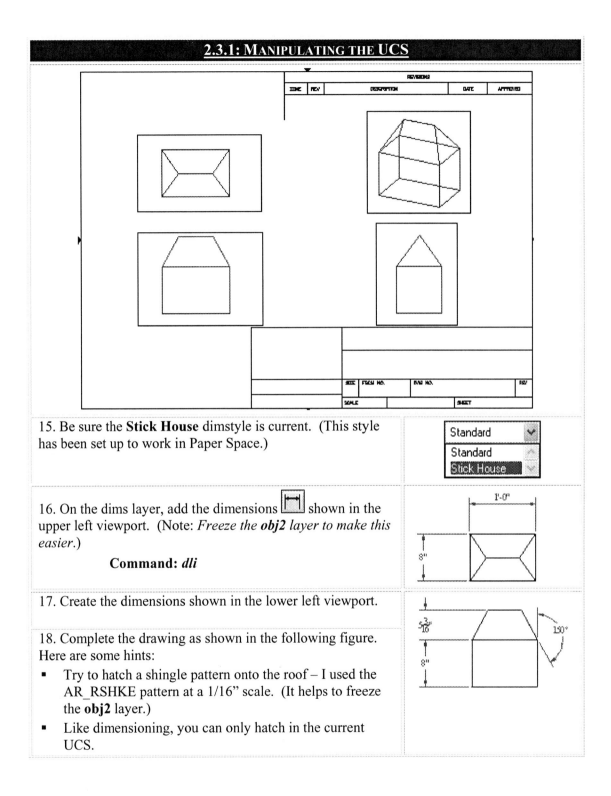

15. Be sure the **Stick House** dimstyle is current. (This style has been set up to work in Paper Space.)

16. On the dims layer, add the dimensions ⊢⊣ shown in the upper left viewport. (Note: *Freeze the obj2 layer to make this easier.*)

    Command: *dli*

17. Create the dimensions shown in the lower left viewport.

18. Complete the drawing as shown in the following figure. Here are some hints:

- Try to hatch a shingle pattern onto the roof – I used the AR_RSHKE pattern at a 1/16" scale. (It helps to freeze the **obj2** layer.)
- Like dimensioning, you can only hatch in the current UCS.

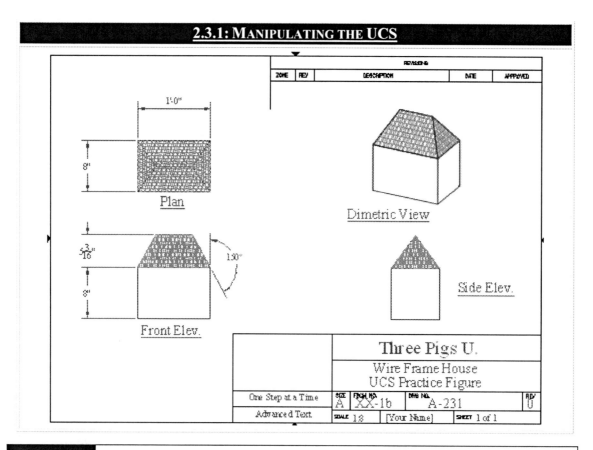

		REVISIONS	
ZONE	REV	DESCRIPTION	DATE	APPROVED

Plan

1'-0"

8"

Dimetric View

3/16"

150°

8"

Side Elev.

Front Elev.

Three Pigs U.
Wire Frame House
UCS Practice Figure

One Step at a Time	SIZE	FSCM NO.	DWG NO.	REV
	A	XX-1b	A-231	U
Advanced Text	SCALE 1:8	[Your Name]	SHEET 1 of 1	

2.4 Advanced Viewing Techniques

We discovered some very useful viewing tools and procedures in our last lesson and have used some of them in this lesson. Indeed, we'll continue to use them throughout our text and our computer-drafting career. But consider this scenario.

A builder is creating an object – we'll use the figure we saw in our *UCS Practice 2* drawing (Exercise 2.1.1) as an example. As he adds a piece here or trims a piece there, he holds the object in his hand and rotates it this way and that to get a better understanding … a better feel for its shape. How can you do the same thing with the computer model *before* our builder creates it?

You can use the viewpoint tool we've been using. You can even speed it up slightly by using preset viewpoints on the View toolbar. But let's face it; at best, this tool is too slow and cumbersome for the scenario just discussed. It won't provide the insights our builder will get by rotating the object at different angles.

For this reason, AutoCAD has provided some extraordinary tools – *3DOrbit*, *3DCOrbit* (3D Continuous Orbit), and *3DFOrbit* (3D Free Orbit). Let's take a look at each.

2.4.1 Controlled Orbiting & Associated Commands

The *3DFOrbit* command (Free Orbit) allows you to rotate a model on the computer screen just as the builder did in his hand.

Hands are marvels of engineering. We use them without a second thought – forgetting the time our infant minds struggled to control them.

Orbit!?

3DFOrbit is also quite a marvel – and it'll also take some time to learn to control it. But we'll soon come to appreciate it almost as much as a builder appreciates his hands!

Access the 3D Free Orbit screen with the *3DFOrbit* command like this:

Command: *3dforbit*

Press ESC or ENTER to exit, or right-click to display shortcut-menu.

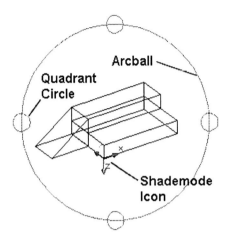

Figure 2.007

AutoCAD displays a sort of three-dimensional compass over the screen (in the current viewport). The compass is called an **Arcball** (Figure 2.007) and will help you control your movements while using the orbiter.

The arcball and smaller quadrant circles allow you to determine how to manipulate the model. It works like this:

WHEN THE CURSOR BEGINS:	DRAGGING THE CURSOR WILL:	THE CURSOR WILL LOOK LIKE:
Inside the arcball	Manipulate the model freely about its center point.	
Outside the arcball	Perform a two-dimensional rotation (called a roll) about an axis extending through the center of the arcball (and outward from the screen).	
Inside the east or west quadrant circle	Rotate the model about the north axis of the arcball.	
Inside the north or south quadrant circle	Rotate the model about the east/west axis of the arcball.	

To reset the original view, right click and select **Reset View** from the cursor menu. (We'll see more on the cursor menu after the next exercise.)

Most of this will become clearer with practice. We'll try an exercise in a minute.

The *3DOrbit* command (aka. **3D *Constrained* Orbit**) operates something like the *3DFOrbit* command except that it lacks the arcball. When using 3DOrbit and dragging left-and-right with your crosshairs, AutoCAD rotates the objects parallel to the XY-plane. When you drag up-and-down, AutoCAD rotates objects along the Z-planes. The benefit of 3D Constrained Orbit is that AutoCAD prevents you from accidentally rotating the object over completely.

Do This: 2.4.1.1	**Three-Dimensional Orbiting**

I.   Reopen the *UCS Practice 2.dwg* file in the C:\Steps3D\Lesson02 folder. (If you didn't save your changes in this drawing, open UCS *Practice 2a.dwg* instead.) Restore the *MyBottom* UCS and set the viewpoint to –1,1.5,-1.

II. Follow these steps.

2.4.1.1: THREE-DIMENSIONAL ORBITING

1. Enter the ***3DFOrbit*** command. Alternately, you can also select **Free Orbit** from the View pull-down menu or pick the **Free Orbit** button 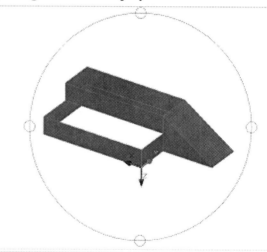 on the Orbit toolbar or Navigation control panel.

   Command: *3dforbit*

2. Place your cursor in the western quadrant circle.

   Press ESC or ENTER to exit, or right-click to display shortcut-menu.

3. With the left mouse button, click and drag to the opposite quadrant circle. Notice how the model rotates. Release the mouse button. Your drawing now looks like this.	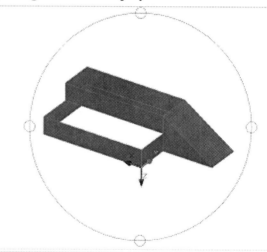
4. Repeat Steps 3 and 4, but this time begin in the upper quadrant circle and end in the lower quadrant circle. Your drawing looks like this. Notice that the UCS icon continues to orient the model for you.	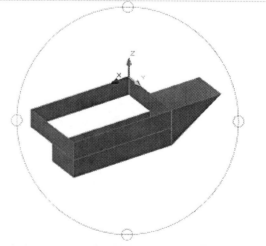

5. Place your cursor outside the arcball near the western quadrant circle. Pick and drag around the arcball to a similar location outside the eastern quadrant circle. (Note: Don't pass through the arcball, as your cursor and the manipulation procedure will change.)

Your drawing looks like this.

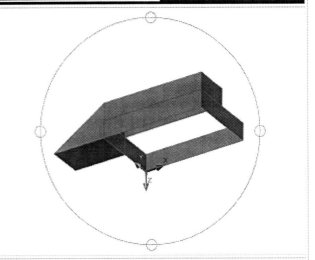

6. Now experiment with the freestyle rotation. Place your cursor inside the arcball and drag it around. Watch and try to control the rotation.

You don't have to drag from quadrant circle to quadrant circle as we did here, but using the quadrant circles makes it a little easier to control what your doing. Feel free, once you've gotten the feel for the *3DFOrbit* command, to rotate as much or as little as you want.

7. Use the cursor menu to change commands from *3dforbit* to constrained orbit (*3DOrbit*).

Notice that the arcball disappears and your cursor changes to one similar to the one you get inside the arcball.

8. Now using your left mouse button, drag from left to right across your screen.

9. Repeat Step 8, but this time, move your cursor up-and-down. Notice that AutoCAD won't allow you to flip the object completely over. The orbit is *constrained*.

10. Complete the command.

Press ESC or ENTER to exit, or right-click to display shortcut-menu. *[enter]*

11. Exit the drawing without saving your changes.

Command: *quit*

As if these procedures alone wouldn't make this a priceless tool in a three-dimensional world, notice that the command prompt offers you the opportunity to **right-click to display shortcut-menu**. There's more!

Let's take a look at the cursor menu (shortcut-menu). Refer to Figure 2.008.

- The top frame contains only one option. Select **Exit** to leave the orbiter.
- The second frame tells you what your current orbiting mode is. It also provides a flyout menu to allow you to change the mode to any of those shown in Figure 2.009. These include:
  - The three orbiting options (**Constrained Orbit**, **Free Orbit**, and **Continuous Orbit**)
  - The **Adjust Distance** option appears to do the same thing that the *3DZoom* command does. (More on 3DZoom in a moment.) The difference is that this option calls the *3DDistance* command, which actually changes the distance between you and the model.

No distortion results from the *3DDistance* command as it may from the *3DZoom* command. The *3DDistance* command even has its own cursor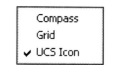

- o The **Swivel** option calls the *3DSwivel* command. This adjusts the view as though a camera, although stationary, is revolving on its tripod. This tool comes in handy when viewing an architectural, structural, or piping drawing from inside the model.

  It also has its own cursor ⟨⟩.

- o **Walk** calls the *3DWalk* command and the Position Locator tool palette. We'll spend some time with this toward the end of our text.

- o **Fly** calls the *3DFly* command. It also calls the Position Locator tool palette. These tools work together and we'll look at them together toward the end of our text.

- o **Zoom** and **Pan** call the dynamic commands. These work as they always have, but a useful trick when working with 3d objects is to select a specific object before entering the command. AutoCAD will hide everything except that object while zooming/panning.

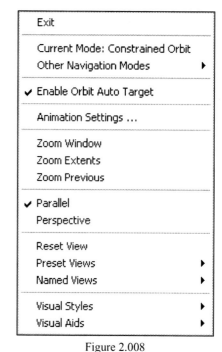

Figure 2.008

- By default, AutoCAD mercifully turns on **Enable Orbit Auto Target** (back on the original menu – Figure 2.008). This causes orbits to revolve around the center of the objects you're viewing rather than the center of the viewport. I'd leave this one alone!

Constrained Orbit	1
Free Orbit	2
Continuous Orbit	3
Adjust Distance	4
Swivel	5
Walk	6
Fly	7
Zoom	8
Pan	9

Figure 2.009: Navigation Mode

Top
Bottom
Front
Back
Left
Right
SW Isometric
SE Isometric
NE Isometric
NW Isometric

Figure 2.010: Preset Views

- **Animation Settings** calls the Animation Settings dialog box. We'll see that one toward the end of the text as well.

3D Hidden
3D Wireframe
Conceptual
Realistic

Figure 2.011: Visual Styles

Compass
Grid
UCS Icon

Figure 2.012: Visual Aids

- **Zoom Window, Extents**, and **Previous** do just that but don't require that you leave the orbiter to do it.

- **Parallel** and **Perspective** change how you see your drawing. **Parallel** works find for most drafting situations; **Perspective** presents a more artistic view.

- **Reset View** is your "Hail Mary" for orbiting. Use it to set the view back to what is was when you started orbiting.

- **Preset Views** presents a flyout list of the basic preset views in AutoCAD (Figure 2.010). You'll find these on the Views toolbar as well.

- **Named Views** does the same thing with any user-named views in the drawing.

- **Visual Styles** presents a flyout list of the visual styles in this drawing (Figure 2.011). You'll find these in the Visual Styles control panel as well.

- Finally, **Visual Aids** calls the menu in Figure 2.012. I can't recommend using the **Compass** called by this option. It tends to clutter the screen. The **Grid** option simply toggles the grid on. The can be useful to help orient you just as the **UCS Icon** can.

2.4.2	**Clipping 3D Objects for Better Viewing**

The *3DClip* command presents the Adjust Clipping Planes dialog box (Figure 2.013) with the model shown at 90° to the current 3D Orbital display. The lines through the center of the window are the clipping planes. Pick and drag to adjust their locations.

Figure 2.013

Control what you see with the five buttons along the top of the dialog box. These are (from the left):

- **Adjust Front Clipping** allows you to move the front clipping plane up or down.
- **Adjust Back Clipping** allows you to move the back clipping plane up or down.
- **Create Slice** allows you to move both clipping planes together.
- **Pan** calls the *Pan* command within the Adjust Clipping Plane window.
- **Zoom** calls the *Zoom* command within the Adjust Clipping Plane window.
- **Front Clipping On/Off** toggles front clipping on or off. When **On**, AutoCAD won't display anything in front of (below) the front clipping plane.
- **Back Clipping On/Off** toggles back clipping on or off. When **On**, AutoCAD won't display anything behind (above) the clipping plane.
- Toggle both clippings off to view the entire model.

Let's look at the orbiter's clipping planes.

Do This: 2.4.2.1	**Using Clipping Planes**

    I.   Reopen the *UCS Practice 2*[or 2a].*dwg* file in the C:\Steps3D\Lesson02 folder.

    II.   Follow these steps.

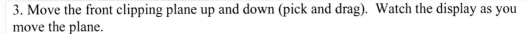

2.4.2.1: USING CLIPPING PLANES

1. Enter the *3DClip* command.
       Command: *3dclip*

2. AutoCAD presents the **Adjust Clipping Planes** window with **Adjust Front Clipping** toggled **On** (refer to Figure 2.013). Toggle the **Front Clipping** On.

3. Move the front clipping plane up and down (pick and drag). Watch the display as you move the plane.

4. Repeat Steps 2 and 3 using the **Back Clipping** plane. (Be sure to toggle **Back Clipping** On and use the **Adjust Back Clipping** toggle .)

5. Let's create a slice. Move both clipping planes fairly close to each other, then pick the

Create Slice button .

6. Move the clipping planes up and down (pick and drag). Watch the display. You're cutting everything before and behind the clipping planes from your view.

7. Close ☒ the Adjust Clipping Planes dialog box.

8. Rotate the object as you did in the previous exercise and watch the effect clipping has on your view.

9. Repeat the **3DClip** command and toggle both the clipping planes off 🔲 and 🔲.

2.4.3	A Continuous Three-Dimensional Orbit – *3DCOrbit*

This tool is guaranteed to razzle-dazzle friends and co-workers (and employers) alike! The **3DCOrbit** command (3D Continuous Orbit) allows you to begin a rotation – and then remove your hands from the keyboard or mouse and watch as AutoCAD continuously rotates the model on the screen.

To use the **3DCOrbit** command, first enter the command or select it from the 3DOrbit toolbar. AutoCAD prompts:

Command: *3dcorbit*
Press ESC or ENTER to exit, or right-click to display shortcut-menu.

Notice that the prompt is the same as the **3DOrbit** command prompt. By right-clicking at any time during the 3D Continuous Orbit, you can access the same cursor menu available through any of the **3DOrbit** commands. Alternately, you can begin a continual orbit of the model. To do this, pick any point on the screen and drag the cursor in the direction you'd like the model to spin. Notice the cursor changes to one of the 3DOrbit cursors (depending on which direction you drag). Release the mouse button and the model continues to spin on its axis – like a planet. The speed at which you drag the cursor determines the speed of the spin.

To stop the spinning, hit either the ENTER or ESC key on the keyboard or right-click and select **Exit** from the cursor menu. The model stops spinning where it is. Use the **Undo** command to return to the orientation it had before the command.

Give it a try.

Do This: 2.4.3.1	**Creating a Continuous Orbit**

    I.   Be sure you're still in the *UCS Practice 2.dwg* file in the C:\Steps3D\Lesson02 folder.
    II.   Follow these steps.

1. Enter the **3DCOrbit** command at the command line or pick the **3D Continuous Orbit**

button 🔲 on the 3DOrbit toolbar or Navigation control panel.
    Command: *3dcorbit*

2. Pick a point on the right side of the screen and drag to the left. Release the mouse button about halfway across the screen but continue the mouse movement (use some follow-through as though you're hitting a golf ball).
    Press ESC or ENTER to exit, or right-click to display shortcut-menu.

2.4.3.1: CREATING A CONTINUOUS ORBIT

3. Watch the model spin before your very eyes!

4. Hit *enter* to stop the rotation.

   Press ESC or ENTER to exit, or right-click to display shortcut-menu. *[enter]*

5. Close the drawing without saving it.

   Command: *quit*

2.5   Extra Steps

It may take some practice to get the feel of the *3DCOrbit* command. Take a few minutes now and repeat the last exercise until you feel comfortable. Change some of the colors for a flashier shown. Try different speeds of rotation.

Can you see how this tool might be useful?

2.6   What Have We Learned?

Items covered in this lesson include:

- *The differences between the UCS and the WCS*
- *How to use the UCS and different working planes*
- *How to use the UCS Dialog Box (Manager)*
- *How to dimension a three-dimensional drawing*
- *How to use AutoCAD's orbiting tools*
- *Commands:*
  - *UCS*
  - *UCSMan*
  - *3DOrbit*
  - *3DPan*
  - *3DZoom*

  - *3DDistance*
  - *3DSwivel*
  - *3DClip*
  - *3DCOrbit*
  - *3DFOrbit*

My chief Grammar and Usage Editor will say this was another full lesson!

But pat yourself on the back! Having made it to this point is no slight accomplishment. In these two lessons, you've mastered the basics for working in Z-Space. Let's take a minute and think about what you can do now that you couldn't do before beginning this text.

- You can maneuver in a drawing from front to back, side to side, and up and down (Spherical and Cylindrical Coordinate Systems, Point Filters).
- You can see your drawing from any point in the universe (*VPoint* and *Plan*).
- You can work on any surface as though it were lying flat on your desk (*UCS*).
- You have a host of new viewing tools to help you see your model from any angle or several angles at one time (*VPoint*, *VPorts*, 3DOrbit tools).
- You can create three-dimensional stick figures (wireframes) and even draw with thickness and elevation.

You've come a long way in a short period of time, but there's still far to go. (Oh, the sights still to see ...) Most of what you learn about Z-space from here will be tools and techniques to make three-dimensional drawing easier, faster, and prettier!

As always, we should practice what we've learned before continuing our study. Do the exercises and answer the questions. Then proceed to our study of Wireframe and Surface Modeling techniques.

2.7   Exercises

1. to 8. Dimension the drawings you created in Exercises 1 through 8 of Section 1.7 (in Lesson 1). Refer to the drawings in Appendix B as a guide. If these drawings are not available, use the corresponding drawing in the C:\Steps3D\Lesson02 folder.

9. [Refer to Section 1.7 of Lesson 1 – Exercise #9.] Open the *My Twisted Y.dwg* file in the C:\Steps3D\Lesson01 folder. [If the *My Twisted Y.dwg* file isn't available, use the *Twisted Y.dwg* file found in the C:\Steps3D\Lesson02 folder.]

    9.1. Place the dimensions shown in Figure 1.018.

    9.2. Save the drawing to the C:\Steps3D\Lesson02 folder.

10. [Refer to Section 1.7 of Lesson 1 – Exercise #10.] Open the *My Block.dwg* file in the C:\Steps3D\Lesson01 folder. [If the *My Block.dwg* file isn't available, use the *Block.dwg* file found in the C:\Steps3D\Lesson02 folder.]

    10.1.   Place the dimensions shown in Figure 1.019.

    10.2.   Save the drawing to the C:\Steps3D\Lesson02 folder.

11. [Refer to Section 1.7 of Lesson 1 – Exercise #11.] Open the *MyGrill.dwg* file in the C:\Steps3D\Lesson01 folder. [If the *My Grill.dwg* file isn't available, use the *Grill.dwg* file found in the C:\Steps3D\Lesson02 folder.]

    11.1.   Place the dimensions shown in Figure 1.020.

    11.2.   Save the drawing to the C:\Steps3D\Lesson02 folder.

12. [Refer to Section 1.7 of Lesson 1 – Exercise #12.] Open the *MyBookEnd.dwg* file in the C:\Steps3D\Lesson01 folder. [If the *MyBookEnd.dwg* file isn't available, use the *BookEnd.dwg* file found in the C:\Steps3D\Lesson02 folder.]

    12.1.   Place the dimensions shown in Figure 1.021.

    12.2.   Save the drawing to the C:\Steps3D\Lesson02 folder.

13. [Refer to Section 1.7 of Lesson 1 – Exercise #13.] Open the *MyMagRack.dwg* file in the C:\Steps3D\Lesson01 folder. [If the *MyMagRack.dwg* file isn't available, use the *MagRack.dwg* file found in the C:\Steps3D\Lesson02 folder.]

    13.1.   Place the dimensions shown in Figure 1.022.

    13.2.   Save the drawing to the C:\Steps3D\Lesson02 folder.

14. [Refer to Section 1.7 of Lesson 1 – Exercise #14.] Open the *My Anchor Stop.dwg* file in the C:\Steps3D\Lesson01 folder. [If the *My Anchor Stop.dwg* file isn't available, use the *Anchor Stop.dwg* file found in the C:\Steps3D\Lesson02 folder.]

    14.1.   Place the dimensions shown in Figure 1.023.

    14.2.   Save the drawing to the C:\Steps3D\Lesson02 folder.

15. [Refer to Section 1.7 of Lesson 1 – Exercise #15.] Open the *My Queen.dwg* file in the C:\Steps3D\Lesson01 folder. [If the *My Queen.dwg* file isn't available, use the *Queen.dwg* file found in the C:\Steps3D\Lesson02 folder.]

    15.1.   Place the dimensions shown in Figure 1.024.

    15.2.   Save the drawing to the C:\Steps3D\Lesson02 folder.

16. [Refer to Section 1.7 of Lesson 1 – Exercise #16.] Open the *My Ring Stand.dwg* file in the C:\Steps3D\Lesson01 folder. [If the *My Ring Stand.dwg* file isn't available, use the *Ring Stand.dwg* file found in the C:\Steps3D\Lesson02 folder.]

    16.1.   Place the dimensions shown in Figure 1.025.

    16.2.   Save the drawing to the C:\Steps3D\Lesson02 folder.

17. Create the drawing in Figure 2.014 according to the following parameters:
    17.1. Start the drawing using *template #2* found in the C:\Steps3D\Lesson02 folder.
    17.2. The Paper Space text is 3/16" and 1/8".
    17.3. Title block text is ¼", 3/16", and 1/8".
    17.4. Text on the blocks uses either AutoCAD's standard text style or a type using the Time New Roman font. Text heights are ¼".
    17.5. Save the drawing as *My Angled Blocks.dwg* in the C:\Steps3D\Lesson02 folder.

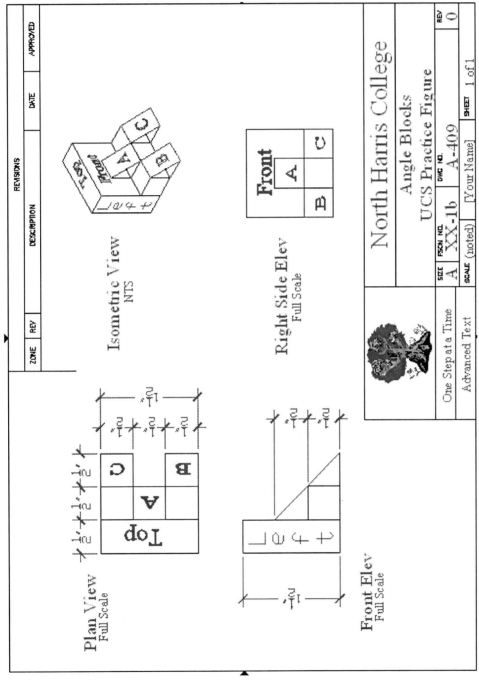

Figure 2.014

18. Create the drawing in Figure 2.015 according to the following parameters:
   18.1.   Start the drawing using *template #1* found in the C:\Steps3D\Lesson01 folder.
   18.2.   The Paper Space text is 3/16" and 1/8".
   18.3.   Title block text is ¼", 3/16", and 1/8". The font is Times New Roman.
   18.4.   Text on the blocks uses AutoCAD's standard text style. Text height is 3/16".
   18.5.   Save the drawing as *My Corner Steps.dwg* in the C:\Steps3D\Lesson02 folder.

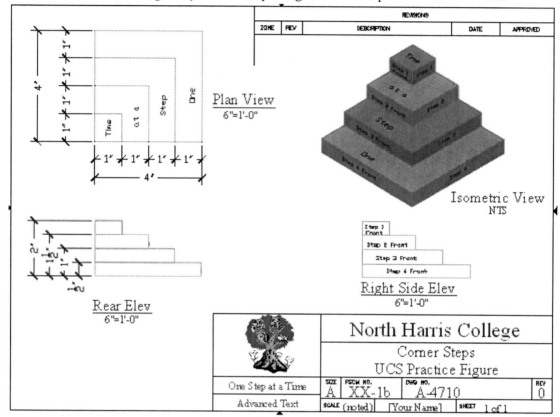

Figure 2.015

19. The drawing in Figure 2.016 is a game of UCS manipulation and the **Array** and **Mirror** commands. Create it according to the following parameters:

   19.1. The tabletop is a 5" width x 5" long polyline drawn with a ½" thickness.
   19.2. Each of the eight legs is made up of eight lines. Each line is 5" long. The original was drawn at 30° in the XY-lane and 60° from the XY-plane. The lines were then arrayed in a 1/16" circle.
   19.3. The eight "feet" are ¼" radius circles. Again, they were arrayed (eight circles in each array).
   19.4. The center ball (at the intersection of the legs) is also an arrayed circle (eight in all) – this one with a ½" radius.
   19.5. The upper legs are mirrored from the bottom.
   19.6. Have fun!
   19.7. Save the drawing as *My Table.dwg* in the C:\Steps3D\Lesson02 folder.

Figure 2.016

20. Create the drawing in Figure 2.017 according to the following parameters:
   20.1.   This is a B-size (11" x 17") layout. Use the appropriate AutoCAD title block/border.
   20.2.   The Paper Space text is 3/16" and 1/8".
   20.3.   Title block text is ¼", 3/16", and 1/8". The font is Times New Roman.
   20.4.   The top is a single polyline drawn with ½ thickness.
   20.5.   Save the drawing as *My Other Table.dwg* in the C:\Steps3D\Lesson02 folder.

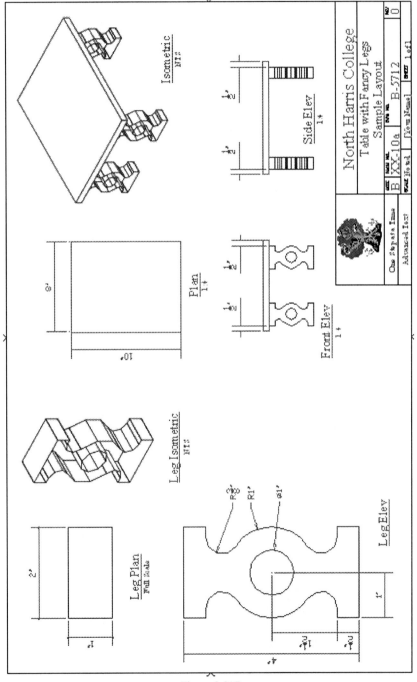

Figure 2.017

21. Create the drawing in Figure 2.018 according to the following parameters:
    21.1.   This is a B-size (11" x 17") layout. Use the appropriate AutoCAD title block/border.
    21.2.   The Paper Space text is 3/16" and 1/8".
    21.3.   Title block text is ¼", 3/16", and 1/8". The font is Times New Roman.
    21.4.   This is a wireframe drawing – use thickness only on the arcs/circles.
    21.5.   Save the drawing as *My Corner Bracket.dwg* in the C:\Steps3D\Lesson02 folder.

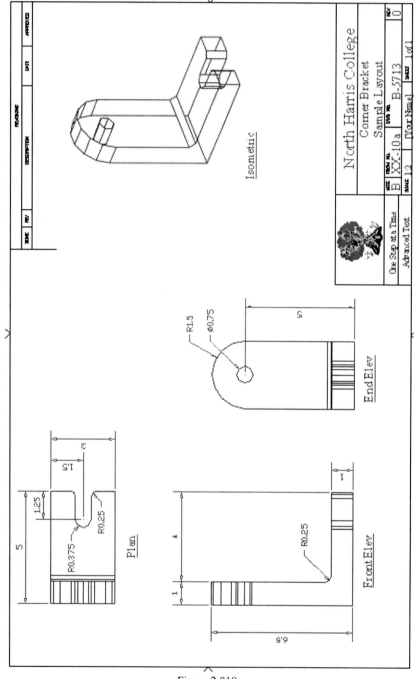

Figure 2.018

22. Create the drawing in Figure 2.019 according to the following parameters:

    22.1.   This is an A-size (8½" x 11") layout. Use the appropriate AutoCAD title block/border.

    22.2.   The Paper Space text is 3/16" and 1/8".

    22.3.   Title block text is ¼", 3/16", and 1/8". The font is Times New Roman.

    22.4.   This is a wireframe drawing – don't use thickness.

    22.5.   You'll need to use the **3DClip** procedures to clean up the views.

    22.6.   Save the drawing as *My Phone Plug.dwg* in the C:\Steps3D\Lesson02 folder.

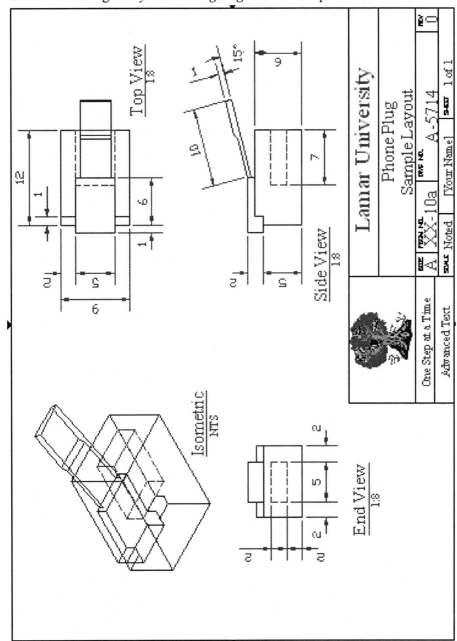

Figure 2.019

23. Create the drawing in Figure 2.020 according to the following parameters:

23.1.   This is a B-size (11" x 17") layout. Use the appropriate AutoCAD title block/border.

23.2.   The Paper Space text is 3/16" and 1/8".

23.3.   Title block text is ¼", 3/16", and 1/8". The font is Times New Roman.

23.4.   This is a wireframe drawing – use thickness only on the arcs/circles.

23.5.   You'll need to use the **3DClip** procedures to clean up the views.

23.6.   Save the drawing as *My Other Corner Bracket.dwg* in the C:\Steps3D\Lesson02 folder.

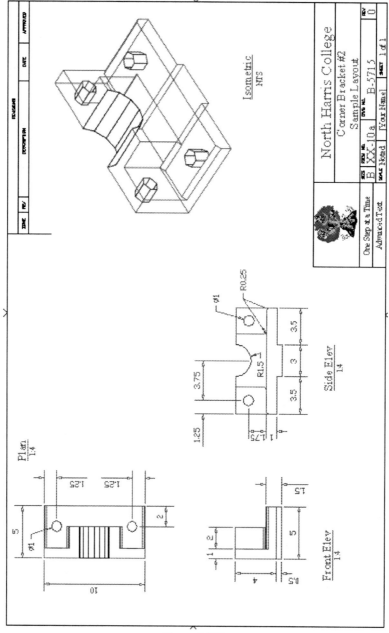

Figure 2.020

2.8   **For Web-Based Review Questions, visit:**
http://www.uneedcad.com/2007/Files/07R2-3D.pdf

Lesson

3

Following this lesson, you will:

- ✓ *Know the differences between a polyline and a three-dimensional polyline*

- ✓ *Know how to project a curved surface in three dimensions*

- ✓ *Know how to create a three-dimensional face (**3DFace**)*

  - o *Know how to make the edges of a face visible or invisible*

- ✓ *Know the differences between solids and regions*

  - o *Know how to create a region with the **Region** command*

  - o *Know how to create a region with the **Boundary** command*

- ✓ *Know how to use the **Subtract** command to remove one region from another*

Wireframes and Surface Modeling

Most textbooks separate Wireframe Modeling and Surface Modeling into two distinct chapters. But the inevitable result is confusion. The two are so closely related that distinguishing between them often causes more bewilderment than just teaching them as they are – two sides of the same coin. Let me make the distinction as simple as possible.

A wireframe model (what we've called a stick figure up until now) is a skeleton drawing. It has all the necessary parts – but no flesh. Drawing a wireframe model is relatively fast (compared to a surface model), but it provides little more than an outline of the model. When used, wireframes generally lead the three-dimensional design process (in the layout stage). Fleshing out the wireframe – turning it into a surface model – comes when the layout is accepted, and you want to turn the skeleton into a production or display drawing.

A surface model essentially stretches some skin over the skeleton. We've seen that visual styles have no effect on wireframe models. Fleshing out the skeleton makes it possible to see surfaces (hence, the name).

In this lesson, we'll learn how to create more complex wireframe models. Then we'll look at some ways to create surfaces.

A quick note about surface modeling before we begin:

AutoCAD is trending away from surface modeling in favor of (far superior) solid modeling. This will benefit most 3-dimensional designers. However, those who wish to continue in the 3D world – into such places as cartooning, animation, gaming, etc. – will do well to learn what they can of surface modeling. Most animation packages – Lightwave, 3D Studio, Maya, Poser, and others – rely heavily on surface models. (I've often found it faster and easier to create a surface model in AutoCAD and transfer it to Lightwave and Poser. I'm sure the same holds true for many Studio users.)

Because of this, we retain Lessons 3 through 5 despite the trend. If you're absolutely sure you'll never need surface models, you can skip Lesson 4, but 3 and 5 have information that will prove useful in any 3D work.

3.1   *3DPoly* vs. *PLine*

Now that you're working with Z-coordinates, you may have noticed a certain limitation in polylines – polylines are two-dimensional creatures. True, you can give a polyline thickness and elevation, but you can't draw a polyline using different points on the Z-axis. That is, when prompted to **Specify next point**, your selection will use the same point on the Z-axis as the first point you identified regardless of any three-dimensional coordinate you give it!

But that doesn't mean that you have to sacrifice the benefits of a polyline ... well, not entirely anyway. AutoCAD provides a three-dimensional version of the polyline call the *3DPoly*. When you need a multi-segmented polyline drawn in Z-space, simply use the *3DPoly* command instead of the *PLine* command.

There are, however, some restrictions to the 3DPoly. Chief among these is that a 3D polyline can't contain width. AutoCAD hasn't added this useful property yet. Additionally, you can't draw a 3D polyline using arcs or linetypes other than continuous.

Bear in mind that, while use of the polyline is restricted in Z-space, use of the spline isn't. You can use the *Spline* command when you want to draw curved lines in three dimensions. However, most surfaces created for a surface model will have flat edges and won't be able to lie flat against a spline.

The benefits of the 3DPoly include the ability to draw it in three dimensions, to edit it with the *PEdit* command, and to spline it.

We'll use the *3DPoly* command in our first exercise.

You may think that wireframe modeling is a fairly easy thing to do. After all, a wireframe model is just stick figures, right?

Of course, you're absolutely right. Stick figures are quite simple to draw – as long as the model you want to draw uses nice straight sticks. But consider the curved panel roof in Figure 3.001. Using the UCS procedures you learned in Lesson 2, you can easily draw the arcs and rooflines. But how would you draw the joint between the roofs? (Uh, oh! Here we go with the hard questions again.)

To draw in three directions at once as this joint requires – (front to back, side to side, and up and down – means that you must identify a series of points where the two roofs intersect. To do this, you must project points – that is, you must identify points by intersection of lines in Z-space.

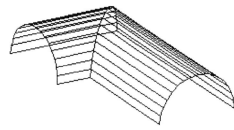

Figure 3.001

This isn't as difficult as it sounds. In fact, it's a lot like duck hunting (or skeet shooting for those with weaker stomachs).

To hit a moving target, you must lead it a bit so that your bullet and the bird (or clay pigeon) arrive at the same place at the same time. What you do when you project points is simply identify where the bird and the bullet will meet. You do this by projecting one line along the bird's flight path and another along the barrel of your rifle. The intersection of the two lines is your actual target – or in drafting terms, your projection point.

Let's see how this works. We'll use our projection technique to identify the intersecting arc of the two roofs and then draw the arc using the 3D polyline.

Remember that all three-dimensional drafting requires precise point identification using one of the methods we've already discussed. You can't pick an "about here" point and get away with it as you might have in two-dimensional drafting.

Do This: 3.2.1	Projections and 3D Polylines

    I.   Open the *Cabin.dwg* file in the C:\Steps3D\Lesson03 folder. The drawing looks like Figure 3.002.

    II.   Follow these steps.

Figure 3.002

3.2.1: PROJECTIONS AND 3D POLYLINES

1. Use the *Divide* command to divide each of the arcs into 16 segments. (If the divisions aren't clearly marked, set the **PDMode** system variable to **3** and regenerate the drawing.)

        Command: *div*

        Select object to divide:

        Enter the number of segments or [Block]: *16*

Notice that the nodes appear in the UCS that was current when the arcs were drawn.

2. Set the **roof** layer current.

3. Draw lines between the corresponding nodes and endpoints as shown. (The lines represent the duck's flight path and the barrel of our rifle.)

(Hint: You may find it easier to draw one line in each direction and then copy it to each of the nodes/endpoints.)

Command: *l*

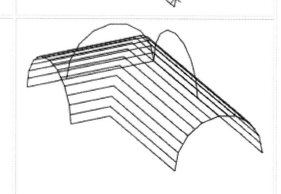

4. Freeze the **Marker2** layer.

5. Carefully trim ⊣ the extra portions of the lines. Start with the nearest intersection – lowest north-south line with lowest east-west line – and work back. (Hint: You may fine it easier to do this from the plan view. But watch the first and last endpoints.)

Command: *tr*

Return to this view (VPoint 2,-1,1) when you've finished. Your drawing looks like this.

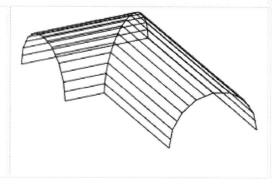

6. Erase ✎ the arcs in the back.

Command: *e*

7. Draw a 3D polyline connecting the intersections of the extension lines as shown. Use OSNAPs! (It might be easier to do this in plan view.)

> **Command: *3dpoly***
> **Specify start point of polyline:**
> **Specify endpoint of line or [Undo]:**
> **Specify endpoint of line or [Undo]:**
> **Specify endpoint of line or [Close/Undo]:**

8. Save the drawing 🖫 but don't exit.

Command: *qsave*

Look closely at the 2D polyline you created. Notice that it's a series of straight lines, not curved like the roof. We might have used a spline instead of the 3D polyline and achieved a nice soft curve, but the tool we'll use to "stretch the skin around our skeleton" doesn't allow for curves. So we're better off using the straighter 3D polyline (as we'll soon see).

3.3 Adding Surfaces – Regions, Solids, and 3D Faces

AutoCAD provides three methods for creating surface models – the ***Region***, ***Solid***, and ***3DFace*** commands. The three are so closely related that it's often difficult to tell the difference:

- You'll draw each as a two-dimensional object.
- Each becomes a 3D solid when extruded (more on the ***Extrude*** command in Lesson 7).

- Each creates an opaque (or solid) surface.

But despite their similarities, each has its place.

- The **Region** command converts a closed object (polygon, circle, two-dimensional spline, etc.) into a surface. A region can't have thickness.
- The **Solid** command fills an area only in the current UCS, but it can have thickness.
- The **3DFace** command draws a true three-dimensional surface (in all of the X-, Y-, and Z-planes). A 3D face can't have thickness.

When would you use one instead of the other two? Let's take a look at each and see.

3.3.1 Creating 3D Faces

Of the three surfacing methods, the **3DFace** command is the most versatile. However, it's also more difficult to use when cutouts are involved. The **3DFace** command makes no allowance for removal of part of the surface (as the **Trim** command allows you to remove part of a line or circle). You can, however, draw a 3D face without concern for the current UCS (provided coordinate entry is precise).

The command sequence looks like this:

> **Command:** *3DFace*
> **Specify first point or [Invisible]:** *[select the first corner point]*
> **Specify second point or [Invisible]:** *[select the second corner point]*
> **Specify third point or [Invisible] <exit>:** *[select the third corner point]*
> **Specify fourth point or [Invisible] <create three-sided face>:** *select the fourth point or hit enter to create a 3D face from the three points already selected]*
> **Specify third point or [Invisible] <exit>:** *[you can continue selecting points or hit enter to exit the command]*

The only option available – **Invisible** – isn't one you really want to use. When creating 3D faces, it'll occasionally be necessary to hide one of the edges (or make it invisible). (This will become apparent in the next exercise.) The command line procedure for doing this involves typing an *I* before the first point selection that defines the edge to be hidden. The edge drawn between the two points that follow the *I* will be invisible. This becomes a real chore when two or more edges must be hidden. We'll look at an easier approach to hiding the edges of 3D faces following the next exercise.

First, let's use the **3DFace** command to place a surface – with a window in it – on one of the walls of our cabin.

> You can also access the **3DFace** command by selecting it from the Draw pull-down menu.
> Follow this path:
>
> *Draw – Modeling – Meshes – 3D Face*

Do This: 3.3.1.1 Surfaces with 3D Faces

I.   Be sure you're still in the *Cabin.dwg* file in the C:\Steps3D\Lesson03 folder. If not, please open it now.

II.   Set UCS = WCS.

III.   Set the **3D Wireframe** visual style for this exercise.

IV.   Thaw the **WALLS** and **MARKER** layers; freeze the **roof** layer. The drawing looks like Figure 3.003.

V.   Follow these steps.

Figure 3.003

71

1. Zoom in 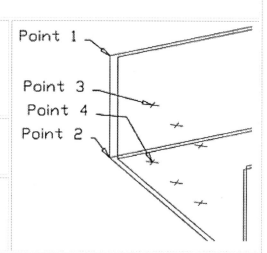 around the protruding part of the cabin – the wall with six nodes (refer to the Step 3 figure).

Command: *z*

2. The front wall consists of two lines drawn with thickness. We can't put a window in these objects, so we'll remove the thickness and replace the lines with 3D faces.

Begin by changing the thickness of both lines (inner and outer walls) to **0**. (Use the Properties Palette .)

Command: *props*

3. Begin the **3DFace** command. Pick Point 1 as your first point.

Command: *3dface*

Specify first point or [Invisible]:
[select Point 1]

4. Pick Point 2 as the second point.

Specify second point or [Invisible]:
[select Point 2]

5. We'll use point filters to locate the third point. Tell AutoCAD to use the XY values of Point 3 …

Specify third point or [Invisible]
<exit>: *.xy*

6. … and the Z value of Point 2.

of (need Z): *[select Point 2]*

7. Again, we'll use point filters to locate the fourth point. Tell AutoCAD to use the X and Y values of Point 4 …

Specify fourth point or [Invisible] <create three-sided face>: *.xy*

8. … and the Z value of Point 1.

of (need Z): *[select Point 1]*

9. Complete the command.

Specify third point or [Invisible]
<exit>: *[enter]*

Your drawing looks like this.

72

10. Repeat Steps 4 through 10 to draw the other end of the wall and the walls above and below the window.

Command: *3dface*

Set the 3D Hidden visual style current. Your drawing will look like this.

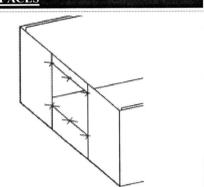

11. Save the drawing ⌷ but don't exit.

Command: *qsave*

You should've noticed three things about the last exercise.

- Although quite useful, the skeleton (wireframe model) isn't required when drawing a surface model.
- The ***3DFace*** command has left lines (edges) above and below the window that don't normally appear on a model (or a wall).
- The current UCS didn't affect placement of the 3D faces.

Let's take a look at those edges.

3.3.2	Invisible Edges in 3D Faces – SPLFrame and the *Edge* Command

Although you can make 3D face edges invisible as you draw them, it's a tedious, time-consuming, and error-prone task. You'll find it much easier to draw the 3D face and then use the ***Edge*** command to hide the edges that you don't want to see.

The command sequence looks like this:

Command: *edge*

Specify edge of 3dface to toggle visibility or [Display]:

Simply select the edge you want to make invisible. How much easier can they make it?

The only option (**Display**) prompts like this:

Enter selection method for display of hidden edges [Select/All] <All>:

Respond by selecting a 3D face whose invisible edges you'd like to see or by hitting ***enter*** to accept the **All** option. The **All** option means that AutoCAD will show all the invisible edges in the display.

Use of the **Display** option allows you to *temporarily* display all invisible edges. Once the command ends, invisible edges are once again invisible.

To display all of the 3D face edges in a drawing, whether visible or not, set the **SPLFrame** system variable to **1**.

Let's make the necessary edges invisible on our new surfaces.

> You can also access the ***Edge*** command by selecting it from the Draw pull-down menu. Follow this path:
>
> *Draw – Modeling – Meshes – Edge*

Do This: 3.3.2.1	**Invisible Edges**

I. Be sure you're still in the *Cabin.dwg* file in the C:\Steps3D\Lesson03 folder. If not, please open it now.

II.   Follow these steps.

3.3.2.1: INVISIBLE EDGES
1. Enter the **Edge** command.   **Command:** *edge*
2. Select the edges below the window and the edges above the window. Also select the upper and lower window edges.   **Specify edge of 3dface to toggle visibility or [Display]:**
3. Complete the command.   **Specify edge of 3dface to toggle visibility or [Display]:** *[enter]*

4. Freeze the **Marker** layer.
Your drawing looks like this.

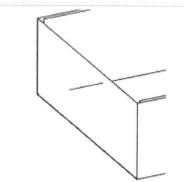

5. Now we'll draw the actual window. First we need to find the edges of our 3D face. Do this by setting the **SPLFrame** system variable to **1**. (Regen the drawing to see the results.)

     Command: *splframe*

     Enter new value for SPLFRAME <0>: *1*

6. Set **Windows** as the current layer.

7. Change the UCS 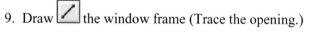 to match the front of the wall (Figure 3.011).

     Command: *ucs*

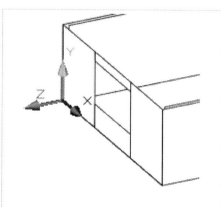

8. Set **Thickness** to **-5.5**.

     Command: *th*

     Enter new value for THICKNESS <0'-0">: *-5.5*

9. Draw the window frame (Trace the opening.)

     Command: *l*

10. Return the **SPLFrame** system variable to zero and remove the hidden lines.

     Command: *splframe*

     Enter new value for SPLFRAME <1>: *0*

Your drawing looks like this.

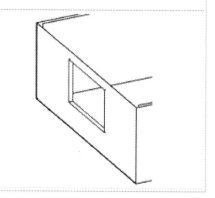

11. Save the drawing but don't exit.

     Command: *qsave*

Of course, you've only drawn the outer surface of the wall. If you'd like, you can repeat the exercise to draw the inner surface as well. Then we can look at another method of Surface Modeling – Regions.

3.3.3	Solids and Regions

Some confusion inevitably arises between the terms *solid* and *3D solid*. Let me clarify the distinction.

A *solid* is a two-dimensional, filled polygon. Use solids when you need to highlight a particular object, building, or area on a drawing. Create a solid using the ***Solid*** command.

AutoCAD has no ***3DSolid*** command. The term 3D solid refers to a family of objects (including spheres, cones, boxes, and more). Although similar objects can be created using surface modeling techniques, those techniques won't create *solid* objects. We'll discuss techniques to create 3D solid objects in Lessons 7 and 8.

There are two real differences between solids and regions. The first is that a solid is a filled two-dimensional polygon (although it can have thickness) while a region is an actual surface. The second is that you can create a solid from scratch while creating a region requires an existing object.

A general rule of thumb to follow when considering solids and regions is this: use a region for a surface and a solid to fill in a two-dimensional object.

Since we looked at solids in the basic text and will spend several lessons on Solid Modeling, we'll concentrate here on regions.

What is a region? Without getting too technical, a region is a two-dimensional surface. It looks very much like a 3D face, but you don't have to hide the edges. You'd use a region anywhere an arc, circle, or hole is required. (Imagine trying to show a round hole with the ***3DFace*** command. Remember that you're restricted to straight edges!)

Let's compare 3D faces with regions.

3D FACE	REGION
Can be drawn from scratch in three dimensions.	Selected objects must be coplanar (share the same UCS). The ***Boundary*** command will only create regions in the current UCS and from existing geometry.
Can't use to show curves or arcs.	Can use to show curves and arcs.
May need to make some edges invisible.	No need to worry about edges.
Can be extruded into a 3D solid.	Can be extruded into a 3D solid.
Create using the ***3DFace*** command.	Create using either the ***Region*** command or the ***Boundary*** command.

As you can see, there are two ways to create a region. Let's consider both.

- The ***Region*** command converts an existing closed object into a region. The objects you can convert include: closed lines, polylines, arcs, circles, splines, and ellipses. Once converted, the original object(s) exists as a region – it's no longer a line, polyline, etc. AutoCAD will create a region from a selected object regardless of the object's relation to the current UCS. The ***Region*** command looks like this:

    Command: *region (or reg)*
    Select objects: *[select the closed object you want to convert]*
    Select objects: *[hit enter to complete the selection]*
    1 Region created. *[AutoCAD tells you how many regions it has created]*

- The ***Boundary*** command uses boundaries to create a region. (We discussed boundaries as part of hatching in the basic text.) No objects are lost or converted with this approach and

AutoCAD uses a dialog box to assist you. For the **Boundary** command to work properly, the objects forming the boundary must be on the zero coordinate of the Z-axis in the current UCS.

We'll use both of these methods to add some more windows in our cabin.

> You can also access the **Region** command by using the **Region** button on the Draw toolbar. Alternately, you can access both the **Region** and **Boundary** commands by selecting them from the Draw pull-down menu.

Do This: 3.3.3.1	Creating Regions

    I.   Be sure you're still in the *Cabin.dwg* file in the C:\Steps3D\Lesson03 folder. If not, please open it now.

    II.   Set the viewpoint to 1,-1,1 (the SE Isometric view).

    III.   Follow these steps.

3.3.3.1: CREATING REGIONS

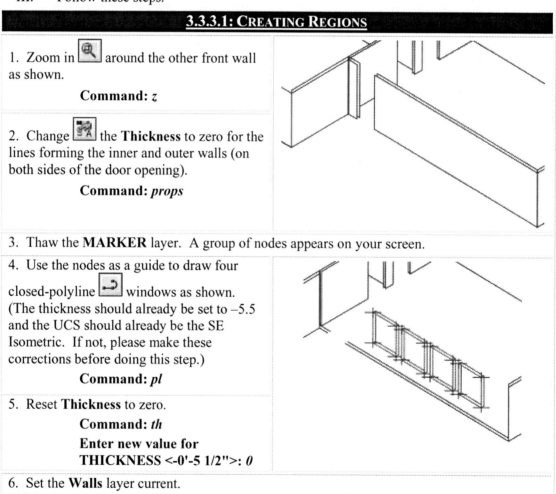

1. Zoom in around the other front wall as shown.

    Command: *z*

2. Change the **Thickness** to zero for the lines forming the inner and outer walls (on both sides of the door opening).

    Command: *props*

3. Thaw the **MARKER** layer. A group of nodes appears on your screen.

4. Use the nodes as a guide to draw four closed-polyline windows as shown. (The thickness should already be set to –5.5 and the UCS should already be the SE Isometric. If not, please make these corrections before doing this step.)

    Command: *pl*

5. Reset **Thickness** to zero.

    Command: *th*

    Enter new value for THICKNESS <-0'-5 1/2">: *0*

6. Set the **Walls** layer current.

7. Use a polyline 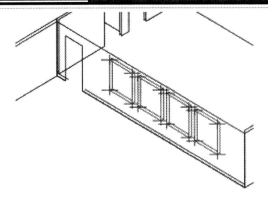 to draw the outline of the outer walls as shown (the height of the door opening is 6'-8"). Be sure to close the polyline.

Command: *pl*

8. Now we'll create our first region. Enter the ***Region*** command 　. (If you haven't entered the command previously, it may take a moment to load.)

Command: *reg*

9. Select the polyline that defines the wall. AutoCAD tells you that it has created a region.

Select objects:
Select objects: *[enter]*
1 loop extracted.
1 Region created.

10. Freeze the **Marker** layer. Your drawing looks like this.

Notice that you can't see through the windows. This is because the wall is a region and there are, as yet, no openings for the windows. We'll deal with that now, first by creating window regions and then by removing the window regions from the wall region.

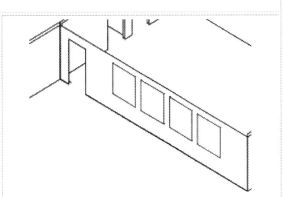

11. Move the current UCS 　 to the lower left corner of the wall as shown.

Command: *ucs*

12. Enter the ***Boundary*** command.

Command: *bo*

AutoCAD presents the Boundary Creation dialog box (see Step 13). You're familiar with the options from your study of hatching in the basic text.

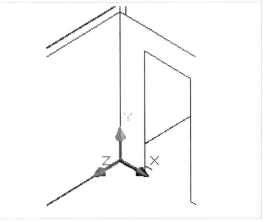

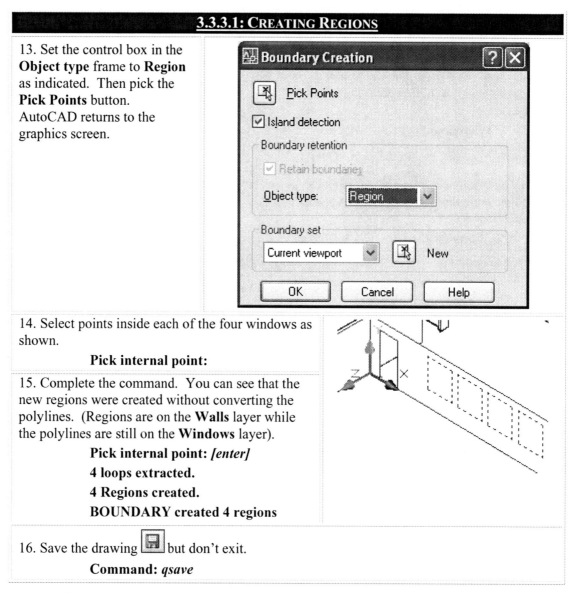

13. Set the control box in the **Object type** frame to **Region** as indicated. Then pick the **Pick Points** button. AutoCAD returns to the graphics screen.

14. Select points inside each of the four windows as shown.

      Pick internal point:

15. Complete the command. You can see that the new regions were created without converting the polylines. (Regions are on the **Walls** layer while the polylines are still on the **Windows** layer).

      Pick internal point: *[enter]*

      4 loops extracted.

      4 Regions created.

      BOUNDARY created 4 regions

16. Save the drawing but don't exit.

      Command: *qsave*

You've used two methods to create your regions. The first – the **Region** command – converted the polyline outlining the wall to a region. That polyline doesn't exist anymore. The second – the **Boundary** command – created regions within the defined boundaries without changing the boundaries themselves (the polylines defining the windows).

But what you haven't done is to use the regions created with your window boundaries to cut holes in the wall for the windows. Right now, you simply have four window regions sitting on top of a wall region. Let's take a look at how we can cut those holes.

We'll use a tool with which we'll become considerably more familiar when we study Solid Modeling. In fact, the tool is one of several modifying tools shared by regions and solid models. The tool we'll use here is the **Subtract** command. It looks like this:

      Command: *subtract (or su)*

      Select solids and regions to subtract from ..

      Select objects: *[select the region or solid from which you'll subtract – in our exercise, this would be the wall]*

      Select objects: *[hit enter to complete the selection]*

Select solids and regions to subtract ..

Select objects: *[select the regions you wish to remove]*

Select objects: *[enter to complete the command]*

You can also begin the **Subtract** command by using the **Subtract** button on the Solid Editing toolbar or the 3D Make control panel. Alternately, you can access the **Subtract** command (and explore other tools shared by regions and solid models) by selecting it from the Modify pull-down menu. Follow this path:

Modify – Solid Editing – Subtract

Let's finish our wall.

Do This: 3.3.3.2	Using Regions to Create Holes

    I.   Be sure you're still in the *Cabin.dwg* file in the C:\Steps3D\Lesson03 folder. If not, please open it now.

    II.   Follow these steps.

3.3.3.2: USING REGIONS TO CREATE HOLES

1. Enter the **Subtract** command .

    Command: *su*

2. AutoCAD needs to know from which surface you'll subtract. Select the wall.

    Select solids and regions to subtract from ..

    Select objects:

3. Now AutoCAD needs to know what to subtract. Select the windows. (Be sure to select the regions and not the polylines.)

    Select solids and regions to subtract ..

    Select objects:

Your drawing looks like the following figure. (Starting to look pretty good, don't you think?)

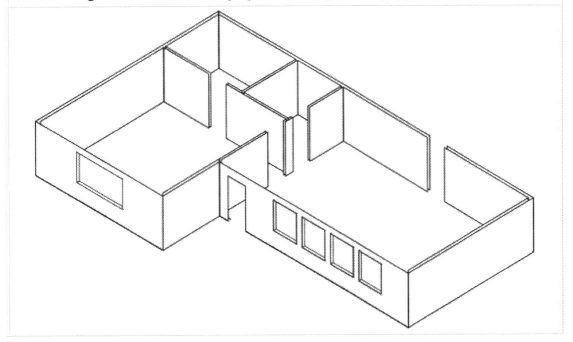

5. Save and close the drawing.

Command: *qsave*

| 3.3.4 | **Which Method Should You Use?** |

Which method of Surface Modeling do you prefer – 3D Face or Regions? Believe it or not, you'll need both.

Consider the model in Figure 3.004. Take a moment to consider each surface. Ask yourself which method of surface modeling you would use to create it. Then (more importantly) ask yourself why you'd use that method.

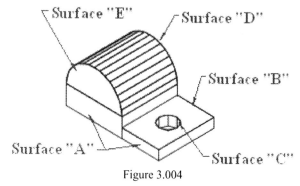
Figure 3.004

Once you've examined each surface, continue to the following explanations.

- You can easily draw **Surface "A"** using lines with thickness. This brings us to the first rule of three-dimensional work: *Never draw a surface when a line will do.* Surfaces are complex objects and take up more drawing memory than simple lines.

- **Surface "B"** has a round hole in it. 3D faces create flat edges so they won't work here. A region will serve best, but which method should you use? Using the Boundary method to create a region, you can pick a point inside the rectangular area (but outside the circle) and let AutoCAD do the rest. This is the best approach.

- **Surface "C"** is the inside surface of the hole. The only method we've seen to create this surface is **Thickness**. But you can't use a circle to create a hole. That will result in a closed cylinder (a drum). Use two arcs with thickness to create the hole.

- **Surface "D"** looks very much like the roof of our cabin. Indeed, it's the same type of construction. You can use a region or solid to create the surfaces over the wireframe, but that would involve setting the UCS flat against the surface to be created for each roof section. There are 16 sections, so you'd have to set the UCS and then draw the surface 16 times. Alternately, you can draw 16 3D faces.

  But look at the surface again. There's an easier way that will provide a more rounded surface. How about drawing an arc with thickness in the proper UCS? This will work on this surface, as there are no intersections with which you have to contend. (Rule #2 of three-dimensional work then might be: *Think about it twice; draw it once.*)

- **Surface "E"** has an odd shape to it. Like Surface "B", the odd shape gives away the answer. Another rule of three-dimensional surface work is: *When faced with an unusual shape or holes in a surface, use the boundary approach to create a region.*

Use Figure 3.004 as a guide in your first steps toward creating three-dimensional surface models. (We'll draw Figure 3.004 in our exercises. Then you can plot it and hang it on your monitor!) Memorize the explanation of each surface and consider each point when determining how to draw a surface on your model.

AutoCAD includes a new command with the '07 release. *XEdges* will create 3D Wireframes from existing 2D solids, regions, and surfaces. That's for those who wish to create the stick figure after the fact!

Did you use the **Subtract** button on the 3D Make control panel in Exercise 3.3.3.2? If you did, you might have noticed that it was grouped with two other buttons – **Union** and **Intersect**. These three buttons work on regions as well as 3D solids. Can you tell from their symbols what they'll do?

We'll discuss them in more detail in Lesson 8, but that doesn't mean that you can't experiment with them now.

Open the *solids & regions.dwg* file in the C:\Steps3D\Lesson03 folder. (It looks like Figure 3.005). Experiment with each of these commands on the objects shown. When you've finished, see Figure 3.006 for the results.

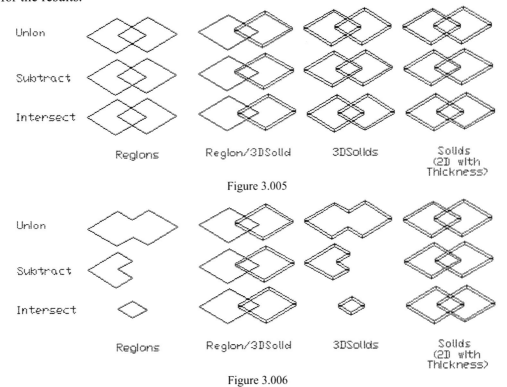

Figure 3.005

Figure 3.006

You'll notice that these commands work on regions or 3D solids. You can't, however, use them to subtract or join (and so forth) different types of objects with each other. Additionally, you'll notice that they don't work at all on simple solids. This is why you should generally use regions and 3D faces when creating surface models.

Let's do one more thing while we're still in the *solids & regions.dwg* file. Use the **Realistic** visual style to color the drawing. Now use the *3DOrbit* command to flip the view (from bottom to top). Notice anything (Figure 3.007)?

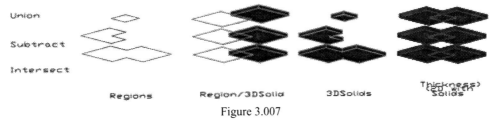

Figure 3.007

You should notice that all of the objects shaded nicely on top and bottom – *except* the regions. This brings up an interesting quirk about regions – you can see the shading on a region only from the top! Does that mean that you can't use a region for a bottom surface?

No! It means that you must draw the bottom region of an object *upside down!* How will you do that? Well, you won't actually draw upside down (face it, there are some things that just weren't meant to be done upside down). You'll use the *UCS* command to tell AutoCAD that down is up (tell AutoCAD to work upside down!). In other words, use the *UCS* command to flip the positive and negative directions of the Z-axis. (Remember this when drawing the cinder block in the Exercises.)

3.5	What Have We Learned?

Items covered in this lesson include:

- *The differences between 3D faces, solids, 3D solids, and regions*
- *The differences between polylines and 3D polylines*
- *Projecting points in three dimensions*
- *The two approaches to creating regions*
  - ○ *Region*   ○ *Boundary*
- *Commands*
  - ○ *3DPoly*   ○ *SPLFrame*
  - ○ *3DFace*   ○ *Boundary*
  - ○ *Region*   ○ *Subtract*
  - ○ *Edge*   ○ *Xedges*

It's taken a few lessons to get comfortable with the basics of Z-space wireframe and surface modeling. At this point, you're either anxious to continue or feeling somewhat overwhelmed by it all (probably a little of both).

I can't overemphasize the importance of practice – if you're uncomfortable with the material thus far, go back and do it again. You shouldn't feel that you're the only person who ever found Z-space difficult to master. But that's the benefit of computer labs and a good textbook! (If you've already changed the files that came from the web, just reload them to start over!)

Are you ready for an easy lesson? Our next chapter – "Predefined Surface Models" – will show you how to create some more complex objects easily. So do the problems that follow … review as necessary to get comfortable … then forward – ever forward!

3.6	Exercises

1. through 8. Add surfaces to the drawings you created in Exercises 1 through 8 of Section 1.7 (in Lesson 1). Refer to the drawings in Appendix B as a guide. If these drawing aren't available use the corresponding drawing in the C:\Steps3D\Lesson\Steps\Lesson03 folder.

9. Open the *My Twisted Y.dwg* file you created in Section 2.7 – Exercise 9 (C:\Steps3D\Lesson02 folder). (If that file isn't available, use the *Twisted Y-3.dwg* file in the C:\Steps3D\Lesson03 folder.) Convert the drawing into a surface model by placing thickness, 3D faces, or regions on the necessary surfaces. See Figure 3.008 for the completed drawing.

10. Open the *My Block.dwg* file you created in Section 2.7 – Exercise 10 (C:\Steps3D\Lesson02 folder). (If that file isn't available, use the *Block-3.dwg* file in the C:\Steps3D\Lesson03

folder.) Convert the drawing into a surface model by placing thickness, 3D faces, or regions on the necessary surfaces. See Figure 3.009 for the completed drawing.

Figure 3.008

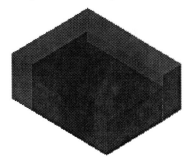

Figure 3009

11. Open the *MyBookEnd.dwg* file you created in Section 2.7 – Exercise 12 (C:\Steps3D\Lesson02 folder). (If that file isn't available, use the *Book End-3.dwg* file in the C:\Steps3D\Lesson03 folder.) Convert the drawing into a surface model by placing thickness, 3D faces, or regions on the necessary surfaces. See Figure 3.010 for the completed drawing.

12. Open the *My Anchor Stop.dwg* file you created in Section 2.7 – Exercise 14 (C:\Steps3D\Lesson02 folder). (If that file isn't available, use the *Anchor Stop-3.dwg* file in the C:\Steps3D\Lesson03 folder.) Convert the drawing into a surface model by placing thickness, 3D faces, or regions on the necessary surfaces. See Figure 3.011 for the completed drawing.

Figure 3.010

Figure 3.011

13. Open the *MyOtherTable.dwg* file you created in Section 2.7 – Exercise 20 (C:\Steps3D\Lesson02 folder). (If that file isn't available, use the *Other Table-3.dwg* file in the C:\Steps3D\Lesson03 folder.) Convert the drawing into a surface model by placing thickness, 3D faces, or regions on the necessary surfaces. See Figure 3.012 for the completed drawing.

14. Open the *My Corner Bracket.dwg* file you created in Section 2.7 – Exercise 21 (C:\Steps3D\Lesson02 folder). (If that file isn't available, use the *corner bracket-3.dwg* file in the C:\Steps3D\Lesson03 folder.) Convert the drawing into a surface model by placing thickness, 3D faces, or regions on the necessary surfaces. See Figure 3.013 for the completed drawing.

83

Figure 3.012

Figure 3.013

15. Open the *My Phone Plug.dwg* file you created in Section 2.7 – Exercise 22 (C:\Steps3D\Lesson02 folder). (If that file isn't available, use the *phone plug-3.dwg* file in the C:\Steps3D\Lesson03 folder.) Convert the drawing into a surface model by placing thickness, 3D faces, or regions on the necessary surfaces. See Figure 3.014 for the completed drawing.

16. Open the *My Other Corner Bracket.dwg* file you created in Section 2.7 – Exercise 23 (C:\Steps3D\Lesson02 folder). (If that file isn't available, use the *other corner bracket-3.dwg* file in the C:\Steps3D\Lesson03 folder.) Convert the drawing into a surface model by placing thickness, 3D faces, or regions on the necessary surfaces. See Figure 3.015 for the completed drawing.

Figure 3.014

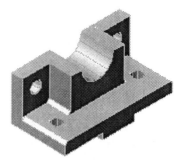

Figure 3.015

17. Open the *projection.dwg* file in the C:\Steps3D\Lesson03 folder. Create the saddle tee shown here. Save the drawing as *My Saddle Tee.dwg* in the C:\Steps3D\Lesson03 folder.

Saddle Tee

18. Create the cinder block shown. The following details will help:

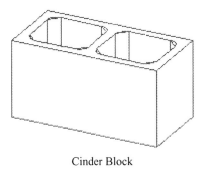

Cinder Block

18.1.   The overall dimensions of a cinder block are 8" x 8" x 16".

18.2.   The holes are 7" x 6½" and are evenly spaced.

18.3.   The fillets in the holes have a 1" radius.

18.4.   Color 164 looks like a cinder block.

18.5.   Remember that a region can only be seen from what was the positive Z-axis direction at the time of its creation.

18.6.   Save the drawing as *My Cinder Block.dwg* in the C:\Steps3D\Lesson03 folder.

19. Draw the demo model shown (refer to Figure 3.004). Use the following details as a guide.

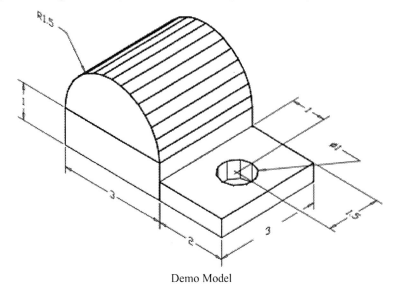

Demo Model

19.1.   Label the types of surfaces as explained in Section 3.3.4.

19.2.   Save the drawing as *Surfaces Model.dwg* in the C:\Steps3D\ Lesson03 folder.

19.3.   Plot the drawing to fit on about one quarter of a standard 8½" x 11" sheet of paper. Cut it out and tape it to the side of your monitor as a reference.

19.4.   You don't have to dimension the drawing.

20. Finish the Cabin drawing we started in this lesson. The final drawing is shown in the figure atop the next page. Use these details as a guide.

20.1.   All the windows are the same size.

20.2.   All the windows are 12" from the top of the walls.

20.3.   Spaced windows are 12" apart.

20.4.   Change the layer for all inner walls to a new **Inner Walls** layer. Then freeze the layer for clarity.

20.5.   Use the *3DClip* command for clarity on the elevations.

20.6.   The scale in each viewport is 1/16"=1'-0" (this layout is set up for an 8½" x 11" sheet).

20.7.   Use the title block of your choice, and plot the drawing.

20.8.   Save the drawing in the C:\Steps3D\Lesson03 folder.

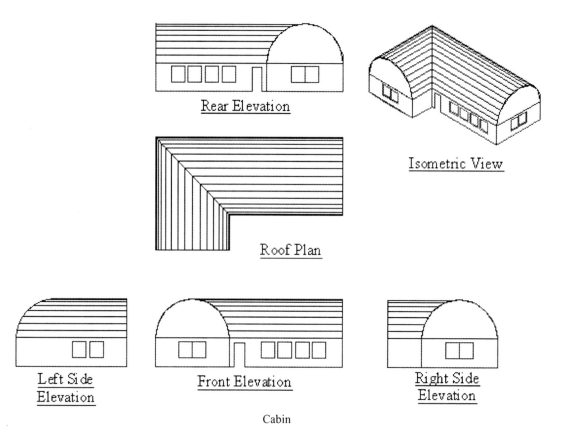

Rear Elevation

Isometric View

Roof Plan

Left Side
Elevation

Front Elevation

Right Side
Elevation

Cabin

21.   Reopen the *Cabin.dwg* file you completed in Exercise 20. We'll add a different roof and a chimney. Follow these guidelines. (The final drawing is shown here).

21.1.   Freeze the **Roof** layer.

21.2.   Add two new layers – **Roof2** and **Chimney**.

21.3.   On the **Roof2** layer, add hexagons at the end walls of the roofs (in the same location where the arcs were found in Exercise 3.2.1).

21.4.   Add the 3D polyline and 3D faces to complete the roof.

21.5.   Place a 4' x 2' rectangle, with a thickness of 24', at coordinates 33',22',0.

21.6.   Use construction lines and UCS manipulation to locate where the chimney penetrates the roof. Draw a

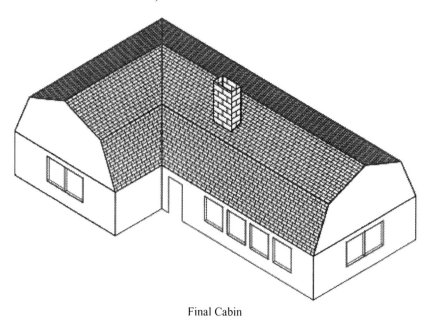

Final Cabin

polyline around the penetration.

21.7. Finish drawing the chimney using wireframe techniques. Erase the rectangle.

21.8. Add 3D faces to the chimney.

21.9. Hatch everything as shown.

21.10. Save and plot the drawing.

3.7   **For Web-Based Review Questions, visit:**
http://www.uneedcad.com/2007/Files/07R3-3D.pdf

Lesson

4

Following this lesson, you will:

✓ *Know how to build and use AutoCAD's predefined surface models*

- o **Box**
- o **Wedge**
- o **Pyramid**
- o **Cone**
- o **Sphere**
- o **Dome**
- o **Dish**
- o **Torus**

✓ *Know how to use the* **3D** *command*

Predefined Surfaces

In our next two lessons, we'll look at some tools that should greatly simplify your work with surface models.

First, in this lesson, we'll learn to use AutoCAD's predefined surface models. Draftsmen at all levels of development can quickly and easily learn to use these remarkable timesaving devices. In fact, I'd be surprised if you hadn't discovered them in your three-dimensional explorations already.

Then in Lesson 5, you'll discover some surprisingly simple tools that you can use to create elaborate, non-uniform surface models.

Let's begin with an overview of the predefined surface modeling tools AutoCAD has provided.

> As I mentioned in our last lesson, AutoCAD appears to be phasing these tools out. Consequently, toolbars which formerly assisted the use of predefined surface models are no longer available. I'll show you command entry methods, but don't be surprised if these tools disappear completely in later releases.

4.1   What Are Predefined Surface Models?

Simply put, predefined surface models are standard geometric shapes that AutoCAD creates for you with a minimal amount of user input. The shapes include (Figure 4.001) a box, a wedge, four types of pyramid, two types of cone, a dome, a dish, a sphere, and a torus. User input for each commonly includes length, width, height, radius, and rotation angle definitions.

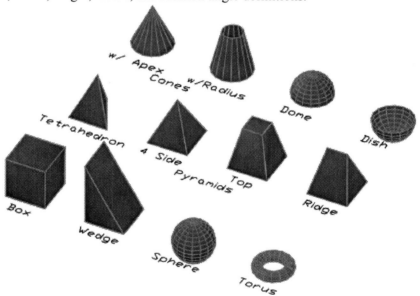

Figure 4.001

You can create each of these models with little effort – simply follow AutoCAD's prompts.

AutoCAD creates each surface model as a 3D mesh (more on 3D meshes in Lesson 5). You can edit a 3D mesh with the **_PEdit_** command (as we'll see in Lesson 6). Additionally, you can explode the model into a series of 3D faces. This enables you to remove part of the model (with the **_Erase_** command) or hide some of the edges (with the **_Edge_** command) without affecting the rest of the faces.

4.2   Drawing Predefined Surface Models

AutoCAD has included a command that enables you to access predefined surface models without difficulty. The command is, simply enough, **_3D_**. It looks like this:

   Command: _3d_

89

Enter an option [Box/Cone/DIsh/DOme/Mesh/Pyramid/Sphere/Torus/Wedge]:

Respond with the type of object you wish to draw. But if the keyboard is too much trouble, AutoCAD provides a toolbar – Surfaces – to make accessing its predefined surface modeling tools even easier.

Let's examine the procedures for drawing each of the predefined surface models.

> Note: We show all the exercises in this section with a **Realistic** visual style, a **Realistic** face style, and showing **Isolines**.

4.2.1	Box

Use the **Box** option of the *3D* command to draw any six-sided box whose sides, top, and bottom are parallel or perpendicular to the current UCS. The command sequence looks like this:

> **Command:** *3d*
>
> **Enter an option [Box/Cone/DIsh/DOme/Mesh/Pyramid/Sphere/Torus/Wedge]:** *b*
>
> **Specify corner point of box:** *[identify the first corner of the box]*
>
> **Specify length of box:** *[tell AutoCAD how long to make the box]*
>
> **Specify width of box or [Cube]:** *[tell AutoCAD how wide to make the box or type C for a cube (all sides equal to the value entered for length)]*
>
> **Specify height of box:** *[tell AutoCAD how tall to make the box – AutoCAD skips this prompt if you opt for Cube in the last step]*
>
> **Specify rotation angle of box about the Z axis or [Reference]:** *[tell AutoCAD how to orient the box using either mouse pick or reference angle]*

Let's try one.

Do This: 4.2.1.1	Creating a 3D Surfaced Box

    I.   Start a new drawing using the *lesson 04 template* file located in the C:\Steps3D\Lesson04 folder.

    II.   Follow these steps.

4.2.1.1: CREATING A 3D SURFACED BOX

1. Enter the *3D* command and select the **Box** option ![Box].
     Command: *3d*
     Enter an option [Box/Cone/DIsh/DOme/Mesh/Pyramid/Sphere/ Torus/Wedge]: *b*

2. Specify the start point of the box as indicated.   **Specify corner point of box:** *1,1*
3. Specify the **length** of the box.   **Specify length of box:** *4*

4. We won't draw a cube this time, so enter the width and height as indicated.
     Specify width of box or [Cube]: *2*
     Specify height of box: *1*

5. And give the box a zero rotation angle.

> **Specify rotation angle of box about the Z axis or [Reference]:** *0*

Your box looks like this.

6. Let's place a cube atop the box. Repeat the command �–ˆ Box ▓.

> **Command:** *[enter]*
>
> **Enter an option [Box/Cone/DIsh/DOme/Mesh/Pyramid/ Sphere/Torus/Wedge]:** *b*

7. Place the first corner atop the first corner of the box.

> **Specify corner point of box:** *1,1,1*

8. Give our cube a **length** of 2 …

> **Specify length of box:** *2*

9. … and tell AutoCAD to use the length dimension for the width and height as well by selecting the **Cube** option ▓ Cube ▓.

> **Specify width of box or [Cube]:** *C*

10. Give the cube the same rotation angle as our first box.

> **Specify rotation angle of box about the Z axis or [Reference]:** *0*

Your drawing looks like this.

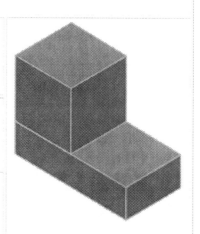

11. Save the drawing 🖫 as *MyBoxes* in the C:\Steps3D\Lesson04 folder.

> **Command:** *save*

12. Perform the *List* command 📋 on the upper box.

> **Command:** *li*

Notice (atop the next page) that each vertex is identified as a polyline.

```
        POLYLINE   Layer:  "obj1"
                   Space:  Model space
              Handle = b6
   Polyface mesh

        VERTEX     Layer:  "obj1"
                   Space:  Model space
              Handle = b7
   Polyface vertex
            at point, X=   1.0000  Y=   1.0000  Z=   0.0000
```

13. Explode 🗡 the upper box.

> **Command:** *x*

14. Repeat Step 12.

> **Command:** *li*

Notice (below) the difference. Now you can use the *Edge* command to hide edges.

```
        3D FACE    Layer:  "obj1"
                   Space:  Model space
             Handle = df
      first point, X=    1.0000   Y=    1.0000   Z=    1.0000
     second point, X=    3.0000   Y=    1.0000   Z=    1.0000
      third point, X=    3.0000   Y=    1.0000   Z=    3.0000
     fourth point, X=    1.0000   Y=    1.0000   Z=    3.0000
```

15. Save and close the drawing.

> **Command:** *qsave*

Wasn't that easier than drawing a stick figure and stretching skin around it? (I love easy!)

Let's try another predefined surface model.

4.2.2	Wedge

You won't find many differences between the *3D* command's **Wedge** and **Box** options. In fact, without the **Cube** option, the **Wedge** option is actually easier! It looks like this:

> **Command:** *3d*
>
> **Enter an option [Box/Cone/DIsh/DOme/Mesh/Pyramid/Sphere/Torus/Wedge]:** *w*
>
> **Specify corner point of wedge:** *[identify the first corner of the wedge]*
>
> **Specify length of wedge:** *[tell AutoCAD how long to make the wedge]*
>
> **Specify width of wedge:** *[tell AutoCAD how wide to make the wedge]*
>
> **Specify height of wedge:** *[tell AutoCAD how tall to make the wedge]*
>
> **Specify rotation angle of wedge about the Z axis:** *[tell AutoCAD how to orient the wedge]*

Does it look familiar? Let's draw one for practice.

Do This: 4.2.2.1	Creating a 3D Surfaced Wedge

    I.   Start a new drawing using the *lesson 04 template* file located in the C:\Steps3D\Lesson04 folder.

    II.   Follow these steps.

1. Enter the *3D* command and select the **Wedge** option [Wedge].

> **Command:** *3d*
>
> **Enter an option [Box/Cone/DIsh/DOme/Mesh/Pyramid/Sphere/Torus/Wedge]:** *w*

2. Identify the starting point of the wedge as indicated.

> **Specify corner point of wedge:** *1,1*

3. Specify the **length, width, height,** and **rotation angle** of the wedge as indicated.

> **Specify length of wedge:** *4*
> **Specify width of wedge:** *2*
> **Specify height of wedge:** *1*
> **Specify rotation angle of wedge about the Z axis:** *0*

Your drawing looks like this.

4. Save the drawing 🖫 as *MyWedge* in the C:\Steps3D\Lesson folder.

> **Command:** *save*

Remember that you can change the UCS prior to creating the wedge to help control the direction of the slope. You can't, however, use negative numbers.

Let's look at something more complex than simple boxes and wedges. Let's look at the **Pyramid** option.

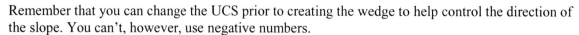

4.2.3	Pyramid

Did you know that there's more than one kind of pyramid?

Technically speaking, a pyramid is a polyhedron – a multi-triangular structure (and you thought pyramid was hard to spell!). The common idea of a pyramid comes from the Egyptian model with a rectangular base (or four triangular sides on a rectangular base). Most of the Egyptian pyramids come to a point at the top.

But there are other pyramids. In fact, the largest pyramid in the world isn't Egyptian at all! Look for it just outside Mexico City. And it has a flat top!

Some pyramids even have triangular bases – or three triangular sides on a triangular base. These are called tetrahedrons. (Sounds like something that ate the bad guys in *Jurassic Park XXIV*.)

You probably didn't realize how complicated the world of pyramids was! But not to worry – AutoCAD provides for drawing each within one simple 3D command option – **Pyramid**. Its command sequence looks like this:

> **Command:** *3d*
>
> **Enter an option [Box/Cone/DIsh/DOme/Mesh/Pyramid/Sphere/Torus/Wedge]:** *p*
> **Specify first corner point for base of pyramid:**
> **Specify second corner point for base of pyramid:**
> **Specify third corner point for base of pyramid:**
> **Specify fourth corner point for base of pyramid or [Tetrahedron]:** *[if the base has four corners, enter the fourth point; otherwise, enter T for a three-sided base (tetrahedron)]*
> **Specify apex point of pyramid or [Ridge/Top]:** *[enter a point in Z-space to identify the point at the top of the pyramid, or tell AutoCAD you wish to create a ridge (2-point) or top (3 or 4 points, depending on the base)]*

It really isn't as complicated as it looks. Let's draw some pyramids and see.

93

Do This: 4.2.3.1	Creating 3D Surfaced Pyramids

I. Start a new drawing using the *lesson 04 template* file located in the C:\Steps3D\Lesson04 folder.

II. Follow these steps.

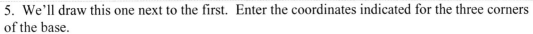

4.2.3.1: CREATING 3D SURFACED PYRAMIDS

1. Enter the *3D* command and select the **Pyramid** option 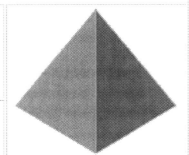.

> **Command:** *3d*
>
> **Enter an option [Box/Cone/DIsh/DOme/Mesh/**
> **Pyramid/Sphere/Torus/Wedge]:** *p*

2. We'll start with a simple, four-sided pyramid that comes to a point at the top. Enter the base coordinates indicated.

> **Specify first corner point for base of pyramid:** *1,1*
>
> **Specify second corner point for base of pyramid:** *@4,0*
>
> **Specify third corner point for base of pyramid:** *@0,4*
>
> **Specify fourth corner point for base of pyramid or [Tetrahedron]:** *@-4,0*

3. An apex point (sharp point at the top) is the default, so enter the three-dimensional coordinate indicated.

> **Specify apex point of pyramid or [Ridge/Top]:**
> *3,3,4*

Your first pyramid looks like this.

4. Let's draw a three-sided pyramid – a tetrahedron. Repeat the command.

> **Command:** *[enter]*
>
> **Enter an option**
> **[Box/Cone/DIsh/DOme/Mesh/Pyramid/**
> **Sphere/Torus/Wedge]:** *p*

5. We'll draw this one next to the first. Enter the coordinates indicated for the three corners of the base.

> **Specify first corner point for base of pyramid:** *11,1*
>
> **Specify second corner point for base of pyramid:** *@0,4*
>
> **Specify third corner point for base of pyramid:** *@-4,-2*

6. When AutoCAD asks for a fourth corner, select the **Tetrahedron** option 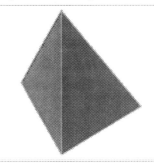.

> **Specify fourth corner point for base of pyramid or [Tetrahedron]:** *T*

7. And place the apex point as indicated.

> **Specify apex point of tetrahedron or [Top]:**
> *9,3,4*

Your drawing looks like this.

8. Now let's draw a four-sided pyramid with a flat top. (Erase the previous pyramids or freeze their layer and set a different one current.) Repeat the command.

    Command: *[enter]*

    Enter an option [Box/Cone/DIsh/DOme/Mesh/Pyramid/Sphere/ Torus/Wedge]: *p*

9. First, draw the base just as you did for the first pyramid. (Toggle dynamic input off – we'll use absolute coordinates for this procedure.)

    Specify first corner point for base of pyramid: *1,1*

    Specify second corner point for base of pyramid: *5,1*

    Specify third corner point for base of pyramid: *5,5*

    Specify fourth corner point for base of pyramid or [Tetrahedron]: *1,5*

10. But instead of identifying an apex point, tell AutoCAD to draw a **Top** on the pyramid.

    Specify apex point of pyramid or [Ridge/Top]: *T*

11. Identifying the points for the top is just like identifying the points for the base – except that the top points must be three-dimensional coordinates. Enter these as indicated.

    Specify first corner point for top of pyramid: *2,2,4*

    Specify second corner point for top of pyramid: 4,2,4

    Specify third corner point for top of pyramid: *4,4,4*

    Specify fourth corner point for top of pyramid: *2,4,4*

    Your drawing looks like this.

> I'm not sure that our next pyramid would qualify as a true pyramid – it only has two triangles, but it also has two quadrilaterals and a rectangular base. Still, it fits better with the pyramid command than any other, and a *Triangles_Quadrilaterals_Rectangle* option might be too much typing even for a pro! (Of course, the last pyramid didn't have any triangles at all!)
>
> Let's draw a ridge.

12. Repeat the command.

    Command: *[enter]*

    Enter an option [Box/Cone/DIsh/DOme/Mesh/Pyramid/Sphere/ Torus/Wedge]: *p*

13. Draw the base as indicated.

    Specify first corner point for base of pyramid: *7,1*

    Specify second corner point for base of pyramid: *11,1*

    Specify third corner point for base of pyramid: *11,5*

    Specify fourth corner point for base of pyramid or [Tetrahedron]: *7,5*

14. But tell AutoCAD to draw a **Ridge** rather than an apex point.

    Specify apex point of pyramid or [Ridge/Top]: *r*

15. Then identify the points on the ridge.

> **Specify first ridge end point of pyramid:** *8,3,4*
>
> **Specify second ridge end point of pyramid:** *10,3,4*

Notice that the ridge is parallel to the first base line you drew.

16. Save the drawing ⌷ as *MyPyramids* in the C:\Steps3D\Lesson04 folder.

> **Command:** *save*

Now let's look at pyramids with round bottoms – let's look at cones.

4.2.4	Cone

Like pyramids, cones are smaller on the top than on the bottom (generally speaking). The top can be pointed like the pyramid's apex point, or it can be flat. But the similarities end there.

> The smaller-top/larger-base definition is simply to help in recognition. It's possible, and at times desirable, to have a pyramid or cone with a larger top than base, or a cone with equal top and base.
>
> You can also use the *3D* command's **Cone** option to draw a surface model cylinder. Simply make the top and base radii the same.

The predefined surface models we've examined so far have all had sides that loaned themselves easily to 3D faces. Beginning with cones, we'll look at several predefined shapes that incorporate circles or arcs in their structures. Because these structures are 3D meshes (and will convert to 3D faces when exploded), we must tell AutoCAD how many faces to use when creating the surfaces of the circles or arcs.

The command sequence for cones is:

> **Command:** *3d*
>
> **Enter an option [Box/Cone/DIsh/DOme/Mesh/Pyramid/Sphere/Torus/Wedge]:** *c*
>
> **Specify center point for base of cone:** *[identify the center point for the base of the cone]*
>
> **Specify radius for base of cone or [Diameter]:** *[identify the radius of the cone or select the diameter option]*
>
> **Specify radius for top of cone or [Diameter] <0>:** *[hit enter to accept zero as the top radius – AutoCAD will draw a cone with a point at the top; or identify the radius for the top and AutoCAD will draw an open top]*
>
> **Specify height of cone:** *[specify the height of the cone]*
>
> **Enter number of segments for surface of cone <16>:** *[tell AutoCAD how many faces to use to create the surface of the cone. Remember that 3D faces are flat, so the more faces you use, the rounder the cone will appear. Remember also that the more faces you use, the larger your drawing becomes. Go for a healthy compromise between appearance and size.]*

We'll draw a couple cones for practice.

Do This: 4.2.4.1	Creating 3D Surfaced Cones

I. Start a new drawing using the *lesson 04 template* file located in the C:\Steps3D\Lesson04 folder.

II. Follow these steps.

4.2.4.1: CREATING 3D SURFACED CONES

1. Enter the *3D* command and select the **Cone** option **Cone**.

   Command: *3d*

   Enter an option [Box/Cone/DIsh/DOme/Mesh/Pyramid/Sphere/Torus/Wedge]: *c*

2. Identify the **center point** and the **radius** of the base as indicated.

   Specify center point for base of cone: *3,3*

   Specify radius for base of cone or [Diameter]: *2*

3. We'll draw a pointed cone first. Accept the default **radius** of zero for the top.

   Specify radius for top of cone or [Diameter] <0>: *[enter]*

4. Specify the **height** of the cone. The height must be a positive number.

   Specify height of cone: *4*

5. Remember – more surface segments mean a rounder appearance; fewer mean a less pronounced curve. Let's accept the default.

   Enter number of segments for surface of cone <16>: *[enter]*

   Your drawing looks like this.

6. Now let's draw a cone with an opening at the top as well as the bottom. Repeat the command **Cone**.

   Command: *[enter]*

7. Locate the base and specify the radius as you did in Step 2.

   Specify center point for base of cone: *9,3*

   Specify radius for base of cone or [Diameter]: *2*

8. But this time, identify a radius for the top as well.

   Specify radius for top of cone or [Diameter] <0>: *1*

9. Specify the height as you did in Step 4.

   Specify height of cone: *4*

10. Let's see what the cone will look like with more surface segments.

> **Enter number of segments for surface of cone <16>:** *32*

11. Save the drawing 🖫 as *MyCones* in the C:\Steps3D\Lesson04 folder.

> **Command:** *save*

For a treat, toggle isolines off in *MyCones.dwg*. Pretty cool, huh?

4.2.5	**Sphere**

Spheres also require you to identify the number of faces required to make up the arc. But with spheres, you must identify the number of latitudinal *and longitudinal* faces. In other words, into how many pieces will you divide the sphere from top to bottom (latitude) and side to side (longitude)? Again, it isn't as difficult as it sounds. The prompts look like this:

> **Command:** *3d*
>
> **Enter an option [Box/Cone/DIsh/DOme/Mesh/Pyramid/Sphere/Torus/Wedge]:** *s*
>
> **Specify center point of sphere:** *[specify the center point of the sphere; unless you want half the sphere to be underground, use a three-dimensional coordinate to do this]*
>
> **Specify radius of sphere or [Diameter]:** *[specify the radius or diameter of the sphere]*
>
> **Enter number of longitudinal segments for surface of sphere <16>:** *[how many divisions will you want from side to side?]*
>
> **Enter number of latitudinal segments for surface of sphere <16>:** *[how many divisions will you want from top to bottom?]*

Let's draw a sphere.

Do This: 4.2.5.1	**Creating a 3D Surfaced Sphere**

  I.   Start a new drawing using the *lesson 04 template* file located in the C:\Steps3D\Lesson04 folder.

  II.   Follow these steps.

1. Enter the *3D* command and select the **Sphere** option [Sphere].

> **Command:** *3d*
>
> **Enter an option [Box/Cone/DIsh/DOme/Mesh/Pyramid/Sphere/ Torus/Wedge]:** *s*

2. Specify the **center point** of the sphere. Be sure to use a three-dimensional coordinate as indicated.

> **Specify center point of sphere:** *3,3,3*

3. Identify the **radius** as indicated.

> **Specify radius of sphere or [Diameter]:** *2*

4. Accept the default number of **longitudinal segments** but increase the number of **latitudinal segments** as indicated (this way, you can see the difference).

> **Enter number of longitudinal segments for surface of sphere <16>:** *[enter]*
>
> **Enter number of latitudinal segments for surface of sphere <16>:** *32*

Your drawing looks like this.

5. Toggle your isolines off [icon]. Your drawing looks like this. Pretty cool!

5. Save the drawing [icon] as *MySphere* in the C:\Steps3D\Lesson04 folder.

> **Command:** *save*

What do you mean you wanted to use the *right half* or *left half* of the sphere?! Some people just have to be difficult!

Well, you can always draw a dome or dish and rotate it using the ***Rotate3d*** command you'll learn in Lesson 6. (Whew!)

4.2.6	Domes and Dishes

So you only need half a sphere, huh? Well, you could draw a sphere, explode it, and then erase what you don't need. But that's too much work; and let's face it, that's not what drafting is all about.

A dome is the upper half of a sphere; a dish is the lower half. The command sequences for both the **Dome** and **Dish** options are identical to the sphere's sequence but result in only half a sphere being drawn.

> **Command:** *3d*
>
> **Enter an option [Box/Cone/DIsh/DOme/Mesh/Pyramid/Sphere/Torus/Wedge]:** *do* [or *di*]
>
> **Specify center point of dome:** *[specify the center point of the dome/dish]*
>
> **Specify radius of dome or [Diameter]:** *[specify the radius or diameter of the dome/dish]*
>
> **Enter number of longitudinal segments for surface of dome <16>:** *[how many divisions will you want from side to side?]*
>
> **Enter number of latitudinal segments for surface of dome <8>:** *[how many divisions will you want from top to bottom?]*

Let's draw one of each.

Do This: 4.2.6.1	Creating 3D Surfaced Domes and Dishes

    I.   Start a new drawing using the *lesson 04 template* file located in the C:\Steps3D\Lesson04 folder.

    II.   Be sure isolines are toggled on.

    III. Follow these steps.

4.2.6.1: CREATING 3D SURFACED DOMES AND DISHES

1. Enter the *3D* command and select the **Dome** option DOme .

   Command: *3d*

   Enter an option [Box/Cone/DIsh/DOme/Mesh/Pyramid/Sphere/ Torus/Wedge]: *do*

2. Use a three-dimensional coordinate for the **center point** as indicated.

   Specify center point of dome: *3,3,5*

3. Specify the **radius**.

   Specify radius of dome or [Diameter]: *2*

4. Accept the default number of **longitudinal** and **latitudinal segments**.

   Enter number of longitudinal segments for surface of dome <16>: *[enter]*

   Enter number of latitudinal segments for surface of dome <8>: *[enter]*

   Your drawing looks like this.

5. We'll draw the dish below the dome. Enter the *3D* command and select the **Dish** option DIsh .

   Command: *3d*

   Enter an option [Box/Cone/DIsh/DOme/Mesh/Pyramid/Sphere/ Torus/Wedge]: *di*

6. Follow the sequence indicated.

   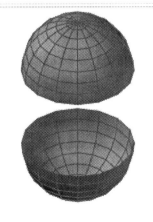

   Specify center point of dish: *3,3,2*

   Specify radius of dish or [Diameter]: *2*

   Enter number of longitudinal segments for surface of dish <16>: *[enter]*

   Enter number of latitudinal segments for surface of dish <8>: *[enter]*

   Your drawing looks like this.

7. Save the drawing [💾] as *MyDome* in the C:\Steps3D\Lesson04 folder.

   Command: *save*

4.2.7	Torus

A torus looks like the inner tube you used at the beach or lake when you were a kid. (Okay, some of you are still young enough to enjoy that type of activity without cracking bones that saw the breakup of Pangaea!) Like the sphere and dome/dish objects, you'll be required to identify the number of segments or faces, as well as the radius. But when drawing a torus, you must identify both the radius of the *torus* and the radius of the *tube*.

> Manipulating the various radii of a torus can lead to some startling (and nifty) results as you'll discover when working with 3D solids in Lesson 7.

The command sequence looks like this:

Command: *3d*

Enter an option [Box/Cone/DIsh/DOme/Mesh/Pyramid/Sphere/Torus/Wedge]: *t*

Specify center point of torus: *[specify the center point of the torus; unless you want half of the torus to be underground, use a three-dimensional coordinate and move it upward on the Z-axis]*

Specify radius of torus or [Diameter]: *[specify the radius or diameter of the torus – this is the distance from the center of your inner tube to the outer edge of the tube (this detail will become important when we look at 3D solid tori)]*

Specify radius of tube or [Diameter]: *[specify the radius or diameter of the tube – this is how big to make the tube itself (how inflated do you want your inner tube?)]*

Enter number of segments around tube circumference <16>: *[how many divisions will you want around the circumference of the tube?]*

Enter number of segments around torus circumference <16>: *[how many divisions will you want along the circumference of the inner tube?]*

Let's give it a try.

Do This: 4.2.7.1	Creating a 3D Surfaced Torus

I. Start a new drawing using the *lesson 04 template* file located in the C:\Steps3D\Lesson04 folder.

II. Follow these steps.

4.2.7.1: CREATING A 3D SURFACED TORUS

1. Enter the *3D* command and select the **Torus** option Torus.

   Command: *3d*

   Enter an option [Box/Cone/DIsh/DOme/Mesh/Pyramid/Sphere/ Torus/Wedge]: *t*

2. Locate the torus using a three-dimensional coordinate.

   Specify center point of torus: *5,5,.5*

3. Specify the radii of the torus and the tube as indicated.

   Specify radius of torus or [Diameter]: *4*

   Specify radius of tube or [Diameter]: *1*

4. Accept the default number of segments around the tube …

   Enter number of segments around tube circumference <16>: *[enter]*

5. ... but increase the number of segments around the torus. This way, you can see the difference.

Enter number of segments around torus circumference <16>: *32*

Your drawing looks like this. Notice the number of segments in each direction.

6. Save the drawing [icon] as *MyTorus* in the C:\Steps3D\Lesson04 folder.

Command: *save*

| **4.3** | **Understanding the Limitations of Predefined Surface Models** |

By now you may be thinking how wonderful predefined surface models are. And you're right to think so. But remember that you've yet to consider their limitations. Let's look at some of these now.

- The surface models discussed in this lesson are objects. Although you can explode them into 3D faces, neither the original objects nor the 3D faces can be easily modified. You can't trim or extend these objects. Nor can you fillet, chamfer, break, lengthen, or offset them. (You can, however, stretch, mirror, array, rotate, and copy them.)

- Neither 3D faces nor 3D meshes have wall thickness. They are, essentially, two-dimensional objects existing in three-dimensional space.

- While you can use these predefined shapes to build many things, you can't combine them as you can solids. (The ***Union***, ***Subtract***, and ***Intersect*** commands won't work on surface models.)

- Not all OSNAPs will work on predefined surface models.

But take heart, AutoCAD has several other commands (that you'll see in our next lesson) to enable you to draw shapes that aren't predefined. Then in Lesson 6, we'll look at some editing tools that do work!

| **4.4** | **Extra Steps** |

You've probably noticed that there are similar predefined models on the 3D Make control panel. These create 3D solid objects. We've spent this lesson studying predefined *surface* objects. Take a few minutes and compare the two. Are they the same? What are the differences? Do they make the same types of models available?

In a new drawing created with the *Lesson 04 Template*, create a box using the surface approach and then create another box using the solid approach. Notice the differences in the command sequences. Repeat this procedure for each of the predefined models.

It's early to be studying Solid Modeling, yet the similarities between solids and surfaces are too tempting to ignore. As you continue your study of Surface Modeling, bear in mind that each procedure probably has a solid modeling equivalent. Then, when we get to Solid Modeling, you'll be a step a head of the game!

4.5	**What Have We Learned?**

Items covered in this lesson include:

- *AutoCAD's predefined surface models*
  - *Box*
  - *Wedge*
  - *Pyramid*
  - *Cone*
  - *Sphere*
  - *Dome*
  - *Dish*
  - *Torus*

This has been a fun lesson. It's nice to know that they're not all difficult!

We've seen several predefined objects designed by AutoCAD to make three-dimensional drafting move more quickly. But you shouldn't limit these objects to their obvious uses. Whenever you have a complex object to build with surface models, think about these predefined tools as basic – and often elastic – building blocks. For example, when you need a cylinder, consider using a cone with equal radii at both ends. Or when you need a ramp and the wedge is too straight, try using a pyramid with an offset ridge.

Practice the exercises at the end of this lesson for experience. Remember to use the UCS and visual styles to assist you. Then try to draw different objects around your desk – how about your mouse or the keyboard?

Our next lesson will cover more complex, user-defined shapes created as surface models. So what you can't draw yet, you'll soon be able to!

4.6	**Exercises**

1. through 8. Recreate the "su" drawing found in Appendix B using the tools found in this lesson to help you. You'll need to explode many of the primitives to get 3D faces to manipulate, but the drawing should be faster. Use cylinders rather than arcs to line the holes.

9. Create the flying saucer drawing shown in the drawing (next page – top figure). The following hints will help:
   - 9.1. Use the *lesson 04 template* to begin.
   - 9.2. Change the layer colors as needed.
   - 9.3. Use these tools: cone, dish, dome, and torus.
   - 9.4. Use clipping planes to create the section.
   - 9.5. Use the direct hatch approach to hatch the section.
   - 9.6. While you're still in Model Space, use the continuous orbit tool to make the saucer fly back and forth across the screen. (Eat your heart out, Marvin the Martian!)
   - 9.7. Save the drawing as *MySaucer* in the C:\Steps3D\Lesson04 folder.

10. Create the aquarium aerator drawing (next page – bottom figure). The following hints will help:
    - 10.1. Use the *lesson 04 template* to begin.
    - 10.2. Change the layer colors as needed.
    - 10.3. Use these tools: box, donut, and dish.
    - 10.4. Viewport scales are a uniform 1:1.
    - 10.5. Text uses the Times New Roman font.
    - 10.6. Save the drawing as *MyAerator* in the C:\Steps3D\Lesson04 folder.

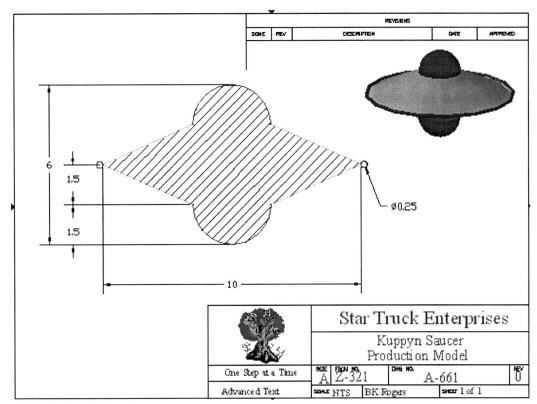

			REVISIONS			
ZONE	REV		DESCRIPTION		DATE	APPROVED

Star Truck Enterprises

Kuppyn Saucer
Production Model

One Step at a Time	SIZE A	FSCM NO. Z-321	DWG NO. A-661	REV 0
Advanced Text	SCALE NTS	BK Rogers	SHEET 1 of 1	

Flying Saucer

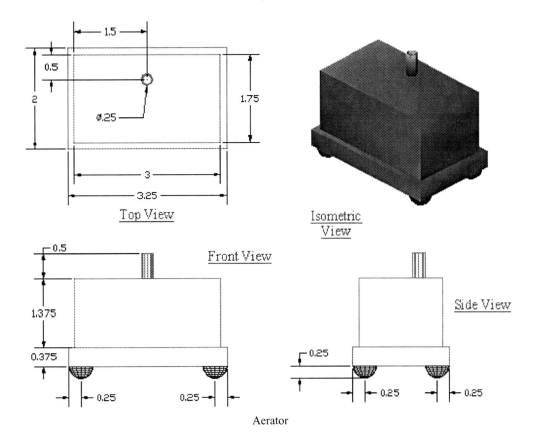

Top View

Isometric View

Front View

Side View

Aerator

11. Create the trailer light drawing shown below. The following hints will help:
    11.1.   Use the *lesson 04 template* to begin.
    11.2.   Change the layer colors as needed.
    11.3.   Use these tools: box, donut, pyramid, and cone.
    11.4.   Viewport scales are a uniform 1:2.
    11.5.   Text uses the Times New Roman font.
    11.6.   Save the drawing as *MyLight* in the C:\Steps3D\Lesson04 folder.

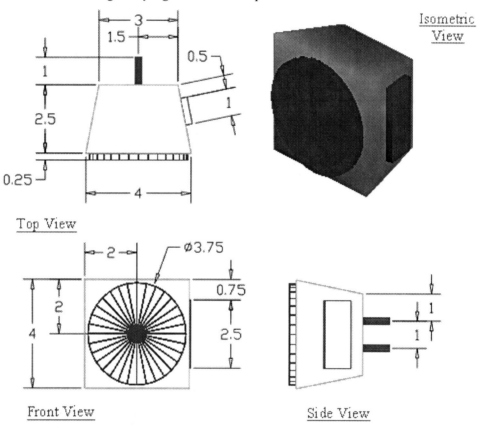

Trailer Light

12. Create the microphone drawing at right. The following hints will help:
    12.1.   Use the *lesson 04 template* to begin.
    12.2.   Change the layer colors as needed.
    12.3.   Use these tools: box, cone, sphere, and wedge.
    12.4.   The UCS is tricky on this one. Align it with the cone to draw the button. Use the UCS to help you rotate the microphone so that it sits atop the wedge.
    12.5.   The wedge is ¼" wide.
    12.6.   Save the drawing as *MyMicrophone* in the C:\Steps3D\Lesson04 folder.

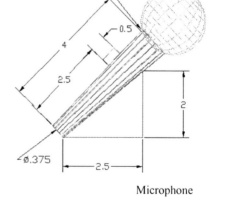

Microphone

13. Create the coffee table drawing. The following hints will help:

   13.1. Use these tools: cone, torus, and region.

   13.2. The torus is 36" diameter and the tube is 1" diameter.

   13.3. The legs are 21" long and extend 2" below the bottom shelf..

   13.4. Save the drawing as *MyCoffeeTable* in the C:\Steps3D\Lesson04 folder.

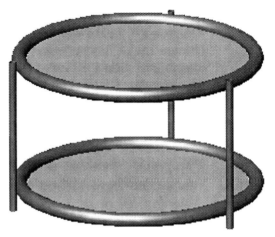

Coffee Table

14. Create the wagon drawing. The following hints will help:

   14.1. Use these tools: cone, torus, box, and dome.

   14.2. The wheel tori are 4" diameter with 1" diameter tubes.

   14.3. The axles are 1" diameter x 8" long cones.

   14.4. The axles are 12" apart.

   14.5. The wagon floor is 18" x 6" x ½".

   14.6. The outer boards are 2½" wide and spaced ½" apart.

   14.7. The inner boards are 1½" wide.

   14.8. Save the drawing as *MyWagon* in the C:\Steps3D\Lesson04 folder.

Wagon

15. Create the pyramid sphere drawing. The following hints will help:

   15.1. Use these tools: sphere, torus, and pyramid.

   15.2. The sphere is 16" diameter. (You'll need to explode it and erase some of the 3D faces.

   15.3. The pyramid is 5" squared on the base x 5" high.

   15.4. The torus is 10" diameter with a 1" diameter tube.

   15.5. The pyramid is hatched to create the brick pattern.

   15.6. Save the drawing as *MyPyrSph* in the C:\Steps3D\Lesson04 folder.

Pyramid Sphere

16. Create the temple drawing below. The following hints will help:
   16.1. Use these tools: wedge, box, and pyramid.
   16.2. The sphere is the drawing we created in Exercise 15. I inserted it as a block at 1/8 scale. (Be sure the UCS in both drawings is equal to the WCS. We'll discuss more on three-dimensional blocks in Lesson 10.)
   16.3. The ramps are 8" x 2" x 2".
   16.4. The center box is 4" x 4" x 2".
   16.5. The pyramid is 4" x 4" x 2" (with a 2" x 2" top).
   16.6. The torus is 10" diameter with a 1" diameter tube.
   16.7. The pyramid is hatched to create the brick pattern.
   16.8. Save the drawing as *MyTemple* in the C:\Steps3D\Lesson04 folder.

Temple

17. Create the lamp drawing. The following hints will help:
   17.1. Use these tools: cone.
   17.2. The center pole is 6' tall x 1" diameter.
   17.3. The base is 12" diameter on the bottom and 1" diameter on the top. It is 2" high.
   17.4. The top is 1" diameter on the bottom and 12" diameter on the top. It is 6" high.
   17.5. The switch is ½" diameter x ½" high. It's located halfway up the center pole.
   17.6. Save the drawing as *MyLamp* in the C:\Steps3D\Lesson04 folder.

Lamp

4.7 **For Web-Based Review Questions, visit:**
http://www.uneedcad.com/2007/Files/07R4-3D.pdf

Lesson

5

Following this lesson, you will:

✓ *Know how to build more complex surface models*

- o **Rulesurf**
- o **Revsurf**
- o **Tabsurf**
- o **Edgesurf**
- o **3DMesh**
- o **Planesurf**
- o **Loft**

✓ *Know how to control the number of surfaces used to draw a surface model*

- o **Surftab1**
- o **Surftab2**

Complex Surface Models

In Lesson 4, you discovered some simple tools that you can use to create surface models. But what if you need a model that doesn't easily translate into one of the predefined surface models? For example, suppose you need to draw an I-Beam, a piping elbow, or an ornate lamp. Which predefined model would you use?

The answer of course, is that none of the predefined tools would help. Well then, would you have to draw a wireframe model (a stick figure) and stretch the surfaces over it? Or would you just give up and wait for Autodesk to develop some more predefined shapes? (Sorry, I don't think any more are coming.)

A wireframe model might work for the I-Beam but not for the piping elbow or the ornate lamp.

The truth is that these tools (wireframe models and predefined surface models) were designed for simple objects, not for complex constructions. But take heart, AutoCAD provides other tools that'll help you deal easily with more intricate designs.

In this lesson, we'll examine tools for creating complex surface models. Here, we'll conclude our study of surface model creation techniques with a look at the procedures needed to put the razzle-dazzle in your three-dimensional drawing.

Let's get started!

5.1 Controlling the Number of Surfaces – Surftab1 and Surftab2

When you drew the sphere, dome, and dish in our last lesson, AutoCAD asked you for the number of segments (or faces) you wanted to use in defining the object. Remember that we defined longitudinal and latitudinal segments differently so that you could see the distinction.

That approach worked well for a predefined shape. But when you draw complex shapes, AutoCAD can't know what you're doing. So, it can't ask you for the number of segments you'll need to define the object. Still, that information will be required for you complex object to take the shape you want.

For this reason, AutoCAD established two system variables to define the number of faces it'll use to create an object. The first – **Surftab1** – defines the number of surfaces AutoCAD will use to create a linear object, or the number of surfaces it will use to create the circumference (axial direction) of a round (or arced) object. The second – **Surftab2** – defines the number of surfaces AutoCAD will use to create latitudinal sections (along the path or rotation) of an object.

Consider the drawing in Figure 5.001. I created this tube (using the *Tabsurf* command) in two steps – the top with a **Surftab1** setting of 20, the bottom with a **Surftab1** setting of 6.

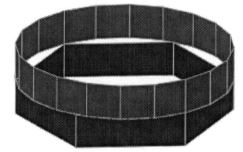

Notice the difference. I created both top and bottom using the same circle object. The only difference is the **Surftab1** setting. On the top, AutoCAD used twenty faces to define the object; on the bottom, AutoCAD used 6. Here you see another important aspect of the **Surftab1**

Figure 5.001

(and **Surftab2**) system variables – *their settings affect the shape of the object being drawn.*

We'll set **Surftab1** and **Surftab2** as needed throughout the exercises in this lesson.

5.2 Different Approaches for Different Goals

AutoCAD provides basic and advanced commands to handle the drawing of complex shapes. You'll probably enjoy the basic commands – they're lots of fun! The advanced commands, however, are more challenging and may take some time to master.

The basic commands all have one thing in common – they all use something two dimensional as a guide to create a three-dimensional object. But remember, a two-dimensional object can exist in Z-space. That is, an object can have any two of the three properties required for a three-dimensional object (length, width, and height). The command you use to create the three-dimensional object will provide the third property. This'll become clear once you've used the commands.

We'll discuss the basic commands in this section and save the advanced commands for the next one. Let's get started.

5.2.1	Follow the Path – The *Tabsurf* Command

Tabsurf is an easy command. You'll need a basic shape – circles, arcs, polylines, and splines make great shapes – and something to indicate a path. AutoCAD will expand the shape into three dimensions along the path you identify.

The command sequence looks like this:

> **Command:** *tabsurf*
>
> **Current wire frame density: SURFTAB1=6** *[AutoCAD reports the Surftab1 settings]*
>
> **Select object for path curve:** *[select the object that'll give shape to your three-dimensional object]*
>
> **Select object for direction vector:** *[select an object that'll tell AutoCAD the direction in which to expand the shape]*

This will become clearer with some practice. (This is a fun project. We'll use the basic commands for drawing complex shapes to create a three-dimensional toy train. So put on your Engineer's hat and let's get started!)

> You can access the *Tabsurf* command (and other complex surface commands discussed in this lesson) from the Surfaces toolbar or from the Draw pull-down menu. Follow this path:
>
> *Draw – Meshes – Tabulated Mesh (or other complex surface command)*

Do This: 5.2.1.1	Using *Tabsurf* to Create a Three-Dimensional Object

I.   Open the *train.dwg* file in the C:\Steps3D\Lesson05 folder. The drawing looks like Figure 5.002.

II. Set **Tank** as the current layer.

III. Follow these steps.

Figure 5.002

5.2.1.1: USING *TABSURF*

1. Set the **Surftab1** system variable to **20** for a more defined shape.

   > **Command:** *surftab1*
   >
   > **Enter new value for SURFTAB1 <6>:** *20*

2. Enter the *Tabsurf* command.

   > **Command:** *tabsurf*

3. AutoCAD wants you to select the object for path curve – the *shape*. Select the circle indicated.

Current wire frame density: SURFTAB1=20

Select object for path curve: *[select the circle]*

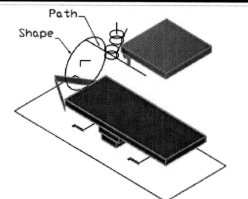

4. AutoCAD wants to know in which direction to expand the shape – the *path*. Select the line indicated. (Select next to where the arrow points in the previous figure.)

Select object for direction vector: *[select the line]*

Your drawing looks like this.

[Note: First AutoCAD determined the path by the selected object. Then it determined the direction for the three dimensional object by where you select on the object for direction vector. Try repeating this step but select the other end of the line. Then undo until your drawing again looks like this.

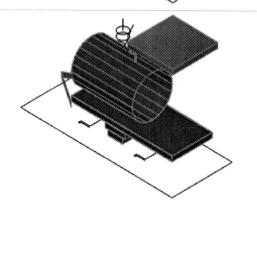

5. Zoom in [icon] around the smokestack (the stacked circles atop the tank) and set the **stack** layer current.

Command: *z*

6. Use the *Tabsurf* command to expand the circles along the lines. Notice that the path is independent of the UCS.

Command: *tabsurf*

Your drawing looks like this.

7. Save the drawing [icon] but don't exit.

Command: *qsave*

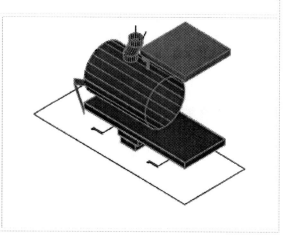

Some things you may have noticed about the *Tabsurf* command and need to remember include:

- The layer of the new object is based on the current layer at the time it is drawn and not on the layer of the original shape or path.

- The part of the path AutoCAD uses to define the new object is the endpoint – *a curved path won't produce a curved object.*
- The original shape and path remain intact after the three-dimensional object is drawn – put them on a separate layer that can be frozen later.
- Where you pick on the path can affect the direction of the expansion.
- The UCS doesn't affect the expansion.

We used circles in our exercise, but **Tabsurf** will work on any predefined shape provided the shape is a single object. Polylines and splines are particularly useful in creating shapes for **Tabsurf** expansion.

Let's take a look at another complex surface modeling command.

5.2.2	Add a Surface Between Objects – The *Rulesurf* Command

Use the **Rulesurf** command when you have two existing objects and want to place a surface between them. It's particularly useful when creating surfaces between uneven objects or objects of different size.

The command sequence is:

> **Command:** *rulesurf*
>
> **Current wire frame density:** SURFTAB1=20 *[AutoCAD reminds you of the current Surftab1 setting; Surftab2 doesn't affect Rulesurf]*
>
> **Select first defining curve:** *[select the first edge of the surface to be created]*
>
> **Select second defining curve:** *[select the opposite edge of the surface to be created]*

There are some similarities between **Rulesurf** and **Tabsurf**, including:

- The layer of the new object is based on the current layer at the time it's drawn and not on the layer of the original shape or path.
- The original edges remain intact after the three-dimensional object is drawn.
- Where you pick on the path can affect the expansion. You should pick in the same vicinity on both edges (toward the same endpoints).
- The UCS doesn't affect the expansion.

Let's try the **Rulesurf** command on our train's cow catcher.

Do This: 5.2.2.1	Using *Rulesurf* to create a Three-Dimensional Object

    I.   Be sure you're still in the *train.dwg* file in the C:\Steps3D\Lesson05 folder. If not, please open it now.

    II.   Restore the **–111** view.

    III.   Set the **tank** layer current.

    IV.   Follow these steps.

5.2.2.1: USING RULESURF

1. Turn the circle in the front of the tank into a region . (This'll improve viewing later.)

> **Command:** *reg*

2. Set the **cow catcher** layer current.

3. Enter the **Rulesurf** command.

> **Command:** *rulesurf*

112

4. AutoCAD needs to know where to draw the surface. Select the edges indicated.

If the surface appears crossed, erase it and try again. When you select the edges, pick in the same general location of each.

(If you have trouble selecting the edges, hold down the control key and select until the edge is found.)

> **Current wire frame density: SURFTAB1=20**
>
> **Select first defining curve:** *[select the first edge]*
>
> **Select second defining curve:** *[select the second edge]*

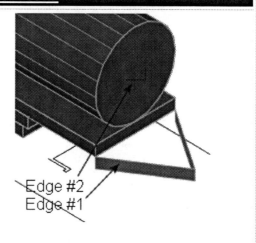

5. Repeat Steps 3 and 4 for the other side of the cow catcher.

> **Command:** *rulesurf*

Your drawing looks like this.

6. Save the drawing [💾] but don't exit.

> **Command:** *qsave*

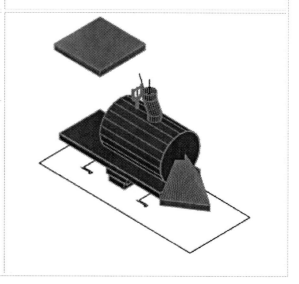

Like *Tabsurf*, any type of object will do for a *Rulesurf* edge – the fancier the original object, the fancier the results!

Speaking of fancy, let's look at the *Revsurf* command!

5.2.3	**Creating Circular Surfaces – The *Revsurf* Command**

Revsurf is one of the more popular of AutoCAD's surface modeling commands. That could be because *Revsurf* is so simple to use; but it's more likely because of the nifty gizmos you can draw with it!

Like the *Tabsurf* command, *Revsurf* begins with an object that'll define its basic shape and another object that'll define its path (or, in the case of *Revsurf*, its axis). Devote some time and care when creating the basic shape since the final object will reflect a well-defined shape. Although other objects may occasionally be required (like a circle as a basic shape to define a piping elbow), I'd use polylines or splines almost exclusively. They tend to produce some truly professional results!

The *Revsurf* command sequence looks like this:

> **Command:** *revsurf*

113

Current wire frame density: SURFTAB1=20 SURFTAB2=6 *[AutoCAD reports the current settings for both Surftab1 and Surftab2. Both will be needed for this procedure.]*
Select object to revolve: *[select the object that defines the basic shape of the object you wish to create]*
Select object that defines the axis of revolution: *[select an object that defines the axis around which you'll revolve the shape]*
Specify start angle <0>: *[specify a starting angle]*
Specify included angle (+=ccw, -=cw) <360>: *[tell AutoCAD if you want a fully or partially revolved shape. The default – 360°-- defines a full revolution. For less than a full revolution, enter the degrees that define the arc you wish to fill.]*

Like *Tabsurf* and *Rulesurf*, the UCS doesn't affect *Revsurf*. However, you might need to adjust it when creating the basic shape you intend to revolve.

Let's take a look at the *Revsurf* command.

Do This: 5.2.3.1	Using *Revsurf* to Create a Three-Dimensional Object

    I.   Be sure you're still in the *train.dwg* file in the C:\Steps3D\Lesson05 folder. If not, please open it now.

    II.   Restore the **bell** view and set the **Stack** layer current.

    III.   Follow these steps.

5.2.3.1: Using *Revsurf*

1. Enter the *Revsurf* command.

    Command: *revsurf*

2. AutoCAD reports the **Surftab1** and **Surftab2** settings. These suit our purpose, so we'll continue.

    Current wire frame density: SURFTAB1=20 SURFTAB2=6

Select the spline rising from the top of the smokestack as the object to revolve.

    Select object to revolve:

3. Select the line rising from the center of the smokestack as your **axis of revolution**.

    Select object that defines the axis of revolution:

4. Accept the **start angle** and **included angle** defaults.

    Specify start angle <0>: *[enter]*

    Specify included angle (+=ccw, -=cw) <360>: *[enter]*

5. Repeat Steps 1 to 4 for the bell assembly (be sure to use the **Bell** layer).

    Command: *revsurf*

The top of your train looks like this.

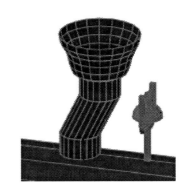

6. Thaw the **MARKER** layer. Notice the nodes, but also notice the lines that appear as axes for the wheel shapes.

Set the **wheels** layer current.

7. Repeat Steps 1 to 4 for both wheels using the lines on the **MARKER** layer as the axes. (Refreeze the **MARKER** layer when you've finished.)

        Command: *revsurf*

Your drawing looks like this.

8. Save the drawing  but don't exit.

        Command: *qsave*

Wasn't that fun?

But remember that I'm providing the basic shapes for these exercises. It's a bit more involved (although not difficult) when you draw them yourself. But just imagine the sense of accomplishment that'll give you!

Our train is starting to take shape (as is our expertise with some cool new commands). Have you tried viewing the model with the isolines toggled off? It looks very nice (especially if you freeze layer **0**).

But we still have to draw the cab and the ground beneath the wheels. Let's not waste a moment – full *steam* ahead!

5.2.4	Using Edges to Define a Surface Plane – The *Edgesurf* Command

Edgesurf is actually one of the simplest of the complex surface commands. But I've placed it at the end of the basic commands because it makes a good transition to the more advanced commands.

Edgesurf creates a surface plane. That doesn't mean that it creates a surface along the X-, Y-, or Z-planes but rather a plane like an open field. It doesn't have to be flat, although it's not the tool for very complex surfaces.

The *Edgesurf* command uses four edges to define a plane. The edges can be parallel to one another or skewed in any direction.

The command sequence simply asks for the four edges:

        Command: *edgesurf*

        Current wire frame density: SURFTAB1=20 SURFTAB2=6 *[AutoCAD reminds you of the Surftab1 and Surftab2 settings. Like Revsurf, both will be needed here.]*

        [Use the next four options to define the edges of the surface.]

        Select object 1 for surface edge:

        Select object 2 for surface edge:

        Select object 3 for surface edge:

        Select object 4 for surface edge:

We'll use *Edgesurf* to create the ground beneath our train's wheels.

Do This: 5.2.4.1	Using *Edgesurf* to Create a Three-Dimensional Object

I. Be sure you're still in the *train.dwg* file in the C:\Steps3D\Lesson05 folder. If not, please open it now.

II. Remain in the **bell** view but zoom out so you can see the ground.

III. Set the **ground** layer current, and freeze the **MARKER** layer.

IV. Follow these steps.

5.2.4.1: USING *EDGESURF*

1. Enter the *Edgesurf* command.

    Command: *edgesurf*

2. AutoCAD reports the current **Surftab1** and **Surftab2** settings and then asks you to select the edges of your object. Select the four lines that form the boundary of the ground (pick one of the shorter lines first).

    Current wire frame density:
    SURFTAB1=20
    SURFTAB2=6

    Select object 1 for surface edge:

    Select object 2 for surface edge:

    Select object 3 for surface edge:

    Select object 4 for surface edge:

Your drawing looks like this.

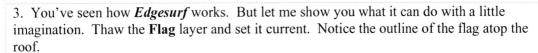

3. You've seen how *Edgesurf* works. But let me show you what it can do with a little imagination. Thaw the **Flag** layer and set it current. Notice the outline of the flag atop the roof.

4. Set **Surftab2** to **20**. This'll enhance our resolution.

    Command: *surftab2*
    Enter new value for SURFTAB2 <6>: *20*

5. Now do an *Edgesurf* using the four sides (two lines and two splines) of the flag as your edges.

    Command: *edgesurf*

Your flag looks like this.

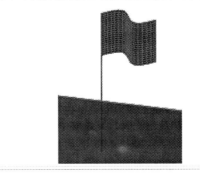

6. Save the drawing 🖫 but don't exit.

    Command: *qsave*

How's that for a bit of razzle-dazzle?!

This concludes the basic Surface Modeling commands. But there's one part of our train we have yet to draw – the hill in front of the train, and the cab. For drawing these surfaces, let's look at some more complex tools, and some newer ones, as well.

5.3	More Complex Surfaces

There are actually several advanced surface model commands – *3DMesh*, *Planesurf*, *Loft*, and *3DFace*. I don't recommend *3DMesh* or *3DFace* for the faint of heart! (In fact, we won't even cover *3DFace* in this text!) The others, however, can be a lot of fun.

AutoCAD invented these commands for you to create objects similar to the predefined surface models so you can manipulate many surfaces as a single object (as in a single sphere rather than dozens of faces). But be forewarned: creating an object with the *3DMesh* command means manually specifying *every vertex on the object*! Besides that, you must identify the vertices *in a specific order*!

Does that sound like a lot of work? It is! But in AutoCAD's defense, I must add that these commands are actually better suited for lisp routines or other third-party programs. You might say that you're on the border where CAD operation ends and CAD programming begins.

> A third-party program is one that's designed to use AutoCAD as a base. In other words, AutoCAD becomes something like a CAD operating system (as Windows is your computer's operating system). The third-party program builds on AutoCAD by providing shortcuts toward a specific end. Popular third-party programs include *Mechanical Desktop*, *Architectural Desktop*, *Propipe*, *ProISO*, and many others.

We'll start with the *3DMesh* command.

5.3.1	Creating Meshes with the *3DMesh* Command

The *3DMesh* command is similar to the *Edgesurf* command. (The similarity is akin to that between a sculptor and a whittler – both will give you a carving. But what the sculptor produces will embarrass the whittler.) Both work well in creating that open field look. But where four edges define the *Edgesurf* object, you have no limit to the number of defined vertices with the *3DMesh* command. As I've mentioned, however, it requires tedious effort to identify each vertex involved.

The command sequence looks like this:

> **Command: *3dmesh***
>
> **Enter size of mesh in M direction:** *[tell AutoCAD how many lines are required to define the columns of faces you'll need]*
>
> **Enter size of mesh in N direction:** *[tell AutoCAD how many lines are required to define the rows of faces you'll need]*
>
> **Specify location for vertex (0, 0):** *[this prompt will repeat for each vertex (intersection) of lines defining the rows and columns]*

Notice that AutoCAD defines the rows and columns in terms of **M** and **N**. This helps avoid any confusion with the X-, Y-, and Z-axes. *3DMesh* works independently of the UCS.

There's an interesting point to remember when defining the size of the mesh in terms of rows and columns. Notice that AutoCAD doesn't ask for the number of rows and columns, but rather, it asks for the number of lines required to define the rows and columns. *You'll be working with the vertices that create the surfaces, not the spaces between the vertices.* The easiest way to determine the number of lines required is simply to add one to the number of rows and columns you want.

This'll become clearer in our next exercise. Let's draw a hill in front of our train (we'll call it *the little engine that could*).

Do This: 5.3.1.1	Using *3DMesh* to Create a Three-Dimensional Object

I.   Be sure you're still in the *train.dwg* file in the C:\Steps3D\Lesson05 folder. If not, please open it now.
II. Thaw the **MARKER** layer and set the **ground** layer current.
III. Begin in the **Bell** view, but pan and orbit so you can see the nodes at the front of the train.
IV. Set your running OSNAPs to **Node**; clear all other settings.
V.   Follow these steps.

5.3.1.1: USING *3DMESH*

1. Enter the *3DMesh* command.

   Command: *3dmesh*

2. (Refer to the figure at right.) Tell AutoCAD you want 5 rows and 5 columns. (Remember that you need 6 lines to define 5 rows or columns.)

   Enter size of mesh in M direction: *6*
   Enter size of mesh in N direction: *6*

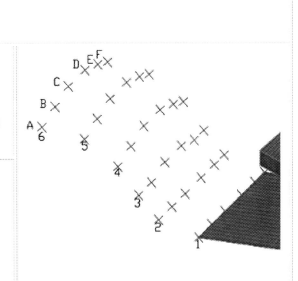

3. Now we'll identify the vertices. Select nodes A-1 through A-6 sequentially. (Hint: Use running OSNAPs.)

   Specify location for vertex (0, 0):
   Specify location for vertex (0, 1):
   Specify location for vertex (0, 2):
   Specify location for vertex (0, 3):
   Specify location for vertex (0, 4):
   Specify location for vertex (0, 5):

4. Follow Step 3 for rows B through F. (Be sure to select the nodes sequentially.)
   Specify location for vertex (1, 0):

5. Freeze the **MARKER** layer. Your drawing looks like this.

6. Save the drawing [icon] but don't exit.

   Command: *qsave*

Note that, once the basic shape of our hill has been defined by using the *3DMesh* command, you can add or remove faces using the *PEdit* command. We'll look at that in more detail in Lesson 6.

Did you find it tedious having to select a node to define each of the 36 vertices? Imagine what it's like defining a large area! Bear in mind that I provided the nodes as a guide for this exercise. Normally, you'll identify the location and place the nodes as well (or enter coordinates at the **Specify location** prompt). Do you see now why I described this command as the edge between CAD operating and CAD programming? You'll often create a 3D mesh using a lisp routine or a Visual Basic program in conjunction with coordinates defined in a database or spread sheet. This is really one of the best ways to create large surfaces (like mountains and valleys).

But wait! There is an easier way!

5.3.2	**Creating Meshes with the *Loft* Command**

With AutoCAD 2007, we have a new command designed to make creation of the ground surface much easier than the procedure we just went through with the ***3DMesh*** command. The new command is ***Loft***, and it makes drawing uneven surfaces a snap.

The sequence looks like this:

> **Command:** *loft*
>
> **Select cross-sections in lofting order:** *[select the lines that will define the curve]*
>
> **Enter an option [Guides/Path/Cross-sections only] <Cross-sections only>:** *[hit enter here or select an option – if you accept the default, AutoCAD will draw the mesh and present the Loft Settings dialog box (Figure 5.003)]*

Okay, it looks deceptively simple, but the real work – drawing the "cross-sections" or defining lines will have already been done by the time you begin the ***Loft*** command. These lines can be just about anything – lines, splines, circles, plines, etc. Further, they can be either open or closed.

> The **DelObj** system variable controls whether or not AutoCAD will delete the original objects once it's drawn the mesh. A setting of **0** tells AutoCAD to delete the objects; **1** tells AutoCAD to leave them.

Let's consider the options.

- **Guides** are guidelines you can use (create) to further define the shape of your wireframe mesh. AutoCAD limits these to lines that intersect each of the defining shapes (cross-sections) and begin and end at the first and last defined shape.

- **Path** defines a single line (spline, etc.) to shape the mesh. While you can use several guides, you're limited to a single path.

- **Cross-sections only** displays the Loft Settings dialog box (Figure 5.003 – next page), which allows you some control of the mesh.
    - **Ruled**, **Smooth Fit**, and **Normal to** control how sharp the mesh will appear.
        - **Ruled** forces the spaces between the defining lines to be flat and sharp.
        - **Smooth Fit** allows a smoother appearance.
        - **Normal to** controls how the mesh behaves at the intersections with the defining lines. **Normal to** options (available in the control box) include:

- ∴ **All cross sections**
- ∴ **Start and end cross sections**
- ∴ **End cross sections**
- ∴ **Start cross sections**

  Accept the default for a smooth surface.
  - o **Draft angles** work something like the start and end vectors of a spline. They'll allow you to control the start and end angles of the mesh.
  - o **Close surface or solid** does just that (much like the **Close** option of the *Line* or *PLine* commands).
  - o **Preview chances**, of course, allows you to see the changes as you define them. It's usually a good idea to leave this box checked.

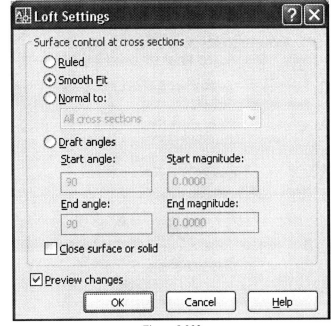

Figure 5.003

Let's use the *Loft* command to create the same surface in front of the train that we created with the *3DMesh* command.

Do This: 5.3.2.1	**Using *Loft* to Create a Three-Dimensional Mesh**

I. Be sure you're still in the *train.dwg* file in the C:\Steps3D\Lesson05 folder. If not, please open it now.

II. Erase the mesh in front of the train.

III. Thaw the **Loft Lines** layer, set the bell view current and adjust the view so you can see the loft lines clearly. Freeze the **Markers** layer and set the **ground** layer current.

IV. Set the UCS to World.

V. Follow these steps.

5.3.2.1: LOFTING

1. Enter the *Loft* command. Alternately, you can pick the Loft button on the 3D Make control panel.

    Command: *loft*

2. Select the east-west splines as your cross-sections. (Hit enter to complete the selection process.)

    Select cross-sections in lofting order:
    Select cross-sections in lofting order: *[enter]*

120

3. AutoCAD wants to know what to do next. Hit enter, and then pick the **OK** button ____OK____ on the Loft Settings dialog box to accept the default.

> **Enter an option [Guides/Path/Cross-sections only] <Cross-sections only>: [enter]**

Your mesh looks like this.

4. Undo the changes ⟲. Let's try this again using a path.

> **Command: *u***

5. Repeat the *Loft* command ⧗.

> **Command: *loft***

6. Select the first and last east-west splines.

> **Select cross-sections in lofting order:**
> **Select cross-sections in lofting order: [enter]**

7. Tell AutoCAD you want to use a **Path** [Path] this time.

> **Enter an option [Guides/Path/Cross-sections only] <Cross-sections only>: *P***

8. And select the center spline as your path.

> **Select path curve:**

Your mesh looks like this.

Notice how the mesh pulls away from the flat ground. You don't have quite as much control using the **Path** option.

9. Undo the changes ⟲. Let's try this again using guides.

Command: *u*

10. Repeat the *Loft* command ⧗.

> **Command: *loft***

11. Select only the first and last east-west splines.

> **Select cross-sections in lofting order:**
> **Select cross-sections in lofting order: [enter]**

12. Tell AutoCAD you'd like to use **Guides** [Guides] this time.

> **Enter an option [Guides/Path/Cross-sections only] <Cross-sections only>: *G***

121

13. Select the north-south lines as your guides.

> **Select guide curves:**
> **Select guide curves:** *[enter]*

Your mesh looks like this. Is there a difference? Which was easier? Faster?

14. Save the drawing ⊞ but don't exit.

Command: *qsave*

5.3.3	Creating a 3D Surface with *Planesurf*

In previous editions of this text, I included a section here that introduced the *PFace* command. This remarkable tool works great for programmers who have a great deal of coordinates to enter and the expertise to create the required programming. For everyday users of AutoCAD, however, it's a nightmare.

We'll use *Planesurf* (a new tool for 2007) to accomplish the same thing quite easily. But for those of you who demand to know the hard way, I'll post the 2006 section on *PFace* on the web at http://www.uneedcad.com/Files. Enjoy!

Planesurf creates a planar surface. (That's a fancy way of saying that it creates a two-dimensional surface, but most surfaces are two-dimensional. Many are drawn with one of the dimensions being in a Z-plane giving the appearance of being three-dimensional.)

The sequence looks like this:

> **Command:** *planesurf*
> **Specify first corner or [Object] <Object>:** *[it's just like drawing a rectangle; pick the first corner ...]*
> **Specify other corner:** *[then pick the opposite corner]*

This may be the easiest surface you'll draw!

Okay, things to remember about *planesurf*:

- *Planesurf* creates surfaces in the XY-plane of the current UCS.
- The **Object** option provides the best approach for using this command. You can convert an existing object to a planar surface in much the same way you can convert a closed object to a region. Convert either closed objects or select multiple objects that form a closed area. Possible object include: lines, circles, arcs, ellipses, elliptical arcs, polylines, planar 3D polylines, planar splines, and regions. This way, you can create a planesurf with a hole in it or with an oddball shape (by selecting a region – you'll see this in our next exercise).
- When using the **Object** option, the surface to be converted does not have to be in the XY-plane of the current UCS.

Let's take a look.

Do This: 5.3.2.2	Using *Planesurf* to Create a Planar Surface

    I.   Be sure you're still in the *train.dwg* file in the C:\Steps3D\Lesson05 folder. If not, please open it now.

   II.   Freeze the **Loft Lines** and **Marker** layers; thaw the **Cabin** layer and set it current; set the **1-11** view current and adjust the view so you can see all three walls of the cabin clearly.

   III.   Set the UCS to World.

   IV.   Follow these steps.

5.3.2.1: USING PLANESURF

1. Enter the **Planesurf** command. Alternately, you can pick the **Planar Surface** button on the 3D Make control panel.

      Command: *planesurf*

2. Tell AutoCAD to use the **Object** option ● Object .

      Specify first corner or [Object] <Object>: *o*

3. Select the three walls of the cabin.

      Select objects:

      Select objects: *[enter]*

Your train looks like this.

4. Restore the -1,1,1 view, and adjust the orbit to improve the view. Remove the isolines and freeze layer **0**. How do you like this look (below)?

5. Save the drawing and exit.

      Command: *qsave*

(That exercise took many more very tedious pages with the **PFace** command! Don't you just love progress?!)

One final note for this lesson:

AutoCAD has also introduced a new command – **ConvToSurface** – designed to convert 2D solids, regions, open polylines with thickness (but zero width), lines with thickness, arcs with thickness, and planar 3D faces. This will accomplish essentially the same thing we did in our last exercise. Remember AutoCAD redundancy!

5.4 Extra Steps

Try to incorporate all you've learned thus far into the train drawing.

- Adjust the views so you can see it from all sides.
- Freeze the **ground** layer and use the Continuous Orbiter to make the train revolve about the screen.
- Set up the train drawing for plotting:
  - o Show it in three views and an isometric.
  - o Dimension it.
  - o Put it on a title block with your school/business name.

5.5 What Have We Learned?

Items covered in this lesson include:

- *Controlling the number of surfaces on a surface model*
- *Basic and Advanced Surface Modeling Commands*
  - o *Surftab1*
  - o *Surftab2*
  - o *Rulesurf*
  - o *Tabsurf*
  - o *Revsurf*
  - o *Edgesurf*
  - o *3DMesh*
  - o *Loft*
  - o *Planesurf*
  - o *ConvToSurface*

Congratulations! You've finished AutoCAD's Wireframe and Surface Modeling commands. You've really come a long way in five lessons!

The decisions you'll now face concern which procedure or method you'll need to create the objects that you want to create. The best help you can get for that is *practice*! So work through the problems at the end of this lesson until you're comfortable with your new abilities.

When you've finished with the exercises, go on to Lesson 6. There we'll discuss the three-dimensional aspects of several editing tools you already know … and some new ones that are specific to three-dimensional drawings. Then, at least where Wireframe and Surface Modeling is concerned, your training will be complete. After that, we'll start a whole new ballgame – we'll learn how to create solid models!

So do the problems, pat yourself on the back for having come this far, and then move onward … ever onward!

1. Create the Window Guide drawing. The following information will help.

    1.1. Use a title block of your choice.

    1.2. Use the Times New Roman font – 3/16" and 1/8".

    1.3. Adjust the dimstyle as needed.

    1.4. Create layers as needed.

    1.5. The object is a tabulated surface model created from a polyline shape.

    1.6. Use either a region or a 3D face to close the ends.

    1.7. Use the **Realistic** visual style with no isolines for the isometric figure.

    1.8. Save the drawing as *MyWinGuide* in the C:\Steps3D\Lesson05 folder.

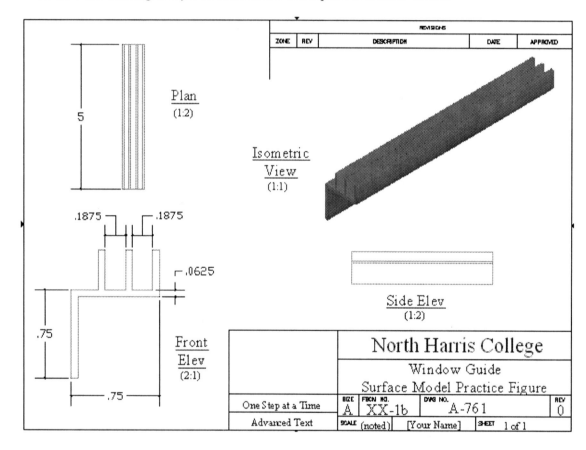

2. Create the Light Fixture drawing. The following information will help.
  2.1. Use a title block of your choice.
  2.2. Use the Times New Roman font – 3/16" and 1/8".
  2.3. Adjust the dimstyle as needed.
  2.4. Create layers as needed.
  2.5. I used a **Surftab1** setting of **32** and a **Surftab2** setting of **6**.
  2.6. The object is a simple revolved surface model. I created the shape on one layer and the revolved surface model on another. I did the cross section by adjusting the viewport and freezing unnecessary layers.
  2.7. Save the drawing as *MyFixture* in the C:\Steps3D\Lesson05 folder.

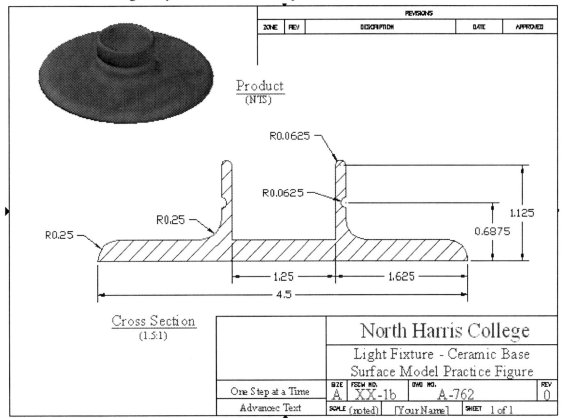

Product
(NTS)

Cross Section
(1.5:1)

R0.0625

R0.0625

R0.25

R0.25

1.125

0.6875

1.25

1.625

4.5

	REVISIONS			
ZONE	REV	DESCRIPTION	DATE	APPROVED

North Harris College

Light Fixture - Ceramic Base
Surface Model Practice Figure

One Step at a Time	SIZE	FSCM NO.		DWG NO.		REV
	A	XX-1b		A-762		0
Advanced Text	SCALE (noted)		[Your Name]	SHEET 1 of 1		

3. Create the Alan wrench drawing. The following information will help.
   3.1. Use a title block of your choice.
   3.2. Use the Times New Roman font – 3/16" and 1/8".
   3.3. Adjust the dimstyle as needed.
   3.4. Create layers as needed.
   3.5. I used the default settings for both surftabs.
   3.6. This object is made up of two tabulated surfaces and a revolved surface. I used six-sided polygons as my basic shapes.
   3.7. Save the drawing as *MyWrench* in the C:\Steps3D\Lesson05 folder.

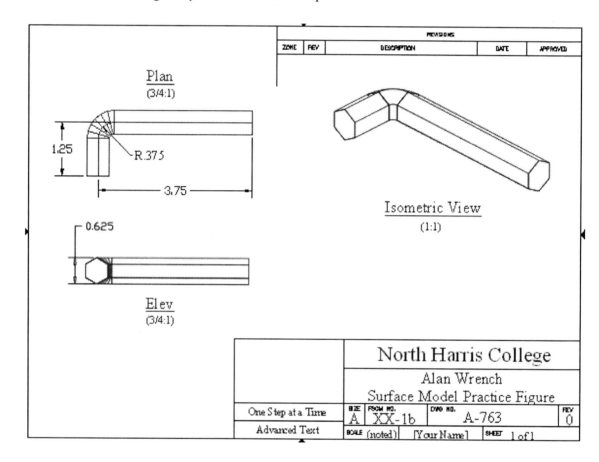

4. Create the caster drawing. The following information will help.
   4.1.   Use the Times New Roman font – 3/16" and 1/8".
   4.2.   Adjust the dimstyle as needed.
   4.3.   Create layers as needed (you may need more than you think).
   4.4.   I used 16 as my setting for both surftabs.
   4.5.   The spindle is a revolved surface.
   4.6.   The upper place is an edged surface.
   4.7.   The axle is a revolved surface.
   4.8.   The wheel is a revolved surface with a hole in it for the axle.
   4.9.   The ball bearings are 1/8" diameter spheres.
   4.10.   To create the sections, use the same technique you used in Exercise 2.
   4.11.   Save the drawing as *MyCaster* in the C:\Steps3D\Lesson05 folder.

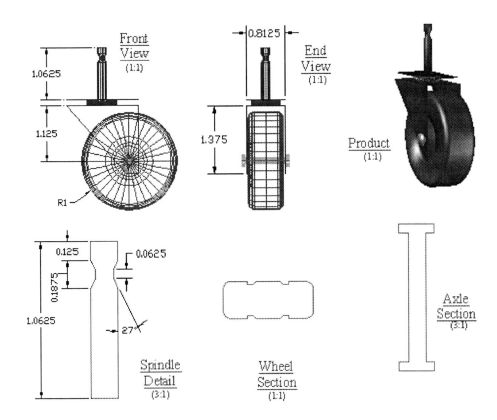

5. Create the toothpaste tube drawing. The following information will help.

Toothpaste Tube

   5.1. The main tube is 7¼" long x 2" wide on the flat end. The round end has an additional ¼" bubble.

   5.2. The round end is 1¼" diameter.

   5.3. The cap is ½" long, 5/8" diameter at the base and ½" diameter at the top.

   5.4. Use *Edgesurf* to create the body of the tube.

   5.5. Use *Revsurf* to create the cap and the bubble-end of the tube.

   5.6. Create layers as needed.

   5.7. Save the drawing as *MyToothpaste* in the C:\Steps3D\Lesson05 folder.

6. Create the lighter drawing. The following information will help.

   6.1. The main bottle is 2¼" tall and is based on an ellipse that is 1" x ½".

   6.2. The top is based on half the bottle's ellipse and is ½" tall.

   6.3. The button is also based on half the bottle's ellipse, is 1/16" thick, and is at an angle of 15°.

   6.4. The striker wheel is 5/16" wide and ¼" diameter.

   6.5. Use *Revsurf* to create the striker wheel.

   6.6. Use *Edgesurf* to create the bottle and the top.

   6.7. Use regions where needed.

   6.8. Save the drawing as *MyLighter* in the C:\Steps3D\Lesson05 folder.

Lighter

7. Create the Remote drawing. The following information will help.

   7.1. The main face is 5¾" long x 2" wide.

   7.2. There's an additional ½" molded arc on the sides and ends.

   7.3. The thickness of the instrument is ½"

   7.4. Round buttons are 3/8" diameter and ¼" diameter domes.

   7.5. Ellipse buttons are ½" x ¼".

   7.6. Other buttons are either pyramids or tabsurfed polylines with regions closing the tops. These are 1/8" high.

   7.7. Use the Times New Roman font at a 1/8" text height.

   7.8. Save the drawing as *MyRemote* in the C:\Steps3D\Lesson05 folder.

8. Create the racer drawing. The ½" grid figure will help. Save the drawing as *MyRacer* in the C:\Steps3D\Lesson05 folder.

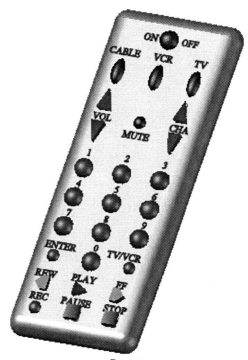

Remote

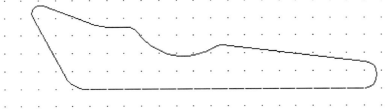

Racer Grid

Racer

5.7   **For Web-Based Review Questions, visit:**
http://www.uneedcad.com/2007/Files/07R5-3D.pdf

Lesson

Following this lesson, you will:

✓ *Know how to use AutoCAD's basic editing tools in Z-Space*

- o **PEdit**
- o **Properties**
- o **Grips**
- o **Trim and Extend**
- o **Align**

✓ *Know how to use basic Z-Space-Specific editing tools*

- o **Rotate3D & 3DRotate**
- o **3DMove**
- o **Mirror3D**
- o **3DArray**

Z-Space Editing

It was just about here in our basic text that we began to look at editing tools. So it's appropriate, I suppose, that we stop now to look at how those editing tools work both on three-dimensional objects and on two-dimensional objects drawn in Z-Space. You'll find little difference in the way some tools and procedures work, but the differences in others may unsettle you. You'll find still others to be brand new (although strangely familiar).

Regardless of their differences or newness, however, you'll find each tool we discuss in this lesson to be invaluable in your three-dimensional efforts. As they did in the two-dimensional world, editing tools will enhance your speed and drawing ability in Z-Space.

To keep it simple (KISS), I'll divide the tools into two categories of study – Familiar (two-dimensional tools with which you're already familiar), and New (three-dimensional tools).

Let's start with the Familiar.

6.1	Three-Dimensional Uses for Familiar (Two-Dimensional) Tools

As we studied editing tools in our basic text, we occasionally came across a prompt that I said would appear in the 3D text. AutoCAD designed these prompts to allow you to continue using some of the more common (and useful) tools when you made the transition into Z-Space. The tools – *Trim*, *Extend*, and *Align* – weren't difficult to learn in the basic book. And now that you're familiar with them, covering their three-dimensional functions will be a snap!

Once we've looked at those, we'll look at the Properties palette and some of the things it can do for a surface model.

Lastly, we'll take a new look at the *PEdit* command and grips. You might be surprised (if not thrilled) at what you find!

Let's start at the beginning.

6.1.1	Trimming and Extending in Z-Space

Trim and *Extend* in Z-Space begin very much like *Trim* and *Extend* in two-dimensional space. In fact, the commands are the same, so all you must learn is the option required to control what gets trimmed/extended in a three-dimensional view.

Remember how the **Edgemode** system variable controlled the **Edge** option in both *Trim* and *Extend* commands? It still holds true in Z-Space, but there's an additional system variable to consider now – **Projmode**. Like **Edgemode**, **Projmode** affects both the *Trim* and *Extend* commands. But where **Edgemode** controls your ability to trim/extend to an imaginary extension of the selected cutting edge/boundary, **Projmode** controls how the *Trim* and *Extend* commands behave in three-dimensional space.

There are two ways to set the **Projmode** system variable – by accessing the **Project** option at the **[Project/Edge/Undo]** prompt of either command, or by entering *Projmode* at the command prompt. The command prompt requires that you enter a number code for the option you wish to use; the **Project** option of the *Trim/Extend* command presents the available settings. The number codes and their corresponding settings follow.

CODE	SETTING	FUNCTION
0	None	This is the *True 3D* setting. It requires that both the cutting edge/boundary and the object to trim/extend be in the same plane. That is, they must actually intersect or, using the **Edgemode** system variable, intersect at an imaginary extension.

CODE	SETTING	FUNCTION
1	UCS	(Default Setting) This setting projects the **cutting edge/boundary** and **object to trim/extend** onto the XY plane of the current UCS and then performs the task as though the objects exist in two-dimensional space.
2	View	This setting causes AutoCAD to project the cutting edge/boundary and object to trim/extend onto the current view as though your monitor's screen is the XY plane. It then performs the task as though the objects exist in two-dimensional space.

Let's see how these settings work in a couple exercises.

Do This: 6.1.1.1	Trimming in Z-Space

I. Open the *trim.dwg* file in the C:\Steps3D\Lesson06 folder. The drawing looks like Figure 6.001.

II. Be sure the **Edgemode** system variable is set to 1.

III. Follow these steps.

Figure 6.001

6.1.1.1: TRIMMING IN Z-SPACE

1. Let's begin by setting the **Projmode** system variable to zero (the *True 3D* setting).

    Command: *Projmode*

    Enter new value for PROJMODE <1>: *0*

2. Now begin the *Trim* command and select the line indicated as your cutting edge.

    Command: *tr*

    Current settings: Projection=None, Edge=Extend

    Select cutting edges ...

    Select objects or <select all>:

    Select objects: *[enter]*

3. Now select the lines indicated to trim. Select the bottom line first.

    Select object to trim or shift-select to extend or [Fence/Crossing/Project/ Edge/ eRase/Undo]:

    Notice that the lower line trims, but the upper line doesn't. With the **Projmode** system variable set to zero, the lines must be on the same plane (as I explained in the chart). The upper line doesn't intersect the cutting edge, so it didn't trim.

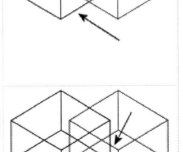

4. Without leaving the command, change **Projmode** Project to the **UCS** setting Ucs as indicated.

    Select object to trim or shift-select to extend or [Fence/Crossing/Project/

133

Edge/eRase/Undo]: *p*

Enter a projection option [None/Ucs/View] <None>: *u*

5. Now trim the line that wouldn't trim previously.

> **Select object to trim or shift-select to extend or [Fence/Crossing/Project/ Edge/eRase/Undo]:**

It trims now because AutoCAD projects the cutting edge and object to trim against the XY plane of the current UCS (as if both lines were drawn in 2D space).

6. Complete the command.

> **Select object to trim or shift-select to extend or [Fence/ Crossing/Project/Edge/eRase/ Undo]:** *[enter]*

Your drawing looks like this.

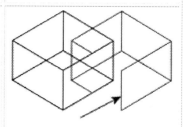

7. Repeat Step 2 .

> **Command:** *[enter]*

8. Select the line indicated to trim.

> **Select object to trim or shift-select to extend or [Fence/ Crossing/Project/Edge/eRase/Undo]:**

Notice that the line won't trim. The **Projmode** system variable setting of **1 (UCS)** means that the lines must intersect in a two-dimensional projection of the current UCS. The line doesn't intersect the cutting edge, so it didn't trim.

9. Change the **Projmode** [Project] to the **View** setting [View] as indicated. (Note: you can use cursor or dynamic input menus if you prefer.)

> **Select object to trim or shift-select to extend or [Fence/Crossing/Project/ Edge/ eRase/Undo]:** *p*
>
> **Enter a projection option [None/Ucs/View] <Ucs>:** *v*

10. Now trim the line that wouldn't trim previously.

> **Select object to trim or shift-select to extend or [Fence/Crossing/Project/ Edge/eRase/Undo]:**

It trims now for two reasons: (1) AutoCAD has projected the **cutting edge** and **object to trim** against your screen (the current view) as if your screen defined the XY plane, and (2) AutoCAD has extended the cutting edge according to the **Edgemode** setting.

11. Complete the command.

> **Select object to trim or shift-select to extend or [Fence/ Crossing/Project/Edge/eRase/ Undo]:** *[enter]*

Your drawing looks like this.

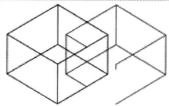

12. Exit the drawing without saving.

> **Command:** *quit*

Now let's look at the *Extend* command.

Do This: 6.1.1.2	Extending in Z-Space

I. Open the *ext.dwg* file in the C:\Steps3D\Lesson06 folder. The drawing looks like Figure 6.002.

II. Be sure the **Edgemode** system variable is set to **1** and the **Projmode** system variable is set to **0**.

Figure 6.002

III. Follow these steps.

6.1.1.2: EXTENDING IN Z-SPACE

1. Begin the *Extend* command 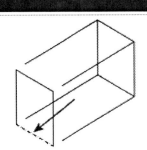 and select the line indicated as your boundary edge.

> **Command:** *ex*
> **Current settings: Projection=None, Edge=Extend**
> **Select boundary edges ...**
> **Select objects or <select all>:**
> **Select objects:** *[enter]*

2. Select the four open-ended lines to extend. Select the bottom lines first.

> **Select object to extend or shift-select to trim or [Fence/Crossing/Project/ Edge/Undo]:**

Notice that the lower lines extend but not the upper lines. As in the *Trim* command, with the **Projmode** set to **0**, the lines must be in the same XY plane. The upper lines don't share the boundary edge's plane, so they didn't extend.

3. Change the **Projmode** Project to the **UCS** setting Ucs.

> **Select object to extend or shift-select to trim or [Fence/Crossing/Project/ Edge/Undo]:** *p*
> **Enter a projection option [None/Ucs/View] <None>:** *u*

4. Now extend the lines that wouldn't extend previously.

> **Select object to extend or shift-select to trim or [Fence/Crossing/Project/ Edge/Undo]:**

They extend now because AutoCAD has projected them against the XY plane of the current UCS.

5. Complete the command.

> **Select object to extend or shift-select to trim or [Fence/Crossing/Project/ Edge/Undo]:** *[enter]*

Your drawing looks like this.

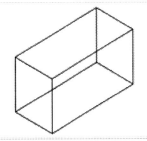

6. Repeat Step 1 [icon], but select the boundary edge indicated here.

        Command: *ex*

7. Select the line indicated here to extend.

        Select object to extend or shift-select to trim or [Fence/Crossing/Project/ Edge/Undo]:

Notice that the line won't extend. With **Projmode** set to **1**, the lines must intersect in a two-dimensional projection of the current UCS. The lines don't, so the selected **object to extend** didn't extend.

8. Change the **Projmode** [Project] to the **View** settings [View].

        Select object to extend or shift-select to trim or [Fence/Crossing/Project/ Edge/Undo]: *p*

        Enter a projection option [None/Ucs/View] <Ucs>: *v*

9. Now extend the line that wouldn't extend previously.

        Select object to extend or shift-select to trim or [Fence/Crossing/Project/ Edge/Undo]:

As with the *Trim* command, it extends now because AutoCAD is looking at the lines projected against your screen (the current view).

10. Complete the command.

        Select object to extend or shift-select to trim or [Fence/Crossing/Project/ Edge/Undo]: *[enter]*

Your drawing looks like this.

11. Exit the drawing without saving.

        Command: *quit*

You've seen that, although still fairly simple to use, the *Trim* and *Extend* commands have some different options with which you must become familiar if you're to use them to full advantage in Z-Space.

But there are some additional things that I should highlight before continuing.

- These commands work on the same objects for which you used them in 2D space – you can't trim/extend a 3D face, 3D mesh, region or solid.
- You can't use a 3D face, 3D mesh, or solid as a cutting edge or boundary edge when trimming/extending.
- You *can*, however, use a region as a cutting edge or boundary edge when trimming or extending.

Let's look at how another 2D command works with three-dimensional objects. Let's look at the *Align* command.

6.1.2	Aligning Three-Dimensional Objects

When you aligned objects in the basic text, you used two source points and two destination points. The main difference between that two-dimensional exercise and aligning three-dimensional objects is that AutoCAD requires three points of alignment for the three-dimensional object.

Another difference lies in your ability to scale the aligned objects as you did in the 2D exercise. You won't have that option with three-dimensional objects. But you can always use the *Scale* command once the objects are aligned.

Let's perform a three-dimensional alignment using AutoCAD's *Align* command.

Do This: 6.1.2.1	Aligning Three-Dimensional Objects

I. Open the *align.dwg* file in the C:\Steps3D\Lesson06 folder. The drawing looks like Figure 6.003. We'll align the eastern face of the ridged pyramid with the top of the box.

II. Follow these steps.

Figure 6.003

6.1.2.1: ALIGNING THREE-DIMENSIONAL OBJECTS

1. Enter the *Align* command.

   Command: *al*

2. Select the wedge.

   Select objects:

   Select objects: *[enter]*

3. (Refer to the left figure below.) Select the alignment points as indicated.

   Specify first source point: *[Point 1a]*
   Specify first destination point: *[Point 1b]*
   Specify second source point: *[Point 2a]*
   Specify second destination point: *[Point 2b]*
   Specify third source point or <Continue>: *[Point 3a]*
   Specify third destination point or [eXit] <X>: *[Point 3b]*

   Your drawing looks like the right figure below.

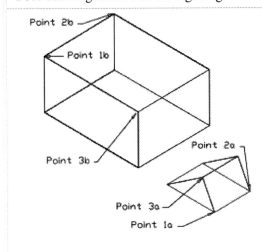

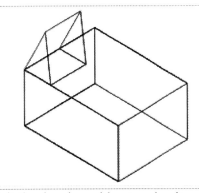

4. Exit the drawing without saving it.

   Command: *quit*

137

I wish they were all that easy!

The really bright side to the *Align* command is that it doesn't care what types of objects are being aligned. You can align the objects you aligned in 2D space or you can align 3D faces, 3D meshes, regions, or solids!

6.1.3	Three-Dimensional Object Properties

When you began creating surface models, you opened the door to a wide variety of new objects – 3D faces, 3D meshes, regions, and solids – that you may need to modify at one time or another.

You can immediately halve your list, however, because regions and three-dimensional solids have no editable properties! Additionally, 3D faces have very few (and very elementary) editable properties, so you can relax in your approach to three-dimensional object properties.

3D meshes can make you long for the simplicity of a two-dimensional world!

We'll spend some time with the different approaches to editing 3D meshes later, but for now, let's begin by examining the 3D face properties AutoCAD makes available in the Properties palette. Refer to Figure 6.004 as we consider the possibilities.

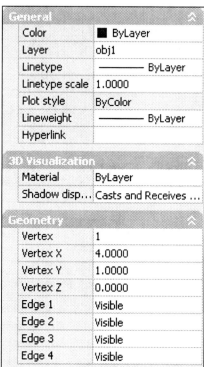

Figure 6.004

- The **General** section contains property information with which you're already familiar from your basic studies.

- **3D Visualization** includes properties we'll discuss in Lesson 11.

- The **Geometry** section contains editable information for the specific 3D face that you've selected.

  o The **Vertex** row identifies a specific vertex (corner) on the 3D face. AutoCAD identifies the vertex on the drawing with an "X" – similar to the way it identifies a vertex when editing with the *PEdit* command's **Edit Vertex** option. When you pick in the **Vertex** row, a set of directional arrows appears in the value column. Use these to scroll through the vertices or type in the number of the vertex you wish to modify.

  o The **Vertex X**, **Vertex Y**, and **Vertex Z** rows present the corresponding coordinate value for that vertex. The coordinate values reflect the current UCS. When you pick one of these rows, AutoCAD presents a **Pick Point** button. You may use this button to pick a point on the screen or you can enter a typed number in the value column to change the location of the vertex.

  o The **Edge** rows provide toggles that you can use to change the visibility of specific 3D face edges.

Let's see how the Properties palette interacts with three-dimensional objects.

Do This: 6.1.3.1	Editing Three-Dimensional Objects with the Properties Palette

I.   Open the *3Dfaces.dwg* file in the C:\Steps3D\Lesson06 folder. The drawing looks like Figure 6.005. (We made the open box using 3D faces; the rectangle is a region, and the other box is a solid.)

II. Follow these steps.

Figure 6.005

6.1.3.1: EDITING THREE-DIMENSIONAL OBJECTS WITH THE PROPERTIES PALETTE

1. Open the Properties palette . Move it to one side and adjust the display so you can see the objects.

Command: *props*

2. Select the region (the flat rectangle).

Notice (right) the **Geometry** section of the palette. It displays two properties for reference, but you can't access either for modification.

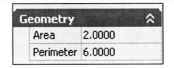

3. Deselect the region [Esc].

4. Select the solid box.

Notice that AutoCAD makes no geometry available for editing or reference.

5. Deselect the solid [Esc].

6. Select the front 3D face on the open box.

Notice the **Geometry** section of the Properties palette (see Figure 6.004).

7. Let's perform some modifications. Change the **Vertex** that you'll edit to *4* [Vertex 4].

Notice an "X" identifies the vertex on the 3D face.

(Note: Set the visual style to 2D Wireframe if you're having trouble seeing grips, highlighting, etc.)

8. Change the value of **Vertex X** to **2.5**. Notice the change on the 3D face. (Note: You must hit *enter* after changing the value for AutoCAD to accept the change.)

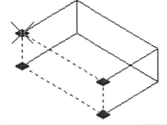

139

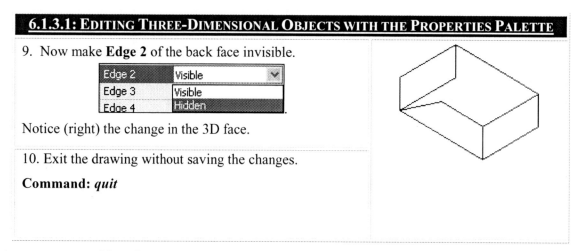

9. Now make **Edge 2** of the back face invisible.

Edge 2	Visible
Edge 3	Visible
Edge 4	Hidden

Notice (right) the change in the 3D face.

10. Exit the drawing without saving the changes.

Command: *quit*

As you can see, although you can't modify a region or solid, modifying a 3D face with the Properties palette is quite easy.

6.1.4	Modifying a 3D Mesh

3D mesh modification is considerably more complicated than 3D face modification primarily because it's a more complex object. When you modify a 3D face, you have only the one object with which to work. That object has three or four vertices and edges. You have nothing else with which to work that might complicate matters.

A 3D mesh, on the other hand, has any number of vertices, several mesh values, and even a polyline fit/smooth value.

Luckily, AutoCAD has provided three methods for modifying 3D meshes – the *PEdit* command, the Properties palette, and grips. Each has its place, and knowing when to use each procedure will go a long way toward preserving your sanity when facing a 3D mesh with dozens (or hundreds) or vertices.

Let's start with the *PEdit* command.

6.1.4.1	Modifying a 3D Mesh – Pedit

Remember how much fun you had with the *PEdit* command in the basic text? I told you then that you'd probably never need the **Edit vertex** tier of options – at least not in the two-dimensional world. Well, you're not in Kansas anymore. But this is where you get the payoff for struggling through the exercise that covered the **Edit vertex** options.

The *PEdit* command looks slightly different when you select a 3D mesh instead of a polyline. This is the sequence:

Enter an option [Edit vertex/Smooth surface/Desmooth/Mclose/Nclose/Undo]:

- **Mclose/Mopen** and **Nclose/Nopen** serve the same function as the **Open/Close** option of the 2D *PEdit* command. But on the 3D mesh, AutoCAD draws a closing line between first and last points of the M-columns or N-rows.

- As always, **Undo** undoes the last modification. (Remember; don't confuse the **Undo** option with the *Undo* command, which undoes the last command.)

- **Smooth surface** creates a curved shape from the 3D mesh. This handy tool is really quite useful for images that'll be rendered (more on rendering in Lesson 11).

  AutoCAD provides three types of smooth surface (Figure 6.006 – next page) – Quadratic B-Spline, Cubic B-Spline, and Bezier. The type of surface created with the **Smooth surface** option depends on the current setting of the **Surftype** system variable (refer to Figure 6.006).

140

Two other system variables control the number of M-columns and N-rows on the smoothed 3D mesh. These are **SurfU** (to control the number of M-columns) and **SurfV** (to control the number of N-rows).

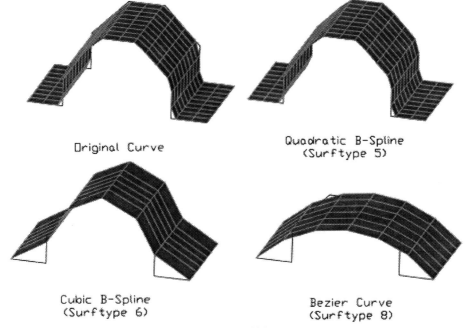

Figure 6.006

- Of course, the **Desmooth** option removes any changes made with the **Smooth surface** option.
- The **Edit vertex** options resemble the same options you received when you selected a two-dimensional polyline. But it has some additional tools. It looks like this:

  Current vertex (0,0).

  Enter an option [Next/Previous/Left/Right/Up/Down/Move/REgen/eXit] <N>:

  o The first thing you'll notice is that AutoCAD identifies the vertex both with an "X" (as it did on the polyline) and by column and row (**M,N**) coordinate at the command prompt.

  o The **Next/Previous** tools work just as they did for a polyline – to maneuver along the mesh from vertex to vertex.

  o The **Left/Right/Up/Down** tools supplement the **Next/Previous** tools, making it easier to maneuver to a specific vertex without having to pass through countless vertices to get there.

  o The **Move** option, of course, allows you to move the currently selected vertex to a new point.

  o **REgen** and **eXit** work the same on 2D and 3D objects. (**REgen** regenerates the mesh/polyline, and **eXit** exits this tier of options.)

Let's experiment with the *PEdit* command and 3D meshes.

Do This: 6.1.4.1.1	Using *PEdit* to Edit 3D Meshes

I. Open the *3DMesh.dwg* file in the C:\Steps3D\Lesson06 folder. The drawing looks like Figure 6.007.

II. Close the Properties palette.

III. Follow these steps.

Figure 6.007

1. Enter the **PEdit** command .

   Command: *pe*

---

2. Select the 3D mesh atop the figure.

   Select polyline or [Multiple]:

---

3. Tell AutoCAD to use the **Edit vertex** option .

   Enter an option [Edit vertex/Smooth surface/ Desmooth/Mclose/Nclose/ Undo]: *e*

---

4. Hit *enter* three times (accepting the **Next** option) to move the locator to the middle of the east end of the 3D mesh (right). (The **Current vertex** will be **0,3**.)

   Current vertex (0,0).

   Enter an option [Next/ Previous/Left/Right/Up/Down/ Move/REgen/eXit] <N>: *[enter]*

   Current vertex (0,1).

   Enter an option [Next/ Previous/Left/Right/Up/Down/ Move/REgen/eXit] <N>: *[enter]*

   Current vertex (0,2).

   Enter an option [Next/ Previous/Left/Right/Up/Down/ Move/REgen/eXit] <N>: *[enter]*

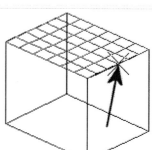

---

5. Use the **Move** option 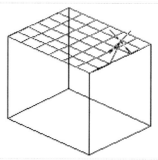 to move the vertex upward 1.5 units as indicated.

   Enter an option [Next/Previous/ Left/Right/Up/Down/Move/ REgen/eXit] <N>: *m*

   Specify new location for marked vertex: *@0,0,1.5*

   Your roof looks like this.

---

6. Use the **Up** option 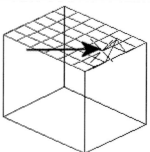 to move the locator to vertex **1,3**.

---

7. Repeat Step 5.

   Enter an option [Next/Previous/ Left/Right/Up/Down/Move/ REgen/eXit] <U>: *m*

   Specify new location for marked vertex: *@0,0,1.5*

8. Repeat Steps 6 and 7 until the entire column has been raised. Your drawing looks like this.

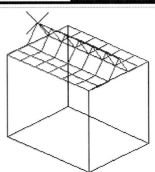

9. Use the **Left** option [Left] to move the locator to vertex **6,2**.

> **Enter an option [Next/ Previous/ Left/Right/Up/Down/Move/REgen / eXit] <U>:** *l*

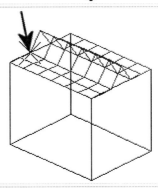

10. Move [Move] the vertex upward three-fourths of a unit.

> **Enter an option [Next/Previous/ Left/Right/Up/Down/Move/ REgen/eXit] <L>:** *m*
>
> **Specify new location for marked vertex:** *@0,0,.75*

11. Move the locator **Down** [Down] to the next vertex and repeat Step 10. Repeat this procedure until the roof looks like this. (You'll use the **Right** option to get to the other side of the ridge.)

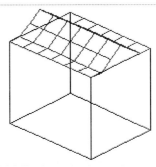

12. Exit the command [eXit].

> **Enter an option [Next/Previous/ Left/Right/Up/Down/Move/ REgen/eXit] <U>:** *x*
>
> **Enter an option [Edit vertex/ Smooth surface/Desmooth/Mclose/Nclose/ Undo]:** *[enter]*

13. Now we'll experiment with different roof shapes. Set the **Surftype** to **5** for a Quadratic B-Spline.

> **Command:** *surftype*
>
> **Enter new value for SURFTYPE <6>:** *5*

14. Set the **SurfU** and **SurfV** system variables as indicated for a more rounded roof.

> **Command:** *surfu*
> **Enter new value for SURFU <6>:** *12*
> **Command:** *surfv*
> **Enter new value for SURFV <6>:** *18*

15. Repeat the *PEdit* command and select the same 3D mesh.

> **Command:** *pe*
> **Select polyline or [Multiple]:**

16. Smooth the surface Smooth surface .

> **Enter an option [Edit vertex/Smooth surface/Desmooth/Mclose/Nclose/Undo]:** *s*

17. Exit the command.

> **Enter an option [Edit vertex/Smooth surface/Desmooth/Mclose/Nclose/Undo]:** *[enter]*

Your drawing looks like this.

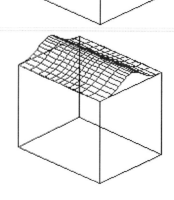

18. Repeat Steps 15 through 17 with the **Surftype** set to **6** (Cubic B-Spline). It'll be difficult to see the difference, but if you look closely (right), you'll notice that the Cubic B-Spline is slightly more curved.

19. Save the drawing , but don't exit.

> **Command:** *qsave*

Experiment with visual styles for each of the different types of roofs. Which do you like best? Let's look next at using the Properties palette to edit the 3D mesh.

6.1.4.2	Modifying a 3D Mesh – The Properties Palette

The Properties palette offers the same options as the *PEdit* command but makes it easier to select a specific vertex if you know its M,N coordinate.

- Vertices work the same as they did when you modified the 3D face in Exercise 6.008. The only difference is the possible number of vertices with which to work.

- Mesh properties include four that you can change and two for reference.

  o **M closed** and **N closed** are toggles. They work like the **Close** option of the *PEdit* command.

  o **M** and **N density** control the density of columns and rows on the 3D mesh. (Remember that the **M** value controls columns of faces and the **N** value controls rows.) AutoCAD bases these on the values of the **SurfU** and **SurfV** system variables, except that they reflect the number of lines defining the rows/columns rather than the number of rows/columns.

  o You can't change the **M vertex count** or **N vertex count**. AutoCAD gives these numbers as a reference only.

- The **Fit/Smooth** option works like the **Smooth vertex** option of the *PEdit* command.

Geometry	
Vertex	1
Vertex X	10.0000
Vertex Y	1.0000
Vertex Z	7.0000

Mesh	
M closed	No
N closed	No
M density	13
N density	19
M verte...	7
N verte...	7

Misc	
Fit/Smo...	Cubic

Figure 6.008

Let's experiment with 3D meshes and the Properties palette.

Do This: 6.1.4.2.1	Modifying a 3D Mesh with the Properties Palette

I. Be sure you're still in the *3DMesh.dwg* file in the *C:\Steps3D\Lesson06* folder. If not, please open it now.

II. Open the Properties palette.

III. Follow these steps.

6.1.4.2.1: MODIFYING A 3D MESH WITH THE PROPERTIES PALETTE

1. Select the roof. Notice that the Properties palette changes to reflect the properties of the 3D mesh (Figure 6.008).

2. Change the type of surface to **Bezier** as indicated. (There's a scroll bar on the left side of the Properties palette. Use it to scroll down until you see the **Misc** section.)

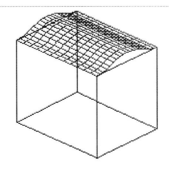

Notice (right) how much softer the curve is than the other two you've seen.

3. We'll use the Properties palette to seal both ends of the roof against the wall. Make **Vertex 3** active. (Select the **Vertex** row and use the directional arrows to change the value to **3**).

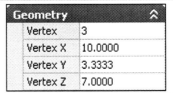

Geometry	
Vertex	3
Vertex X	10.0000
Vertex Y	3.3333
Vertex Z	7.0000

145

4. Change the value of **Vertex Z** to **7** (see the previous figure).

Notice the change on the drawing.

5. Repeat Steps 3 and 4 for vertices 4, 5, 45, 46, and 47. (Normally, you'd use the arrow keys in the **Vertex** row while watching the locator "X", but I've already determined the vertices you'll need to change. I list them here to save time.)

Your drawing looks like this.

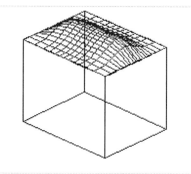

6. Save the drawing ⊞, but don't exit.

         Command: *qsave*

Again, experiment with the visual styles. Orbit the view to see the building from all sides and then return to this view.

Which procedure do you like best so far? Certainly the Properties palette is easiest, but let's take a look at grips next.

6.1.4.3	Using Grips to Modify a 3D Mesh – Grips

There's very little to add to what you've already learned about grips (Lesson 16 of *AutoCAD 2007: One Step at a Time*). But I want to show you how easy it is to modify a 3D mesh using these marvelous tools.

Let's get right to it.

Do This: 6.1.4.3.1	Using Grips to Modify a 3D Mesh

    I.   Be sure you're still in the *3DMesh.dwg* file in the C:\Steps3D\Lesson06 folder. If not, please open it now.

    II.   Select the roof and set the **Fit/Smooth** option (on the Properties palette) to **None**.

    III.   Set the running OSNAP to **Node** and clear all other settings. Thaw the **Marker** layer (notice the nodes above the roof).

    IV.   Follow these steps.

1. Select the roof. Notice the grips.

2. Pick the center grip at the top of the roof (use the coordinate display to the left on the status bar – the grip is at coordinate 5.5, 4.5, 8.5).

3. Stretch the 3D mesh to the center node above the roof.

4. Stretch the 3D mesh using the grip at point 7, 4.5, 8.5 to the east-most node and the grip at point 4, 4.5, 8.5 to the west-most node.

146

5. Freeze the **Marker** layer, set the **Fit/Smooth** option to **Quadratic**, and set the **Realistic** visual style current. Remove the isolines. Your drawing looks like this.

6. Save the drawing .

> **Command:** *qsave*

You can see how much easier it is to move a vertex using grips than any other method. The only requirement is that you know the destination point!

6.2   Editing Tools Designed for Z-Space

You've seen how AutoCAD has adapted several modification tools you already knew to help you in Z-Space and with three-dimensional objects. It's good to maintain some familiarity between the 2D and 3D worlds.

In this section, we'll look at some new tools designed specifically for working in Z-Space, but as their names imply (***Rotate3d***, ***3DRotate***, ***3DMove***, ***Mirror3d***, and ***3DArray***), they serve familiar functions. The major difference between these and their two-dimensional counterparts involves the use of axes rather than base or rotation points.

Let's look at each.

6.2.1   Moving in Z-Space – The *3DMove* Command

You might think that moving objects in Z-space would be simple enough using Cartesian coordinates – just add the Z! Okay, it really is. But AutoCAD does include a command that makes moving to a general location fairly simple. What's more, it really doesn't require a lot of adjustment to use.

Here's the sequence:

> **Command:** *3dmove*
> **Select objects:** *[select the object(s) to move]*
> **Select objects:** *[enter to confirm the selection]*
> **Specify base point or [Displacement] <Displacement>:** *[pick a base point]*
> **Specify second point or <use first point as displacement>:** *[pick a target point]*

Look familiar? It should – it's exactly the same as the *Move* command! Then why use it at all? Notice the tool for the *3DMove* command (shown). This handy gizmo – oddly called a *grip* tool – appears after you've identified your base point or accepted the **Displacement** option. It will help you relocate objects in Z-space.

How?

3DMove
Grip Tool

- When you place your cursor on one of the axes, AutoCAD will move the object along that axis. It even provides a ghost line to let you know which axis it's using.
- When you move the grip over a 3D Face or the face of a solid object with the dynamic UCS toggled on, AutoCAD will automatically change the UCS to assist your move.

True, you can also enter X,Y,Z coordinates in a Cartesian format, but you can do that with the standard *Move* command.

Try this.

Do This: 6.2.1.1	Moving Objects in Z-Space

    I.   Reopen the *align.dwg* file in the C:\Steps3D\Lesson06 folder.

    II.   Follow these steps.

6.2.1.1: MOVING OBJECTS IN Z-SPACE

1. We want to move the wedge to "about" the center of the top of the block. You can do it with the *Move* command – use OSNAPs to move it adjacent to one of the sides, then eyeball a second move to about the center of the block. But let's see how we can do it with the

3DMove command. Enter the command. Alternately, you can pick the **3D Move** button on the 3D Make control panel.

             Command: *3dmove*

---

2. Select the wedge.

             Select objects:

---

3. Select a convenient base point.

             Specify base point or [Displacement] <Displacement>:

Notice that the *3DMove* grip appears.

---

4. Place your cursor over the east-west grip axis as shown. When you see the ghost line, pick with the left mouse button and move the object to the center of the bottom of the block. Pick where you want the wedge and AutoCAD relocates it.

             Specify second point or <use first point as displacement>:

---

5. Repeat the command , and select the wedge and a convenient base point again.

---

6. This time, place your cursor over the blue Z-axis grip as shown. Move the wedge to the top of the block.

             Specify second point or <use first point as displacement>:

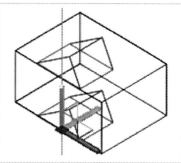

7. Repeat the *3DMove* command to roughly center the wedge on the top of the block. Your drawing looks like this.	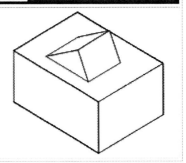
8. Exit the drawing without saving.	

Frankly, I'm not all that impressed by the *3DMove* command – I prefer *Move* with Cartesian coordinates or OSNAPs. (Of course, you can also use Cartesian coordinates or OSNAPs with 3DMove, but then, what's the point?) Still, you may find it just the ticket!

6.2.2	## Rotating About an Axis – The *Rotate3D* and *3DRotate* Commands

Okay, before you get nervous, they both do the same thing – with slightly different approaches. We used to use the command line with *Rotate3D*; AutoCAD gave us the more visual *3DRotate* with the 2007 release. We'll look at both.

First the Olde Way – *Rotate3D*.

Rotating about a base point was easy – you simply selected what to rotate and a base point. Then you told AutoCAD what angle you wanted.

Rotating about an axis is slightly more complex. But if you ever need to rotate an object in Z-Space, you'll find the *Rotate3d* command quite handy. (Earlier editions of this text called it irreplaceable – maybe I won't be quite so dogmatic in the future!) It works like this:

> **Command:** *rotate3d*
>
> **Current positive angle: ANGDIR=counterclockwise ANGBASE=0** *[AutoCAD reminds you how the drawing was set up]*
>
> **Select objects:** *[select the object(s) you want to rotate]*
>
> **Select objects:** *[confirm completion of the selection set]*
>
> **Specify first point on axis or define axis by**
>
> **[Object/Last/View/Xaxis/Yaxis/Zaxis/2points]:** *[select a point on the axis about which you wish to rotate the objects]*
>
> **Specify second point on axis:** *[select a second point to identify the axis]*
>
> **Specify rotation angle or [Reference]:** *[tell AutoCAD how much to rotate the object(s)]*

It might look frightening compared with the *Rotate* command, but once you've used it, you'll find it fairly simple and straightforward. Let's consider each of the axis-defining options.

- The default option is to specify **2points** on the axis. AutoCAD needs you to define the axis of rotation by picking any two points on it. Once you've done that, AutoCAD will prompt you to

  > **Specify rotation angle or [Reference]:**

  Then tell AutoCAD how much to rotate the selected objects.

- The **Object** option is probably the easiest. If you have an object drawn that can serve as an axis, all you have to do is select it. When you choose this option, AutoCAD prompts

  > **Select a line, circle, arc, or 2D-polyline segment:**

  o   If you select a line, AutoCAD uses the line as your axis of rotation.

o If you select a circle or arc, AutoCAD rotates the objects parallel to the plane of the circle or arc and about an imaginary axis drawn through the center of it.

o AutoCAD treats a straight 2D-polyline segment as a line, and a 2D-polyline arc as an arc.

- The **Last** option refers to the last axis you used in the *Rotate3d* command.

- When you use the **View** option, AutoCAD rotates the objects about an imaginary axis drawn perpendicular to your monitor's screen.

- The **Xaxis/Yaxis/Zaxis** options align the axis of rotation with the X-, Y-, or Z-axis that runs through a selected point. AutoCAD prompts:

    Specify a point on the X [or Y or Z] axis <0,0,0>:

    Enter the point's coordinates or pick it (with an OSNAP) on the screen.

Before we try it, let's look at the New Way – *3DRotate*.

You'll accomplish the same thing using *3DRotate* as you did with *Rotate3D*, but *3DRotate* uses a more visual, on-screen approach.

The command sequence begins the same way as *Rotate3D*:

> **Command: *3drotate***
>
> **Current positive angle in UCS: ANGDIR=counterclockwise ANGBASE=0**
>
> **Select objects:** *[select the object(s) you want to rotate]*
>
> **Select objects:** *[confirm completion of the selection set]*

At this point, the prompts change and AutoCAD presents the *3DRotate* grip tool appears. This tool works in much the same way the 3DMove grip tool worked – place your cursor over one of the axes and AutoCAD will rotate the selected objects about that axis.

Here are the remaining prompts:

3DRotate Grip Tool

> **Specify base point:** *[put the grip in the center of the grip tool over the point about which you want to rotate]*
>
> **Pick a rotation axis:** *[select one of the axes – just as you selected an axis with the 3DMove grip tool]*
>
> **Specify angle start point:** *[pick a starting point]*
>
> **Specify angle end point:** *[the objects rotate dynamically, so rotate until you're happy and pick the ending point]*

Now, let's give both these commands a try.

> The *3DRotate* command (and most of the other 3D commands in this section) can also be found in the Modify pull-down menu. Follow this path:
>
> > *Modify – 3D Operation – Rotate 3D*
>
> Unfortunately, the *Rotate3D* command has no such convenient tools.

Do This: 6.2.2.1	Rotating Objects in Z-Space

I. Open the *ro3d.dwg* file in the C:\Steps3D\Lesson06 folder. The drawing looks like Figure 6.009.

II. Follow these steps. (We'll start with the Olde tool and move on to the new one.)

Figure 6.009

150

1. Enter the *Rotate3d* command.

    Command: *rotate3d*

2. Select the handle.

    Select objects:

    Select objects: *[enter]*

3. We'll begin by selecting two points to define the axis of rotation (the default). Select the node at the end of the line in front of the handle …

    Specify first point on axis or define axis by [Object/Last/View/Xaxis/ Yaxis/Zaxis/2points]:

4. … and then select the node at the other end of the line.

    Specify second point on axis:

5. Rotate the handle 45°.

    Specify rotation angle or [Reference]: *45*

    The drawing looks like this.

    Notice that the handle rotated downward. When we selected points on the axis, AutoCAD assumed the direction we defined (from the first node to the second) to be the positive Z-direction of our rotation. It then rotated the object counterclockwise. (Use the right-hand rule to verify this for yourself.)

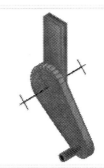

6. We'll use an object to define our axis of rotation this time. Repeat the command.

    Command: *[enter]*

7. Select the handle again.

    Select objects:

    Select objects: *[enter]*

8. Now choose the **Object** option [Object].

    Specify first point on axis or define axis by [Object/Last/View/Xaxis/ Yaxis/Zaxis/2points]: *o*

9. Select the line between the two nodes. (Note: I drew the line from the front node to the rear node – thus defining the positive Z-direction for the object).

    Select a line, circle, arc, or 2D-polyline segment:

10. Rotate the handle -45°.

    Specify rotation angle or [Reference]: *-45*

    The handle returns to its original position.

11. Next we'll try the **View** option. Reset the viewpoint to 0,-1,0 for a front view of the objects. (Caution: Do *not* use the **Front View** button on the View toolbar, as this will also change the UCS.)

    Command: *vp*

12. Repeat Steps 1 and 2.

13. Select the **View** option [View].

    Specify first point on axis or define axis by [Object/Last/View/Xaxis/

Yaxis/Zaxis/2points]: *v*

14. Select the node in the center of the large end of the handle.
    Specify a point on the view direction axis <0,0,0>:

15. Rotate the handle 135°. This time, AutoCAD assumes the view represents a plan view of the drawing (with +Z rising outward from the monitor).
    Specify rotation angle or [Reference]: *135*

16. Restore the previous view .

    Command: *z*
    Your drawing looks like this.

17. Next, we'll rotate the handle about the Y-axis (the axis along which the line is drawn). Repeat Steps 1 and 2.
    Command: *rotate3d*

18. Choose the **Yaxis** option .

    Specify first point on axis or define axis by[Object/Last/View/Xaxis/ Yaxis/Zaxis/2points]: y

19. Select one of the nodes on the line …
    Specify a point on the Y axis <0,0,0>:

20. … and tell AutoCAD to rotate the handle 135°. Then handle returns to its original position.
    Specify rotation angle or [Reference]: *135*

21. Now let's see how the other half lives – enter the **3DRotate** command. Alternately, you can pick the **3D Rotate** button ⊕ on the 3D Make control panel.
    Command: *3drotate*

22. Select the handle.
    Select objects:
    Select objects: *[enter]*

23. Pick the node in the center of the handle.
    Specify base point:
    The 3D Rotate grip tool appears.

24. Place your cursor over the (green) Y-axis and hover until AutoCAD presents the ghost line.

Pick a rotation axis:

Notice that the selected axis changes colors to help identify which one you've selected.

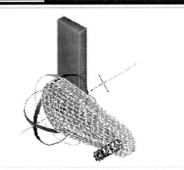

25. Pick a point in the center of the small end of the handle.

Specify angle start point: _cen of

26. Move your cursor up and down. Notice that the handle moves dynamically. Pick a rotation you like.

Specify angle end point:

21. Exit the drawing without saving it.

Command: *quit*

As you can see, the only real difficulty in three-dimensional rotations is deciding which tool and which option to use! Which tool do you prefer?

6.2.3	Mirroring Three-Dimensional Objects – The *Mirror3d* Command

The differences between the ***Rotate3d*** and ***Rotate*** commands are really quite similar to the differences between the ***Mirror3d*** and ***Mirror*** commands. Rather than selecting a point around which to rotate an object in 2D space, you had to pick two points on an axis to satisfy the ***Rotate3d*** command. Rather than picking two points on a mirror *line* as you did in 2D space, you must pick three points to identify a mirror *plane* (the actual face of the mirror) when you use the ***Mirror3d*** command.

The options offered by the ***Mirror3d*** command are also very similar to those presented by the ***Rotate3d*** command.

> **Command:** *mirror3d*
>
> **Select objects:** *[select the object(s) you want to mirror]*
>
> **Select objects:** *[confirm the selection set]*
>
> **Specify first point of mirror plane (3 points) or**
>
> **[Object/Last/Zaxis/View/XY/YZ/ZX/3points] <3points>:** *[use these three options to identify the mirror plane]*
>
> **Specify second point on mirror plane:**
>
> **Specify third point on mirror plane:**
>
> **Delete source objects? [Yes/No] <N>:** *[this option is the same as the 2D* Mirror *command – hit enter to keep the source objects or enter* **Y** *to remove them]*

Let's get right to an exercise.

Do This: 6.2.3.1	Rotating Objects in Z-Space

I.   Open the *Star.dwg* file in the C:\Steps3D\Lesson06 folder. The drawing looks like Figure 6.010.

II.   Set the **Endpoint** running OSNAP.

III.   Follow these steps.

Figure 6.010

6.2.3.1: ROTATING OBJECTS IN Z-SPACE

1. Enter the *Mirror3d* command.

    Command: *mirror3d*

---

2. Select the star.

    Select objects:

    Select objects: *[enter]*

---

3. We'll use the default **3points** approach first. Pick the points indicated.

    Specify first point of mirror plane (3 points) or [Object/Last/Zaxis/View/XY/YZ/ZX/ 3points] <3points>:

    Specify second point on mirror plane:

    Specify third point on mirror plane:

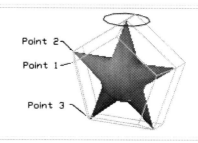

---

4. Don't delete the source objects.

    Delete source objects? [Yes/No] <N>: *n*

Your drawing looks like the one of the left (below). The star has been mirrored along the plan you identified. Rotate the view to see it from above (lower right figure) for a better understanding of the angles.

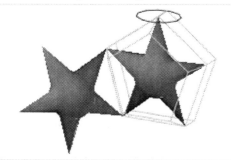
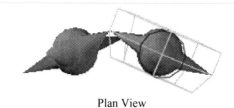

Plan View

---

5. Erase the new star [icon].

    Command: *e*

---

6. Let's use the **Object** option to stand the star on its head. Repeat Steps 1 and 2.

    Command: *mirror3d*

---

7. Choose the **Object** option [Object].

    Specify first point of mirror plane (3 points) or [Object/Last/Zaxis/View/ XY/YZ/ZX/3points] <3points>: *o*

154

6.2.3.1: Rotating Objects in Z-Space

8. Select the star's halo (the circle).

Select a circle, arc, or 2D-polyline segment:

9. This time, delete the source objects.

Delete source objects? [Yes/No] <N>: y

Your drawing looks like this. The star has been mirrored using the plane in which the circle was drawn.

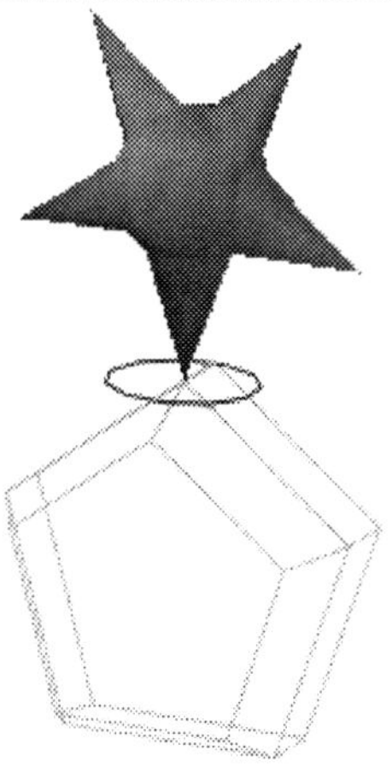

10. Now we'll mirror the star using the YZ plane. Repeat Steps 1 and 2. (Turn on the UCS icon to help identify the YZ plane.)

Command: *[enter]*

11. Choose the **YZ** option and select the leftmost point of the star.

Specify first point of mirror plane (3 points) or [Object/Last/Zaxis/View/XY/YZ/ZX/3points] <3points>: *yz*
Specify point on YZ plane <0,0,0>:

12. Don't delete the source objects.

Delete source objects? [Yes/No] <N>:

Your drawing looks like this.

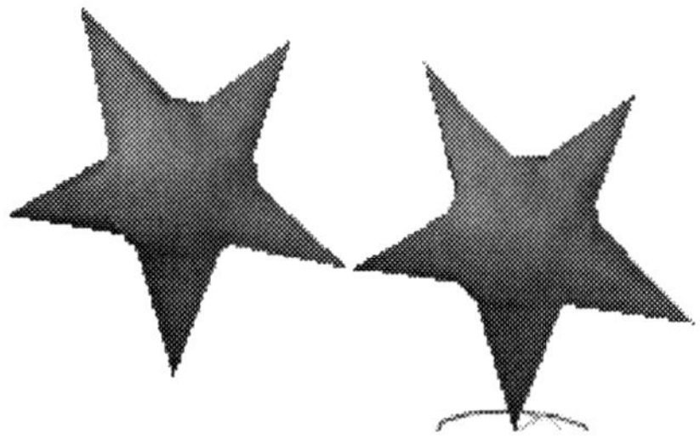

13. Exit the drawing without saving your changes.

Command: *quit*

If there were only one suggestion I could make about both the ***Rotate3d*** and ***Mirror3d*** commands, it would be to always check your image from more than one viewpoint (preferably three or four). Remember that, in Z-Space, object positions seen from one angle are not necessarily true three-dimensional positions.

6.2.4 Arrayed Copies in Three Dimensions – The *3DArray* Command

Of the three modification commands in this section, the ***3DArray*** command most closely resembles its two-dimensional counterpart (well, the command line approach of its 2D counterpart anyway). In fact, the most important difference between the two-dimensional rectangular array and the three-dimensional rectangular array is the addition of prompts for number and spacing of levels. The most important difference between the two-dimensional polar array and the three-dimensional polar array is that, rather than selecting a center point of the array, you must identify two points on an axis.

I should mention another important difference between the ***Array*** and ***3DArray*** commands. ***3DArray*** has no dialog box with which to work. But if you're comfortable with the Array dialog box, the command line prompts and options will be familiar to you.

Let's array some objects in Z-Space.

> A notable difference between ***3DArray*** and the other modification commands in this section is that ***3DArray*** has a hotkey – ***3a***.

Do This: 6.2.4.1	Arraying Objects in Z-Space – Rectangular Arrays

I. We'll begin this exercise by creating a three-dimensional piperack. Open the *3darray-rec.dwg* file in the C:\Steps3D\Lesson06 folder. The drawing looks like Figure 6.011.

II. Follow these steps.

Figure 6.011

6.2.4.1: ARRAYING OBJECTS IN Z-SPACE – RECTANGULAR ARRAY

1. Enter the **3DArray** command.

   Command: *3a*

2. Select the vertical 10' I-Beam.

   Select objects:
   Select objects: *[enter]*

3. Accept the default **Rectangular** type of array.

   Enter the type of array [Rectangular/Polar] <R>: *[enter]*

4. Tell AutoCAD you want two rows, three columns, and two levels.

   Enter the number of rows (---) <1>: *2*
   Enter the number of columns (|||) <1>: *3*
   Enter the number of levels (...) <1>: *2*

5. Specify the distances as shown.

   Specify the distance between rows (---): *9'*

   Specify the distance between columns (|||): *15'*

   Specify the distance between levels (...): *11'*

   Your drawing looks like this. (Adjust your view as required to see the entire drawing.)

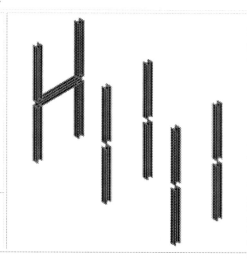

6. Now we'll array the horizontal support. Repeat the **3DArray** command.

   Command: *[enter]*

7. Select the horizontal support.

   Select objects:

8. Accept the default **Rectangular** type of array.

   Enter the type of array [Rectangular/Polar] <R>: *[enter]*

9. You'll want to create one row, three columns, and two levels ...

   Enter the number of rows (---) <1>: *[enter]*
   Enter the number of columns (|||) <1>: *3*
   Enter the number of levels (...) <1>: *2*

10. …at the spacing indicated.

> **Specify the distance between columns (‖):** *15'*
>
> **Specify the distance between levels (…):** *11'*

Your drawing looks like this.

---

11. Save the drawing as *MyPiperack.dwg* in the C:\Steps3D\Lesson08 folder, and then exit.

> **Command:** *saveas*

Do This: 6.2.4.2	Arraying Objects in Z-Space – Polar Arrays

I. Now we'll use the **Polar** option of the *3DArray* command. Open the *3darray-polar.dwg* file in the C:\Steps3D\Lesson06 folder. The drawing looks like Figure 6.012.

II. Set the **Intersection** and **Endpoint** running OSNAPs. Clear all other settings.

III. Freeze the **obj2** layer to temporarily remove the sphere.

IV. Follow these steps.

Figure 6.012

1. Enter the *3DArray* command.

> **Command:** *3a*

---

2. Select the nozzle.

> **Select objects:**
> **Select objects:** *[enter]*

---

3. Tell AutoCAD you wish to create a **Polar** array ⬚ Polar ⬚.

> **Enter the type of array [Rectangular/Polar] <R>:** *p*

---

4. We'll create four copies of the nozzle and fill a full circle.

> **Enter the number of items in the array:** *4*
> **Specify the angle to fill (+=ccw, -=cw) <360>:** *[enter]*

---

5. We do want to rotate the nozzles as they're copied.

> **Rotate arrayed objects? [Yes/No] <Y>:** *[enter]*

---

6. Select the intersection of the guidelines as the **center point of array**.

> **Specify center point of array:**

7. Pick the rightmost endpoint of the north-south horizontal line (the one running from lower left to upper right). **Specify second point on axis of rotation:** Your drawing looks like this.	
8. Repeat Steps 2 through 8, but this time select an endpoint on the vertical line in Step 8. Your drawing looks this.	
9. Thaw the **obj2** layer and freeze the **marker** layer. Your drawing looks like this.	
10. Save the drawing as *Weird Vessel.dwg* in the C:\Steps3D\Lesson06 folder, and then exit. **Command:** *saveas*	

6.3	Extra Steps

Create several 3D meshes – similar to those shown in Figure 6.006. Use different shapes to begin – hat or stair shapes are good as starters, but don't limit yourself. Use the *Edgesurf* command to help you.

Once you have four or five meshes, experiment with the different **Smooth surface** options of the *PEdit* command.

It's an important step in your training to combine the different tools you've learned.

- Try editing each mesh before and after you've smoothed it. Note the differences in outcome.
- Try doing the same editing chores using different visual styles. Which style is easier? Which editing tool (*PEdit*, Properties palette, or grips) is easiest for each of the settings?

| 6.4 | **What Have We Learned?** |

Items covered in this lesson include:

- *Two-dimensional modification tools used on three-dimensional objects*
  - o *PEdit*
  - o *Trim*
  - o *Extend*
  - o *Align*
  - o *Grips*
  - o *The Properties palette*
- *Tools designed specifically for Z-Space*
  - o *Surftype*
  - o *SurfV and SurfU*
  - o *Rotate3D and 3DRotate*
  - o *Mirror3D*
  - o *3DMove*
  - o *3DArray*

This has been a busy (and full) lesson, but you've learned so much!

When combined with your knowledge of wireframe and surface modeling (and some practice), these tools will enable you to create almost any structure you wish to draw. With some creative use of visual styles, you can produce professional-quality, colorful drawings of almost anything for any industry!

But what must you have that I can't provide?

PRACTICE ... PRACTICE ... PRACTICE!

Remember: Only through practice does training become experience. And it's experience that creates successful, efficient, economical, and sound designs; and it's experience that earns top dollar!

So repeat any lesson as needed for the proper training, and then work through the exercises at the end of the lesson for experience.

Our next lesson begins the wonderful world of Solid Modeling. There, you'll see things that are guaranteed to amaze and confound, bemuse and befuddle. But above all, you'll see why Solid Modeling is the future of CAD.

| 6.5 | **Exercises** |

1. Using the *Star-Root.dwg* file in the C:\Steps3D\Lesson06 folder, create the star drawing we used in Exercise 6.2.2.1. (Hint: Grips make this exercise much easier.)

2. Create the conveyor belt drawing shown below. Follow these guidelines:
   2.1. Draw only one shaft and one roller (use the ***Revsurf*** command for best results).
   2.2. Use the 3D commands from this lesson to arrange the guides and the rollers on the guides.
   2.3. Use splines and the ***Rulesurf*** command to create the belt.
   2.4. I used a **Surftab1** setting of **18** or the shaft and roller, and **Surftab1** setting of **100** and **Surftab2** setting of **36** when I created the belt.
   2.5. Save the drawing as *MyBelt.dwg* in the C:\Steps3D\Lesson06 folder.

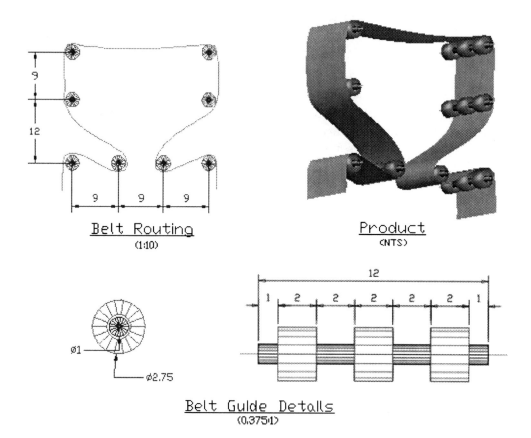

Belt Routing
(1:10)

Product
(NTS)

Belt Guide Details
(0.375:1)

3. Starting with the *MyPiperack.dwg* file you created in Exercise 6.2.3.1 (or the *Piperack.dwg* file if that one isn't available), create the piping drawing. Follow these guidelines:

3.1. The tank has a 15' diameter and a 10' height. The top has a 3' pointed cone.

3.2. Pipe is 12" diameter (12.75" ID, or outer diameter).

3.3. Elbows are 18" from open face to centerline of bend.

3.4. There's a 1/8" gasket between the flange and the nozzle at the tank.

3.5. **Surftab1** and **Surftab2** values are 16.

3.6. The dike wall around the tank is 2' high. The top of the wall is one mesh grid wide.

3.7. I used **Revsurf** to create the elbows and **Rulesurf** to create the pipe.

3.8. Save the drawing as *MyPipingPlan.dwg* in the C:\Steps3D\Lesson06 folder.

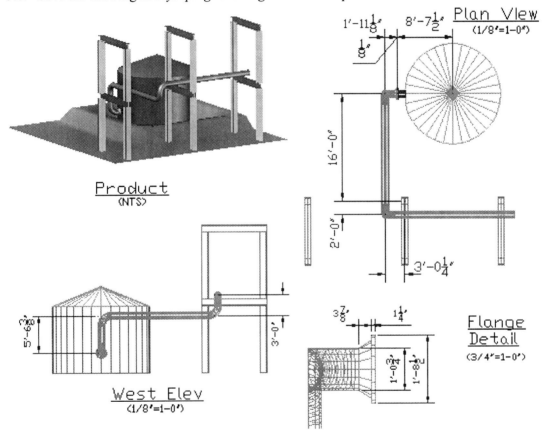

Product
(NTS)

Plan View
(1/8"=1-0")

West Elev
(1/8"=1-0")

Flange Detail
(3/4"=1-0")

4. Create the propeller drawing shown below. Follow these guidelines:

4.1. The blade is a three-dimensional curve – use a spline as the arc and rise to the end of the upper line as shown in the *top blade detail*. Use as many vertices a you need – but I wouldn't use less than five.

4.2. I used a **Surftab1** setting of **8** to create the hub, and a **Surftab1** setting of **16** and **Surftab2** setting of **18** to create the blade.

4.3. Once you've drawn the blade, turn it into a block. Insert the block into its proper place on the hub, but then explode it.

4.4. Use the *Rotate3d* command to rotate the blade 105° on the hub.

4.5. Use the 3D mesh editing tools you learned in this lesson to attach the ends of the blade to the hub.

4.6. (Hint: The *Stretch* command works as well in Z-Space as it did in 3D space.)

4.7. Save the drawing as *MyProp.dwg* in the C:\Steps3D\Lesson06 folder.

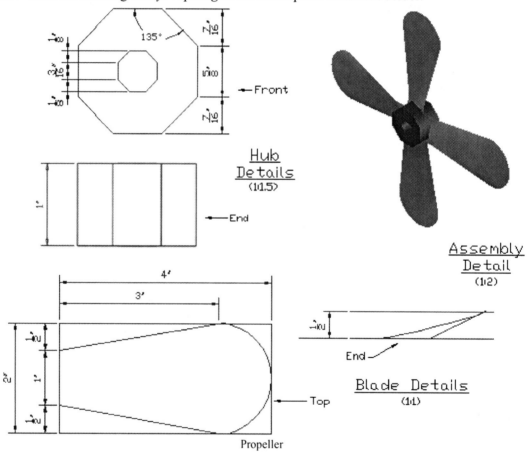

Propeller

162

5. Create the three-dimensional chess board. Follow these guidelines:
   5.1. Each square is 1½".
   5.2. The boards are rotated at 15° increments.
   5.3. The post is 1" diameter.
   5.4. The frames are ½" wide x ¾" deep.
   5.5. The boards are 8" apart.
   5.6. Save the drawing as *My3DChess.dwg* in the C:\Steps3D\Lesson06 folder.

3D Chess Board

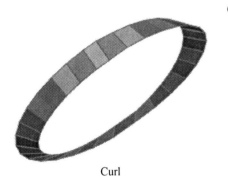

Curl

6. Here's another challenge! Create the curl drawing shown here. Follow these guidelines:
   6.1. I started with a 1" line.
   6.2. There are 30 faces in all.
   6.3. The ring is ~4¼" diameter (I started with a line at 1,1 and arrayed it about point 4,4).
   6.4. I used three layers and two colors.
   6.5. The faces rotate 180°.
   6.6. Save the drawing as *MyCurl.dwg* in the C:\Steps3D\Lesson06 folder.

7. Create the sailboat drawing shown at right. Follow these guidelines:
   7.1. This is a toy sailboat. The boat itself is 6 "x 2" x ¾".
   7.2. The keel is 3" below the bottom of the boat.
   7.3. The mast is 7" long x 1/8" diameter.
   7.4. The boom is 5" long x 1/8" diameter.
   7.5. Save the drawing as *MySBoat.dwg* in the C:\Steps3D\Lesson06 folder.

| 6.6 | **For Web-Based Review Questions, visit:**
http://www.uneedcad.com/2007/Files/07R6-3D.pdf |

Lesson

7

Following this lesson, you will:

✓ *Know how to create AutoCAD's Solid Modeling Building Blocks*

    o **Box**

    o **Wedge**

    o **Cone**

    o **Sphere**

    o **Cylinder**

    o **Torus**

    o **Extrude**

    o **Revolve**

✓ *Know how and why to use AutoCAD's Isolines system variable*

✓ *Creating 3D Object from 2D Objects*

Solid Modeling Creation Tools - Basic

Understanding some of the history of three-dimensional AutoCAD might help you prepare for this lesson.

AutoCAD began its trek into Z-Space by creating the Z-axis. The Z-axis gave us the ability to create three-dimensional lines and circles for the first time. AutoCAD called this development Wireframe Modeling.

But although the creation of a Z-axis was no small feat for programmers, Wireframe Modeling came up short in its usefulness to draftsmen. After all, a skeleton without skin is a fairly transparent accomplishment.

AutoCAD "covered" the need by developing Surface Modeling. Here, we gained the 3DFace (and related) commands that could be used to "stretch a blanket" over the wireframe. This appeared to solidify AutoCAD's three-dimensional experiment. But the success, like its models, was hollow.

AutoCAD programmers still dreamed of a model that would be "just like the real thing." That is, they wanted the computer to be able to reflect mass properties – solids where the object was solid, and spaces where the solid was empty. They wanted a solid object to be a solid object – not a loose conglomeration of circles and lines. So AutoCAD developed Solid Modeling.

Obviously, I couldn't give you the full history in these few paragraphs. The reason for these paragraphs, then, is to let you know that developers of Solid Modeling had Wireframe and Surface Modeling on which to build.

What does that mean to you now? Simply that having studied the intricacies of the more primitive modeling techniques, you're well prepared (better, perhaps, than you might think) for tackling this newest – and most remarkable – of AutoCAD's modeling tools.

7.1	**What Are Solid Modeling Building Blocks?**

Most people refer to Solid Modeling building blocks as primitive solids. But frankly, that term isn't as descriptive as it might be. Building blocks are toys with which we all played as children. You're already familiar with their basic shapes – box, wedge, cone, cylinder, sphere, and torus. You studied all these, except cylinder, as part of your predefined surface models. (A cylinder is simply a cone with equal radii at both ends.)

Additionally, we'll include homemade shapes as part of our building blocks (didn't you wish you could do that when you were a child?). To create these, we'll use the solids equivalent of the *Revsurf* command – *Revolve* – and a command that turns 2D objects into 3D solids – *Extrude*.

Therefore, to answer the question, "What are Solid Modeling building blocks?" (for the test), let me give you a quick definition. Solid Modeling building blocks are predefined and user-defined solid shapes with which you build your model.

Let's look at each of them.

7.2	**3D Solids from 2D Regions and Solids**
7.2a	***Thicken***

You have a few ways to convert existing structures – surfaces, faces, and closed objects – into solid objects. These commands – *Thicken*, *Extrude*, and *PressPull* – work on different types of existing objects and knowing which is which will save a lot of frustration.

Thicken works on surfaces only. That sounds simple enough, but be aware that it doesn't work on 3D Faces or meshes (the source of potential aggravation). You must have created the surface using one of the surface tools – *ConvToSurface* (good on 2D solids, regions, lines/arcs/polylines with thickness, and *planar* faces) or *Planesurf.*

The command goes like this:

Command: *thicken*

Select surfaces to thicken: *[select the surface(s) to thicken]*

Select surfaces to thicken: *[confirm the selection set]*

Specify thickness <0.0000>: *[tell AutoCAD how thick to make it]*

That's simple enough! But be aware that thicken doesn't allow for anything other than a straight path along the current UCS.

7.2b	*Extrude*

One of the easiest ways to create a three-dimensional solid is simply to *extrude* a two-dimensional object. This means that AutoCAD will take the two-dimensional object and "stretch" it or "pull" it into Z-Space. The objects on which AutoCAD can perform this engineering marvel are 3D faces, closed polylines, circles, ellipses, closed splines, donuts, regions, and 2D solids. The results may surprise you!

The command sequence looks like this:

Command: *extrude* (or *ext*)

Current wire frame density: ISOLINES=4

Select objects to extrude: *[select the object(s) you want to extrude]*

Select objects to extrude: *[confirm the selection set]*

Specify height of extrusion or [Direction/Path/Taper angle] <5.0000>:*[tell AutoCAD how far into Z-Space you want to extrude the object or select one of the other options]*

There aren't many options to confuse you, but what they can do will astound you. Let's look at each line.

- AutoCAD first lets you know how many *isolines* it'll use to display the object.

  Let me explain isolines.

  Remember when you drew surface models? You had to identify the number of faces to use by answering some prompts or adjusting the values of the **Surftab1** and **Surftab2** system variables.

  When drawing a solid object, the shape is unaffected by the surftab settings. A round solid object is round regardless of the number of lines AutoCAD uses to show that it's round. But using a large number of lines to show something is round takes a bit more memory and regeneration time, so AutoCAD allows you to control the number.

  You'll control the number of lines used to show a rounded solid object with the **Isolines** system variable. (You can toggle isolines on or off with the **Isolines** button in the Visual Styles control panel.)

  This will become clearer in our next exercise.

- The first option occurs right after the **Select objects** prompts. With the **Direction** option, you can pick two points to identify direction and length of the extrusion.

- Next, you can select an object that'll define the extrusion **Path**. The path object can be a line, arc, or 3DPoly. The results can be quite elaborate.

- Another option that can produce elaborate results is the **taper for extrusion** option. The default (**0**) produces a nice straight extrusion. An angle entry, however, can turn a box into a pyramid!

With the 2007 release, AutoCAD will also extrude *open* polylines and other open objects – but the object produced will be a *surface* rather than a *solid*. The sequence and options are the same, so be careful what you select as it will have a profound effect on what you produce.

7.2c	*PressPull*

If you thought *Thicken* and *Extrude* were easy, take a look at *PressPull*. Here's the sequence:

> **Command:** *presspull*
> **Click inside bounded areas to press or pull.**

All you do with *PressPull* once you've picked inside a bounded area is to push or pull until the 3D object is as big as you want it! It works on polylines, regions, 3D faces, and 2D solids to create a 3D solid. What's more – you can use it to press or pull any face of an existing 3D solid! Sooo cool!

Let's make some 3D solid objects.

Do This: 7.2.1	From 2D to 3D – Without Kicking and Screaming!

    I.   Open the *regions & solids.dwg* file in the C:\Steps3D\Lesson07 folder. The drawing looks like Figure 7.001. (The top two I-Beam are regions, the third I-Beam is a polyline, the square is a solid, and the circle is a circle. The oddball shape is a region and the rectangle is a polyline drawn with thickness.)

Figure 7.001

    II.   Set the **obj1** layer current.

    III.   Set the **Isolines** system variable is set to **4**.

    IV.   Follow these steps.

7.2.1: FROM 2D TO 3D

1. Enter the *Extrude* command. Alternately, you can pick the **Extrude** button on the 3D Make control panel.

> **Command:** *ext*

2. Select the lower-left I-Beam.

> **Current wire frame density: ISOLINES=4**
> **Select objects to extrude:**
> **Select objects to extrude:** *[enter]*

3. Enter a **height of extrusion** of **5**.

> **Specify height of extrusion or [Direction/Path/Taper angle] <5.0000>:**

The I-Beam looks like this. Notice that the original object disappears and that the new 3D solid object is created on the current layer.

4. Repeat the *Extrude* command .

5. Select the I-Beam directly behind the first (the one with the straight line rising from it).
   Select objects to extrude:

6. Tell AutoCAD to use a **Path** [Path] to guide the extrusion ...
   Specify height of extrusion or [Direction/Path/Taper angle] <5.0000>: *p*

7. ... and select the line in the center of the I-Beam.
   Select extrusion path or [Taper angle]:

   The beams look like this.

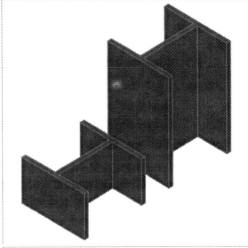

8. Repeat Steps 4 through 7 for the other I-Beam using the 3D polyline as the path.
   Command: *[enter]*

   The beams look like this. Notice the difference when the path isn't straight.

11. Now let's look at the last prompt. Repeat the *Extrude* command [icon] and select the solid (the square).

12. Let's taper [Taper angle] this one ...
    Specify height of extrusion or [Direction/Path/Taper angle] <-0.9132>: *t*

13. ...at a 30° angle.
    Specify angle of taper for extrusion <0>: *30*

14. Make it 5 units tall.
    Specify height of extrusion or [Direction/Path/Taper angle] <-0.9132>: *5*

    How's this one?

15. Let's try something cool – enter the *PressPull* command. Alternately, you can use the **Press Pull** button [icon] on the 3D Make control panel.
    Command: *presspull*

168

16. Try it on some of the faces of the pyramid we made in the last step.

> **Click inside bounded areas to press or pull.**

It may look something like this – kind've odd, but awfully easy to do!

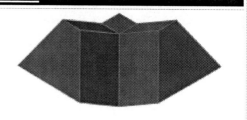

17. Enter the ***ConvToSolid*** command. (We'll use it to convert the polyline rectangle to a 3D solid.)

> **Command: *convtosolid***

18. Select the polyline rectangle.

> **Select objects:**
>
> **Select objects: *[enter]***

Not much to that one, is there?

19. Only one command left – but we have to convert the oddball region to a surface first. Use the ***ConvToSurface*** command and select it now.

> **Command: *convtosurface***

20. Now thicken it.

> **Command: *thicken***
>
> **Select surfaces to thicken:**
>
> **Select surfaces to thicken: *[enter]***

Give it a thickness of about one inch.

> **Specify thickness <0.0000>: *1***

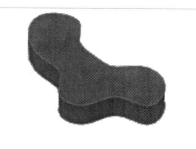

14. Save the drawing 💾.

Command: *qsave*

Draw an open line or polyline anywhere in the drawing and extrude it. Notice the difference? The open object produces a surface!

You may think we're on to something with these new commands, but as Jolson said, "You ain't seen nothin yet!"

7.3   Drawing the Solid Modeling Building Blocks

Extruding two-dimensional objects into Z-Space is handy. But solids offer many of the same predefined shapes that you used in Surface Modeling – plus some additional shapes. We'll look at these now, and then we'll look at the ***Revolve*** command. But the real marvels of Solid Modeling – the nifty tricks that make it so very valuable – will have to wait for our remaining lessons.

Let's look at the predefined Solid Modeling shapes and, when applicable, their similarities to (and differences from) their Surface Modeling counterparts.

7.3.1	Box

Use the *Box* command to draw any size box whose sides are parallel or perpendicular to the current UCS. This is the command sequence:

Command: *box*
Specify first corner or [Center]: *[identify the first corner of the box]*
Specify corner or [Cube/Length]: *[identify the opposite corner of the box]*
Specify height or [2Point]<0.0000>: *tell AutoCAD how tall to make the box]*

The first thing you probably noticed is that the command sequence is shorter than the *3D* command's **Box** option. Indeed, the *Box* command has only four prompts to the surface command's five. But the *Box* command's prompts offer more options.

Let's look at each line.

- The first prompt asks for a **corner** of the box. Satisfy this prompt by picking a point on the screen or entering a coordinate.

  The alternative to specifying the first corner is to specify the **Center** of the box. Access this option by typing *C*. AutoCAD will ask you to specify the center of the box:

  Specify center:

  Once you locate the center of the box, AutoCAD will continue with the remaining prompts.

- Next, AutoCAD asks you to specify the opposite corner of the box. A rubber band box on the screen helps you select corners. AutoCAD will use the point you select to determine the length and width of the box. It'll then prompt you for the height.

  The **Cube** option on this line will prompt you to **Specify length** and use the value you enter as length, width, and height for the cube.

  The **Length** option will also ask you to **Specify length** but will follow that request with prompts for **width** and **height** as well.

- The last prompt also includes an option. AutoCAD will provide a rubber band "box" to help you determine the height of your box. Alternately, with the **2Point** option, you can give AutoCAD the height by picking two points on the screen.

We'll draw some boxes in our exercise to see these options.

You can also access the *Box* command (as well as the other commands in this lesson) using the Draw pull-down menu. Follow this path:

Draw – Modeling – [command]

Do This: 7.3.1.1	Drawing Solid Boxes

    I.   Start a new drawing using the 3D Objects template in the C:\Steps\Lesson07 folder.

   II.   Be sure polar snap is on and that the **Polar distance** is set to *.5*. Set polar tracking to **Track using all polar angle settings**.

  III.   Follow these steps.

7.3.1.1: DRAWING SOLID BOXES

1. Enter the *Box* command. Alternately, you can pick the **Box** button on the 3D Make control panel.

    Command: *box*

7.3.1.1: DRAWING SOLID BOXES

2. Specify the corners of the box as shown.

> **Specify first corner or [Center] <0,0,0>:** *4,4*
> **Specify other corner or [Cube/Length]:** *@4,2*

3. Use polar tracking to give it a **height** of **1.5** units as indicated.

> **Specify height:**

That was simple, wasn't it?

Polar: 1.5000 < +Z

4. This time, let's draw a cube. Repeat the command ▢.

> **Command:** *[enter]*

5. We'll use the **Center** option ▣ Center .

> **Specify first corner or [Center]:** *C*

6. And place the center as indicated.

> **Specify center:** *5,5,2.5*

7. Tell AutoCAD to draw a **Cube** ▣ Cube .

> **Specify corner or [Cube/Length]:** *c*

8. Make the sides of the cube **2** units.

> **Specify length:** *2*

Your drawing looks like this. Notice that the center we indicated is the center of the box along all three axes – X, Y, and Z.

9. We'll draw one more to see the **Length** option. Repeat the command ▢.

> **Command:** *[enter]*

10. Pick the bottom corner of the upper box (at coordinates 6,4,1.5) as the first **corner**.

> **Specify first corner or [Center]:**

11. Use the **Length** option ▣ Length .

> **Specify corner or [Cube/Length]:** *l*

12. Finally, specify the length, width, and height as shown.

> **Specify length <2.0000>:** *2*
> **Specify width:** *2*
> **Specify height or [2Point] <2.000>:** *2*

Your drawing looks like this.

13. Save the drawing ▣ as *MyBlocks-Boxes.dwg* in the C:\Steps3D\Lesson07 folder.

> **Command:** *save*

Does it remind you of playing with blocks when you were a child? Well, now you can make a living playing with those blocks!

7.3.2 Wedge

The similarities between the ***3D*** command's **Box** and **Wedge** options hold true for the ***Box*** and ***Wedge*** commands as well. The command sequence for the ***Wedge*** command looks like this:

> **Command: *wedge* (or *we*)**
> **Specify first corner or [Center]: *[identify the first corner of the wedge (this will be the right-angled corner)]***
> **Specify other corner or [Cube/Length]: *[identify the opposite corner of the wedge]***
> **Specify height or [2Point]<>: *[tell AutoCAD how tall to make the wedge]***

Look familiar? The prompts and the options are identical to those of the ***Box*** command. The only additional information you need to know is that the first corner of the wedge identifies the right angle.

We'll draw a couple of wedges for practice.

Do This: 7.3.2.1 Drawing Solid Wedges

I. Start a new drawing using the 3D Objects template in the C:\Steps\Lesson07 folder.

II. Follow these steps.

7.3.2.1: DRAWING SOLID WEDGES

1. Enter the ***Wedge*** command. Alternately, you can pick the **Wedge** button on the 3D Make control panel.

   Command: *we*

2. Start the wedge as shown.

   Specify first corner or [Center]: *1,1*

3. Point the wedge away from the screen by using a negative X value, as shown, and give it a height of 1.5 units.

   Specify other corner or [Cube/Length]: *@-4,2*

   Specify height or [2Point]<2.000>: *1.5*

   Your wedge looks like this.

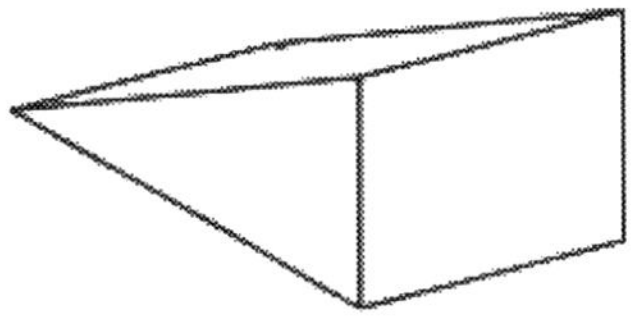

4. Let's try the **Cube** option. Repeat the command.

   Command: *[enter]*

5. Pick the bottom corner (at coordinate 1,1) as the **first corner**.

   Specify first corner or [Center]:

6. Use the **Cube** option Cube...

   Specify corner or [Cube/Length]: *C*

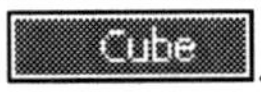

7. ... and give it a length of **2**.

   Specify length <2.000>: *[enter]*

   Your drawing looks like this.

   Obviously, you haven't drawn a cube but a wedge (the diagonal half of a cube) based on the cube you specified.

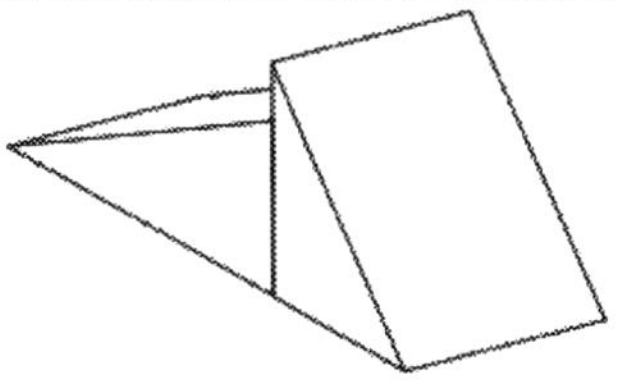

8. Save the drawing 🖫 as *MyBlocks-Wedges.dwg* in the C:\Steps3D\Lesson07 folder.
    Command: *save*

You probably noticed that the *Wedge* command doesn't have a rotation angle prompt like the surface method did. You can orient the solid wedge as you draw it (using positive or negative numbers), or you can rotate it to point it in the desired direction.

7.3.3	Cones and Cylinders

The command sequence for solid cones (or cylinders) is slightly different from their surface model counterpart. But the differences contain some new opportunities.

The differences between the two include these.

- You can draw a solid cylinder with the *Cone* command as you could draw a surface cylinder, or you can use the *Cylinder* command to draw a solid cylinder faster.

- It's possible to draw an *elliptical* solid cone but not an elliptical surface model cone.

- Drawing a solid cone or cylinder is very similar to drawing a 2-dimensional circle or ellipse (using the same familiar options) making the learning curve very short.

- You can't create a hollow cone using the solid approach, although you can use the *Subtract* command to hollow a cone. (You'll see some other ways later in this text.)

The *Cone* and *Cylinder* command sequences are almost identical.

Command: *cone or cylinder (or cyl)*
Specify center point of base or [3P/2P/Ttr/Elliptical]: *[identify the center point for the base of the cone]*
Specify base radius or [Diameter]: *[identify the radius of the cone's base]*
Specify height or [2Point/Axis endpoint/Top radius] <1.0000>: *[tell AutoCAD how tall to make the cone; the cylinder command doesn't offer the Top radius option]*

The options are fairly straightforward. Let's take a look.

- The first prompt, as well as its options, is identical to the *Circle* command's prompt and options except that the Cone/Cylinder command includes an **Elliptical** option. This option changes to prompts to mirror those of the *Ellipse* command.

- The next option allows you to specify a base radius or diameter.

- The last line of prompts asks for a **height**. Enter this on the keyboard or use the 2Point option to pick a couple points on the screen. Alternately, you can identify an **Axis endpoint**, which allows you to draw cones or cylinders that aren't straight up and down, or (with the *Cone* command) tell AutoCAD that you'd like to define the **Top radius**.

Try your hand at the solid approach to cones and cylinders in an exercise.

Do This: 7.3.3.1	Drawing Solid Cones and Cylinders

I. Start a new drawing using the 3D Objects template in the C:\Steps\Lesson07 folder.
II. Set the visual style to **Realistic**.
III. Follow these steps.

173

7.3.3.1: DRAWING SOLID CONES AND CYLINDERS

1. Enter the *Cone* command. Alternately, you can pick the **Cone** button on the 3D Make control panel.

   Command: *cone*

2. We'll use default options on the first cone/cylinder. Place the first cone at coordinate **2,8** (the first cylinder at coordinate **8,8**).

   Specify center point of base or [3P/2P/Ttr/Elliptical]: *2,8*

3. Give the cone/cylinder a base radius of **2** and a height of **4**.

   Specify base radius or [Diameter]: *2*

   Specify height or [2Point/Axis endpoint/Top radius]<2.000>: *4*

4. Repeat Steps 1 through 3 using the *Cylinder* command .

   Command: *cyl*

   Your drawing looks like this.

5. Let's use our new commands to draw an elliptical cone and then an elliptical cylinder. Repeat the *Cone* command .

   Command: *cone*

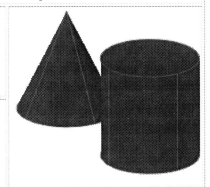

6. Choose the **Elliptical** option .

   Specify center point of base or [3P/2P/Ttr/Elliptical]: *e*

7. Place the **endpoint of first axis** at coordinate **0,4**. (Place the **endpoint of first axis** of the cylinder at **6,4**.)

   Specify endpoint of first axis or [Center]: *0,4*

8. Place the **other endpoint of first axis** at coordinate **4,4**. (Place the **other endpoint of first axis** for the cylinder at **10,4**.)

   Specify other endpoint of first axis: *4,4*

9. Place the **endpoint of second axis** 1" to the north.

   Specify endpoint of second axis: *@1<90*

10. Finally, make the cone (cylinder) 4" tall.

    Specify height or [2Point/Axis endpoint/Top radius] <4.0000>: *4*

11. Repeat Steps 5 through 10 using the *Cylinder* command .

    Command: *cyl*

    The ellipse cone/cylinder looks like this.

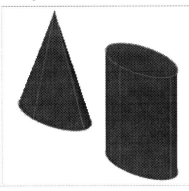

12. Now use the **Top radius** option to change the end of the cone. Repeat the *Cone* command .

    Command: *cone*

13. Place the base point of the cone at **2,0**.

    Specify center point of base or [3P/2P/Ttr/Elliptical]: *2,0*

14. Use the **Diameter** option `Diameter` to give the cone a diameter of 4".

    Specify base radius or [Diameter] <2.0000>: *d*
    Specify diameter <4.0000>: *4*

15. Now use the **Top radius** option `Top radius` to define the top radius at 1".

    Specify height or [2Point/Axis endpoint/Top radius] <4.0000>: *t*
    Specify top radius <0.0000>: *1*

16. Finally, give it a height of 4".

    Specify height or [2Point/Axis endpoint] <4.0000>: *4*

The cone now looks like this.

17. Save the drawing as *MyBlocks-Cones.dwg* in the C:\Steps3D\Lesson07 folder.

    Command: *save*

Of course, you can also use the other options made familiar by your 2-dimensional use of the *Circle* and *Ellipse* commands. It's interesting that these commands use the same procedures to produce such similar objects. Perhaps, in the future, AutoCAD will reduce them to one command with a **Cone/Cylinder** option.

7.3.4	Sphere

The sphere is another object whose production was greatly simplified between creation of the *3D* command's **Sphere** option and the solid *Sphere* command. Indeed, we've gone from five prompts and three options to two prompts and one option! And the option is the common radius/diameter choice available in so many commands.

Here's the solid *Sphere* command sequence:

    Command: *sphere*
    Specify center point or [3P/2P/Ttr]: *[locate the center of the sphere]*
    Specify radius or [Diameter] <2.0000>: *[how big do you want it to be?]*

You're already familiar with the options from your use of the *Circle* command.

Although AutoCAD doesn't prompt for the number of longitudinal or latitudinal segments, it's a good idea to set the **Isolines** system variable to a large enough number for proper viewing (unless you're using the **Realistic** visual style as we are, or the **Conceptual** visual style). But that's something you should do early in the drawing session. It doesn't have to be repeated for each command.

Draw a sphere.

Do This: 7.3.4.1	Drawing a Solid Sphere

    I.   Start a new drawing using the 3D Objects template in the C:\Steps\Lesson07 folder.
    II. Set the visual style to **Realistic** and remove isolines.
    III. Follow these steps.

1. Enter the *Sphere* command. Alternately, you can pick the **Sphere** button  on the 3D Make control panel.

> **Command:** *sphere*

2. Locate the **center of sphere** as indicated …

> **Specify center point or [3P/2P/Ttr]:** *4,4,4*

3. … and give it a **radius** of **2**.

> **Specify radius or [Diameter] <2.0000>:** *2*

Your drawing looks like this.

4. Save the drawing as *MyBlocks-Sphere.dwg* in the C:\Steps3D\Lesson07 folder.

> **Command:** *save*

There's nothing else to show you about spheres. AutoCAD simplicity – what a marvel!

7.3.5	Torus

There's a subtle difference in the way you drew the surface model torus and how you'll draw a solid torus. But the difference will drive you crazy if you're not aware of it.

The difference lies in the way you size the torus itself (as opposed to sizing the tube of the torus). When you gave a radius or diameter for the surface model torus, you were indicating how large it would be from the center to the outer edge of the torus. When you give a radius or diameter for a solid torus, you're indicating the distance from the center of the torus to the center of the tube that forms it.

Consider the tori in Figure 7.002. The torus on the left is a surface model; the torus on the right is a solid model. Both have a torus diameter of 4 and a tube diameter of 1. But the torus diameter of the surface model measures the distance to the outer

Figure 7.002

edge of the tube, whereas the diameter of the solid model measures the distance to the center of the tube. Bear this in mind when drawing surface or solid tori.

The command sequence for a solid torus (like the other solid sequences) is shorter than its surface model counterpart. It looks like this:

> **Command:** *torus* (or *tor*)
> **Specify center point or [3P/2P/Ttr]:** *[locate the center of the torus]*
> **Specify radius or [Diameter] <10.0000>:** *[indicate the size of the torus]*
> **Specify tube radius or [2Point/Diameter]:** *[indicate the size of the tube that will make up the torus]*

As with the *Sphere* command, the options reflect those of the *Circle* command.

Draw a torus.

Do This: 7.3.5.1	Drawing a Solid Torus

I.   Start a new drawing using the 3D Objects template in the C:\Steps\Lesson07 folder.

II. Set the visual style to **Realistic**.

III. Follow these steps.

7.3.5.1: DRAWING A SOLID TORUS

1. Enter the *Torus* command. Alternately, you can pick the **Torus** button  on the 3D Make control panel.

   Command: *tor*

2. Locate the torus as indicated.

   Specify center point or [3P/2P/Ttr]: *4,4,1*

3. Size the torus and the tube as indicated.

   Specify radius or [Diameter] <2.0000>: *3*

   Specify tube radius or [2Point/Diameter]: *.5*

   Your drawing looks like this.

4. The *Torus* command cries for experimentation. Let's play a little. What happens when the tube diameter is larger than the torus diameter?

   Repeat the *Torus* command  (let's find out).

   Command: *[enter]*

5. Let's put this torus in the center of the first one.

   Specify center point or [3P/2P/Ttr]: *4,4,1*

6. Just for fun, let's give the radius of the torus a negative number …

   Specify radius or [Diameter] <3.0000>: *-3*

7. … and the tube a larger (absolute) number.

   Specify tube radius or [2Point/Diameter] <0.5000>: *6*

   Your drawing looks like this. (Whoa, cool! See what you can discover with a bit of experimentation!)

8. Save the drawing 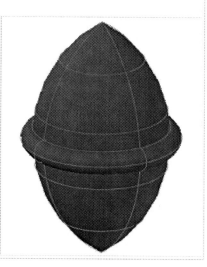 as *MyBlocks-Torus.dwg* in the C:\Steps3D\Lesson07 folder.

   Command: *save*

Oh, the fun you can have with AutoCAD, time, and a little imagination!

7.3.6	*PolySolid*

Here's a handy command that doesn't use the circle prompts. Use *Polysolid* to create three-dimensional walls or other solids on the run.

It looks like this:

> **Command:** *polysolid*
>
> **Specify start point or [Object/Height/Width/Justify] <Object>:** *[pick a start point]*
>
> **Specify next point or [Arc/Undo]:** *[continue picking points as you would with the* **Line** *or* **PLine** *commands]*
>
> **Specify next point or [Arc/Undo]:**
>
> **Specify next point or [Arc/Close/Undo]:**

Polysolid looks and acts a lot like the *PLine* command, but the differences are remarkable.

- The **Object** option provides a quick and easy way to convert existing objects to polysolids. Objects available for conversion include: lines, arcs, 2D polylines, and circles. (Note that multilines are *not* included on the list.) Objects can be open or closed.

- **Width** provides the same opportunity as the *PLine* **width** option, but **Height** allows the same opportunity for Z-space.

- **Justify** works much like the same option in the *Mline* command, although the options it offers go by different names (**Left, Center, Right** – justification based on the direction of the first line segment).

Height, Width, and **Justify** options all affect how AutoCAD draws the polysolid even when you use the **Object** option.

Do This: 7.3.6.1	**Drawing a Polysolid**

IV. Open the *2DFlrPln.dwg* file in the C:\Steps\Lesson07 folder. (Users of *AutoCAD: One Step at a Time* may recognize the floor plan as the one they drew in the basic book. I've converted the outer walls of the multiline to polylines for this exercise.)

V. Follow these steps.

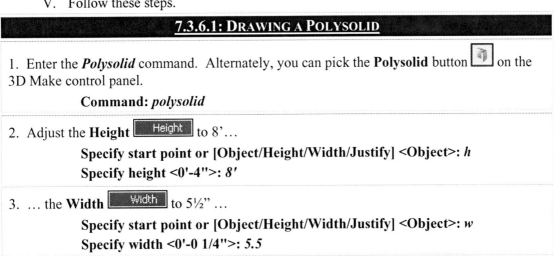

7.3.6.1: DRAWING A POLYSOLID

1. Enter the *Polysolid* command. Alternately, you can pick the **Polysolid** button on the 3D Make control panel.

> **Command:** *polysolid*

2. Adjust the **Height** [Height] to 8'...

> **Specify start point or [Object/Height/Width/Justify] <Object>:** *h*
>
> **Specify height <0'-4">:** *8'*

3. ... the **Width** [Width] to 5½" ...

> **Specify start point or [Object/Height/Width/Justify] <Object>:** *w*
>
> **Specify width <0'-0 1/4">:** *5.5*

4. ... and the **Justification** to left.

> **Specify start point or [Object/Height/Width/Justify] <Object>:** *j*
> **Enter justification [Left/Center/Right] <Right>:** *l*

5. Now use the **Object** 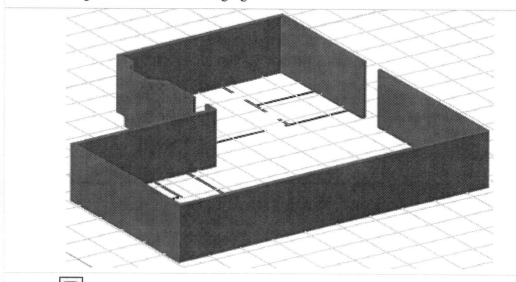 option ...

> **Specify start point or [Object/Height/Width/Justify] <Object>:** *[enter]*

... to select the outer polyline along the left side of the floor plan.

6. Repeat the **Object** option ![Object] to select the outer polyline along the right side of the floor plan.

> **Command:** *[enter]*

Your drawing looks like the following figure.

7. Save ![save icon] and exit the drawing.

Command: *qsave*

You could have drawn the outline from scratch, but I find it easier to do the layout in 2D and then make the conversion. You can now do the inner walls and use the commands you'll find in Lesson 8 to add openings for doors and windows. Use the information in Lesson 10 to add the actual 3-dimensional door and window blocks.

There are some things to remember about this procedure:

- AutoCAD drew the wall on the object's original layer – *not* the current layer.
- AutoCAD deleted the original object after it created the polysolid.
- AutoCAD will convert arcs as well as lines.

| 7.3.7 | **The Solid *Pyramid*** |

I suppose it's only fair; you can draw surface pyramids so why not solid ones?

As with most children (the surface pyramid came first), this command vaguely resembles its parents. Although in the case of the solid *Pyramid* command, it might look more like its mother (the *Polygon* command – although I think the *Cone* command might have slipped in there as well).

It works like this:

> **Command:** *pyramid* (or *pyr*)
>
> **4 sides Circumscribed** *[AutoCAD gives you some starting setup information]*
>
> **Specify center point of base or [Edge/Sides]:** *[pick the center point of your pyramid]*
>
> **Specify base radius or [Inscribed]:** *[tell AutoCAD what the radius is that you'll be working around (you're working with the default* Circumscribed *setup)]*
>
> **Specify height or [2Point/Axis endpoint/Top radius]:** *[how tall should it be?]*

The options should be familiar from both the *Polygon* command and the surface *Pyramid* command.

- As you can do with the *Polygon* command, you can define the pyramid by defining its edges with the **Edge** option. AutoCAD prompts:

  > **Specify first endpoint of edge:**
  >
  > **Specify second endpoint of edge:**

- Use the **Sides** option to tell AutoCAD how many sides you'd like your pyramid to have. You're allowed from 3 to 32 sides (more than that and you might consider the *Cone* command instead).

- You'll draw your pyramid base circumscribed around the outside of an imaginary circle whose radius you'll provide in the next prompt. Alternately, you can create your pyramid **Inscribed**, or within, an imaginary circle.

- Now our prompts switch over to the surface pyramid approach (sort of). You can identify the **height** by picking a point on the screen, coordinate input, using the **2Point** approach (pick two points on the screen), or you can redefine the orientation of the pyramid by using the **Axis endpoint** option. AutoCAD also allows you to change the pointed top by providing a **Top radius** option.

Let's draw some pyramids and see if this approach is any more fun than the surface approach.

Do This: 7.3.7.1	Drawing a Solid Pyramid

    I. Start a new drawing using the 3D Objects template in the C:\Steps\Lesson07 folder.

   II. Follow these steps.

7.3.7.1: DRAWING A SOLID PYRAMID

1. Enter the *Pyramid* command. Alternately, you can pick the **Pyramid** button ▲ on the 3D Make control panel.

   > **Command:** *pyr*

2. AutoCAD lets you know what you're working with and asks you to locate the pyramid. Put it at the location indicated.

   > **4 sides Circumscribed**
   >
   > **Specify center point of base or [Edge/Sides]:** *0,0*

3. Use polar entry to tell AutoCAD that you want a 10" radius `Polar: 10.0000 < 0°`.

   > **Specify base radius or [Inscribed] <14.1421>:**

4. Again, use polar entry to tell AutoCAD that you want a height of 15" `Polar: 15.0000 < +Z`. Your pyramid looks like this.

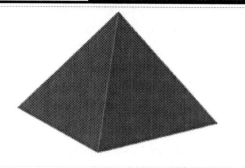

5. Okay, that's the basic way; let's see what some of the other options do. Repeat the command.

       Command: *[enter]*

6. Let's do something the ancients never did, let's give our pyramid twelve sides `Sides`.

       Specify center point of base or [Edge/Sides]: *s*
       Enter number of sides <4>: *12*

7. Better put it a good distance from the first one.

       Specify center point of base or [Edge/Sides]: *30,0*

8. And we'll inscribe `Inscribed` this one in a 10" radial circle `Polar: 10.0000 < 0°`.

       Specify base radius or [Inscribed] <14.1421>: *I*
       Specify base radius or [Circumscribed] <14.1421>: *10*

9. Let's give this one a flat top `Top radius` in a radius of 4".

       Specify height or [2Point/Axis endpoint/Top radius] <15.0000>: *t*
       Specify top radius <0.0000>: *4*

10. Finally, give it an **Axis endpoint** `Axis endpoint` as indicated.

       Specify height or [2Point/Axis endpoint] <15.0000>: *a*
       Specify axis endpoint: *@30,0,15*

Your drawing looks like this.

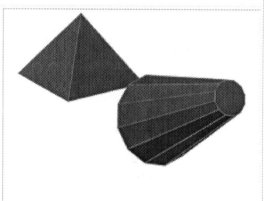

11. Save the drawing with a convenient name, and close it.

Command: *save*

One more basic command – but this one's a doozy!

7.3.8	**Creating a *Helix***

This one's been a long time in the making; and boy, has it been anxiously anticipated!

Ever try to draw a spring or a coil? Prior to the '07 release, it was a nightmare for those few courageous souls who dared the attempt. But those were the olde days.

Here's how we do it now:

       Command: helix

       Number of turns = 3.0000   Twist=CCW *[some basic setup information]*

       Specify center point of base: *[where do you want it?]*

Specify base radius or [Diameter] <1.0000>: *[how big do you want the base?]*

Specify top radius or [Diameter] <1.0000>: *[how big do you want the top?]*

Specify helix height or [Axis endpoint/Turns/turn Height/tWist] <1.0000>: *[how tall do you want it?]*

Interestingly, most of the options appear at the end of the command. The first three prompts contain no surprises. Let's look at that last one.

- **Specify helix height** is pretty straightforward. Tell AutoCAD how tall to make the helix.

- **Axis endpoint** – no real difficulty here either. As you did with other commands, pick or identify an axis endpoint for the end opposite the one you identified in the first prompt. If necessary, AutoCAD will lean the helix over to reach the point you identify.

- **Turns** is a unique option. Use this to redefine the number of turns you want in your helix. (The default is 3 as indicated in the informational line that began the command.)

- **turn Height** refers to the distance covered by a single turn. If you use this option, AutoCAD will automatically adjust the number of turns to reach the indicated height. If you've entered a desired number of turns (the **Turn** option), you can't also enter a **turn Height**.

- **tWist** just wants to know which way to go with the helix – clockwise (CW) or counterclockwise (CCW). It prompts:

Enter twist direction of helix [CW/CCW] <CCW>:

Let's give it a try.

Do This: 7.3.8.1	Drawing a Helix (Spring or Coil)

    I. Open *Helix.dwg* in the C:\Steps\Lesson07 folder.

    II. Follow these steps.

7.3.8.1: DRAWING A HELIX

1. Enter the *Helix* command. Alternately, you can pick the **Helix** button [icon] on the 3D Make control panel.

    Command: *helix*

2. AutoCAD gives you some starting information, then asks where to put the helix. Locate it as indicated.

    Number of turns = 3.0000 Twist=CCW

    Specify center point of base: *0,0*

3. Give is a base radius of 2 …

    Specify base radius or [Diameter] <1.0000>: *2*

… and a top radius to match.

    Specify top radius or [Diameter] <2.0000>: *[enter]*

4. Make it 6" tall.

    Specify helix height or [Axis endpoint/Turns/turn Height/tWist] <1.0000>: *6*

The helix looks like this.

5. Okay, let's try some options. Repeat the command 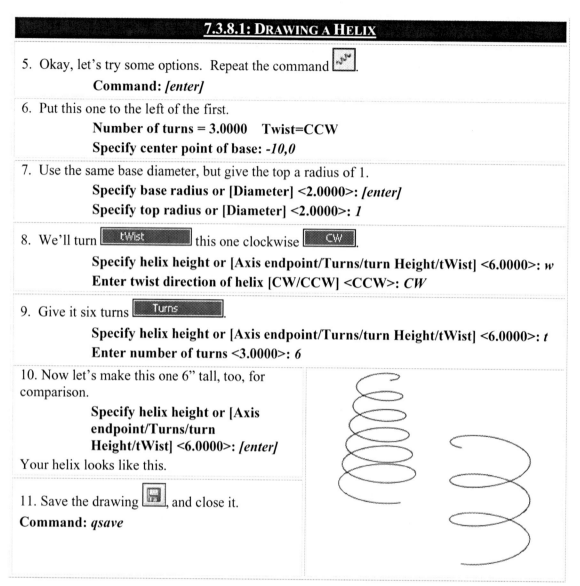.

   Command: *[enter]*

6. Put this one to the left of the first.

   Number of turns = 3.0000   Twist=CCW

   Specify center point of base: *-10,0*

7. Use the same base diameter, but give the top a radius of 1.

   Specify base radius or [Diameter] <2.0000>: *[enter]*

   Specify top radius or [Diameter] <2.0000>: *1*

8. We'll turn ▮ tWist ▮ this one clockwise ▮ CW ▮.

   Specify helix height or [Axis endpoint/Turns/turn Height/tWist] <6.0000>: *w*

   Enter twist direction of helix [CW/CCW] <CCW>: *CW*

9. Give it six turns ▮ Turns ▮.

   Specify helix height or [Axis endpoint/Turns/turn Height/tWist] <6.0000>: *t*

   Enter number of turns <3.0000>: *6*

10. Now let's make this one 6" tall, too, for comparison.

    Specify helix height or [Axis endpoint/Turns/turn Height/tWist] <6.0000>: *[enter]*

    Your helix looks like this.

11. Save the drawing 💾, and close it.

    Command: *qsave*

A helix, coil, or spring drawn like this doesn't provide much to a drawing. After all, it's still a two-dimensional object (a line) even if it does twist through Z-space. We'll reopen this drawing in our next section and I'll show you how to give it some true 3-dimensional qualities.

7.4	**Creating More Complex Solids**
7.4.1	**Using the *Revolve* Command**

After we studied the predefined surface model objects in Lesson 4, we spent another lesson studying several commands that helped us create more complex surface models.

In our solids studies, we've replaced *Tabsurf* easily with the *Extrude* command that we saw at the beginning of this lesson. But it may please you know that most of the surface-specific commands have no direct equivalents in the solids world. Of course, that being said, now I'll tell about the exceptions to that statement!

183

The first exception involves your favorite command (and mine) – **Revsurf.** Remember the nifty shapes we created on our train back in Lesson 5 (the top of the smokestack, the wheels, and the bell)? It'd be a shame not to be able to create such objects as solids.

For that reason, AutoCAD has provided the **Revolve** command. But unlike the other solid commands and their Surface Modeling counterparts, **Revolve** is just a bit more difficult to use than **Revsurf.** But this is mostly because of the additional options involved. Here's the command sequence:

> **Command:** *revolve* **(or** *rev***)**
>
> **Current wire frame density: ISOLINES=64**
>
> **Select objects to revolve:** *[select the object that defines the basic shape of the object you wish to create – you may select multiple objects]*
>
> **Select objects to revolve:** *[confirm the selection set]*
>
> **Specify axis start point or define axis by [Object/X/Y/Z] <Object>:** *[select a point on the axis of revolution]*
>
> **Specify axis endpoint:** *[select another point to define the axis]*
>
> **Specify angle of revolution or [STart angle] <360>:** *[tell AutoCAD how much of a revolution you want]*

> **Revolve** has also undergone some changes with the '07 release. If your selection of objects to revolve involves closed objects, **Revolve** will create a 3D solid. Now, however, if your selection involves open objects, Revolve will actually create a surface object! (Look out, **Revsurf**! You may be replaced!)
>
> Most objects to be revolved are 2D objects. You can, however, also revolve the face of a 3D solid ... or even a 3D face!

The first options don't occur until AutoCAD prompts for an **axis** (of revolution). Then you have four!

- The default option requires that you specify a point on the axis. AutoCAD will then ask you to specify another point to define the axis.
- You can also define the axis by **Object.** When you choose this option, AutoCAD asks you to **Select an object.** Select an object that exists in the current XY plane and AutoCAD will do the rest.
- The **X/Y/Z (axis)** options will revolve the object about the selected axis using coordinate 0,0 as the center of the revolution.
- AutoCAD presents the last prompt after you've made the revolution **axis** decision. This prompt allows you to control the **angle of revolution** (how much of a revolution do you want?). Simply enter an angle in degrees. You can also define **Start angle** of your revolution.

Let's see the **Revolve** command in action.

Do This: 7.4.1.1	Drawing a 3D Solid with the *Revolve* Command

I. Open the *finial.dwg* file in the C:\Steps3D\Lesson07 folder. The drawing looks like Figure 7.003.

II. Notice the orientation of the UCS and where it's centered; then turn off the UCS icon.

III. Be sure the **obj1** layer is current.

IV. Follow these steps.

Figure 7.003

1. Enter the *Revolve* command. Alternately, you can pick the **Revolve** button  on the 3D Make control panel.

       Command: *rev*

2. Select the shape.

       Select objects to revolve:

3. Using OSNAPs, pick the endpoints of the vertical line to define your **axis** (of revolution). (Pick the bottom endpoint first.)

       Specify axis start point or define axis by [Object/X/Y/Z] <Object>:

4. Revolve the object **270°**.

       Specify angle of revolution or [STart angle] <360>: *270*

Your drawing looks like this (isolines removed for clarity). Notice that AutoCAD creates the solid on the current layer.

5. Undo the change.

       Command: *u*

6. Let's use an object to define our axis. Repeat Steps 1 and 2.

       Command: *rev*

7. Tell AutoCAD you'll use an **Object** [● Object] to define the **axis.**

       Specify axis start point or define axis by [Object/X/Y/Z] <Object>: *o*

8. Then select the vertical line.

       Select an object:

9. Accept the default **360°** this time.

       Specify angle of revolution or [STart angle] <360>: *[enter]*

Remove the isolines, and your drawing looks like this.

10. Undo the change.

       Command: *u*

11. Let's use the X-axis to define our axis of revolution. Repeat Steps 1 and 2.

       Command: *rev*

12. Tell AutoCAD to revolve the objects about the Y-axis [x].

       Specify axis start point or define axis by [Object/X/Y/Z] <Object>: *x*

13. Accept the **360°** default rotation.

Your drawing again looks like this. (Okay. See if you can rotate it to look like that. Hint: Use the ***3DOrbit*** command.) Your finial has become an ashtray! Doesn't that deserve another "Whoa, cool"?.

14. Undo the changes 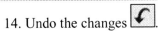.

Command: *u*

To see how ***Revolve*** works with open objects (it does the same things as it did in our last exercise – but it creates surfaces rather than solids), follow these steps while you're still in the *finial.dwg* file:

Freeze all layers that don't end in -sur. Conversely, thaw all layers that do end in   -sur. Repeat the last exercise.

The object that you'll revolve now is an open object.

7.4.2	Using the *Sweep* Command

Sweep works something like ***Revolve*** except that you're not restricted to moving around an axis. With Sweep, you can "sweep" an object along a path to create a solid. You can sweep open or closed objects, including: lines, arcs (straight and elliptical), 2D polylines and splines, circles, ellipses, 2D solids, regions, and planar surfaces, faces and solids. Sweep the objects along a path made of: lines, arcs (straight and elliptical), 2D polylines and splines, 3D polylines and splines, helices, and edges of solids or surfaces.

Wow, that's quite a versatile tool! It works like this:

Command: *sweep*

Current wire frame density: ISOLINES=4

Select objects to sweep: *[select the object you want swept – this is the object that will define the shape of your object]*

Select objects to sweep: *[confirm the selection]*

Select sweep path or [Alignment/Base point/Scale/Twist]: *[select the object that will define the path of your sweep]*

Options include:

- **Alignment** allows you to adjust the object to be tangent to the path (default) or not.
- The **Base point** option allows you to define the base point of the object as it is swept along the path.
- **Scale**, of course, allows you to adjust the size of the object being swept. AutoCAD will apply the scale uniformly along the path.
- With the **Twist** option, you can control the angle of the object being swept or, by default, allow banking of the object as it follows the path.

Let's take a look.

Do This: 7.4.2.1	Drawing a 3D Solid with the *Revolve* Command

I. Reopen the *helix.dwg* file in the C:\Steps3D\Lesson07 folder.

II. Follow these steps.

7.4.2.1: *SWEEP*

1. Enter the *Sweep* command. Alternately, you can pick the **Sweep** button 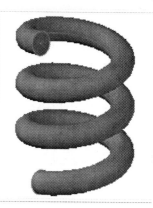 on the 3D Make control panel.

      Command: *sweep*

2. Select the tiny circle in front of the helix on the right.

      Select objects to sweep:

      Select objects to sweep: *[enter]*

3. Select the helix on the right.

      Select sweep path or [Alignment/Base point/ Scale/Twist]:

Your swept spring looks like this. Notice that AutoCAD removed the object you selected to sweep.

4. Undo the changes.

      Command: *u*

5. Let's look at the **Scale** option. Repeat Steps 1 and 2.

      Command: *[enter]*

6. Select the **Scale** option Scale.

      Select sweep path or [Alignment/Base point/Scale/Twist]: *s*

7. Scale the object by ½, and select the helix on the left as your path.

      Enter scale factor or [Reference]<1.0000>: *.5*

      Select sweep path or [Alignment/Base point/Scale/ Twist]:

The results look like this.

8. Save the drawing.

      Command: *qsave*

Experiment with the other shape if you wish.

A few things to remember about the sweep command include:

- AutoCAD places the new object on the current layer.
- AutoCAD removes the original of the object being swept.
- AutoCAD doesn't remove the object that forms the path of your sweep.

| 7.5 | **Extra Steps** |

- Read through the *3D Solids – Creating* section of the *User's Guide*. (Follow this path: Help – Help; then on the **Index** tab, enter **3D Solids** and double-click on some of the options beneath **Creating**.) You can pick up some tips here on each of the tools we've covered in this lesson … and some that are yet to come. Don't forget to try some of the procedures outlined on the **Procedures** tab.
- Experiment with the *Loft* command (Section 5.3.2) with solids.

| 7.6 | **What Have We Learned?** |

Items covered in this lesson include:
AutoCAD's Solid Modeling building blocks

    o *Extrude*   o *Revolve*
    o *Box*   o *Polysolid*
    o *Wedge*   o *Helix*
    o *Cone*   o *Pyramid*
    o *Sphere*   o *Thicken*
    o *Cylinder*   o *Sweep*
    o *Torus*   o *ConvToSolid*

- *Support for the building blocks*
  - o *Isolines*

This has been another fun lesson! (We need these occasionally.) The commands have been simple and straightforward.

In Lesson 7, you saw how to draw familiar shapes as solids rather than simple surface models. You also had the opportunity to do some 2D-to-3D conversions. Did you feel like a kid again – opening a new box of blocks for the first time and exploring each wooden shape? Did your mind slip ever so slightly into that thin mist that inevitably precedes any great discovery? Did you start to create vague mental objects using the shapes as building blocks? How many times did you begin a thought with the words, "I can use this for …" or "This is a lot easier than …"?

The Solid Modeling bug has bitten you!

Actually, you may not be quite bit … yet. But wait until you finish Lessons 8 and 9! There you'll get to play with your new building blocks in ways you never dreamed possible back in your nursery. You'll see ways to combine blocks … ways that were simply not possible until the advent of the computer. Wait until you see …

But I'm getting ahead of myself. First, we must finish this lesson. Do the exercises. Get some practice. Answer the review questions. And then we can proceed!

| 7.7 | **Exercises** |

To get the opportunity to compare Solid Modeling with Surface Modeling, repeat the exercises you did in Lesson 3, 4, 5, and 6. Use solids whenever possible.

1. through 6. Create the drawings in Exercises 4.6.9 through 4.6.14 using solids instead of surface models. Save the drawings to the C:\Steps3D\Lesson07 folder.

7. through 12. Create the drawings in Exercises 5.6.1 through 5.6.3, and Exercises 5.6.6 through 5.6.8 using solids instead of surface models. Save the drawings to the C:\Steps3D\Lesson07 folder.

13. Create the paper clip drawing shown here.
    13.1.   The drawing is set up and dimensioned using metrics.
    13.2.   The paper clip is a single solid object.
    13.3.   Save the drawing as *MyClip.dwg* in the C:\Steps3D\Lesson07 folder.

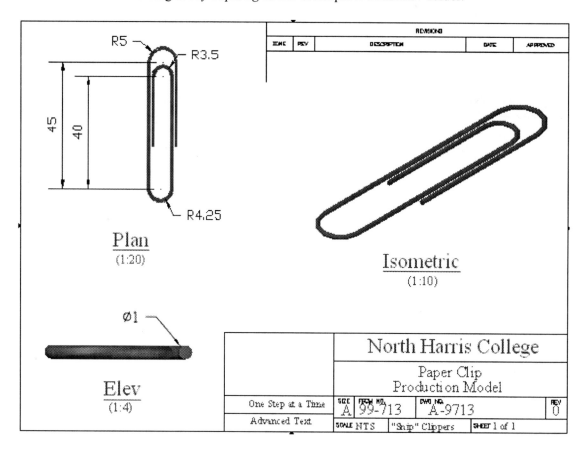

Plan
(1:20)

Isometric
(1:10)

Elev
(1:4)

		REVISIONS		
ZONE	REV	DESCRIPTION	DATE	APPROVED

	North Harris College			
	Paper Clip Production Model			
One Step at a Time	SIZE A	FSCM NO. 99-713	DWG NO. A-9713	REV 0
Advanced Text	SCALE NTS	"Snip" Clippers	SHEET 1 of 1	

189

14. Create the fan cover drawing below.
    14.1.   Each of the wires is 1/16" in diameter (including the torus around the frame).
    14.2.   The center plate is 1/8" thick.
    14.3.   Save the drawing as *MyFanCover.dwg* in the C:\Steps3D\Lesson07 folder.

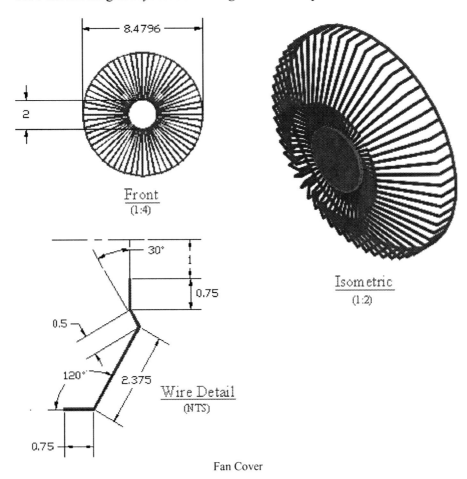

Front
(1:4)

Isometric
(1:2)

Wire Detail
(NTS)

Fan Cover

15. Create the round planter drawing. Follow these guidelines.
    15.1. Use the *ANSI A Title Block* in AutoCAD's template folder.
    15.2. Text size is 3/16" and 1/8".
    15.3. Save the drawing as *MyPlanter.dwg* in the C:\Steps3D\Lesson07 folder.

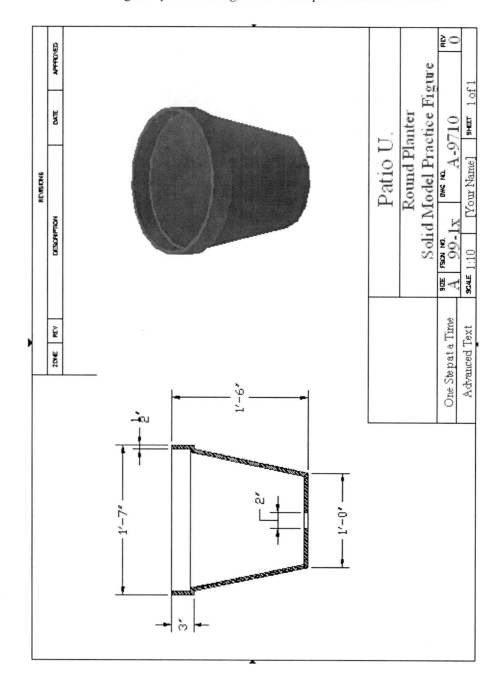

16. Create the double helix drawing. Follow these guidelines.
    16.1.   The balls are 1" diameter.
    16.2.   The rods are 1/8" diameter x 1" long.
    16.3.   Each pairing rotates 15°.
    16.4.   Save the drawing as *MyGenes.dwg* in the C:\Steps3D\Lesson07 folder.

Double Helix

Hex Head
Bolt

17. Try the Hex Head bolt shown at left. I used a ¼"dia cylinder as the core and a 3-sided polygon as the shape that I swept for the threads. This is a first attempt for me, maybe you'll do better!

18. Create the fence drawing. Follow these guidelines.
    18.1.   The posts are 4 x 4s (3½" x 3½").
    18.2.   The slats are 1 x 4s (¾" x 3½"). (I started with splines and turned them into regions.)
    18.3.   The fence is 6" above the ground.
    18.4.   The center rail is a 1 x 2 (¾" x 1½").
    18.5.   Save the drawing as *MyFence.dwg* in the C:\Steps3D\Lesson07 folder.

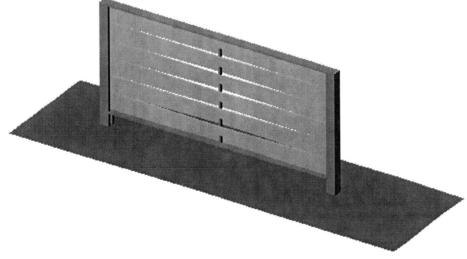

Fence

19. Create the patio planter box drawing shown in Figure 7.029. Follow these guidelines.
    19.1.   Use the *ANSI A Title Block* found in AutoCAD's template folder.
    19.2.   Text size is 3/16" and 1/8".
    19.3.   Save the drawing as *MyPlanterBox.dwg* in the C:\Steps3D\Lesson07 folder.

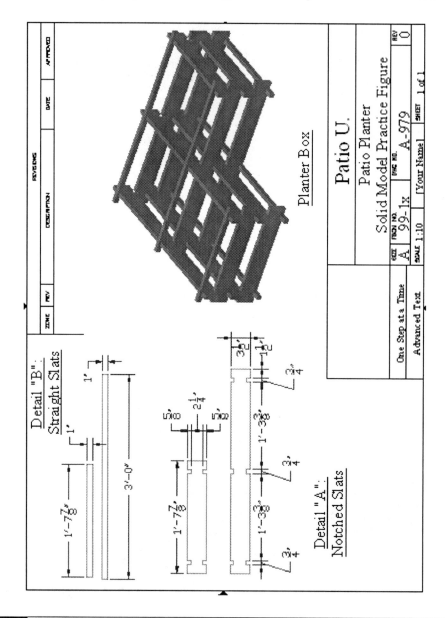

7.8	For Web-Based Review Questions, visit: http://www.uneedcad.com/Files/06R7-3D.pdf

193

Lesson 8

Following this lesson, you will:

✓ *Know how to create composite solids from AutoCAD's solid building blocks using these commands:*

- o **Union**
- o **Subtract**
- o **Intersect**
- o **Slice**
- o **Interfere**

✓ *Know how to calculate mass properties of a solid*

✓ *Know how to create a cross section using the **Section** and **SectionPlane** commands*

✓ *Know how to shape solids using these commands:*

- o **Fillet**
- o **Chamfer**

Composite Solids

You've made it through the beginnings of Solid Modeling. You've experienced successes and near misses throughout your study, but the semester is half over. You may be tired and thinking more about Christmas or Easter or Labor Day than AutoCAD. You may be wondering, "Why AutoCAD … why school … why spend all this time and money to educate (or reeducate) myself?"

Let's pause for a paragraph or two for some words of encouragement. Let me tell you where you are in the overall scheme of (AutoCAD) things.

In all professions, there's a turning point – the point where the draftsman becomes the engineer, where the painter becomes the artist, the idea becomes the design. In every life there is (hopefully) a time where adolescence gives way to adulthood. In the world of computer drafting, you're at that turning point. You're about to leave the CAD Draftsman designation behind and become a true CAD Operator.

In the next few lessons, you'll discover how to take the building blocks – 3D solids and all of the basic and advanced modifying tools you've learned (and some you'll learn now) – and create *objects*. (Notice I didn't say, "create *drawings*.") You'll show the objects you create *in* drawings, but be assured that you'll be creating objects.

Once you've accomplished that very doable goal, I'll show you how to apply materials to those objects – how to show the wood grain on a table or make glass transparent. We'll cover this in the lesson on presentation.

But for now, let me offer these words of encouragement: Approach these lessons with the confidence of a graduate moving into graduate school. You've many successes under your belt, but the best is yet to come!

---

*I'll group the remaining solid construction tools into loose categories to help your understanding. These include Construction/Shaping Tools (**Slice**, **Section**, **Interfere**, **Union**, **Subtract**, **Intersect**, **Fillet**, and **Chamfer**), Solid Editing Tools (the multifaceted **Solidedit** command, grips and the Properties palette), and some Print Setup commands exclusively for use with solid objects (**Solprof**, **Soldraw**, **Solview**, and **Flatshot**).*

*We'll consider the Construction/Shaping tools in Lesson 8, and the many editing tools – including those hidden within the **Solidedit** command in Lesson 9. We'll save the Print Setup commands for Lesson 10.*

8.1   Solid Construction Tools

When you were a child, did you ever wish you could fuse your playing blocks together in order to preserve a particularly clever building effort? You wanted to keep that castle or tower forever to demonstrate your prowess with the tools of your trade. You wanted your family and friends to be able to see – years from now – how you built the perfect model!

And then your sister rode through on her tricycle and your dreams were shattered.

Well, the programmers at AutoCAD had sisters, too. So they created a way to permanently fuse their computer blocks so that no one could ever disassemble them. Then they followed their childhood fantasies and created ways to remove parts of their blocks by using different shapes to define the carving. And they invented ways to find interferences between their blocks and to create cross sections …

… and their childhood dreams became reality in Solid Modeling Construction Tools.

195

Let's see how they work.

8.1.1	Union

The *Union* command behaves very much like a computer-controlled welding rod. It combines two solid objects into one. But unlike the welding rod, it leaves no seams that can break!

It's one of the simplest tools you'll ever hope to find. The command sequence is

> **Command:** *union* (**or** *uni*)
> **Select objects:** *[select the solids you wish to weld]*
> **Select objects:** *[confirm the selection]*

They just don't come any easier. But the value of the *Union* command can't be overstated. It turns simple objects like cylinders and boxes into production models like flanges, tools, doorstops, doorknobs, and much, much more.

We have to try this one. We'll create a flange over the next few exercises by using two construction tools and several cylinders.

> You can also access the *Union* command (as well as the *Subtract* and *Intersect* commands) using the Modify pull-down menu. Follow this path:
>
> *Modify – Solid Editing – Union*

Do This: 8.1.1.1	Welding Solid Objects with the *Union* Command

I. Open the *flange.dwg* file in the C:\Steps3D\Lesson08 folder. The drawing looks like Figure 8.001.

II. Follow these steps.

Figure 8.001

8.1.1.1: WELDING SOLID OBJECTS WITH THE UNION COMMAND

1. Enter the *Union* command. Alternately, you can pick the **Union** button  on the 3D Make control panel.

> **Command:** *uni*

2. Select the three cylinders indicated.

> **Select objects:**

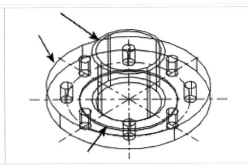

3. Confirm the selection and switch to the
Realistic [Realistic ▼] visual style.

Select objects: *[enter]*

Your drawing looks like this. The selected
cylinders have become a single unit. (You can try
to erase one of them to verify this.)

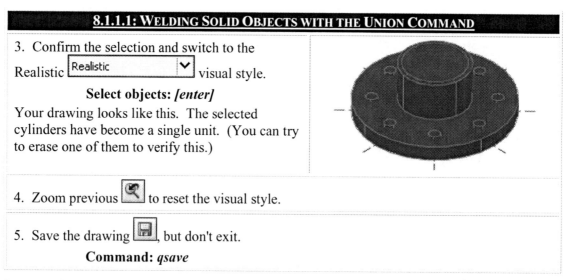

4. Zoom previous [⟲] to reset the visual style.

5. Save the drawing [💾], but don't exit.

Command: *qsave*

Of course, the **Union** command is only one side of the coin. If you can add objects to each other, you should be able to remove one object from another as well.

Let's look at the **Subtract** command.

8.1.2	Subtract

We created a solid flange in our last exercise, but a flange has little use if nothing can flow through it. Enter the **Subtract** command.

You're already familiar with the **Subtract** command from Lesson 3. We used it in Section 3.3.3 to put windows in our walls. Subtract works the same on 3D solids as it did on regions.

We'll use it to remove the boltholes and the core of our flange.

Do This: 8.1.2.1	Removing One Solid from Another

    I.   Be sure you're still in the *flange.dwg* file in the C:\Steps3D\Lesson08 folder. If not, please open it now.

    II.   Follow these steps.

1. Enter the **Subtract** command. Alternately, you can pick the **Subtract** button [⊙] on 3D Make control panel.

Command: *su*

2. AutoCAD asks you to select the object from which you wish to remove something. Select the solid you created in our last exercise (select the outermost cylinder). Confirm the selection.

Select solids and regions to subtract from ..

Select objects:

Select objects: *[enter]*

3. AutoCAD now wants to know what to remove. Select the innermost cylinder and each of the smaller cylinders arrayed about the flange (the bolt holes). Confirm this selection as well, and reset the Realistic Realistic ⌄ visual style.

> **Select solids and regions to subtract ..**
> **Select objects:**
> **Select objects:** *[enter]*

Your drawing looks like this.

4. Save 🖫 and close the drawing.

> **Command:** *qsave*

These first two exercises have been fairly easy and straightforward. But take a moment and fill in the blanks in the following sentences with as many answers as you can. (Time yourself and see how many answers you can find in 60 seconds.)

> I can use the ***Union*** command to create _____ out of _____ .
>
> I can use the ***Subtract*** command to create _____ out of _____ .

Here are some hints:

* Look about the room and consider objects on the desk, floor, walls, and shelves.
* Imagine that you have the blocks with which you played as a child, but now you have a bottle of glue, a drill, and a chisel, as well.

Are you beginning to see the possibilities?

8.1.3	Intersect

The ***Intersect*** command comes in handy when creating intricate multisided figures. It works by removing everything that doesn't intersect something else. This will become clearer with an exercise, but first look at the command sequence.

> **Command:** *intersect* (**or** *in*)
> **Select objects:** *[select objects that intersect each other]*
> **Select objects:** *[confirm the selection set]*

If only all commands accomplished as much – as easily!

Let's see what we can do with the ***Intersect*** command.

Do This: 8.1.3.1	Creating Objects at Intersections

I.   Open the *emerald.dwg* file in the C:\Steps3D\Lesson08 folder. The drawing looks like Figure 8.002. (It's two octogons extruded at 30° to become solid objects. We mirrored the objects to have the four solids you see now.)

II. Follow these steps.

Figure 8.002

1. Enter the ***Intersect*** command. Alternately, you can pick the **Intersect** button ⊚ on 3D

Make control panel.

> **Command:** *in*

2. Select the four octagon solids.
    Select objects:
    Select objects: *[enter]*
Your drawing looks like this.

4. Save the drawing 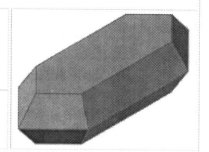, but don't exit.   **Command:** *qsave*

Wow! What else can we do?!

8.1.4	**Slice**

Did you know that the value of precious stones often increases when they're cut just right? Let's cut our emerald.

The command we'll use is called *Slice*. Use the *Slice* command to make a straight cut or remove a piece of an object as if cutting it away with a knife. The sequence offers more options than the others we've seen in this lesson, but that means more opportunities to cut it the way you want it cut.

It looks like this:

> **Command:** *slice* (or *sl*)
>
> **Select objects to slice:** *[select the solid object to cut]*
>
> **Select objects to slice:** *[confirm the selection set]*
>
> **Specify start point of slicing plane or [planar Object/Surface/Zaxis/View/XY/ YZ/ZX/3points]** <3points>: *[pick two points on the object to define the slicing plane]*
>
> **Specify second point on plane:**
>
> **Specify a point on desired side or [keep Both sides]** <Both>: *[pick a point on the side of the object you wish to keep]*

The options should be familiar from your study of the *Rotate3d* and *Mirror3d* commands, but let's go over them again to be sure.

- The default option requires that you select two points (a **start point** and a **second point** on the plane) to define a slicing plane. This is like drawing the knife blade that'll be slicing through the object.

- The **3points** option (enter 3 or just hit enter to accept the default option) requires that you select three points to define the slicing plane. It allows a bit more precision in your slicing.

- The **planar Object** option is still the easiest. If you have an object (circle, ellipse, arc, spline, or polyline) drawn through the object you want to slice, you can select it as your slicing plane.

- The **Surface** option works in the same way as the **planar Object** option except that you can use a surface as a cutting plane. The results may surprise you!

- The **Zaxis** option is difficult to follow. It prompts like this:

> **Specify a point on the section plane:**
>
> **Specify a point on the Z-axis (normal) of the plane:**

- o The first prompt is asking for a point on the slicing plane.

o The next prompt is asking for a point on the Z-axis of the slicing plane. Use this point to orient the slicing plane – essentially by picking a point to define which way is "up" if you're standing on the slicing plane.

- The **XY/YZ/ZX** options allow you to define the slicing plane by identifying a single point on the chosen plane. AutoCAD defines these planes according to the current UCS.
- The last option occurs at the final prompt. It allows you to keep either a selected piece or both pieces of the object after you've sliced it.

Let's cut our gemstone.

> You can also access the **Slice** command (and the **Interfere** command) using the Modify pull-down menu. Follow this path:
>
> *Modify – 3D Operations – Slice*

Do This: 8.1.4.1	Slicing 3D Solid Objects

I. Be sure you're still in the *emerald.dwg* file in the C:\Steps3D\Lesson08 folder. If not, please open it now.

II. Follow these steps.

8.1.4.1: SLICING 3D SOLID OBJECTS

1. Enter the **Slice** command. Alternately, you can pick the **Slice** button ![icon] on the 3D Make control panel.

> **Command:** *sl*

2. Select the emerald.

> **Select objects to slice:**
> **Select objects to slice:** *[enter]*

3. Accept the **3Point** option and then select the points indicated.

> **Specify start point of slicing plane or [planar Object/Surface/Zaxis/ View/XY/YZ/ ZX/3points] <3points>:** *[enter]*
> **Specify first point on plane:**
> **Specify second point on plane:**
> **Specify third point on plane:**

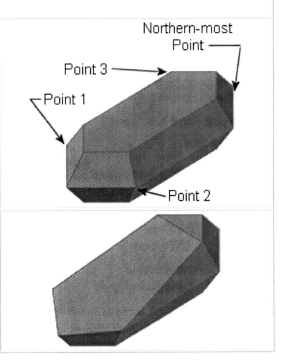

Northern-most Point

Point 3

Point 1

Point 2

4. Pick the northernmost endpoint on the emerald (indicating that you want to keep that section of the gem).

> **Specify a point on desired side or [keep Both sides] <Both>:**

Your drawing looks like this.

5. Undo the changes ⟲.

6. Let's try the **planar Object** option
   planar Object . First, thaw the **obj1** layer.
   Notice the circle that intersects the emerald.
   Command: *sl*

7. Repeat Steps 1 🗡 and 2.
   Command: *sl*

8. Choose the **planar Object** option planar Object .

   Specify start point of slicing plane or [planar Object/Surface/Zaxis/View/XY/YZ/ZX/3points] <3points>: *O*

9. Select the circle ...

   Select a circle, ellipse, arc, 2D-spline, 2D-polyline to define the slicing plane:

10. ... and pick the northernmost point on the emerald.

    Specify a point on desired side or [keep Both sides] <Both>:
    Your drawing looks like this.

11. Undo the changes ⟲.
    Command: *u*

12. Let's try the **Surface** option. First, thaw the **obj4** layer. Notice the surface that intersects the emerald.

13. Repeat Steps 1 🗡 and 2.
    Command: *sl*

14. Choose the **Surface** option Surface .

    Specify start point of slicing plane or [planar Object/ Surface/Zaxis/View/XY/YZ/ ZX/3points] <3points>: *s*

15. Select the surface ...

    Select a surface:

16. ... and keep both sides of the emerald.

Specify a point on desired side or [keep Both sides] <Both>: *[enter]*

17. Erase 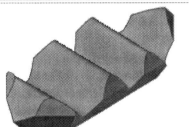 the surface and the top of the emerald. Your drawing looks like this. (Pretty cool? Imagine what you can do with a really involved surface!)	

18. Undo the changes ⟲.

Command: *u*

19. Save the drawing 💾.

           Command: *qsave*

We've seen the most common uses of the **Slice** command, but take some time and experiment with the other options. As I said, the **Slice** command is slightly more involved than the commands we learned earlier, but you can see why.

Most people find one method of doing things easier than other methods. With the **Slice** command, AutoCAD gives you plenty of methods from which to choose. Knowing all the ways to accomplish an intended goal, however, may save you some time and hassle later when the preferred method refuses to work.

> Suppose you had to determine the volume of the object we created in our last exercise (the cut emerald). Can you think of an easy way?
>
> AutoCAD provides a tool to make the calculations downright easy – **Massprop**. The **Massprop** command will compute not only the volume of the selected object but also the mass, bounding box, centroid, moments and products of inertia, radii of gyration, and principle moments and directions about the centroid. All you have to do is enter the command and select the object! (And your boss spent all those years in engineering school learning how to do this on a slide rule!)

8.1.5	**Interferences**

Using the **Interfere** command, you can identify problems cheaply and easily *before* construction finds them.

Interfere identifies places in a drawing where one solid interferes with another. You'll use it more as a checking tool once you've completed the drawing than as a drawing tool itself – although you can use it to draw an interference.

The command sequence looks like this:

        Command: *interfere* (or *inf*)

        Select first set of objects or [Nested selection/Settings]: *[identify the solids you want to check]*

        Select first set of objects or [Nested selection/Settings]: *[confirm the selection]*

        Select second set of objects or [Nested selection/checK first set] <checK>: *[identify a second set of solids if you wish to check one against the other (otherwise, AutoCAD will check all the objects in the first set against each other)]*

At this point, AutoCAD presents the Interference Checking dialog box (Figure 8.004).

Let's take a look at our options; then we'll look at the dialog box.

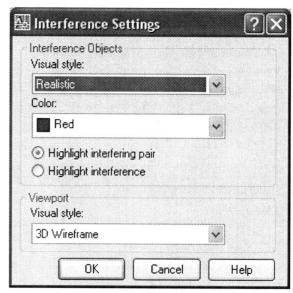

Figure 8.003

- **Select first set of objects** is fairly straightforward. Pick the object you wish to check for interferences. But what about those other options?
  - o **Nested selection** allows you to select objects that reside in blocks or Xrefs for checking.
  - o **Settings** calls the Interference Settings dialog box (Figure 8.003). Here you can set which visual style and color you'd like AutoCAD to use when showing interferences. You can also have AutoCAD highlight the entire interfering pair or just the interference using the radio boxes. In the **Viewport** frame, you can tell AutoCAD which visual style to use for the viewport where you're checking. It's a good idea to use different visual styles in these frames to make it easier to see your interferences.

- **Select second set of objects** allows you to select a second set of objects to check against the set you selected at the first prompt. It might be easier just to select all the objects you want to check against each other during the first prompt, and then use the **checK first set** option. This way, AutoCAD checks everything in the selection set against everything else in the selection set. It might bog down in a very large drawing; otherwise, it's a bit easier on you.

Once AutoCAD has completed its check, it presents the Interference Checking dialog box (Figure 8.004). This one is easier than it looks.

- The **Interfering objects** frame tells you how many interfering objects it found in your selection sets. Then it tells you how many interfering pairs it found.

- The **Highlight** frame makes it easier for you to see the interferences – even allowing you to move between them with the **Previous** and **Next** buttons. A check next to **Zoom to pair** makes your efforts more rewarding. You can also use the three buttons to the left of the Highlight frame – **Zoom dynamic, Pan**, and **3D Orbit** – to assist your viewing.

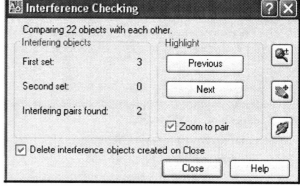

Figure 8.004

- Finally, when you check for interferences, AutoCAD will automatically create an object where the interferences occur. (This is something like using the *Intersect* command, but AutoCAD doesn't delete anything.) You can keep this object to further study the interference, or you can **Delete interference objects on close** with a check in the box.

Let's see this one in action.

Do This: 8.1.5.1	**Finding Interferences**

I.   Open the *pipe08.dwg* file in the C:\Steps3D\Lesson08 folder. The drawing looks like Figure 8.005. (It's a simple piping plan with a two-level piperack. Can you see any interferences?)

II. Follow these steps.

Figure 8.005

8.1.5.1: FINDING INTERFERENCES

1. Begin the ***Interfere*** command. (The button ⬚ is on the 3D Make control panel.)
   Command: *inf*

2. We'll check the entire drawing for interferences. At the prompt, type ***all***.
   Select first set of objects or [Nested selection/Settings]: *all*
   Select first set of objects or [Nested selection/Settings]: *[enter]*

3. We'll check all of the solids against each other, so hit ***enter*** at the prompt.
   Select second set of objects or [Nested selection/checK first set] <checK>: *[enter]*

4. (Refer to Figure 8.004.) AutoCAD found three solids hitting each other in two instances of interference.

5. Use the **Previous** [Previous] and **Next** [Next] buttons to examine each of the interferences. Interference **2 of 2** is shown at right. (Notice that AutoCAD shows the interference with a Red Realistic visual style as was indicated in the settings dialog box - Figure 8.003.)

6. Complete the command [Close].

7. Exit the drawing without saving it.
   Command: *quit*

In a few simple steps, you've located a problem that might have cost tons of money in redesign and construction costs.

We have another timesaver to see, but first, let's visit some old friends.

8.2	**Using Some Old Friends on Solids – *Fillet* and *Chamfer***

Remember how much fun you had drawing the outhouse door back in Lesson 8 of the basic text? You used the ***Fillet*** and ***Chamfer*** commands to make the corners (twice). Where would you be if you couldn't use those convenient tools on 3D solids?

Luckily, AutoCAD saw the need to round and mitre corners on solid objects and made the tools available – with a few necessary adjustments. Look at the command sequences when these two are used on solids (we'll begin with the *Fillet* command):

> **Command:** *fillet* (or *f*)
>
> **Current settings: Mode = TRIM, Radius = 0.5000**
>
> **Select first object or [Undo/Polyline/Radius/Trim/Multiple]:** *[select a solid]*
>
> **Enter fillet radius <0.5000>:** *[enter the desired radius]*
>
> **Select an edge or [Chain/Radius]:** *[select the edge to fillet]*

The command begins just as it did when you studied it in the basic text. But when you select a solid object at the **Select first object** prompt, AutoCAD recognizes the solid and asks for some different input.

- It immediately prompts for a **radius** – something it didn't do for a two-dimensional object.
- You can hit *enter* at the **Select an edge** prompt and AutoCAD will assume that you intend to fillet the edge you selected at the **Select first object** prompt. It'll then proceed to fillet that edge. Alternately, you can choose one of the other options:
  - When you pick a single edge on the surface of a solid while using the **Chain** option, AutoCAD should pick the other lines on that surface that are sequential and tangential to the one you selected. [Frankly, I've never been impressed by the way this works (or doesn't work).]
  - The **edge** option (the default) simply allows you to select the edges to fillet one at a time.
  - The **Radius** option allows you to change the radius of each edge you select.

The command sequence for the *Chamfer* command is

> **Command:** *chamfer* (or *cha*)
>
> **(TRIM mode) Current chamfer Dist1 = 0.5000, Dist2 = 0.5000**
>
> **Select first line or [Undo/Polyline/Distance/Angle/Trim/mEthod/Multiple]:** *[select a solid]*
>
> **Base surface selection...**
>
> **Enter surface selection option [Next/OK (current)] <OK>:** *[each edge naturally has two surfaces that are next to it; hit* enter *if the correct surface is highlighted or type* N *to toggle between the surfaces until the appropriate one highlights]*
>
> **Specify base surface chamfer distance <0.5000>:** *[enter the chamfer distances]*
>
> **Specify other surface chamfer distance <0.5000>:**
>
> **Select an edge or [Loop]:** *[select the edge to chamfer]*

- The first option, as explained, allows you to select the correct surface to chamfer.
- The next two options – **Specify base surface chamfer distance** and **specify other surface chamfer distance** – allow you to accept or change the chamfer distances (notice that there's no **Angle** option here as there is for two-dimensional objects).
- The last option – **Select an edge or [Loop]** – allows you to pick the edges to chamfer individually or, when you use the **Loop** option, collectively around the entire surface.

Let's try the *Fillet* and *Chamfer* commands on a solid.

Do This: 8.2.1	Solid Fillets and Chamfers

    I.   Open the *flange.dwg* file in the C:\Steps3D\Lesson08 folder. If you haven't completed it yet, open the *Flange-done.dwg* file instead. We'll countersink the boltholes, mitre the weld neck (the upper cylinder), and fillet the edge.

II.   Follow these steps.

8.2.1: SOLID FILLETS AND CHAMFERS

1. Let's begin with a simple fillet. Enter the **Fillet** command ▣.

    Command: *f*

2. Select the top surface of the base of the flange.

    Current settings: Mode = TRIM, Radius = 0.5000

    Select first object or Undo/Polyline/Radius/Trim/Multiple]:

3. Set the radius to ¼ unit.

    Enter fillet radius <0.5000>: .25

4. Complete the command.

    Select an edge or
    [Chain/Radius]: *[enter]*

    Your drawing looks like this.

5. Now we'll mitre the weld neck. Enter

    the **Chamfer** command ▣.

    Command: *cha*

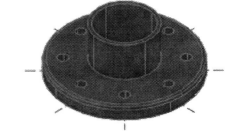

6. Select the upper cylinder …

    (TRIM mode) Current chamfer Dist1 = 0.5000, Dist2 = 0.5000

    Select first line or [Undo/Polyline/Distance/Angle/Trim/mEthod/Multiple]:

7. … and adjust the surface selected until just the outer circle of
    the cylinder is highlighted.

    Base surface selection...

    Enter surface selection option [Next/OK (current)]
    <OK>: *n*

    Enter surface selection option [Next/OK (current)]
    <OK>: *[enter]*

8. Set the chamfer distances to 1/8 unit.

    Specify base surface chamfer distance <0.5000>: *.125*

    Specify other surface chamfer distance <0.5000>: *.125*

9. Select the outer edge of the upper
    cylinder and then confirm the selection.

    Select an edge or [Loop]:

    Select an edge or [Loop]:
    [enter]

    Your drawing looks like this.

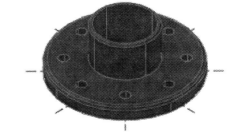

10. Now countersink the bolt holes.

    Repeat the **Chamfer** command ▣.

    Command: *[enter]*

206

11. Select the upper surface of the base of the flange.

> **(TRIM mode) Current chamfer Dist1 = 0.1250, Dist2 = 0.1250**
>
> **Select first line or [Undo/Polyline/ Distance/Angle/Trim/mEthod/ Multiple]:**
>
> **Base surface selection...**
>
> **Enter surface selection option [Next/OK (current)] <OK>:** *[enter]*

12. Set the chamfer distances to ¼ unit.

> **Specify base surface chamfer distance <0.1250>:** *.25*
>
> **Specify other surface chamfer distance <0.1250>:** *.25*

13. Select the upper circle around each of the bolt holes.

> **Select an edge or [Loop]:**

14. Complete the command and remove the isolines.

> **Select an edge or [Loop]:**
>
> *[enter]*

Your drawing looks like this.

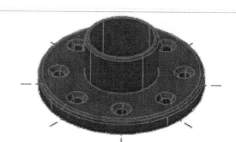

15. Save the drawing , but don't exit. Save it a second time as *MyFlange10* in the C:\Steps3D\Lesson10 folder. (We'll do more with it later).

> **Command:** *qsave*
>
> **Command:** *saveas*

Close the drawing.

Now let's look at that other timesaver – the *Section* command.

8.3	Creating Cross Sections with *Section* and *SectionPlane*
8.3.1	**The *Section* Command**

Have you ever completed the tedious cross section of an object only to discover that you missed something (perhaps a line or an arc that was difficult to see)? Well, AutoCAD has just the tool for you!

The *Section* command creates cross sections of solid objects. And it's one of AutoCAD's easiest commands to master!

The command sequence is

> **Command:** *section* **(or** *sec***)**
>
> **Select objects:** *[select one of more solids to section]*
>
> **Select objects:** *[confirm the selection]*
>
> **Specify first point on Section plane by [Object/Zaxis/View/XY/YZ/ZX/3points]**
>
> **<3points>:** *[identify three points on the section plane (to define it)]*
>
> **Specify second point on plane:**
>
> **Specify third point on plane:**

It's really just that simple. AutoCAD does the rest and places the section inside the object(s) being sectioned. Move it to a suitable place on the drawing, add section (hatch) lines, and you're finished!

Some things to note about the *Section* command:

- The options for defining the section plane are identical to those used to define a slice plane.
- The section that AutoCAD creates is a region. You can hatch a region, or you can explode it into lines and arcs.
- The section created is aligned with the section plane – rotate it as necessary to align it to the UCS.
- AutoCAD creates the section on the current layer.

We'll create a cross section of our flange. Then we'll look at another command.

Do This: 8.3.1	Creating Cross Sections with *Section*

  I.   Reopen the *flange.dwg* file (or the *flange-done.dwg* file) in the C:\Steps3D\Lesson08 folder.
 II.   Set the **obj1** layer current.
III.   Follow these steps.

8.3.1: CREATING CROSS SECTIONS WITH SECTION

1. Enter the *Section* command.

   Command: *sec*

2. Select the flange.

   Select objects:

3. Pick the westernmost endpoint of the east-west centerline.

   Specify first point on Section plane by [Object/Zaxis/View/XY/YZ/ZX/ 3points] <3points>:

4. Pick the other endpoint of the same line.

   Specify second point on plane:

5. Pick the center of the top of the flange (use OSNAPs).

   Specify third point on plane:

6. Move ⊕ the section, as indicated, to see it better. (I selected the last item created and moved it using the displacement method.)

   Command: *m*
   Select objects: *l*
   Select objects: *[enter]*
   Specify base point or displacement: *12,0*
   Specify second point of displacement or <use first point as displacement>: *[enter]*

7. Adjust the view to see the objects from the front.

   Command: *-vp*
   Current view direction: VIEWDIR=1.0000,-1.0000,1.0000
   Specify a view point or [Rotate] <display compass and tripod>: *0,-1,0*

Your drawing looks like the following one.

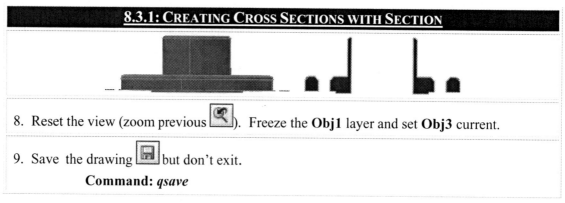

8. Reset the view (zoom previous). Freeze the **Obj1** layer and set **Obj3** current.

9. Save the drawing but don't exit.

   Command: *qsave*

How does that compare to drawing a cross section from scratch? But wait (don't order yet!); there's more!

8.3.2	The *SectionPlane* Command

SectionPlane also creates sections, but *SectionPlane* is a bit more dynamic than the *Section* command.

Let's see.

> **Command:** *sectionplane*
>
> **Select face or any point to locate section line or [Draw section/Orthographic]:** *[locate the section plane]*
>
> **Specify through point:** *[pick a second point on the plane]*

That looks deceptively simple. What about those options?

- **Draw section** allows you to define your section with multiple points – producing something of a jogged section. It prompts:

  > **Specify start point:**
  >
  > **Specify next point:**
  >
  > **Specify next point or ENTER to complete:**

- Orthographic lets you pick from some preset settings to make a straight section plane. It prompts:

  > **Align section to: [Front/bAck/Top/Bottom/Left/Right] <Front>:**

But the really cool part of the *SectionPlane* command occurs after you've created the section plane. You can move it around adjusting the section. You can even use grips to adjust what you see in terms of **Section Plane, Section Boundary,** and **Section Volume.**

- **Section Plane** is the plane of the section.

- A **Section Boundary** shows the XY extent of the section (with a boundary box). The Z-extent is infinite.

- **Section Volume** uses a 3D box to show the extent of the section in all directions.

> The *SectionPlane* command doesn't look like much when you use it. You need to "activate" the section first with the *LiveSection* command. You'll see this in action in our exercise.

This command will become a lot clearer with an example.

| Do This: 8.3.2 | Creating Cross Sections with *SectionPlane* |

I. Be sure your still in the *flange.dwg* file (or the *flange-done.dwg* file) in the C:\Steps3D\Lesson08 folder.

II. Follow these steps.

8.3.2: CREATING CROSS SECTIONS WITH SECTIONPLANE

1. Enter the *SectionPlane* command. Alternately, you can pick the **Section Plane** button on the 3D Make control panel.

> **Command:** *sectionplane*

2. Let's draw a jogged section. Use the **Draw Section** option `Draw section`.

> **Select face or any point to locate section line or [Draw section/Orthographic]:** *d*

3. Start west of the flange, move to the center, then move to the north.

> **Specify start point:** *[start due west of the flange]*
> **Specify next point:** _cen of *[use an OSNAP to get the center of the flange]*
> **Specify next point or ENTER to complete:** *[move to the north]*
> **Specify next point or ENTER to complete:** *[enter]*

4. Now tell AutoCAD which part of the flange you want to see. Pick somewhere in the northwest area.

> **Specify point in direction of section view:**

The results look like this. (Doesn't look like much yet, does it?)

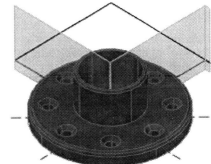

5. Enter the *LiveSection* command and select the section you just drew.

> **Command:** *livesection*
> **Select section object:**

Now you can see the section.

6. Undo the changes and we'll create a section plane we can do a little more with.

> **Command:** *undo*

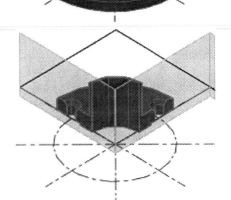

7. Enter the *SectionPlane* command .

> **Command:** *sectionplane*

8. Create a **Front** ● Front **Orthographic** Orthographic section plane.

> **Select face or any point to locate section line or [Draw section/Orthographic]:** *o*
>
> **Align section to: [Front/bAck/Top/Bottom/Left/Right] <Front>:** *f*

Notice that the *LiveSection* works automatically here.

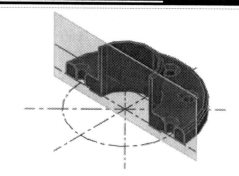

9. Now we can have some fun. Pick on the plane and notice the grips. Use the center arrow grip to move the plane back and forth. Notice that the section changes dynamically relative to the position of the plane. (This works easier if you turn off your OSNAPs.)

10. Use the other center arrow to flip the section. (Flip it back after you've experimented.)

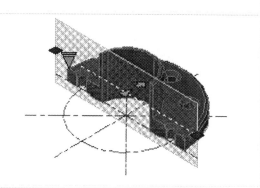

11. Remember, you're working with grips. Right click on the center grip and select **Rotate** Rotate from the menu.

12. Rotate the section about 45° around the center of the flange.

> **Specify base point:**
>
> **Specify rotation angle or [Copy/Reference] <0>:** *45*

Notice that the section itself rotates – not the object being sectioned.

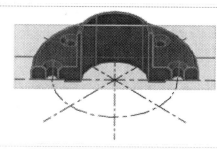

13. We like this section, so let's keep it. Right click on the section line (the gray line through the center of the plane), and select **Generate 2D/3D section** from the menu.

Live section settings...
Generate 2D/3D section...
Add jog to section

14. AutoCAD helps you out with a dialog box. Take a minute to explore the possibilities here, then generate a 3D section.

15. Place the section next to the flange for comparison.

> **Units: Inches   Conversion: 1.0000**
>
> **Specify insertion point or [Basepoint/Scale/X/Y/Z/Rotate]:**
>
> **Enter X scale factor, specify**

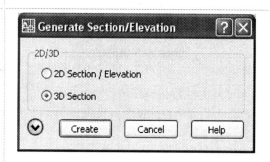

211

opposite corner, or [Corner/XYZ] <1>: *[enter]* **Enter Y scale factor <use X scale factor>:** *[enter]* **Specify rotation angle <0>:** *[enter]*	
It looks like the figure below.	

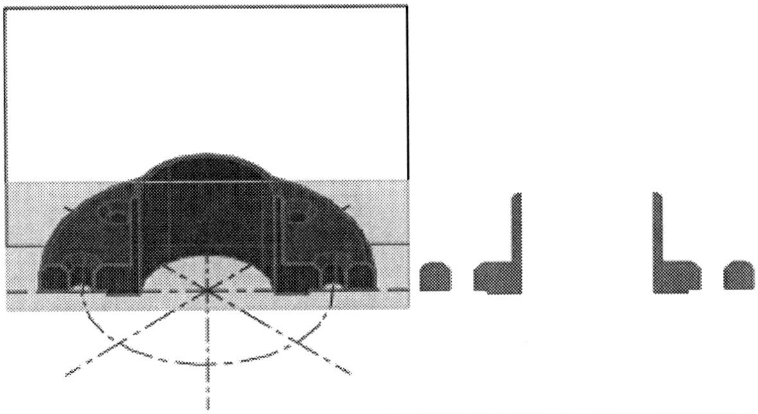

16. Save the drawing ⊞. **Command:** *qsave*	

8.4   Extra Steps

Go back to the list of items you created at the end of Section 8.1.2. Take a few hours (or an afternoon) and see how many of them you can create in AutoCAD using the tools you learned in this lesson. I can't think of a better way to gain experience (or identify questions).

Some hints for this exercise:

- Don't attempt to draw anything that won't fit in a shoebox.
- One of those flexible, 6" rulers with inches on one side and millimeters on the other will serve you well (now and in the future).
- Try (at first) to limit yourself to objects that'll require no more than three of the basic shapes you've learned.
- You'll find other terrific objects to draw in garages and kitchens.

8.5   What Have We Learned?

Items covered in this lesson include:

- *Tools used to create composite solids*
  - *Union*
  - *Subtract*
  - *Intersect*
  - *Slice*
  - *Interfere*
- *Tools used to shape solids*
  - *Fillet*
  - *Chamfer*
- *Other Solid Modeling tools*

212

○ *Section & SectionPlane*　　　　　　○ *Massprop*

Well, what do you think? Wouldn't it have been fun to have these tools when you were playing with blocks as a child?

As I promised, you've stopped drawing pictures of things and have actually begun creating objects using the tools in AutoCAD's "shop." I hope you can sense the potential of these tools from what you've seen here.

> When I was in junior high school, I read a book by Jack London called *Call of the Wild*. It was about a dog that was taken from an easy life in the Northwest and forced to pull a sled in the Klondike during the Gold Rush. Buck (the dog) had many adventures (learning experiences) as he adapted to the wild frontier life of the arctic. But all the while – with increasing intensity – he felt a call from the wild to move out on his own. He experimented with the urging – often leaving camp for days at a time to explore the wilderness. In the end, after learning all that he could in the safety and comfort of the camps, he answered the call and moved out to live with the other wild creatures.
>
> At this point in your AutoCAD training, you should be experimenting on your own, just as Buck did. You'll find thrills – and chills – as you discover things about the software that even the masters don't know. You'll make some mistakes, but the adventure lies in overcoming the mistakes (that's what makes learning fun!).
>
> In a few short chapters, you'll be on your own (with the other wild creatures in the design world). Learn all that you can now!

8.6　Exercises

1. through 8. Create the "su" drawings in Appendix B using solids. Use solid primitives and the composite solid creation tools you learned in this lesson to make each drawing a single object. Save the drawings in the C:\Steps3D\Lesson08 folder.

9. Create the hinge. Refer to the following guidelines.

　9.1. The hinge is a single solid object.

　9.2. Fully dimension the hinge as shown.

　9.3. Place it with the title block of your choice on an 11" x 8½" sheet of paper.

　9.4. Save the drawing as *MyHinge. dwg* in the C:\Steps3D\ Lesson08 folder.

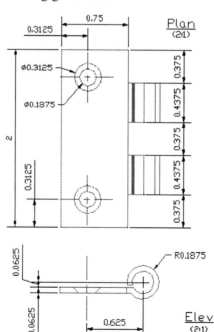

Product
(1.5:1)

Hinge

213

10. Create the flange below. Refer to the following guidelines.

   10.1. The flange is a single solid object.

   10.2. Place it with the title block of your choice on an 11" x 8½" sheet of paper.

   10.3. Bold holes are 3/8" diameter.

   10.4. The center hole is 2¼" diameter.

   10.5. Save the drawing as *MyFlange.dwg* in the C:\Steps3D\Lesson08 folder.

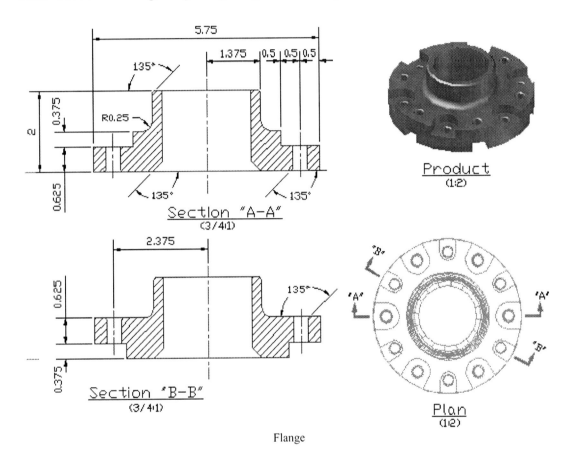

Flange

11. Create the flange gear below. Refer to the following guidelines.
    11.1.   The flange gear is a single solid object. (Hint: I created the top of the brace with wedges whose length and height were 4".)
    11.2.   Fully dimension the object as shown.
    11.3.   Place it with the title block of your choice on an 11" x 8½" sheet of paper.
    11.4.   Save the drawing as *MyAnchor.dwg* in the C:\Steps3D\Lesson08 folder.

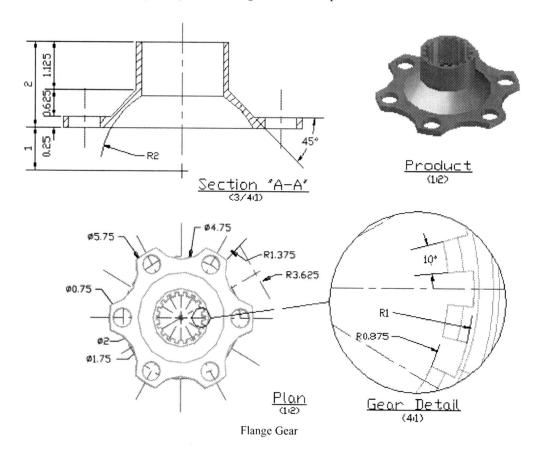

Section "A–A"
(3/4:1)

Product
(1:2)

Plan
(1:2)

Gear Detail
(4:1)

Flange Gear

215

12. Create the floating support and anchor below. Refer to the following guidelines.
    12.1.   Each piece is a single solid object.
    12.2.   Fully dimension the object as shown.
    12.3.   Place it with the title block of your choice on an 11" x 8½" sheet of paper.
    12.4.   Save the drawing as *MyFlangeGear.dwg* in the C:\Steps3D\Lesson08 folder.

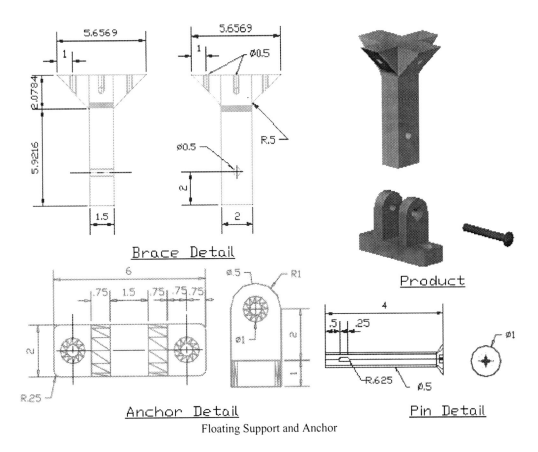

Brace Detail

Anchor Detail

Product

Pin Detail

Floating Support and Anchor

13. Create the dining chair. Refer to the following guidelines.
    13.1. Each leg begins at 1" diameter, but balloons to 1½" in the middle.
    13.2. The leg bracing is ¾" diameter; the back dowels are ½" diameter.
    13.3. The back support is 1" squared.
    13.4. Fully dimension the object as shown.
    13.5. Place it with the title block of your choice on an 11" x 8½" sheet of paper.
    13.6. Save the drawing as *MyDiningChair.dwg* in the C:\Steps3D\Lesson08 folder.

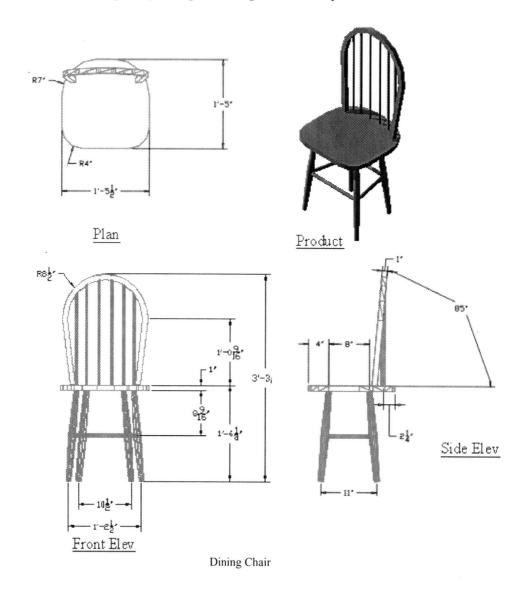

Plan

Product

Front Elev

Side Elev

Dining Chair

217

14. Create the table lamp. Refer to the following guidelines.
    14.1. The base is a solid object.
    14.2. The top is 1/8" thick hollow glass ball.
    14.3. Fully dimension the object as shown.
    14.4. Place it with the title block of your choice on an 11" x 8½" sheet of paper.
    14.5. Save the drawing as *MyTableLamp.dwg* in the C:\Steps3D\Lesson08 folder.

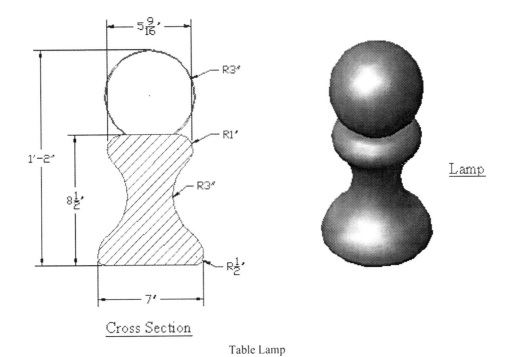

Cross Section

Lamp

Table Lamp

15. Create the fountain shown in Figure 8.029. Refer to the following guidelines.
    15.1.   Each piece (including the water) is a separate solid object.
    15.2.   Fully dimension the objects as shown.
    15.3.   Save the drawing as *MyFountain.dwg* in the C:\Steps3D\Lesson08 folder.

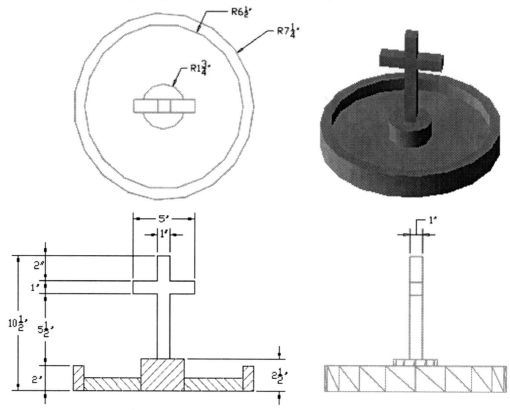

Thanks to Casey Peel for permission to use this drawing.

Following this lesson, you will:

✓ *Know how to edit 3D Solids with Grips*

✓ *Know how to use the subcommands of AutoCAD's **SolidEdit** command:*

o **Face**
  - **Extrude**
  - **Move**
  - **Rotate**
  - **Offset**
  - **Taper**
  - **Delete**
  - **Copy**
  - **coLor**

o **Edge**
  - **Copy**
  - **coLor**

o **Body**
  - **Imprint**
  - **seParate solids**
  - **Clean**
  - **Shell**

✓ *Know how to use the **SolidCheck** system variable*

Lesson

9

Editing 3D Solids

*Over the course of your studies, I've pointed out many of AutoCAD's redundant features. (Indeed, by now you know me to be a great advocate of AutoCAD redundancy.) In this lesson, we'll present a feature that duplicates some other features of 3D solid editing. But this command – **SolidEdit** – has some routines and twists that make it a favorite to solid modelers everywhere.*

*Unfortunately, **SolidEdit** is not a simple command. In fact, it's a command in the tradition of **PEdit** or **Splinedit**. In other words, expect a multi-tiered command with multiple options per tier.*

On the fortunate side, however, AutoCAD has greatly increased the involvement of grips in its solid editing arsenal. These might make you a bit more comfortable with an otherwise daunting task!

*I'll show you both approaches; I'll begin with the **SolidEdit** command approach, and then show you what grips can do.*

Let's get started.

9.1   A Single Command, But It Does So Much - *SolidEdit*

Actually, as a command by itself, **SolidEdit** doesn't accomplish a thing. The **SolidEdit** command should be considered a ticket into a realm where many new commands dwell – each capable of something beneficial to the solid modeler.

If we tried to study **SolidEdit** as a single command, we might find it somewhat overwhelming. But luckily, AutoCAD divided the command options into three categories – **Face**, **Edge**, and **Body**. In fact, AutoCAD's **SolidEdit** command prompt looks like this:

> **Enter a solids editing option [Face/Edge/Body/Undo/eXit] <eXit>:**

Each of the options (categories) presents a separate tier of choices designed to help modify a solid object. (The other two options – **Undo** and **eXit** – are the standard options for most commands.) We'll use these natural divisions to study each option as a category, or grouping of several routines.

AutoCAD also provides a Solids Editing toolbar with buttons that quickly access each of the commands in the categories. We'll use these buttons throughout our lesson.

> Most of you won't remember that AutoCAD's original dimensioning tool called a Dim prompt. From there, you issued one of the many dimension commands (linear, angular, etc.). Think of what dimensioning looks like today, and then imagine what the future might hold for the **SolidEdit** command.

9.2   Changing Faces – The Face Category

The Face Category contains the bulk of **SolidEdit**'s commands. This category includes routines (or command options) designed to alter the faces of a solid.

> Don't confuse the face on a 3D solid with a 3D face. Remember, you'll find a 3D face on a *surface model*. A solid model has a 3D *solid* face.

To get to the Face Category's options, follow this sequence:

> **Command:** *Solidedit*
>
> **Solids editing automatic checking: SOLIDCHECK=1**
>
> **Enter a solids editing option [Face/Edge/Body/Undo/eXit] <eXit>: f**
>
> **Enter a face editing option**
>
> **[Extrude/Move/Rotate/Offset/Taper/Delete/Copy/coLor/mAterial/Undo/eXit] <eXit>:**

You can then select the routine you wish to use.

Of course, an easier way to access a specific **SolidEdit** routine would be simply to pick the desired choice on the Solids Editing toolbar.

Let's look at each of the routines as though they were individual commands.

9.2.1	Changing the Thickness of a 3D Solid Face – the Extrude Option

Have you tried to stretch a 3D solid? If so, you may have noticed that, once created, you can't change the shape or dimensions of individual sides (faces) of the 3D solid. Even the Properties palette doesn't help much. And, if you've tried to extrude a 3D solid, you've seen that you can't.

So how do you change the individual faces of a 3D solid?

Well, one way is by using the **Extrude** option of the Face Category. The option works identically to the *Extrude* command – but only on selected faces.

Here's the sequence:

> **Command:** *solidedit*
>
> **Solids editing automatic checking: SOLIDCHECK=1**
>
> **Enter a solids editing option [Face/Edge/Body/Undo/eXit] <eXit>:** *f*
>
> **Enter a face editing option**
> **[Extrude/Move/Rotate/Offset/Taper/Delete/Copy/coLor/mAterial/Undo/eXit] <eXit>:**
> *e [select the Extrude option]*
>
> **Select faces or [Undo/Remove]:** *[pick a face or an edge(s) of the face you wish to extrude – AutoCAD will highlight the two faces that form that edge]*
>
> **Select faces or [Undo/Remove/ALL]:** *r [unless you wish to extrude both faces, tell AutoCAD you wish to Remove a face]*
>
> **Remove faces or [Undo/Add/ALL]:** *[select the face you don't wish to extrude]*
>
> **Remove faces or [Undo/Add/ALL]:** *[confirm the selection set]*
>
> **Specify height of extrusion or [Path]:** *[these last two options are identical to the Extrude command's sequence]*
>
> **Specify angle of taper for extrusion <0>:**

AutoCAD will extrude the selected face and return to the Face Category of the *SolidEdit* command. Let's give it a try.

> The Extrude option of the *SolidEdit* command (as well as the other options discussed in this lesson) can also be reached via the Modify pull-down menu. Follow this path:
>
> *Modify – Solids Editing – Extrude Faces (or the desired option)*

Do This: 9.2.1.1	Extruding a 3D Solid Face

I. Open the *SE-Box.dwg* file in the C:\Steps3D\Lesson09 folder. The drawing is a simple box. (The current viewpoint is 1, -2,1).

II. Follow these steps.

9.2.1.1: EXTRUDING A 3D SOLID FACE

1. Enter the command sequence shown to access the **Extrude** option of the Face Category.

Alternately, you can pick the **Extrude Faces** button on the Solids Editing toolbar. (Note: Picking the **Extrude Faces** button replaces the entire sequence shown in this step.)

> **Command:** *solidedit*
>
> **Solids editing automatic checking: SOLIDCHECK=1**
>
> **Enter a solids editing option [Face/Edge/Body/Undo/eXit] <eXit>:** *f*

Enter a face editing option
[Extrude/Move/Rotate/Offset/Taper/Delete/Copy/coLor/mAterial/Undo/
eXit] <eXit>: *e*

2. Select the upper face.

Select faces or [Undo/Remove]:

3. Confirm the selection set.

Select faces or [Undo/Remove/ ALL]:
[enter]

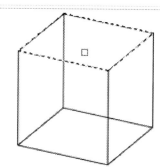

4. Tell AutoCAD to use an extrusion height of **1** and a taper angle of **30°**.

Specify height of extrusion or [Path]: *1*
Specify angle of taper for extrusion <0>:
30

5. By default, AutoCAD validates that the task you've outlined is possible and then extrudes the object.

Hit *enter* twice to exit the command.

Solid validation started.

Solid validation completed.

Enter a face editing option

[Extrude/Move/Rotate/Offset/Taper/
Delete/Copy/coLor/mAterial/Undo/eXit]
<eXit>: *[enter]*

Solids editing automatic checking:
SOLIDCHECK=1

Enter a solids editing option
[Face/Edge/Body/Undo/eXit] <eXit>:
[enter]

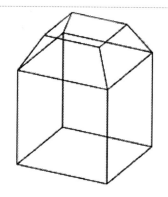

Your drawing looks like this.

6. Save the drawing 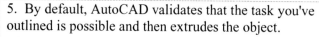.

Command: *qsave*

Let's look at a similar option.

9.2.2   Moving a Face on a 3D Solid

The **Move** routine of the Face Category proves to be quite handy when it becomes necessary to relocate part of a 3D solid – such as a bolt hole – that was improperly placed.

The command sequence looks like this:

Command: *solidedit*
Solids editing automatic checking: SOLIDCHECK=1
Enter a solids editing option [Face/Edge/Body/Undo/eXit] <eXit>: *f*
Enter a face editing option

[Extrude/Move/Rotate/Offset/Taper/Delete/Copy/coLor/mAterial/Undo/eXit] <eXit>: *m [select the Move option]*

Select faces or [Undo/Remove]: *[the face selection options are the same as those in the Extrude option]*

Select faces or [Undo/Remove/ALL]:

Specify a base point or displacement: *[the next options are identical to the basic two-dimensional Move command's options]*

Specify a second point of displacement:

AutoCAD will then move the selected face and return to the Face Category of the *SolidEdit* command.

Let's give it a try.

Do This: 9.2.2.1	Moving a 3D Solid Face

I.   Be sure you're still in the *SE-Box.dwg* file in the C:\Steps3D\Lesson09 folder. If not, please open it now.

II. Thaw the **obj2** layer. Notice the cylinder that appears inside the box.

III. Follow these steps.

9.2.2.1: MOVING A 3D SOLID FACE

1. Use the *Subtract* command ⊚ to remove the cylinder from the box.

        Command: *su*

Your drawing looks like this. (I've shown it here using the **3D Hidden** visual style.)

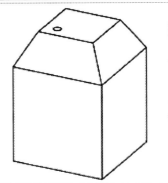

2. Enter the command sequence shown to access the **Move** option of the Face Category.

Alternately, you can pick the **Move Faces** button ⊡ on the Solids Editing toolbar.

        Command: *solidedit*

        Solids editing automatic checking: SOLIDCHECK=1

        Enter a solids editing option [Face/Edge/Body/Undo/eXit] <eXit>: *f*

        Enter a face editing option [Extrude/Move/Rotate/Offset/Taper/Delete/ Copy/coLor/mAterial/Undo/eXit] <eXit>: *m*

3. Select the cylinder inside the box (restore the **3D Wireframe** visual style if necessary).

        Select faces or [Undo/Remove]:

        Select faces or [Undo/Remove/ ALL]: *[enter]*

4. I'll use the displacement method to move the hole **1** unit east and **1** unit north on the 3D solid.

        Specify a base point or displacement: *1,1*

        Specify a second point of displacement: *[enter]*

224

5. As with the **Extrude** routine, AutoCAD validates the procedure before actually moving the hole.

Hit *enter* twice to exit the command.

> **Solid validation started.**
>
> **Solid validation completed.**
>
> **Enter a face editing option [Extrude/Move/ Rotate/Offset/Taper/Delete/Copy/coLor/ mAterial/Undo/eXit] <eXit>:** *[enter]*
>
> **Solids editing automatic checking: SOLIDCHECK=1**
>
> **Enter a solids editing option [Face/Edge/Body/ Undo/eXit] <eXit>:** *[enter]*

Your drawing looks like this (3D Hidden visual style shown).

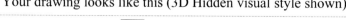

6. Save the drawing , but don't exit.

> **Command:** *qsave*

Sorry, there's no grip approach for moving faces like that. Rotating faces, however, is a different story!

9.2.3	**Rotating Faces on a 3D Solid**

Like the other Face Category options, **Rotate** emulates another command. But in the case of the **Rotate** routine, it doesn't emulate the *Rotate* command but rather the *Rotate3d* command. In other words, you'll have the opportunity to rotate a 3D solid face about an axis (as opposed to a point).

The command sequence looks like this:

> **Command:** *solidedit*
>
> **Solids editing automatic checking: SOLIDCHECK=1**
>
> **Enter a solids editing option [Face/Edge/Body/Undo/eXit] <eXit>:** *f*
>
> **Enter a face editing option**
>
> **[Extrude/Move/Rotate/Offset/Taper/Delete/Copy/coLor/mAterial/Undo/eXit] <eXit>:** *r*
>
> **Select faces or [Undo/Remove]:** *[the Select faces routine is identical to that of the Extrude and Move routines]*
>
> **Select faces or [Undo/Remove/ALL]:**
>
> **Specify an axis point or [Axis by object/View/Xaxis/Yaxis/Zaxis] <2points>:** *[the rest of the options are identical to the Rotate3d command's options]*
>
> **Specify the second point on the rotation axis:**
>
> **Specify a rotation angle or [Reference]:**

(Don't you just love commands that are based on routines you already know?!) Let's give it a try.

Do This: 9.2.3.1	**Rotating a 3D Solid Face**

I.   Be sure you're still in the *SE-Box.dwg* file in the C:\Steps3D\Lesson09 folder. If not, please open it now.

II. Thaw the **obj3** layer. Notice the object that appears inside the box. (This might be easier using the **3D Wireframe** visual style.)

III. Use the ***Subtract*** command to remove the new object from the box. (It'll leave a slot.)

IV. Follow these steps.

9.2.3.1: ROTATING A 3D SOLID FACE

1. Enter the command sequence shown to access the **Rotate** option of the Face Category.

Alternately, you can pick the **Rotate Faces** button [⟲] on the Solids Editing toolbar.

> **Command:** *solidedit*
> **Solids editing automatic checking: SOLIDCHECK=1**
> **Enter a solids editing option [Face/Edge/Body/Undo/eXit] <eXit>:** *f*
> **Enter a face editing option [Extrude/Move/Rotate/Offset/Taper/Delete/Copy/coLor/mAterial/Undo/eXit] <eXit>:** *r*

2. Select the four faces forming the slot.

> **Select faces or [Undo/Remove]:**
> **Select faces or [Undo/Remove/ALL]:** *[enter]*

3. Select the upper- and lower-center points indicated. (Pick the lower-center point first to properly set the Z-axis.)

> **Specify an axis point or [Axis by object/View/Xaxis/Yaxis/Zaxis] <2points>:**
> **Specify the second point on the rotation axis:**

4. Rotate the slot 45°.

> **Specify a rotation angle or [Reference]:** *45*
> **Solid validation started.**
> **Solid validation completed.**

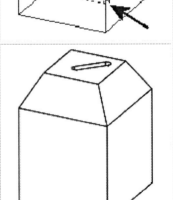

5. Complete the command.

> **Enter a face editing option [Extrude/Move/Rotate/Offset/Taper/Delete/Copy/coLor/mAterial/Undo/ eXit] <eXit>:** *[enter]*
> **Solids editing automatic checking: SOLIDCHECK=1**
> **Enter a solids editing option [Face/Edge/Body/Undo/eXit] <eXit>:** *[enter]*

Your drawing looks like this.

6. Save the drawing [💾].

> **Command:** *qsave*

Imagine the trouble you'd have had accomplishing this task without the ***SolidEdit*** command!

9.2.4   Offsetting Faces on a 3D Solid

The **Offset** routine of the Face Category works very much like the two-dimensional command. There are, however, some quirks about it that you must know to avoid frustration.

The first of these quirks lies in the direction of the offset. When using the two-dimensional command, you pick the direction of the offset on the screen or by coordinate input. In Z-Space, this might present problems (since picking a point on the screen doesn't work well in Z-Space). Instead, you'll control the direction of the offset by using a positive or negative number to identify the distance of the offset. But here's the quirk: the positive number doesn't increase the size of the face being offset (it won't increase the size of the slot, as you'll see). Rather, it increases the *volume of the solid* (thus *decreasing* the size of the slot). A negative number, of course, has the opposite effect.

Another quirk is actually an omission on AutoCAD's part. Whereas you can offset an object through a point in two-dimensional space (using the ***Offset*** command), no such option is presented when using the ***SolidEdit*** command. You'll miss this convenience. (Hopefully, AutoCAD will remedy this oversight in the future.)

The command sequence for the **Offset** option is

> **Command:** *solidedit*
> **Solids editing automatic checking: SOLIDCHECK=1**
> **Enter a solids editing option [Face/Edge/Body/Undo/eXit] <eXit>:** *f*
> **Enter a face editing option**
> **[Extrude/Move/Rotate/Offset/Taper/Delete/Copy/coLor/mAterial/Undo/eXit] <eXit>:** *o*
> **Select faces or [Undo/Remove]:** *[the* **Select faces** *routine is identical to that of the* ***SolidEdit*** *routines you've already seen]*
> **Select faces or [Undo/Remove/ALL]:**
> **Specify the offset distance:** *[enter the distance you wish to offset the selected faces]*

Try enlarging the slot a bit.

Do This: 9.2.4.1	Offsetting a 3D Solid Face

I. Be sure you're still in the *SE-Box.dwg* file in the C:\Steps3D\Lesson09 folder. If not, please open it now.

II. Follow these steps.

9.2.4.1: OFFSETTING A 3D SOLID FACE

1. Enter the command sequence shown to access the **Offset** option of the Face Category.

Alternately, you can pick the **Offset Faces** button [image] on the Solids Editing toolbar.

> **Command:** *solidedit*
> **Solids editing automatic checking: SOLIDCHECK=1**
> **Enter a solids editing option [Face/Edge/Body/Undo/eXit] <eXit>:** *f*
> **Enter a face editing option [Extrude/Move/Rotate/Offset/Taper/Delete/ Copy/coLor/mAterial/Undo/ eXit] <eXit>:** *o*

2. Select the four faces forming the slot.

> **Select faces or [Undo/Remove]:**
> **Select faces or [Undo/Remove/ ALL]:** *[enter]*

3. We want to increase the size of the slot (decreasing the volume of the solid). We'll enter a negative number. Offset the slot by 1/8" as indicated.

> **Specify the offset distance:** *-.125*

4. Complete the command.

> **Solid validation started.**
>
> **Solid validation completed.**
>
> **Enter a face editing option**
> **[Extrude/Move/Rotate/Offset/Taper/Delete/**
> **Copy/coLor/Undo/ eXit] <eXit>:** *[enter]*
>
> **Solids editing automatic checking:**
> **SOLIDCHECK=1**
>
> **Enter a solids editing option [Face/**
> **Edge/Body/Undo/eXit] <eXit>:** *[enter]*

Your drawing looks like this (3D Hidden visual style shown).

5. Save the drawing , but don't exit.

> **Command:** *qsave*

9.2.5   Tapering Faces on a 3D Solid

Tapering a face on a 3D solid isn't difficult, but you'll need to watch the positive and negative numbers just as you did when you offset a face. The command sequence is

> **Command:** *solidedit*
>
> **Solids editing automatic checking: SOLIDCHECK=1**
>
> **Enter a solids editing option [Face/Edge/Body/Undo/eXit] <eXit>:** *f*
>
> **Enter a face editing option**
> **[Extrude/Move/Rotate/Offset/Taper/Delete/Copy/coLor/mAterial/Undo/eXit] <eXit>:** *t*
>
> **Select faces or [Undo/Remove]:** *[the* Select faces *routine is identical to that of the* SolidEdit *routines you've already seen]*
>
> **Select faces or [Undo/Remove/ALL]:**
>
> **Specify the base point:** *[the base point doesn't have to be on the face itself; essentially, you're using the base point and second point to identify a direction, or axis, for the taper]*
>
> **Specify another point along the axis of tapering:** *[identify a second point along the axis]*
>
> **Specify the taper angle:** *[tell AutoCAD how much of an angle you wish to create]*

Let's taper a hole in our solid.

Do This: 9.2.5.1	Tapering a 3D Solid Face

I.   Be sure you're still in the *SE-Box.dwg* file in the C:\Steps3D\Lesson09 folder. If not, please open it now.

II. Thaw the **obj4** layer. Notice the cylinder that appears inside the box.

III. Subtract the new cylinder from the box.

IV. Follow these steps.

1. Enter the command sequence shown to access the **Taper** routine of the Face Category.

Alternately, you can pick the **Taper Faces** button 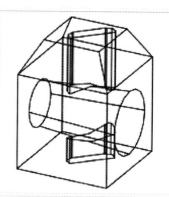 on the Solids Editing toolbar.

> **Command:** *solidedit*
> **Solids editing automatic checking: SOLIDCHECK=1**
> **Enter a solids editing option [Face/Edge/Body/Undo/eXit] <eXit>:** *f*
> **Enter a face editing option [Extrude/Move/Rotate/Offset/Taper/Delete/ Copy/coLor/ mAterial/Undo/eXit] <eXit>:** *t*

2. Select one of the isolines defining the large hole. (This is easier with a 3D Wireframe visual style.)

> **Select faces or [Undo/Remove]:**
> **Select faces or [Undo/Remove/ ALL]:** *[enter]*

3. Use the center of the large eastern (right) hole as the base point and the center of the other end as the other **point along the axis of tapering**.

> **Specify the base point:**
> **Specify another point along the axis of tapering:**

4. We'll reduce the size of the hole as it moves westward. Enter a negative **taper angle** of *5°* as indicated.

> **Specify the taper angle:** *-5*

5. Complete the command (hit enter twice).
Your drawing looks like this.

6. Save the drawing 💾, but don't exit.

> **Command:** *qsave*

9.2.6	**Deleting 3D Solid Faces**

Our next routing provides a method for removing some faces (like fillets, chamfers, holes, etc.) from a 3D solid. The command sequence is one of the easiest (no points or axes to identify).

> **Command:** *solidedit*
> **Solids editing automatic checking: SOLIDCHECK=1**
> **Enter a solids editing option [Face/Edge/Body/Undo/eXit] <eXit>:** *f*
> **Enter a face editing option**
> **[Extrude/Move/Rotate/Offset/Taper/Delete/Copy/coLor/mAterial/Undo/eXit] <eXit>:** *d*
> **Select faces or [Undo/Remove]:** *[the Select faces routine is identical to that of the SolidEdit routines you've already seen]*
> **Select faces or [Undo/Remove/ALL]:** *[enter]*

Suppose we want to get rid of the large hole altogether. We'll use the **Delete** routine.

Do This: 9.2.6.1	Deleting a 3D Solid Face

I. Be sure you're still in the *SE-Box.dwg* file in the C:\Steps3D\Lesson09 folder. If not, please open it now.

II. Follow these steps.

9.2.6.1: DELETING A 3D SOLID FACE

1. Enter the command sequence shown to access the **Delete** routine of the Face Category. Alternately, you can pick the **Delete Faces** button 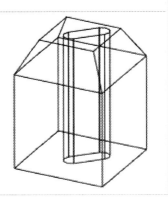 on the Solids Editing toolbar.

   Command: *solidedit*
   Solids editing automatic checking: SOLIDCHECK=1
   Enter a solids editing option [Face/Edge/ Body/Undo/eXit] <eXit>: *f*
   Enter a face editing option [Extrude/Move/Rotate/Offset/ Taper/Delete/ Copy/coLor/mAterial/Undo/ eXit] <eXit>: *d*

2. Select the large, tapered hole (you'll fine it easier to either select inside the hole or to select one of the internal isolines defining the inside face of the hole).

   Select faces or [Undo/Remove]:

3. Complete the command.
Your drawing looks like this.

4. Save the drawing ⊟, but don't exit.

   Command: *qsave*

9.2.7	Copying 3D Solid Faces as Regions or Bodies

Use the **Copy** routine of the Face Category to create copies of one or more faces of a 3D solid. AutoCAD creates the copies as regions or bodies, which you can explode into individual lines, arcs, circles, and so forth, extrude into new 3D solid objects, or convert to surfaces (*ConvToSurface*). Unlike the results of the *Copy* command, however, the new objects exist on the layer that was current when the copies were created.

A *body* is any structure that represents a solid or a Non-Uniform Rational B-Spline (NURBS) surface.

It's as easy to use as the *Copy* command. The command sequence is

   Command: *solidedit*
   Solids editing automatic checking: SOLIDCHECK=1
   Enter a solids editing option [Face/Edge/Body/Undo/eXit] <eXit>: *f*
   Enter a face editing option
   [Extrude/Move/Rotate/Offset/Taper/Delete/Copy/coLor/mAterial/Undo/eXit] <eXit>: *c*

Select faces or [Undo/Remove]: *[the* Select faces *routine is identical to that of the* SolidEdit *routines you've already seen]*

Select faces or [Undo/Remove/ALL]: *[enter]*

Specify a base point or displacement: *[the last prompts are the same as the* Copy *command's prompts]*

Specify a second point of displacement:

We'll copy the top faces of our solid.

Do This: 9.2.7.1	Copying a 3D Solid Face

I. Be sure you're still in the *SE-Box.dwg* file in the C:\Steps3D\Lesson09 folder. If not, please open it now.

II. Follow these steps.

9.2.7.1: COPYING A 3D SOLID FACE

1. Enter the command sequence shown to access the **Copy** routine of the Face Category.

    Alternately, you can pick the **Copy Faces** button ![icon] on the Solids Editing toolbar.

    Command: *solidedit*

    Solids editing automatic checking: SOLIDCHECK=1

    Enter a solids editing option [Face/ Edge/ Body/Undo/eXit] <eXit>: *f*

    Enter a face editing option [Extrude/Move/Rotate/Offset/Taper/Delete/ Copy/coLor/mAterial/Undo/eXit] <eXit>: *c*

2. Select the top face and the four angled faces around it.

    Select faces or [Undo/Remove]:

    Select faces or [Undo/Remove/ ALL]: *[enter]*

3. Use the displacement method to copy the faces five units to the right as indicated.

    Specify a base point or displacement: *5,0*

    Specify a second point of displacement: *[enter]*

4. Complete the command.

    The copy looks like this.

5. Convert the bodies to surfaces.

    Command: *convtosurface*

    Select objects:

    The surfaces look like this (shown with a **Realistic** visual style for clarity.)

    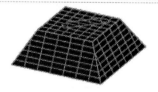

5. Save the drawing ![icon], but don't exit.

    Command: *qsave*

Cool!

9.2.8	Changing the Color of a Single Face

The **coLor** routine of the Face Category is useful if you intend to shade or remove hidden lines from your drawing. It helps to distinguish between the different faces.

The command sequence is

> **Command:** *solidedit*
>
> **Solids editing automatic checking: SOLIDCHECK=1**
>
> **Enter a solids editing option [Face/Edge/Body/Undo/eXit] <eXit>:** *f*
>
> **Enter a face editing option [Extrude/Move/Rotate/Offset/Taper/Delete/Copy/coLor/mAterial/Undo/eXit] <eXit>:** *l*
>
> **Select faces or [Undo/Remove]:** *[the* **Select faces** *routine is identical to that of the* **SolidEdit** *routines you've already seen]*
>
> **Select faces or [Undo/Remove/ALL]:** *[enter]*
>
> *[AutoCAD presents the Color Selection dialog box; select the color you wish the face(s) to be]*

Let's make the slot a different color and view our 3D solid using the **Realistic** visual style.

Do This: 9.2.8.1	Changing the Color of a 3D Solid Face

I. Be sure you're still in the *SE-Box.dwg* file in the C:\Steps3D\Lesson09 folder. If not, please open it now.

II. Delete the 3D faces you created in the last exercise.

III. Follow these steps.

9.2.8.1: CHANGING THE COLOR OF A 3D SOLID FACE

1. Enter the command sequence shown to access the **coLor** routine of the Face Category.

   Alternately, you can pick the **Color Faces** button on the Solids Editing toolbar.

   > **Command:** *solidedit*
   >
   > **Solids editing automatic checking: SOLIDCHECK=1**
   >
   > **Enter a solids editing option [Face/ Edge/ Body/Undo/eXit] <eXit>:** *f*
   >
   > **Enter a face editing option [Extrude/Move/Rotate/Offset/Taper/Delete/ Copy/coLor/mAterial/Undo/ eXit] <eXit>:** *c*

2. Select the faces that form the slot.

   > **Select faces or [Undo/Remove]:**
   >
   > **Select faces or [Undo/Remove/ALL]:** *[enter]*

3. AutoCAD presents the Select Color dialog box. Select **Green**.

4. Complete the command.

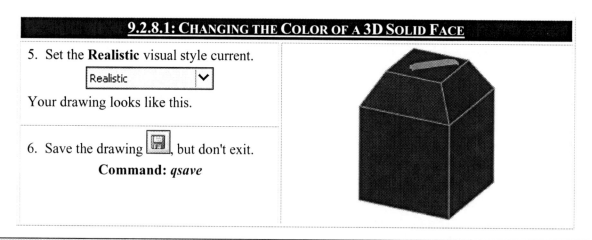

5. Set the **Realistic** visual style current.

| Realistic | ∨ |

Your drawing looks like this.

6. Save the drawing 🖫, but don't exit.

    Command: *qsave*

You'll notice a **Materials** option in the Face category. We'll look at materials when we get to the lesson on Rendering.

9.3   Modifying Edges – The Edge Category

The Edge Category contains only two real options (besides the **Undo/eXit** options). Both of these – **Copy** and **coLor** – repeat options found in the Face Category. But here they're for use on single edges rather than entire faces.

The command sequence to access the **Edge** options of the *SolidEdit* command is

    Command: *solidedit*
    Solids editing automatic checking: SOLIDCHECK=1
    Enter a solids editing option [Face/Edge/Body/Undo/eXit] <eXit>: *e*
    Enter an edge editing option [Copy/coLor/Undo/eXit] <eXit>:

Prompts for both the **Copy** option and the **coLor** option are identical to their counterparts in the Face Category.

Let's look at each in an exercise.

Do This: 9.3.1	Changing Edges on a 3D Solid

    I.   Be sure you're still in the *SE-Box.dwg* file in the C:\Steps3D\Lesson09 folder. If not, please open it now.

    II.   Change the visual style setting back to **3D Wireframe**.

    III.   Set **const** as the current layer.

    IV.   Follow these steps.

1. Enter the command sequence shown to access the **coLor** routine of the Edge Category.

Alternately, you can pick the **Color Edges** button 🔲 on the Solids Editing toolbar.

    Command: *solidedit*
    Solids editing automatic checking: SOLIDCHECK=1
    Enter a solids editing option [Face/ Edge/Body/Undo/eXit] <eXit>: *e*
    Enter an edge editing option [Copy/coLor/Undo/eXit] <eXit>: *l*

2. Select the four and easternmost edges of the box.

> **Select edges or [Undo/Remove]:**
> **Select edges or [Undo/Remove]:** *[enter]*

3. AutoCAD presents the Select Color dialog box. Select **Red**.

4. AutoCAD changes the color of the selected lines (right) and then returns to the **edge editing option** prompt. Tell it you want to **Copy** [Copy] an edge as shown. (Alternately, you can pick the **Copy Edges** button [icon] on the Solids Editing toolbar).

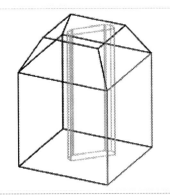

> **Enter an edge editing option**
> **[Copy/coLor/Undo/eXit] <eXit>:** *c*

5. Select the same edges as in Step 2.

> **Select edges or [Undo/Remove]:**
> **Select edges or [Undo/Remove]:** *[enter]*

6. Use the displacement method to copy the edges five units to the east, as indicated.

> **Specify a base point or displacement:** *5,0*
> **Specify a second point of displacement:** *[enter]*

7. Complete the command.

Your copies look like this. Notice that the copies exist on the current layer and adopt the settings of that layer.

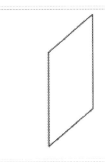

8. Save the drawing [icon], but don't exit.

Command: *qsave*

How could you turn the new lines into a 3D face?[*]

So you see that not much difference occurs between these procedures and their counterparts in the Face Category – except for the obvious effect on edges rather than faces.

Our next category, however, will be quite different!

9.4	**Changing the Whole 3D Solid – The Body Category**

The Body Category includes routines to modify a 3D solid as a whole. None of its five options (except the **Undo/eXit** options) has a counterpart in the 2D or 3D modification worlds. We'll look at each.

To access the Body Category's options, follow this sequence:

> **Command:** *solidedit*
> **Solids editing automatic checking:** **SOLIDCHECK=1**
> **Enter a solids editing option [Face/Edge/Body/Undo/eXit] <eXit>:** *b*

---

[*] You could use the *Edgesurf* or *Planesurf* command

Enter a body editing option
[Imprint/seParate solids/Shell/cLean/Check/Undo/eXit] <eXit>:

| 9.4.1 | Imprinting an Image onto a 3D Solid |

The **Imprint** routine of the Body Category "imprints" (or draws) an image of a selected object – arc, circle, line, 2D or 3D polyline, ellipse, spline, region, or body – onto a 3D solid. Essentially, the imprint is a two-dimensional representation of the object on one of the faces of the 3D solid.

Once the impression has been made, *the line (or arc, spline, etc.) actually becomes a defining edge of a new face on the 3D solid.* So you can use this to help create new faces where they're needed.

The command sequence to use the Imprint option is

> **Command:** *solidedit*
> **Solids editing automatic checking: SOLIDCHECK=1**
> **Enter a solids editing option [Face/Edge/Body/Undo/eXit] <eXit>:** *b*
> **Enter a body editing option**
> **[Imprint/seParate solids/Shell/cLean/Check/Undo/eXit] <eXit>:** *i*
> **Select a 3D solid:** *[select the 3D solid on which you wish to make the impression]*
> **Select an object to imprint:** *[select the object you wish to imprint]*
> **Delete the source object [Yes/No] <N>:** *[AutoCAD allows you the opportunity to keep or delete the object you're using to create your impression]*
> **Select an object to imprint:** *[you can continue to imprint objects if you wish]*

This will become clearer with an exercise. Let's see what we can do with it.

| Do This: 9.4.1.1 | Imprinting Edges on a 3D Solid |

   I.   Be sure you're still in the *SE-Box.dwg* file in the C:\Steps3D\Lesson09 folder. If not, please open it now.
   II. Follow these steps.

9.4.1.1: IMPRINTING EDGES ON A 3D SOLID

1. Draw a line [⟋] between the midpoints of the vertical edges defining the western face of the 3D solid. We'll use this line to imprint a new edge.

> **Command:** *l*

2. Enter the command sequence shown to access the *Imprint* routine of the Body Category. Alternately, you can pick the **Imprint** button [⟲] on the Solids Editing toolbar.

> **Command:** *solidedit*
> **Solids editing automatic checking: SOLIDCHECK=1**
> **Enter a solids editing option [Face/Edge/Body/ Undo/eXit] <eXit>:** *b*
> **Enter a body editing option [Imprint/seParate solids/Shell/cLean/Check/Undo/eXit] <eXit>:** *i*

3. Select the 3D solid.

> **Select a 3D solid:**

4. Select the line you created in Step 1.

   Select an object to imprint:

5. We won't need the line after we make the impression, so allow AutoCAD to delete it.

   Delete the source object [Yes/No] <N>: *y*

6. We can continue to imprint objects, but we won't need to do so now. Complete the command.

   Select an object to imprint: *[enter]*

7. Follow the procedure outlined in Exercise 9.2.3.1 to rotate the new face 30°.

   Command: *solidedit*

Your drawing looks like this.

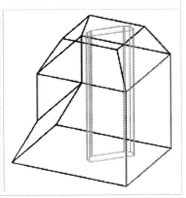

6. Save the drawing.

   Command: *qsave*

You can probably see that **Imprint** will be one of the more useful of the *SolidEdit* command's options. You may find it easier to imprint and modify than to create a new 3D solid and join it (via the *Union* command) to an existing 3D solid.

9.4.2	**Separating 3D Solids with the seParate Solids Routines**

At first glance, the **seParate solids** option looked very promising – after all, it separates 3D solids into their constituencies. Simply put, this means that, if you created a 3D solid from a box and a cylinder, it would separate the 3D solid into the box and cylinder again. The way it works, however, *you can only separate the constituent objects when they don't actually touch.*

Still, there will be times when you find the **seParate solids** option quite handy. You'll see this in our exercise.

The command sequence is one of the simplest:

   Command: *solidedit*
   Solids editing automatic checking: SOLIDCHECK=1
   Enter a solids editing option [Face/Edge/Body/Undo/eXit] <eXit>: *b*
   Enter a body editing option
   [Imprint/seParate solids/Shell/cLean/Check/Undo/eXit] <eXit>: *p*
   Select a 3D solid: *[select the solid you wish to separate]*

Let's take a look.

Do This: 9.4.2.1	**Separating Parts of a 3D Solid**

I.   Open the *SE-Box-2.dwg* file in the C:\Steps3D\Lesson09 folder. The drawing looks like the one we've been working, but has an additional object.

II. Use the *List* command to verify that all objects shown are part of a single 3D solid.

III. Follow these steps.

236

1. Enter the command sequence shown to access the *sePrate solids* routine of the Body Category. Alternately, you can pick the **Separate** button 🔲 on the Solids Editing toolbar.

> **Command:** *solidedit*
> **Solids editing automatic checking: SOLIDCHECK=1**
> **Enter a solids editing option [Face/Edge/Body/Undo/eXit] <eXit>:** *b*
> **Enter a body editing option**
> **[Imprint/sePrate solids/Shell/cLean/Check/Undo/eXit] <eXit>:** *p*

2. Select either of the objects on the screen (as you've seen, although they don't touch, they're both part of a single 3D solid).

> **Select a 3D solid:**

3. Complete the command.

4. Erase 🖊 the object on the left to verify that the 3D solids have separated.

> **Command:** *e*

5. Save the drawing 💾, but don't exit.

> **Command:** *qsave*

That's easy enough – although it doesn't have a lot of use. It can, however, separate things that you joined inadvertently.

9.4.3	Clean

The **Clean** option of the Body Category removes extra (redundant) edges and vertices – including imprinted and unused edges – from a 3D solid. Use it as a final cleanup tool once you've completed your 3D solid.

The command sequence is identical to that of the **sePrate solids** option – and is, therefore, one of AutoCAD's simplest.

Did you notice the extra circular edge at the top of the new 3D solid? We imprinted it there by mistake and we don't need it. Let's use the **Clean** option to remove it.

Do This: 9.4.3.1	Cleaning Up a 3D Solid

    I.   Be sure you're still in the *SE-Box-2.dwg* file in the C:\Steps3D\Lesson09 folder. If not, please open it now.

    II.   Follow these steps.

1. Enter the command sequence shown to access the *Clean* routine of the Body Category.

Alternately, you can pick the **Clean** button 🔲 on the Solids Editing toolbar.

> **Command:** *solidedit*
> **Solids editing automatic checking: SOLIDCHECK=1**
> **Enter a solids editing option [Face/Edge/Body/Undo/eXit] <eXit>:** *b*
> **Enter a body editing option**

[Imprint/seParate solids/Shell/cLean/Check/Undo/eXit] <eXit>: *l*

2. Select the 3D solid.

   Select a 3D solid:

3. Complete the command.

   The object looks like this. Notice that AutoCAD has removed the extra circular edge on the top.

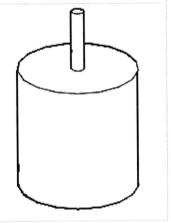

4. Save the drawing ![floppy disk icon], but don't exit.

   Command: *qsave*

9.4.4	**Shell**

The **Shell** routine is one of the niftiest in the ***SolidEdit*** stable. With it, you can convert a 3D solid into a solid object similar to a surface model. In other words, you can convert a 3D solid into a hollow "shell" made up of a single 3D solid object.

To better understand this, consider your computer's monitor. Imagine the monitor with all the "guts" taken out – leaving just the plastic shell. The shell is a single object. The programmers at AutoCAD designed the **Shell** routine to create such objects!

The command sequence resembles those in the Face Category:

> **Command:** *solidedit*
> **Solids editing automatic checking: SOLIDCHECK=1**
> **Enter a solids editing option [Face/Edge/Body/Undo/eXit] <eXit>:** *b*
> **Enter a body editing option**
> **[Imprint/seParate solids/Shell/cLean/Check/Undo/eXit] <eXit>:** *s*
> **Select a 3D solid:** *[select the 3D solid you wish to shell]*
> **Remove faces or [Undo/Add/ALL]:** *[select an edge of the face(s) you wish to remove]*
> **Remove faces or [Undo/Add/ALL]:** *[complete the selection]*
> **Enter the shell offset distance:** *[this figure defines the thickness of your shell]*

Let's create a shell from our original object.

Do This: 9.4.4.1	**Shelling a 3D Solid**

I. Be sure you're still in the *SE-Box-2.dwg* file in the C:\Steps3D\Lesson09 folder. If not, please open it now.

II. Change the viewpoint to 1,-2,-1.

III. Follow these steps.

1. Enter the command sequence shown to access the ***Shell*** routine of the Body Category. Alternately, you can pick the **Shell** button  on the Solids Editing toolbar.

> **Command:** *solidedit*
> **Solids editing automatic checking: SOLIDCHECK=1**
> **Enter a solids editing option [Face/ Edge/Body/Undo/eXit] <eXit>:** *b*
> **Enter a body editing option**
> **[Imprint/seParate solids/Shell/ cLean/Check/ Undo/eXit] <eXit>:** *s*

2. Select the 3D solid.
> **Select a 3D solid:**

3. Remove the bottommost face (pick in the middle of the face – not on an edge).
> **Remove faces or [Undo/Add/ALL]:**
> **Remove faces or [Undo/Add/ALL]:** *[enter]*

4. Make the shell thickness 1/8".
> **Enter the shell offset distance:** *.125*

5. Complete the command.

Your drawing looks like this (shown with a **Realistic** visual style).

4. Save the drawing.
> **Command:** *qsave*

9.4.5   Checking to Be Certain You Have an ACIS Solid

Have you noticed this note at the beginning of each of the options you've used in the ***SolidEdit*** command?

> **Solids editing automatic checking: SOLIDCHECK=1**

This is telling you that the **SolidCheck** system variable has been set to **1** (that is, it's been activated). This means that AutoCAD will automatically check any 3D solid objects selected for editing to verify that they're valid ACIS solids.

To keep it simple, this just means that other software than uses ACIS can use 3D solids created in AutoCAD. If the object fails the verification, it's a good idea to redraw it.

9.5   Editing 3D Solids with Grips

Is there anyone left in the AutoCAD world who doesn't think grips are cool? (Okay, how about anyone who's been using AutoCAD for more than a month?)

Well, just wait until you see what you can do to 3D solids with grips!

You already know the four command routines that work with grips – Stretch, Move, Rotate, Scale and Mirror. Well, they all work with 3D solids as well. No big deal, you say? Okay, you can also use them with individual faces of 3D solids!

Check it out!

Do This: 9.5.1	Finally, Coming to Grips with 3D Solids!

    I.   Reoptn the *SE-Box.dwg* file in the C:\Steps3D\Lesson09 folder. If the surfaces are still there from your experiments with the *SolidEdit* copy routines, erase them.

   II. Follow these steps.

9.5.1: GRIPS AND 3D SOLIDS

1. You can select the object and see its grips, but we don't want them all. Hold down the CTRL key on your keyboard and move your cursor over the eastern side of the box. Notice that you can pick just the side. Do that now. You'll notice that a single grip appears for the side – and the grip tool you used with the **3DMove** command also appears to assist you.	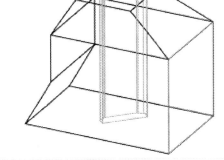
2. Pick the grip (make it hot) and notice the normal grip prompts on the command line. Using the default **Stretch** command, move the grip an inch to the east. `Polar: 1.0000 < 0°` Clear the grip. The box looks like this.	
3. Repeat Step 1.	

4. Pick the grip and use the SPACEBAR to change to the **Rotate** grip command. Rotate the face -30°.
 	
      ** ROTATE **
      Specify rotation angle or [Base point/Undo/Reference/eXit]: *-30*
 	
Clear the grip. The box looks like this.
	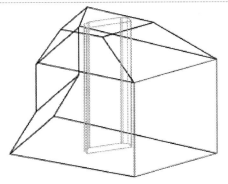

5. This time select the box without holding down the CTRL key. Notice that all the grips show.	

6. Select a grip and use the SPACEBAR to change to the Scale grip command. Scale the object 1½ times.

      Specify scale factor or [Base point/Copy/Undo/Reference/eXit]: *1.5*

Notice that now the entire object scales.

Take some time and experiment with grips on other 3D solid objects you've drawn. We've just scratched the surface here!

9.6	Extra Steps

- Just for fun, use the *ACISOut* command to create an ACIS text file (AutoCAD will automatically export the file with a .sat extension). Select one of the three-dimensional objects in the last drawing you had open.

  Once you've created the file, open it with **Notepad**. Scan the text; it sure takes a lot to create a three-dimensional object!

- Select an object and open the Properties palette. The information is fairly straightforward and about what you'd expect. Of course, you can change the settings that aren't grayed out. The Properties palette, then, provides another approach to editing 3D solids. But now, try to select just a single wall of the 3D solid. (Hold down the CTRL key as we did in our last exercise.)

  What happens to the Properties palette? You can't do quite as much now. I suppose you'd better practice up with grips then!

9.7	What Have We Learned?

Items covered in this lesson include

- *Grips*
- *Tools used to edit 3D Solid Faces, including*
  - *Extrude*
  - *Move*
  - *Rotate*
  - *Offset*
  - *Taper*
  - *Delete*
  - *Copy*
  - *coLor*
- *Tools used to edit 3D Solid Edges, including*
  - *Copy*
  - *coLor*
- *Tools used to edit 3D Solid Bodies, including*
  - *Imprint*
  - *seParate solids*
  - *Clean*
  - *Shell*
- *The SolidCheck system variable*

Wow! What a lesson! Did you ever imagine a single command could have so many different options?!

You've learned many ways to create and modify 3D solids. As I promised, you're no longer simply a CAD draftsman. By experience and training, you've become a CAD operator. You no longer draw. Now you create actual objects in the computer. There's very little left in the three-dimensional world for you to learn! (Okay. Don't get too excited – we still have two more chapters!)

In our next lesson, I'll show you how to handle blocks in Z-Space. I'll also show you some tools to help you plot the objects you've learned to create. It'll be an easier and less involved lesson than this one, so you can relax a bit. After that, we'll look at rendering the objects you create (making them look "real" by assigning materials to them).

But first, as always, let's practice what we've learned.

1. Open the *Slotted Guide #1.dwg* file in the C:\Steps3D\Lesson09 folder. Using only the procedures discussed in this lesson, create the drawing.

    1.1. Remember that a negative number entered as an extrusion height will extrude *into* the object.

    1.2. Remember that a negative number entered as a tapering angle will angle outward.

    1.3. Add a 8½" x 11" title block.

    1.4. Save the drawing as *MySG#1.dwg* in the C:\Steps3D\Lesson09 folder.

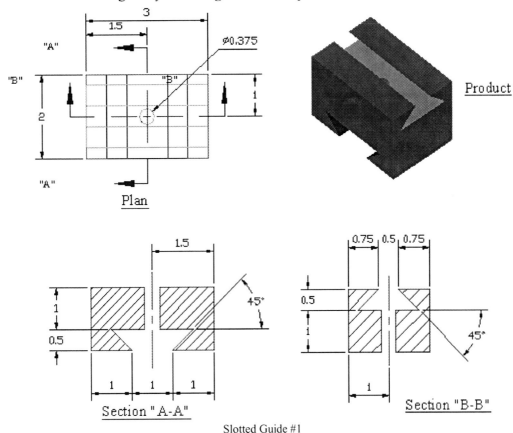

Slotted Guide #1

2. Open the *Slotted Guide #2.dwg* file in the C:\Steps3D\Lesson09 folder. Using only the procedures discussed in this lesson, create the drawing.
    2.1. Add a 8½" x 11" title block.
    2.2. Save the drawing as *MySG#2.dwg* in the C:\Steps3D\Lesson09 folder.

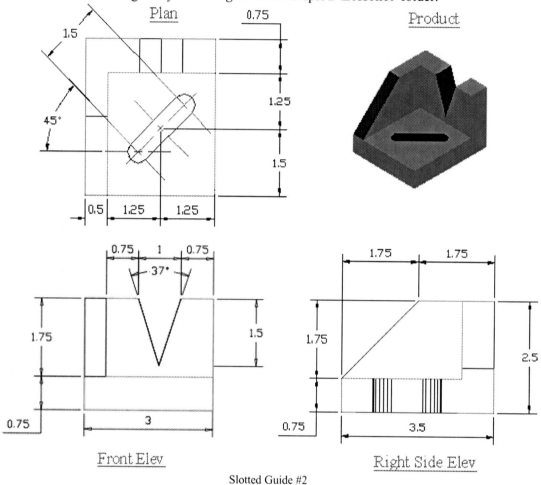

Slotted Guide #2

3. Create the corner bracket drawing.
   3.1. Use a 1/16" fillet along the edges.
   3.2. The rounded indentations are visible front and back.
   3.3. Add a 8½" x 11" title block.
   3.4. Save the drawing as *MyCB.dwg* in the C:\Steps3D\Lesson09 folder.

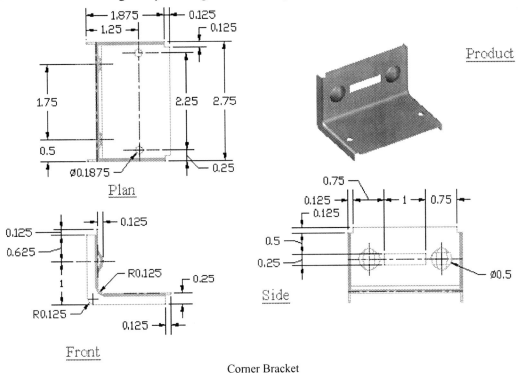

Corner Bracket

4. Create the lid drawing below.
   4.1. Add a 8½" x 11" title block.
   4.2. Save the drawing as MyLid.dwg in the C:\Steps3D\Lesson09 folder.

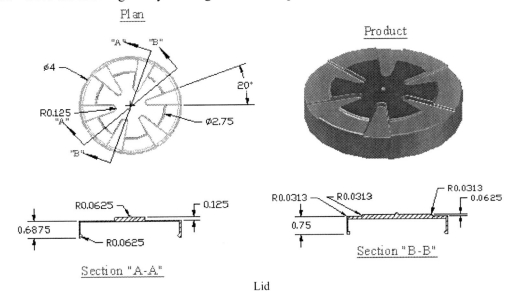

Lid

244

5. Create the plug drawing.

    5.1.   Add a 8½" x 11" title block.

    5.2.   Save the drawing as *MyPlug.dwg* in the C:\Steps3D\Lesson09 folder.

Thanks to George Gilbert of G. Gilbert EngineeringServices Ltd. for permission to use this drawing. For more on G. Gilbert Engineering Services Ltd., and more of George's drawings, visit his web site at: http://ourworld.compuserve.com/homepages/george_gilbert/

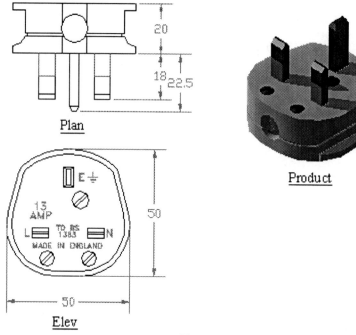

Plug

6. Create the power switch drawing.
    6.1.   Add a 8½" x 11" title block.
    6.2.   Save the drawing as Switch.dwg in the C:\Steps3D\Lesson09 folder.

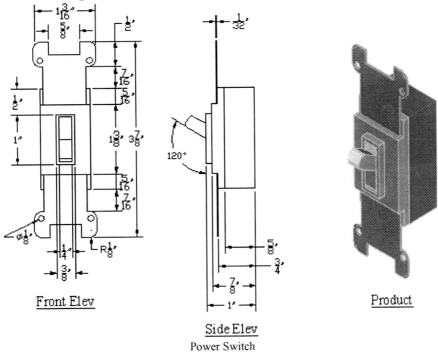

Front Elev   Side Elev   Product

Power Switch

7. Create the level drawing.
    7.1.   Don't join the glass pieces to the body of the level.
    7.2.   Add a 8½" x 11" title block.
    7.3.   Save the drawing as *MyLevel.dwg* in the C:\Steps3D\Lesson09 folder.

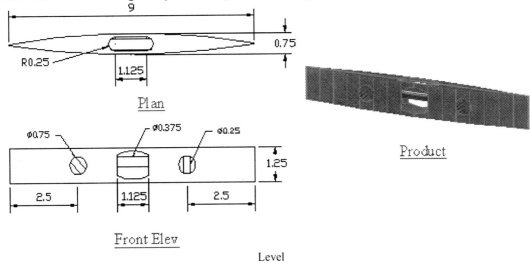

Plan   Product

Front Elev

Level

8. Create the wheel drawing.
   8.1. Place this drawing on a C-size (22" x 17") sheet of paper. Use a title block of your choice.
   8.2. Fillet the rim and hub with a ¼" fillet.
   8.3. Save the drawing as *MyWheel.dwg* in the C:\Steps3D\Lesson09 folder.

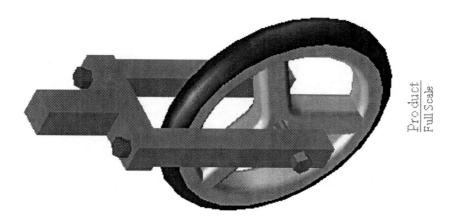

Product
Full Scale

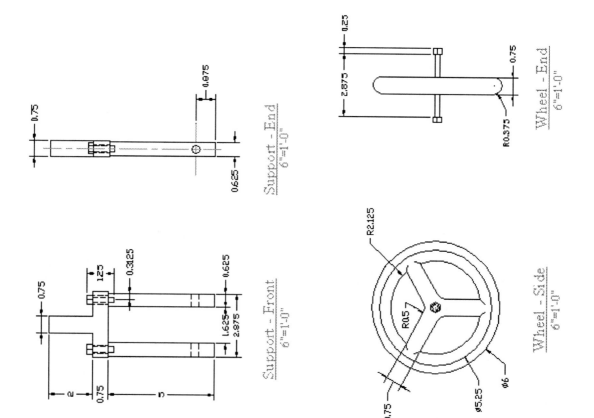

For Web-Based Review Questions, visit:
http://www.uneedcad.com/2007/Files/07R9-3D.pdf

9.8

Lesson

10

Following this lesson, you will:

✓ *Know how to use blocks in Z-Space*
- o *Creating three-dimensional blocks*
- o *Inserting three-dimensional blocks*

✓ *Know how to use the Solid Plotting Tools*
- o **Solview**
- o **Soldraw**
- o **Solprof**
- o **Flatshot**

Three-Dimensional Blocks and Three-Dimensional Plotting Tools

As I mentioned when concluding the last lesson, there's very little left for you to learn with respect to creating three-dimensional objects in AutoCAD. This lesson, then, will serve as a wrap-up of Z-Space methods and techniques before we move on to our discussion of presentation tools.

In Lesson 10, we'll first consider the behavior of blocks in a three-dimensional world. While the differences between two-dimensional blocks and three-dimensional blocks can be dramatic, they don't necessarily have to be difficult. We'll consider the effects of Z-Space and working planes on creation and insertion of blocks as well as the use of attributes on a three-dimensional block.

Then we'll discuss some special tools designed to help you set up and plot 3D solids with considerably less difficulty than you might have had previously.

Let's begin.

10.1	**Using Blocks in Z-Space**

As with two-dimensional blocks, three-dimensional blocks can save you a tremendous amount of time and effort. But there are a few things the three-dimensional operator must consider.

10.1.1	**Three-Dimensional Blocks and the UCS**

First among these considerations is the working plane (the current UCS). *AutoCAD creates blocks against the plane of the current UCS* (Figure 10.001) – *not* the WCS. In other words, the XYZ values of the current UCS (the X-axis, Y-axis, and Z-axis values of the object) become part of the block definition.

Likewise, AutoCAD inserts bocks by matching the axis values of the block to the current UCS (Figure 10.002).

We'll see this in a series of exercises. First, we'll create two blocks – an elbow and some pipe. Our blocks will have two simple attributes defining what they are and their size. Second, we'll utilize our UCS and insertion scale factors to insert the blocks in a simple piping configuration. Third, we'll extract attribute data that'll give us a running total of the amount of pipe we've used.

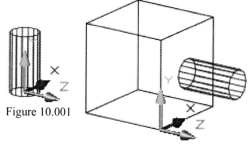

Figure 10.001

Figure 10.002

Let's begin.

Do This: 10.1.1.1	**Creating 3-Dimensional Blocks**

    I.   Open the *Blocks.dwg* file in the C:\Steps3D\Lesson10 folder. The drawing looks like Figure 10.003.

    II.   Notice that the elbow is open in the +X and +Y directions. Note also that the elbow and the pipe are drawn to scale as 4" fittings, and that the height of the pipe is 1".

    III. Follow these steps.

Figure 10.003

10.1.1.1: CREATING 3-DIMENSIONAL BLOCKS

1. Make a note of the current UCS. Then make blocks (use the ***WBlock*** command) from the two objects you see.

Call the block on the left *Pipe*. Use the node as the insertion point (include the node and the two attributes in the block).

Call the block on the right *Ell*. Use the node inside the eastern opening of the elbow as the insertion point (include all three nodes and the two attributes in the block).

Be sure to write both blocks to the C:\Steps3D\Lesson10 folder.

> **Command:** *w*

2. Close the drawing.

Now we'll look at some new variations of the *Insert* command.

10.1.2	**Inserting Three-Dimensional Blocks**

The second three-dimensional block consideration involves the insertion scale of the block. In two-dimensional drafting, you could scale a block along the X- or Y-axis. Now you'll have an additional axis along which you can scale the block. You should give special attention to the use of a three-dimensional block because of the effect scale might have. Consider the figures below. We'll have an opportunity to use the scale options and see how the UCS affects the insertion when we insert our new blocks into a drawing.

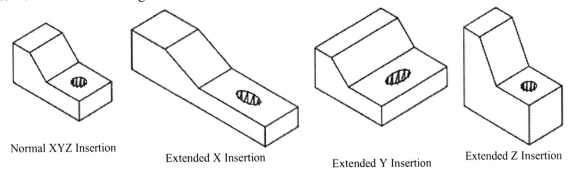

Normal XYZ Insertion   Extended X Insertion   Extended Y Insertion   Extended Z Insertion

Let's get started.

Do This: 10.1.2.1	**Inserting 3-Dimensional Blocks**

I. Open the *Piping Configuration.dwg* file in the C:\Steps3D\Lesson10 folder. (I set the nodes to help guide you through the block insertions. The **UCSIcon** system variable has been set to **ORigin**.)

II. Set the running OSNAP to **Node**. Clear all other settings.

III. Set the current layer to **Pipe** and the current visual style to **Realistic**.

IV. Follow these steps.

1. Change the UCS [icon]. (Hint: Rotate the UCS 90° on the X-axis and then 270° on the Z-axis.) Relocate the UCS to the upper right node as shown.

> **Command:** *ucs*

2. Insert the *Ell* block at the 0,0,0 coordinate of the current UCS. (You created this block and placed it in the C:\Steps3D\Lesson10 folder in our last exercise.) Use a scale of 1 for each axis. Accept the default 4" size.

The elbow looks like this.

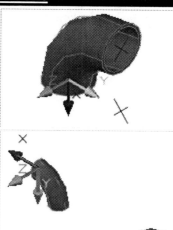

3. Add the rest of the elbows. (Place the UCS at each node and insert the elbows at 0,0,0.)

Your drawing looks like this. (Your UCS icon may be in a different location.)

4. Reset the UCS to the WCS 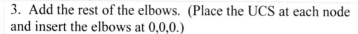.

        Command: *ucs*

5. Now we'll insert the pipe using a scale factor to make it fit between the elbows. Tell AutoCAD you wish to insert the *Pipe* block. Use the settings shown below. (The distance between the elbows we'll use is 8' – or 96".)

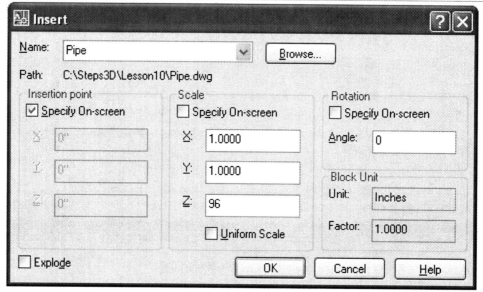

6. Insert the block at the upper node of the lower-right elbow.

        Specify insertion point or [Basepoint/Scale/X/Y/Z/Rotate]:

7. Accept the default size of the pipe.

        Enter attribute values

        What is the size of the unit? <4">:

8. Repeat Steps 5 through 7 for the other vertical run of pipe.

Your drawing looks like the one of the left below.

9. Adjust the UCS as needed to add the final run of pipe. The distance between the two elbows is 12".

Your drawing looks like the one on the right below.

10. Save the drawing ⊞, but don't close it.

        Command: *qsave*

10.1.3   Making Good Use of Attributes

The last (and possibly most rewarding) things we should consider when using three-dimensional blocks is the possible use of attributes. When combining the abilities you've already seen in this lesson with a clever use of attributes, you'll discover a remarkably useful way to create a bill of materials for most projects.

We'll extract the attribute data to our blocks to see that the *Pipe* blocks contain data about the length of each piece of pipe. This data is accurate enough to be used on a cutting list!

Sound nifty? Let's try it!

Do This: 10.1.3.1	**Extracting the Attributes**

    I.   Be sure you're still in the *Piping Configuration.dwg* file in the C:\Steps3D\Lesson10 folder. If not, please open it now.

    II.   Set the UCS = World and restore the plan view (0,0,1).

    III.   Zoom out to about .25x and set the **Text** layer current.

    IV.   Follow these steps.

1. Begin the attribute extraction wizard.

        Command: *Eattext*

2. Accept the defaults on page 1 (Begin) and page 2 (Select Drawings) of the wizard
| Next > |
.

3. (Refer to the figure below.)
- Deselect **Ell** in the **Blocks** list box.
- Clear the check box next to **Exclude general block properties**. (AutoCAD will list the blocks' general properties – such as scale and position.)
- Clear the check box next to **UNIT** in the **Properties for checked blocks** list box.
- Place a check next to **Scale Z** in the **Properties for checked blocks** list box. (This will give us our pipe lengths.)

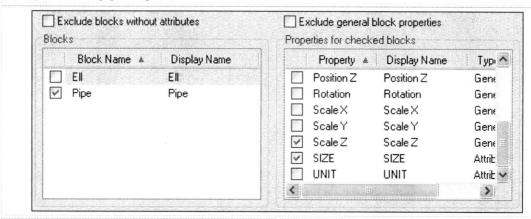

4. Go on to the next page | Next > |, (Refer to the figures at right.)
- Rename the **Scale Z** column to **Length**.
- Rearrange the columns as shown.

Quantity	Name	SIZE	Length ▲
1	Pipe	4"	12.0000
2	Pipe	4"	96.0000

5. Go on to Page 5 and (referring to the figure at right):
- Enter a title for your table as shown.
- Use the Pipe Length Table (already created for you).

6. Go to Page 6 | Next > | and complete the wizard | Finish |.

Table Style settings

Enter a title for your table:
Cut Lengths of Pipe

Select table style:
Pipe Length Table ▾ ...

☑ Display tray notification when data needs refreshing

Title	
Header	Header
Data	Data
Data	Data

7. Place the table in a convenient location. It looks like this.

8. Save and exit the drawing.

Cut Lengths of Pipe

Quantity	Name	SIZE	Scale Z
1	Pipe	4"	12.0000
2	Pipe	4"	96.0000

How's that for convenience?

> Although we used pipe in our exercise, this method works as well when tracking board feet or lengths of steel. How might you use it in your profession?

10.2 Plotting a 3D Solid

We'll conclude our study of 3D solids with a group of special commands that AutoCAD designed to make plotting solid models easier.

First, we'll look at a new command in the plotting stable – *Flatshot*. *Flatshot* works something like taking a 2-dimensional photograph of a 3D solid object. You may find it handy for illustrations.

Next, we'll conquer the "Sol Group" – a group of paper space plotting tools that consists of three commands: *Solview*, *Soldraw*, and *Solprof*. (You won't find a finer example of teamwork in the CAD world.) You'll use the first command – *Solview* – to set up the layout (the Paper Space viewports). Then you'll use the other two commands – *Soldraw* and *Solprof* – to create the actual drawings that go into the viewports.

Let's get started.

10.2.1 The *Flatshot* Command

I think Autodesk designed *Flatshot* primarily as a detail-creation tool. It works well for just such a goal. I found, however, that you can also use it to convert 3-dimensional drawings to 3D drawing for plotting in Model Space. It takes a two-dimensional "photo" (image) of all three-dimensional objects in the current viewport.

This oddball command really presents nothing in the way of a command sequence – enter *Flatshot* at the command prompt, set up the Flatshot dialog box (Figure 10.004) as desired, and follow the command line sequence for insertion of a block. (AutoCAD inserts the flatshot as a block for easy manipulation.)

So let's look at the Flatshot dialog box.

Figure 10.004

- The **Destination** frame offers three radio options.
  - **Insert as new block** means that AutoCAD will create and insert the detail as a new block, which it gives a default name. Use the *BEdit* command to change the name if you wish.
  - You can also use the Flatshot to **Replace** [an] **existing block**. When you place the bullet next to this option, AutoCAD makes the **Select block** button available for you to choose the block you'll replace.

- o Using the **Export to a file** option works much like the *WBlock* command. Use the **Filename and path** box to name and locate the new block. You can edit the new block as a drawing of its own, or you can insert it into another file.
- Use the next two frames – **Foreground lines** and **Obscured lines** – to set the **Color** and **Linetype** of lines within the new block. You don't have to show the **Obscured lines** (lines behind objects), but if you do, use the options in this frame to make the lines appear hidden (use the **Hidden** line type).

Let's create a flatshot of our flange.

Flatshot actually projects the *current* view of the 3D objects in the *current* viewport against the XY-plane of the *current* UCS. That's a lot of "currents"; and that makes for a very dynamic command. This can cause a bit of confusion at first; but there's no substitute for experience!

Practice Practice Practice

Do This: 10.2.1.1	Creating a Flatshot Detail

I. Open the *MyFlange10a.dwg* file in the C:\Steps3D\Lesson10 folder. If that one isn't available, open *Flange 10.dwg*.
II. Set the **obj1** layer current.
III. Follow these steps.

10.2.1.1: CREATING A FLATSHOT DETAIL

1. Enter the *Flatshot* command. Alternately, you can pick the **Flatshot** button 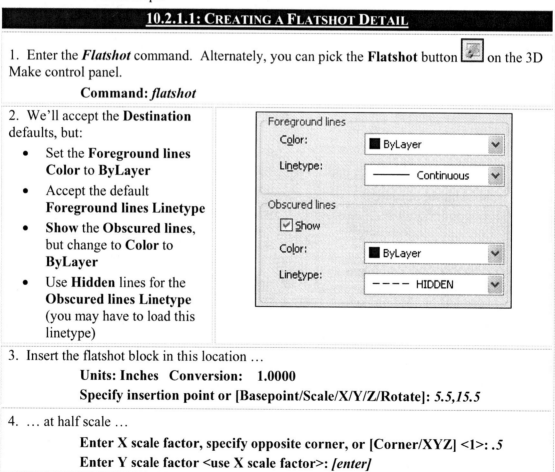 on the 3D Make control panel.

      Command: *flatshot*

2. We'll accept the **Destination** defaults, but:

- Set the **Foreground lines Color** to **ByLayer**
- Accept the default **Foreground lines Linetype**
- **Show** the **Obscured lines**, but change to **Color** to **ByLayer**
- Use **Hidden** lines for the **Obscured lines Linetype** (you may have to load this linetype)

3. Insert the flatshot block in this location …

      Units: Inches   Conversion: 1.0000

      Specify insertion point or [Basepoint/Scale/X/Y/Z/Rotate]: *5.5,15.5*

4. … at half scale …

      Enter X scale factor, specify opposite corner, or [Corner/XYZ] <1>: *.5*

      Enter Y scale factor <use X scale factor>: *[enter]*

5. … and at a 45° angle.
 	
    Specify rotation angle
    <0>: *45*
 	
Your drawing looks like this.
	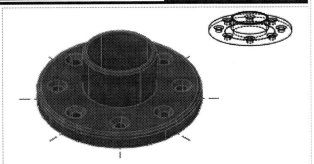

6. Let's try another one. Repeat Steps 1 and 2, but this time, don't **Show** the **Obscured lines.**	

7. Insert the flatshot block in this location …

    Units: Inches   Conversion: 1.0000

    Specify insertion point or [Basepoint/Scale/X/Y/Z/Rotate]: *14,7.5*

8. … at half scale …

    Enter X scale factor, specify opposite corner, or [Corner/XYZ] <1>: *.5*

    Enter Y scale factor <use X scale factor>: *[enter]*

9. … and at a 45° angle.
 	
    Specify rotation angle <0>:
    45
 	
Your drawing looks like this.
 	
10. Save the drawing 💾.
 	
    Command: *qsave*
	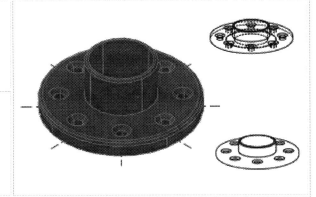

You can plot this drawing in Model space, but for a better approach (as paper space advocates will insist) follows!

10.2.2   Setting Up the Plot – the *Solview* Command

Paper space plotting tools for 3D solids include: ***Solview*, *Soldraw*,** and ***Solprof.*** Of the three, ***Solview*** is the most complex command. It creates viewports according to your input. You can define the viewports by the XY-plane or a user-defined UCS, or by calculating orthographic projections, auxiliary projections, and cross sections from a UCS viewport. ***Solview*** places the viewports on the **VPorts** layer (which it creates if necessary). It also creates viewport-specific layers for visible lines (*Viewname-vis*), hidden lines (*Viewname-hid*), dimensions (*Viewname-dim*), and hatching (*Viewname-hat*).

You must enter the ***Solview*** command while a **Layout** tab is active. AutoCAD responds with the initial ***Solview*** prompt:

    Command: *solview*

    Enter an option [Ucs/Ortho/Auxiliary/Section]:

Let's consider each option.

- The **UCS** option creates a two-dimensional profile view of the object. It uses the XY-plane of a user-specified UCS to define the profile. AutoCAD responds to selection of the UCS option with the prompt:

  Enter an option [Named/World/?/Current] <Current>: *[enter]*
  Enter view scale <1.0000>: *[enter the scale for the view (if incorrect, you can rescale the view later using Zoom XP or the Scale control box on the Viewports toolbar)]*
  Specify view center: *[pick a point where you'd like to place the center point of the view]*
  Specify view center <specify viewport>: *[reposition the view, if necessary, or hit enter to continue]*
  Specify first corner of viewport: *[define the viewport by specifying opposite corners]*
  Specify opposite corner of viewport:
  Enter view name: *[give the viewport a unique name]*

  The same sequence applies to the **Named** and **World** options, except that AutoCAD will precede the **Named** option sequence with a request for the name of the UCS to use. Use the **?** option to list the named UCSs available for use. Use the **UCS** option to create the first viewport – usually a front view or plan view of the 3D solid.

- Use the **Ortho** option (back at the first *Solview* prompt) to create orthographic projections from an existing view. The command sequence is the same as with the **UCS** option.

- Creating an auxiliary view – a view perpendicular to an inclined face – is as easy as drawing an orthographic projection for AutoCAD. AutoCAD responds to selection of the **Auxiliary** option with

  Specify first point of inclined plane: *[specify two points that define the inclined plane]*
  Specify second point of inclined plane:
  Specify side to view from: *[pick a point from where you wish to see the inclined plane]*

  AutoCAD continues with the options to size and locate the viewport.

- The **Section** option creates a cross section complete with section lines. (It takes the *Soldraw* command to actually create the section.) The sequence is

  Specify first point of cutting plane:
  Specify second point of cutting plane:
  Specify side to view from:

  Again, AutoCAD continues with the options to size and locate the viewport.

All of these options will become much clearer with an exercise.

> You'll notice in our next exercise that, in fact, none of these options creates a drawing. What they do is *set up* a viewport for the orthographic, auxiliary, or cross sectional drawings that you'll create later with the *Soldraw* command. You'll see the actually 3D solid in each viewport until you use the *Soldraw* command.

Let's begin.

> You can access all of the *Sol...* commands through the Draw pull-down menu. Follow this path:
> *Draw – Modeling – Setup – (Drawing, View, or Proflie)*

257

Do This: 10.2.2.1	Using *Solview* to Set Up a Layout

I. Open the *Sol1.dwg* file in the C:\Steps3D\Lesson10 folder. It looks like Figure 10.005.

II. Activate the **Layout1** tab. Erase any viewports that appear.

Figure 10.005

10.2.2.1: USING SOLVIEW TO SET UP A LAYOUT

1. Enter the *Solview* command.

    Command: *solview*

2. Select the **UCS** option ![Ucs].

    Enter an option [Ucs/Ortho/Auxiliary/Section]: *u*

3. Tell AutoCAD to use the **Named** UCS option ![Named], and use the UCS called *Front*.

    Enter an option [Named/World/ ?/Current] <Current>: *n*

    Enter name of UCS to restore: *front*

4. We'll use a three-quarter scale for our viewport.

    Enter view scale <1.0000>: *.75*

5. Center the viewport on Paper Space coordinate 3,3.5.

    Specify view center: *3,3.5*

    Specify view center <specify viewport>: *[enter]*

6. Size the viewport as indicated (you can pick approximate coordinates).

    Specify first corner of viewport: *1,4.5*

    Specify opposite corner of viewport: *@4,-2*

7. Call the view *Front*.

    Enter view name: *Front*

8. Complete the command.

    Enter an option [Ucs/Ortho/Auxiliary/ Section]: *[enter]*

    Your drawing looks like this.

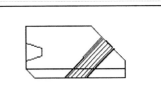

9. Repeat the command.

    Command: *[enter]*

10. Now tell AutoCAD to create an orthographic projection ![Ortho].

    Enter an option [Ucs/Ortho/Auxiliary/Section]: *o*

11. Pick a point on the right side of the existing viewport (notice that AutoCAD automatically uses the midpoint OSNAP) ...

    Specify side of viewport to project:

12. ... and center the viewport about 3 units to the right of the UCS view.

    Specify view center: *@3<0*

    Specify view center <specify viewport>: *[enter]*

258

13. Locate the viewport at about the coordinates indicated.

      Specify first corner of viewport: *6.5,4.5*

      Specify opposite corner of viewport: *@3,-2*

14. Call the viewport *Right*, and complete the command.

      Enter view name: *Right*

      Enter an option [Ucs/Ortho/ Auxiliary/Section]: *[enter]*

15. Repeat Steps 10 through 14 to create a Top viewport as shown in the following figure.

      Command: *[enter]*

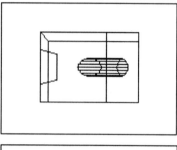

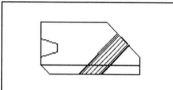 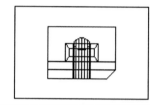

16. Now we'll create an **Auxiliary** view ▮Auxiliary▮ of the inclined surface.

      Command: *[enter]*

      Enter an option [Ucs/Ortho/Auxiliary/Section]: *a*

17. In the original viewport (*Front*), pick the endpoints of the inclined surface. (Pick anywhere in the Front viewport to activate it.)

      Specify first point of inclined plane:

      Specify second point of inclined plane:

18. Tell AutoCAD that you wish to view the surface from the upper-right corner of the viewport.

      Specify side to view from:

19. Pick a point about even with the center of the upper viewport (*Top*).

      Specify view center:

      Specify view center <specify viewport>: *[enter]*

20. Place the viewport around the auxiliary image (don't worry that the viewports overlap), and name the view *Aux*.

      Specify first corner of viewport:

      Specify opposite corner of viewport:

      Enter view name: *Aux*

      UCSVIEW = 1 UCS will be saved with view

Complete the command.

21. Move 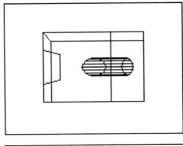 the new viewport to the position shown below.

    Command: *m*

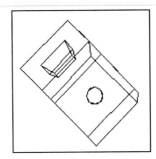
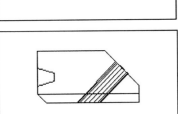
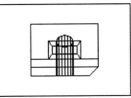

22. Save the drawing ▦.

    Command: *qsave*

23. Repeat the **Solview** command.

    Command: *solview*

24. Select the **Section** option Section.

    Enter an option [Ucs/Ortho/Auxiliary/Section]: *s*

25. In the upper-left viewport (*Top*), specify the cutting plane as shown (use Ortho).

    Specify first point of cutting plane:

    Specify second point of cutting plane:

    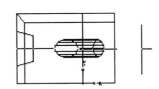

26. View the object from the lower half of the viewport, and accept the default view scale.

    Specify side to view from:

    Enter view scale <0.7500>: *[enter]*

27. Center the sectional viewport below the original (*Front*) viewport.

    Specify view center:

    Specify view center <specify viewport>: *[enter]*

28. Place the viewport around the image, and call the view **Sect**.

    Specify first corner of viewport:

    Specify opposite corner of viewport:

    Enter view name: *Sect*

260

29. Complete the command.

UCSVIEW = 1 UCS will be saved with view

Enter an option [Ucs/Ortho/Auxiliary/Section]: *[enter]*

Your drawing looks like the following figure.

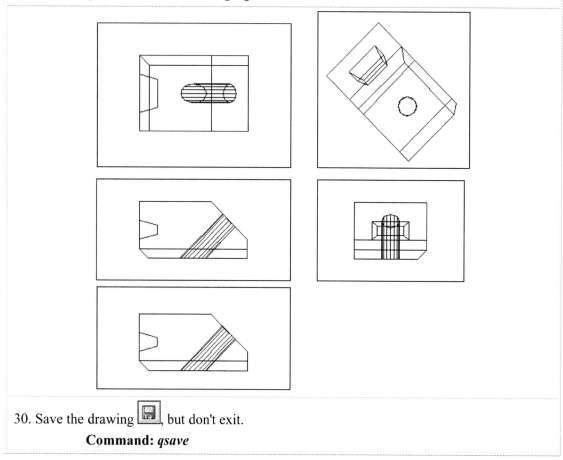

30. Save the drawing 💾, but don't exit.

Command: *qsave*

How's that for a quick way to set up several viewports? If you look a little further than your immediate screen, you'll find that AutoCAD has also set up layers specific to each viewport.

Obviously, however, the drawing isn't yet ready to plot – each viewport still shows the full 3D solid. To complete the drawing, we need to show profiles in each viewport. Let's look at the *Soldraw* and *Solprof* commands next.

10.2.3	Creating the Plot Images – The *Soldraw* and *Solprof* Commands

Both *Soldraw* and *Solprof* create profiles in a viewport. The biggest difference is that the programmers designed *Soldraw* to work specifically with viewports created by the *Solview* command. *Solprof* will create a profile (see insert) in a viewport created by the *MView* or *MVSetup* commands. Additionally, *Soldraw* will create cross sections where they were set up with the *Solview* command.

A profile shows only those edges and/or silhouettes of a 3D solid that are visible in the specified viewport when hidden lines are removed.

An important thing to remember about the Sol… commands is that they were designed to work only with solids. They won't work with surfaces or blocks.

261

The command sequence for *Soldraw* is one of AutoCAD's simplest:

> **Command:** *soldraw*
> **Select viewports to draw..**
> **Select objects:**

AutoCAD does the rest automatically. Try it.

Do This: 10.2.3.1	Using *Solview* to Set Up a Layout

    I.   Be sure you're still in the *Sol1.dwg* file in the C:\Steps3D\Lesson10 folder. If not, please open it now.

    II.   Follow these steps.

10.2.3.1: USING SOLVIEW TO SET UP A LAYOUT

1. Enter the *Soldraw* command.

> **Command:** *soldraw*

2. Select each of the viewports.

> **Select viewports to draw...**
> **Select objects:**
> **Select objects:** *[enter]*

AutoCAD creates the profiles and sections.

Your drawing looks like the figure below.

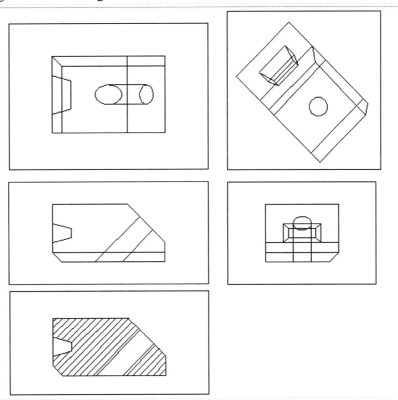

3. Not quite satisfied? Freeze all of the **[Name]-hid** layers except **Front-hid**.

4. Load the **Hidden** linetype and assign it to the **Front-hid** layer.

Your drawing lows like the following figure.

262

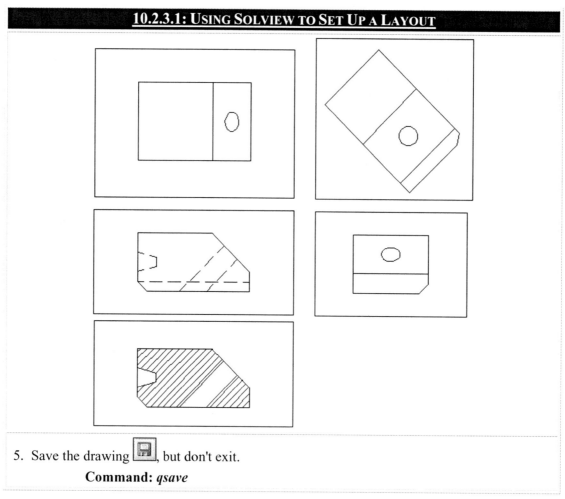

5. Save the drawing 🖫, but don't exit.

   Command: *qsave*

Solprof works almost as easily, but the profiles it creates are actually blocks. Here's the command sequence:

   Command: *solprof*
   Select objects:
   Select objects:
   Display hidden profile lines on separate layer? [Yes/No] <Y>:
   Project profile lines onto a plane? [Yes/No] <Y>:
   Delete tangential edges? [Yes/No] <Y>:

Let's look at the options.

- The first option – **Display hidden profile lines on separate layer** – asks if you'd like to place all profile lines on one layer or place the hidden lines on a separate layer. The default is to place hidden lines on a separate layer.

  When you accept the default (generally a good idea), AutoCAD places visible lines on layer *PV-[viewport handle]* and hidden lines on layer *PH-[viewport handle]*. By using the AutoCAD-assigned viewport handle as part of the layer, AutoCAD assures you of a unique layer name. This way, you can freeze the layer or change the linetype of the hidden lines.

- The next option – **Project profile lines onto a plane** – allows you to create a two-dimensional profile by projecting the lines onto the view plane (the default), or to create three-dimensional lines.

- The last option – **Delete tangential edges** – allows you to remove tangential lines. These are objects (lines) that show the transition between arcs or circles. They're essentially the same things as isolines, except that they're actual objects.

Let's use the *Solprof* command to create an isometric view of our object.

Do This: 10.2.3.2	Using *Solprof* to Set Up a Layout

    I.   Be sure you're still in the *Sol1.dwg* file in the C:\Steps3D\Lesson10 folder. If not, please open it now.

    II.   Create a new viewport in the lower-right corner of the layout. (Use the *MView* command.)

    III.   Activate the new viewport and set up an isometric view (1,1,1),

    IV.   Follow these steps.

10.2.3.2: USING SOLPROF TO SET UP A LAYOUT

1. Enter the *Solprof* command.

    Command: *solprof*

2. Select the 3D solid in the new viewport.

    Select objects:

    Select objects: *[enter]*

3. Accept the defaults for the next three prompts.

    Display hidden profile lines on separate layer? [Yes/No] <Y>: *[enter]*

    Project profile lines onto a plane? [Yes/No] <Y>: *[enter]*

    Delete tangential edges? [Yes/No] <Y>: *[enter]*

4. Freeze the **PH-[viewport handle]** layer. (The viewport handle will vary.)

5. Freeze the **obj1** layer in the active viewport.

The figure looks like this.

6. Save the drawing.

    Command: *qsave*

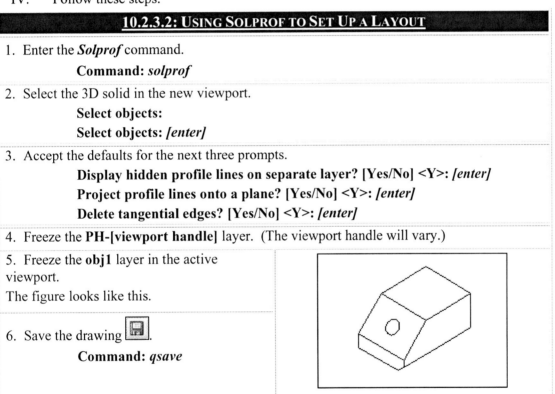

Now you can use the other techniques you've learned to dimension each view, add appropriate text, and otherwise complete the drawing.

10.3	**Extra Steps**

Return to any of the drawings you created in the exercises at the end of Lessons 8 and 9. Create the plotting layouts shown in the exercises (if you created layouts, open **Layout2** and recreate them). This will work best if you use drawings for which you've already created layouts – it'll help you compare the method you used previously with the *Sol...* commands.

Items covered in this lesson include:

- *Three-dimensional uses and techniques for blocks*
- ***Flatshot***
- *The **Sol...** tools used to set up plots for 3D solid*
  - ***Solview***
  - ***Soldraw***
  - ***Solprof***

In this lesson, you discovered some easier ways to set up a Paper Space plot and some new (and useful) techniques for working with blocks. And you wrapped up your study of three-dimensional drafting and modeling techniques. You can relax for two minutes and pat yourself on the back for having accomplished quite a lot of often-difficult material. Then tackle the exercises at the end of the lesson.

In Lesson 11, you'll learn some presentation tricks. While not always useful as a drafting tool, presentation takes you one step further – to adding material qualities to your objects. This means having a table that shows wood grain or a glass lamp that appears transparent. You'll see how to show your drawing in perspective rather than isometric mode. You'll create photographic-quality images suitable for brochures or posters, and much more!

So, complete the exercises and hurry into that place where AutoCAD meets computer graphics!

| 10.5 | Exercises |

1. Open the *slotted guide.dwg* file in the C:\Steps3D\Lesson10 folder. Create the layout.
    1.1. Hint: The ***Sol...*** commands work best when the object is viewed through a 2D Shademode.
    1.2. Save the drawing as *MySG.dwg* in the C:\Steps3D\Lesson10 folder.

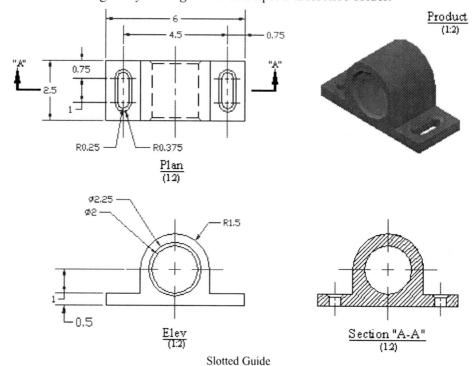

Slotted Guide

2. Open the *ExFlange 10.dwg* file in the C:\Steps3D\Lesson10 folder. Create the layout.
   2.1. Most of the centerlines already exist on layer **Cl**.
   2.2. Save the drawing as *MyFlg.dwg* in the C:\Steps3D\Lesson10 folder.

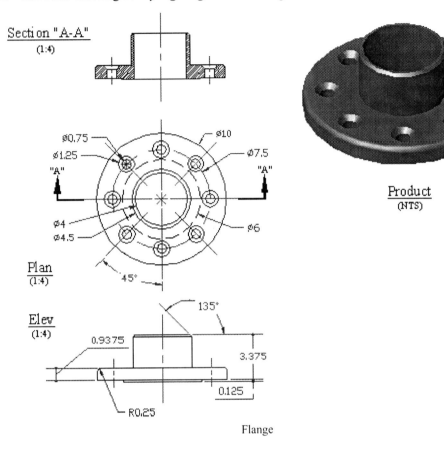

Section "A-A"
(1:4)

Ø0.75
Ø1.25
"A"

Ø10
Ø7.5
"A"

Ø4
Ø4.5

Ø6

Plan
(1:4)

45°

Product
(NTS)

Elev
(1:4)

135°

0.9375

3.375

0.125

R0.25

Flange

3. Open the *Jig.dwg* in the C:\Steps3D\Lesson10. Create the layout.
   3.1. Set up the drawing on a 17" x 11" sheet of paper.
   3.2. Save the drawing as *MyJig.dwg* in the C:\Steps3D\Lesson10 folder.

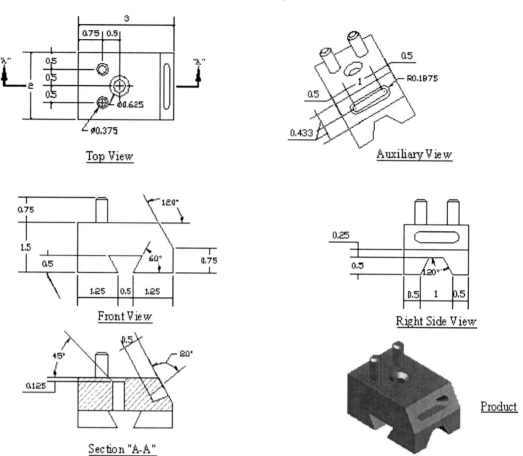

Top View

Auxiliary View

Front View

Right Side View

Section "A-A"

Product

Jig

4. Open the *Thermometer.dwg* file in the C:\Steps3D\Lesson10 folder. Create the layout.

    4.1. Set up the drawing on an 11" x 17" sheet of paper.

    4.2. Save the drawing as *MyThermometer.dwg* in the C:\Steps3D\Lesson10 folder.

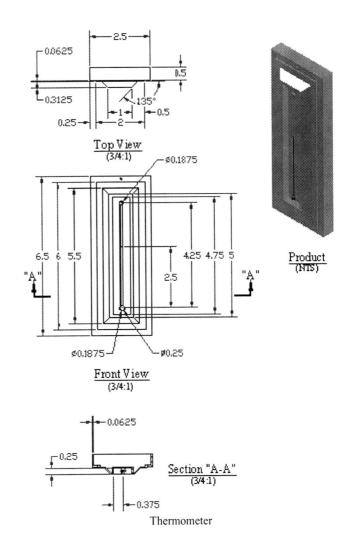

Thermometer

5. Create the service cart drawing shown below.
    5.1. Create the layout on an 11" x 17" sheet of paper.
    5.2. Adjust the Z-Space and UCS as needed to use a single 2" x 2" block to build the frame.
    5.3. Use the caster you created in Lesson 4 (or the *Caster.dwg* file in the C:\Steps3D\Lesson10 folder) for the caster block.
    5.4. Use attributes and the ***Attext*** command to create the cutting list.
    5.5. You'll notice that the ***Sol...*** commands won't work properly on blocks, so you'll have to use the ***MView*** or ***MVSetup*** command to create your viewports.
    5.6. Save the drawing as *MyCart.dwg* in the C:\Steps3D\Lesson10 folder.

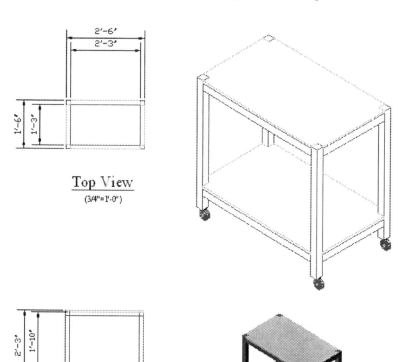

Top View
(3/4"=1'-0")

Side View
(3/4"=1'-0")

Product
(NTS)

Service Cart

Cutting List		
Quantity	Item	Scale Z
4	2x2	15
8	2x2	27
4	caster	1

269

6. Create the *½" Ell* drawing.

    6.1. Make sure the base point of the elbow is as indicated. (Use the **Base** command to move it, if necessary).

    6.2. Be sure the UCS = WCS when you finish.

    6.3. Save the drawing as *My1_2Ell.dwg* in the C:\Steps3D\Lesson10 folder.

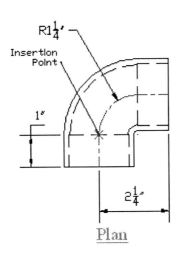

Plan

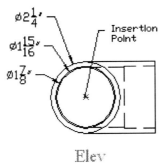

Elev

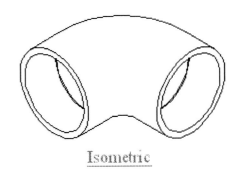

Isometric

½" Ell

7. Create the *½"Tee* drawing.

    7.1. Make sure the base point of the tee is as indicated.

    7.2. Be sure the UCS = WCS when you finish.

    7.3. Save the drawing as *My1_2Tee.dwg* in the C:\Steps3D\Lesson10 folder.

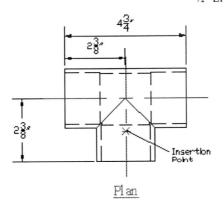

Plan

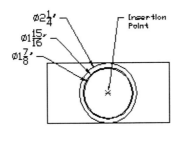

Elev

Isometric

½" Tee

8. Create the bike rack.

    8.1. Use the elbow you created in Exercise 6. (If this isn't available, use the *1_2Ell* drawing found in the C:\Steps3D\Lesson10 folder.)

    8.2. Use the *1_2Pipe* drawing to provide the pipe between the elbows (just as you did in Exercise 10.1.2.1).

    8.3. Be sure the UCS = WCS when you finish.

    8.4. Save the drawing as *MyBikeRack.dwg* in the C:\Steps3D\Lesson10 folder.

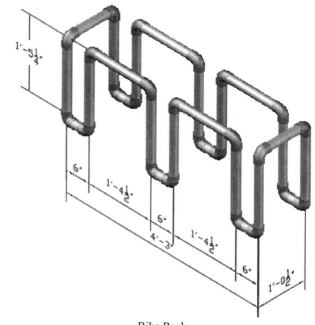

Bike Rack

9. Create the lawn chair.

    9.1. Use the elbow you created in Exercise 6. (If this isn't available, use the *1_2Ell* drawing found in the C:\Steps3D\Lesson10 folder.)

    9.2. Use the tee you created in Exercise 7. (If this isn't available, use the *1_2Tee* drawing found in the C:\Steps3D\Lesson10 folder.)

    9.3. Use the *1_2Pipe* drawing to provide the pipe between the elbows (just as you did in Exercise 10.1.2.1).

    9.4. Be sure the UCS = WCS when you finish.

    9.5. Save the drawing as *MyLawnChair.dwg* in the C:\Steps3D\Lesson10 folder.

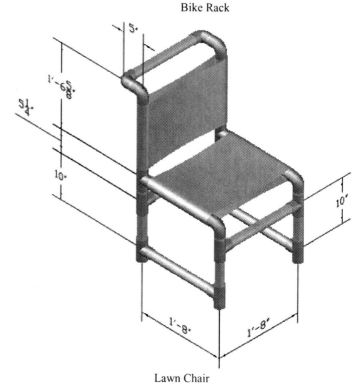

Lawn Chair

271

10. Create the patio scene.

   10.1.   Use the equipment you created in Lesson 10's Exercises. (If these aren't available, use the corresponding drawing found in the C:\Steps3D\Lesson10 folder.)

   10.2.   You created the garden fence in Lesson 7 and the fountain in Lesson 8. (Both are provided in the C:\Steps3D\Lesson10 folder if you didn't save your drawings.)

   10.3.   Save the drawing as *MyPatioScene* in the C:\Steps3D\Lesson10 folder.

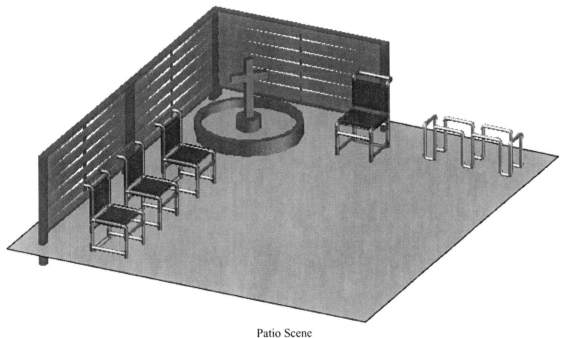

Patio Scene

10.6	For Web-Based Review Questions, visit: http://www.uneedcad.com/2007/Files/07R10-3D.pdf

Lesson

11

Following this lesson, you will:

✓ *Know how to render an AutoCAD drawing*
  - o *Rendering*
  - o *Assigning materials*
  - o *Adding lights*

✓ *Be Able to Create Animations*

Presentation Tools

> *From childhood's hour I have not been*
>
> *As others were – I have not seen*
>
> *As other saw.*
>
> *Alone* – Edgar Allan Poe

> *Far better it is to dare mighty things, to win glorious triumphs, even though checkered by failure, than to take rank with those poor spirits who neither enjoy much nor suffer much, because they live in the gray twilight that knows not victory nor defeat.*
>
> Theodore Roosevelt

> *The measure of one's soul is calculated*
>
> *not in successes or failures, but in the number of*
>
> *attempts one is willing to make.*
>
> Anonymous

As you might guess from the three preceding quotes, you now face the most challenging of the lessons you'll undertake in our One Step at a Time series. So before you start, think back to what you knew when you began Lesson 1 of AutoCAD 2007: One Step at a Time. You began each lesson with anticipation and a touch of anxiety, but you finished each knowing more than you did when you started. It hasn't always been easy, but you've persevered (or else you wouldn't be here). Consider your accomplishments. And take Teddy's advice and "dare mighty things" in Lesson 11.

11.1   What Is Rendering and Why Is It So Challenging?

Rendering is a procedure that takes the objects you've created and gives them properties to make them appear "real." The degree to which they appear real depends on a host of user-defined settings and assignments, including materials, types and positions of lights, and light intensity.

Why is rendering so challenging? Consider what Edgar Allan Poe said in the quote that began this lesson. Every individual will "see" a scene in a different way. Translating what your mind sees to what appears on the screen involves often subtle manipulation of several variables.

Remember Lesson 5 – I told you that we'd reached the edge between CAD operating and CAD programming. Well, in Lesson 11, you've reached the edge between CAD operating and art. Just as not every whittler is a sculptor, not every draftsman is an artist. (A fact I found myself repeating … and repeating … to my employer back when I designed those nifty little houses that Santa sits in down at the mall.) This is where you face the challenge.

11.2   Beyond Visual Styles – The *Render* Command

It may fortify you to know that you've been using a rudimentary form of rendering all along when you used visual styles. But here again, consider the whittler and the sculptor. Whereas visual styles have a few settings from which to choose, rendering presents (quite literally) infinite possibilities. Fortunately, we'll navigate the possibilities using tool palettes and dialog boxes. (This should make you appreciate the fact that you're not using one of the earlier – primitive – releases of AutoCAD!)

Let's begin with the Render Presets (refer to the Render Presets dialog box in Figure 11.001 – next page). Access the dialog box by entering the *RenderPresets* command at the command prompt or by selecting **Manage Render Presets** from the **Select Render Preset** control box in the Render control panel. Make yourself comfortable; we're going to spend some time with this one.

Let's get started.

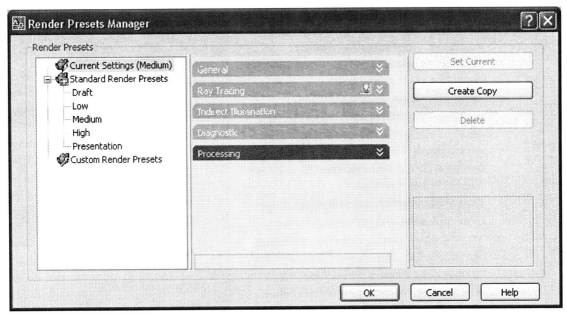

Figure 11.001

- We'll start with the selection box on the left.
  - o It begins with an informational item giving you the **Current Settings**. (In this case, it shows the default – **Medium**.)
  - o Below the informational item, you'll see the list of Standard Render Presets. Here, the list graduates from **Draft** quality renderings to **Presentation** quality. Until you have some experience rendering, you'll find it easier to begin with **Medium** quality renderings and adjust from there.
  - o The last item in the list reads **Custom Render Presets**. These are the rendering setups you'll create. Begin with a preset, **Create** [a] **Copy** (use the button to the right), and then make your adjustments on the Property Panel in the middle of the dialog box.
- The Property Panel in the middle of the dialog box can (and will) be frightening the first time you see it (unless you're a closet photographer or artist). We're going to spend some time here, but if you don't fully absorb it all, it won't be the end of the world. Remember, the folks at Autodesk have worked hard to keep their baby user-friendly. The default list provides just about everything you'll need in the way of presets. You'll use that scary settings list more for tweaking than anything else.

You'll find similar settings on the Advanced Render Settings palette. Access it with the *RPref* command. Using the palette, you can change the current preset or even the settings of your rendering on the fly.

  - o The **General** tab (Figure 11.002 – next page) of the Property Panel contains settings for **Materials**, **Sampling** and **Shadows**.
    - We'll spend time later in this lesson discussing **Materials**. For now, know that you can toggle their application on or off here. More important, perhaps, is the ability to force materials to appear on one or two sides of the host object. Forcing materials to appear where they won't be seen wastes system resources, while not seeing materials where you should can ruin your presentation.
    - **Sampling** has taken a major leap between AutoCAD releases – at least in options! Let me try to make it simple. Sampling speeds the rendering process by rendering only a ratio of the pixels on your screen the more the samples (pixels rendered), the

finer (and slower) the rendering. The number of **Min samples** can't exceed the number of **Max samples**. Lower numbers produce faster but lower quality renderings.

Filters determine how AutoCAD expresses multiple samples in a single pixel. You have a choice of five **Filter types** (listed from fastest and lowest quality): **Box, Triangle, Gauss, Mitchell**, and **Lanczos**.

Larger **filter width** and **height** settings slow rendering and soften and image.

The **Contrast** settings can be confusing, but simply put, they control the color and amount of contrast your rendered image will have. Zero settings indicate black, one settings indicate fully opaque colors.

- Notice the light bulb atop the **Shadows** tab? This sneaky toggle determines whether or not your rendering will show shadows.

General	
Materials	
Apply materials	On
Texture filtering	On
Force 2-sided	On
Sampling	
Min samples	1
Max samples	4
Filter type	Gauss
Filter width	3.0000
Filter height	3.0000
Contrast color	0.0500, 0.0500, 0.0500, …
Contrast red	0.0500
Contrast blue	0.0500
Contrast green	0.0500
Contrast alpha	0.0500
Shadows	
Mode	Simple
Shadow map	Off

Figure 11.002

Shadow **Modes** include: **Simple** (random shadows), **Sorted** (shadows generated in order from the object to the light), and **Segment** (generates shadows along the ray of light). As usual, the simpler shadows are faster but don't produce as high a quality image.

A **Shadow map** controls the accuracy of a shadow. Using shadow maps can greatly slow a rendering, but you'll almost always like the results.

o **Ray Tracing** (Figure 11.003) also involves shadows, and by inference, light. Luckily, this complicated tool has only three options beyond the on/off toggle on the tab itself.

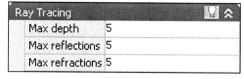

Ray Tracing	
Max depth	5
Max reflections	5
Max refractions	5

Figure 11.003

- The **Max depth** setting limits the total reflections and refractions allowed during the rendering. The setting of 5 (shown here) means that the total reflections and refractions that actually occur will be less than their settings allow.

- **Max reflections** controls how many times light will bounce off of a surface.

- **Max refractions** controls how many times light will bend as a result of collision with a surface.

o **Indirect Illumination** (Figure 11.004 – next page) also contains three tabs that deal with light.

- Toggle **Global Illumination** on or off with the light bulb on its tab. Then use its settings to control your scene's lighting.

  Photons/sample sounds Star Truckkie – but it isn't quite that terrifying. It controls the intensity of global light (ambient light). Higher numbers slow renderings and make the scene more blurry but less noisy. (The dictionary defines Photon using words like *particle* and *antiparticle* – let's avoid that discussion, shall we?)

When it's on, **Use radius** works with **Radius** to control the use and size of your photons. Normally, AutoCAD uses ten sources of ambient light – so each photon is 1/10 the size of the scene. Larger sizes mean slower renders (and possible detection by Romulan war birds!)

The last three options are the same as those found on the **Ray Tracing** tab.

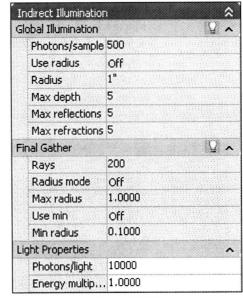

Figure 11.004

- **Final Gather** (when you've toggled the light bulb on) continues AutoCAD's efforts in controlling global illumination.

  The **Rays** setting determines how many rays of light AutoCAD will use in a final "gathering" before rendering. Higher numbers mean slower renders but less noise.

  The **Radius mode** (**On**, **Off**, or **View**) determines whether or not AutoCAD will use the **Max radius** setting for the final gather. **View** let's you set the mode in terms of pixels or world units.

  Increasing the **Max radius** here will give you a better rendering, but it'll take longer.

  Use min and **Min radius** are similar to **Radius mode** and **Max radius**.

- **Light Properties** affect how indirect light behaves. You only have a couple settings about which to concern yourself.

  We've already looked at **Photons/light**.

  The **Energy Multiplier** multiples the global illumination, ambient light, and intensity. Put more simply, it can make your image sharper.

- **Diagnostic** settings (Figure 11.005) can help you figure out why the renderer isn't doing exactly what you expected it to do.

  Grid toggles a grid on or off. The grid shows coordinate spacing of **Objects**, the **World**, or a **Camera**. **Grid size** determines how large a grid to use.

  Use **BSP** to check for **Depth** or **Size** problems when your renderer seems to be going particularly slow.

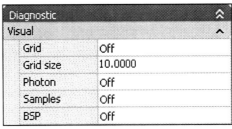

Figure 11.005

- When you render, you'll notice a "tile" moving about the screen producing an image. Use options on the **Processing** tab (Figure 11.006) to adjust how this works.

  - Larger tiles (**Tile size**) decrease render time but produce fewer image updates.

Figure 11.006

  - **Tile order** controls the render order AutoCAD uses to render individual tiles. Most of the options are obvious, but **Spiral** spirals outward from the center, and **Hilbert** (the default) moves to whichever tile will be quickest.

277

- Finally, the **Memory limit** is how much of your system memory (RAM) AutoCAD will use to do the render. If you reach your limit, AutoCAD will discard some geometry in favor of others.
- The three buttons on the right side of the Render Presets Manager require little explanation. But understand that, in order to create a new preset, you must make a copy of an existing one with which to begin.

There's one more thing we have to view before we do create our first rendering – the Rendering Window (Figure 11.007).

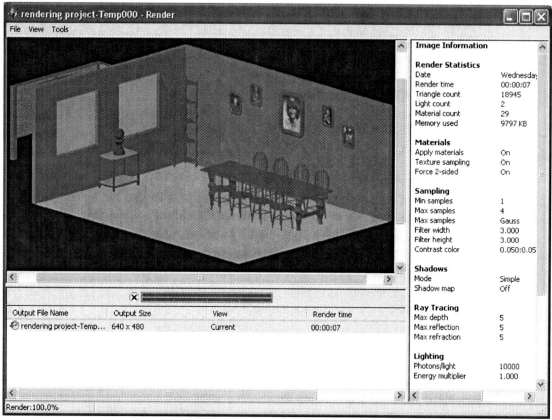

Figure 11.007

This window is an anomaly – one that's a lot simpler than it looks! (I love it when they're easy!) The rendering appears in the upper left corner (the dominant feature of the window). Below, you'll find an informational pane about the rendered image. To the left, you'll find the **Statistics** pane containing information about how the rendered image was created.

- Save the rendered image via the **Save** commands in the File pull down menu.
- Hide the Statistics pane and/or the Status bar with options in the View pull down menu.
- Zoom in or out with options in the Tools pull down menu.

Well, we have to begin someplace. Let's do a basic rendering just to see how it works.

You can also access all of the commands in this lesson via the View pull-down menu. Follow this path:

View – Render – [command]

Do This: 11.2.1	Discovering Rendering

I. Open the *rendering project.dwg* file in the C:\Steps3D\Lesson11 folder. The drawing looks like Figure 11.008.

II. Follow these steps.

Figure 11.008

11.2.1: DISCOVERING RENDERING

---

1. Enter the ***Render*** command. Alternately, you can pick the **Render** button  on the Render toolbar or the Render control panel.

       Command: *rr*

AutoCAD presents the rendered image seen in Figure 11.007.

---

2. Save the rendering as *MyFirstRender.jpg* in the C:\Steps3D\Lesson11 folder. (Use the JPEG Image type.)

File name:	MyFirstRender	▾	Save
Files of type:	JPEG(*.jpeg;*.jpg)	▾	Cancel

---

3. Now let's try it again at a higher resolution. We'll use the Advanced Rendering Settings palette (it's faster). Enter the ***RPref*** command. Alternately, you can pick the **Advanced Render Settings** button on the Render toolbar or the Render control panel.

       Command: *rpref*

---

4. Select **Presentation** `Presentation ▾` in the control box atop the Advanced Rendering Settings palette.

---

5. Repeat Step 1.

AutoCAD presents the following rendered image. Compare it to the image you saved in Step 2. You should find it to be a higher quality.

279

6. Take a few minutes to experiment with some of the other settings before continuing.

We could easily spend a hundred pages exploring the rest of the possibilities, but you should have the general idea. Take some time (once you complete the lesson) to continue exploring on your own.

You've seen the basics of the *Render* command, but so far, the rendered drawing is fairly unimpressive. It still looks like a cartoon – bright and colorful but not real. Next we'll begin to add reality to our image by assigning material values to the various objects.

> In previous releases, we'd use a series of landscape tools to add plants and the images in the frames. These commands have been retired in the current release in favor of better tools. (I used the *ImageAttach* command to attach the family photos in the file. These now have the benefit of being visible even when not rendered.

Let's proceed.

11.3	Adding Materials to Make Your Solids Look Real
11.3.1	Adding Materials via Layers

As you'll soon see, adding materials to an object can mean the difference between colorful cartoon images and images that come close to photographic realism. And luckily, you can accomplish it quite easily.

To understand materials, think of them as paint (or wallpaper). The object doesn't actually become wood (or granite, etc.). Rather, it has the image of wood painted onto it. AutoCAD achieves this by attaching an image file to the surfaces of the objects. The only trick involved for you, then, is to know which image file to use. AutoCAD provides a library full of possible images from which to choose. If these don't satisfy your needs, however, AutoCAD helps to create new images (or modify old ones)!

AutoCAD comes with a library of existing materials accessed via the Visual Styles – Materials palette (Figure 11.009). Open it by selecting **Materials** from the Properties menu of the tool palettes. (Pick the **Properties** button, then select **Materials** from the menu that appears.)

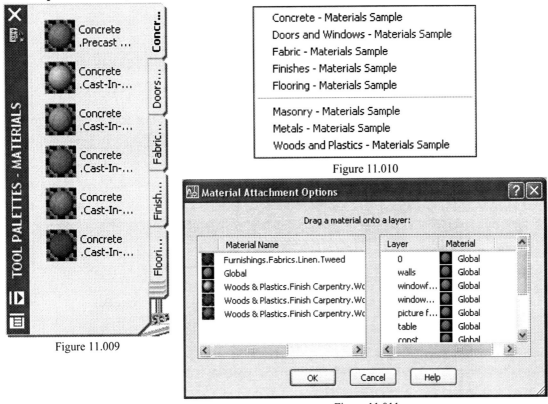

Figure 11.009

Figure 11.010

Figure 11.011

Right click on one of the overlapping tabs to produce a convenient menu (Figure 11.010) listing the other tabs available on this palette. Attaching a material to an object can be as easy as dragging and dropping a material from the palette to the desired object in your drawing. This procedure actually "loads" the material into the drawing and attaches it to the object at the same time. You can also right click on a material and select **Add to current drawing** from the cursor menu to load the material without actually attaching it. We'll look at why this might be useful after the next exercise.

Another approach for attaching materials (the preferred approach) covers more distance at once that having to individually select objects. You can use the *MaterialAttach* command to attach materials to entire layers. This command calls the Material Attachment Options dialog box (Figure 11.011). Just follow the instructions at the top – drag a material onto a layer – and AutoCAD does the rest!

Let's attach some materials before we look any deeper into materials.

You'll notice, when attaching materials, that nothing appears to happen. Materials won't appear until you render the drawing, as you'll see in this exercise.

Do This: 11.3.1.1	Attaching Materials

    I.   Be sure you're still in the *rendering project.dwg* file in the C:\Steps3D\Lesson11 folder.

   II.   If tool palettes aren't open, open them now.

  III.   Follow these steps.

11.3.1.1: ATTACHING MATERIALS

1. We'll begin by loading several materials. Pick the **Properties** button ▣ on the tool palette and select **Materials** [✔ Materials] from the menu. AutoCAD opens the Tool Palettes – Materials tool palettes (Figure 11.009).

2. Right click on the bunched up tabs at the bottom of the palette and select **Doors and Windows** [Doors and Windows - Materials Sample] from the menu (Figure 11.010). AutoCAD places that palette atop the others.

3. Right click on Doors – Windows. Glazing.Glass. Clear and select **Add to current drawing** [Add to Current Drawing] from the menu.

4. Repeat this procedure to add the following materials to your drawing.

MATERIAL	TAB
Doors - Windows. Metal Doors and Frames.Steel.Galvanized	Doors and Windows
Woods - Plastics.Finish Carpentry.Wood.Paneling.1	Woods and Plastics
Finishes.Flooring.Carpet.Loop.5	Flooring
Finishes.Plaster.Stucco.Troweled.White	Finishes

5. Now you have several materials available, let's attach them to your layers. (We'll still have to do some tweaking, but this will complete most of the material assignments for your drawing.)

Enter the *MaterialAttach* command. Alternately, you can pick the **Attach by layer** button ⊗ on the Materials control panel.

Command: *materialattach*

AutoCAD presents the Material Attachment Options dialog box (Figure 11.011).

6. Drag the materials from the left window to the layer in the right window. Use the following chart to assist you.

MATERIAL	LAYER(S)
Doors - Windows. Metal Doors and Frames.Steel.Galvanized	Windowframe
Woods - Plastics.Finish Carpentry.Wood.Paneling.1	Picture frame Table Obj1 Lamp Corner shelf
Finishes.Flooring.Carpet.Loop.5	Floor
Finishes.Plaster.Stucco.Troweled.White	Walls
Doors - Windows.Glazing.Glass.Clear	Windowpane

7. Pick the **OK** button [OK] to complete the procedure.

282

8. Save the drawing 💾.

9. Render the drawing 🖼️.

    Command: *rr*

It now looks like the following figure. (Not exactly photographic quality, is it? Not to worry; we haven't finished yet!)

10. Save the rendering as *Render1.jpg* to the C:\Steps3d\Lesson11 folder. You can use it for comparison later.

We still need to tweak the materials to see the floor properly, wood grains and glass. We'll create a blue glass for the globe and lamp table shelving. That'll help – but it won't quite finish our efforts. Still, we'll get there *one step at a time*!

11.3.2	**Creating and Tweaking Materials – and Another Method of Assigning Them to Objects**

The title of this section makes it sound very busy, but these things all work together. It won't be as difficult as it sounds – we'll do the work from the Materials tool palette (Figure 11.012 – next page). AutoCAD divides the palette into two primary frames – the top for creation and manipulation of materials, the bottom for editing materials.

- Starting the top frame, you'll find a large area listing (pictorially) the materials available in the drawing. To the right of the title bar, you'll see a toggle ■ that will provide larger images if you need them, but larger images restrict the number of items that AutoCAD can show at one time.

  Several buttons reside below the images. From the left, these include:

  o A **Swatch Geometry** toggle – use this to view materials attached to a sample sphere 🔵, box 📦, or cylinder 🛢️.

283

- A **Checkered Underlay** toggle 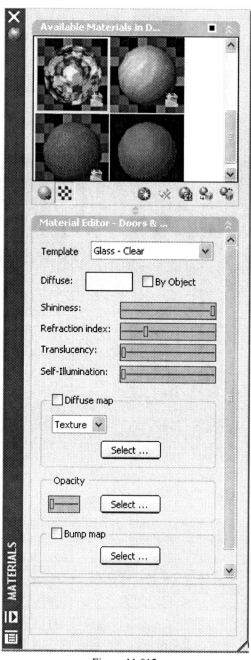 – use this to toggle the checkered background in the sample images on or off.

- The **Create New Material** button – this will open the Create New Material dialog box (Figure 11.013) where you'll name and (optionally) provide a description of your new material. We'll use this procedure to create the blue glass for our lamp's globe.

- A **Purge from Drawing** button which comes in handy when your drawing gets too cramped with unused materials.

- The **Indicate Materials in Use** button updates the display. Materials in use will display an icon in the lower right corner of the image.

- The **Apply Material to Objects** button allows you to apply the currently selected material to selected objects in the drawing. It prompts with a **Select objects** prompt and replaces the cursor with this one: n

- Use the **Remove Materials from Selected Objects** button to remove materials from selected objects. This also prompts with a **Select objects** prompt and uses the same cursor as the Apply Material procedure uses.

- The lower frame begins by naming the currently selected material in the title bar. It then provides many opportunities.

  - The **Template** control box provides access to many templates (Figure 11.014 – next page) you can use as the basis for new materials.

  - The **Diffuse** options shown in Figure 11.012 work for **Realistic** and **Realistic Metal** templates. (Diffusion softens edges.) You can diffuse by color or by object.

Figure 11.012

Figure 11.013

284

- To assign a color, pick in the color box. AutoCAD presents the standard color selection dialog box.
- To diffuse by object, put a check in the check box for that option. Diffusing by object means that AutoCAD will diffuse materials according to the color of the object.

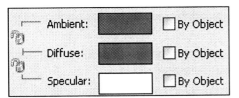

Figure 11.015

Figure 11.014

   o When using the Advanced or Advanced Metal templates, AutoCAD replaces the **Diffuse** options in Figure 11.012 with those shown in Figure 11.015.

- Use the color box or the **By Object** check box next to **Ambient** to control the color reflected by faces lit only by ambient light.
- Use the color box or the **By Object** check box next to **Diffuse** to control the main color reflected by the object.
- Use the color box or the **By Object** check box next to **Specular** to control the color reflected by shiny objects.

   o Use the slider bars below the **Diffuse** options to adjust the look of your materials.

- Shiny material reflects light in fewer directions. The lower the **Shininess** setting, the softer the reflected light.
- **Refraction**, you recall, is the bending of light. Use this setting on non-metal templates to control how much refraction you'll get through transparent materials.
- A translucent object both scatters and transmits light. The higher the value, the lower the translucence. **Translucency** isn't available for metal templates.
- **Self-illumination** makes an object appear to give off light independent of the drawing's light settings.

   o A **Diffuse Map** is an image file attached to the object. You can use the following image files: TGA, BMP, PNG, JPG, TIF, GIF, or PCX. Alternately, you use the control box to select either Wood or Marble procedural materials.

   Use the **Select** button to select a diffuse map. Once you do, AutoCAD makes a couple buttons available for editing the

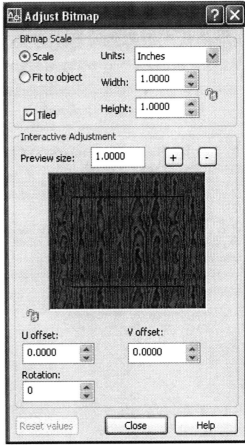

Figure 11.016

285

map.

- The **Adjust Scale/Tiling, Offset, and Rotation Values** button ⊞ calls the Adjust Bitmap dialog box (Figure 11.016). Here you can adjust the **Scale**, **Offset**, and **Rotation** of the image. You also determine whether or not the image will be **Tiled**. (Note that you can **Reset values** when things get out of hand!)
- The **Delete map information from drawing** button ⊠ removes the image from the material definition.
  - When used, **Opacity** areas of a material can be transparent. Use the slider to control just how transparent – larger numbers mean the image will be more opaque.
  - Use a **Bump Map** to make a material appear to have surface characteristics – ridges and/or valleys. Use the **Select** button to select a bump map file. When a bump map file is present, AutoCAD provides the same buttons (with the same functions) as it did with the **Diffuse Map**.

In our next exercise, we'll create and attach a blue glass material for our lamp globe, and make some needed adjustments to the materials we've already assigned.

Do This: 11.3.2.1	Creating and Tweaking Materials

    I.   Be sure you're still in the *rendering project.dwg* file in the C:\Steps3D\Lesson11 folder.

   II. If tool palettes aren't open, open them now.

  III. Follow these steps.

11.3.2.1: ATTACHING MATERIALS

1. Open the Materials tool palette (Figure 11.012). You can enter the command on the command line or pick the Materials button 🔲 on the Materials control panel.

    Command: *materials*

2. Pick the **Create New Material** button 🔵. AutoCAD presents the Create New Material dialog box (Figure 11.013).

3. Call the new material *Blue Glass* and give it a description if you wish. Pick the **OK** button OK to continue.

4. Notice that AutoCAD creates a new material and highlights it in the upper section of the Materials palette. We'll define it now.	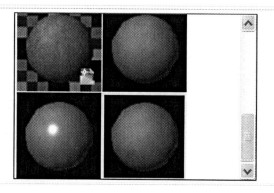

5. Use these settings:

- Use the **Glass-Clear** template.
- Set a **Diffuse** color of blue. (Diffuse by color.)
- Use default settings for **Shininess** and **Refraction** index.
- Set the **Translucency** to ~75 and the **Self-Illumination** to ~15. This will make our glass shine a touch brighter than normal.
- Don't use a **Diffuse map** or a **Bump map**. We don't need either for clear glass.
- Set your **Opacity** to ~ 15.

Congratulations! You've created a material! Now let's attach it to something.

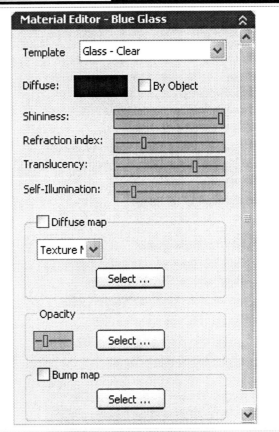

6. Pick the **Apply Material to Object** button .

AutoCAD returns to the drawing and asks you to select object.

7. Select the lamp's globe and the upper and lower shelf of the lamp table. Complete the command.

> **Select objects:**
> **Select objects:** *[enter]*

8. Render the drawing to check your settings.

> **Command:** *rr*

The lamp and table should look like this. (Notice the transparency of the glass.)

9. Save the rendering as you did previously. Compare it to previous renderings. Notice the changes?

10. Save the drawing 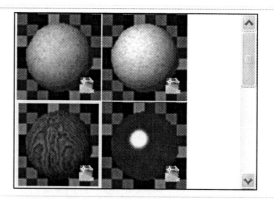, but don't exit.

11. Have you noticed that the window glass looks solid. Have you noticed that the wall doesn't look textured, the floor looks empty and no wood grain shows on the table (or anything else)?

We'll do something about these problems now using the same tools we used to create our blue glass material.

Select the Panel1 material.

12. Make these changes to the settings:
- Set **Shininess** to ~75 (this'll give us some nice polished furniture)
- Increase the **Refraction** to 1.200
- Set the **Diffuse map** to ~75 …
- … and the **Bump map** to ~10.

Accept the other defaults here.

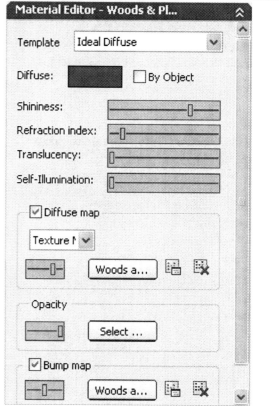

13. We need to do a little more to the **Diffuse map**. If you render now, you'll notice that the wood grain goes in the wrong direction. Pick the **Adjust scale/tiling, offset, and rotation** button in the **Diffuse map** frame.

AutoCAD opens the Adjust Bitmap dialog box (see the Step 14 figure).

288

14. Make these adjustments:

- Change the **Width** and **Height** to the drawing's scale factor (48). This may make the preview image appear blurry, but don't let it bother you. It'll look fine once you render the drawing.
- Change the **Rotation** angle to 90 to make the grain go the right way on the table.

15. Close [Close] the Adjust Bitmap dialog box.

16. Save the drawing [💾], but don't exit.

17. Render the drawing [🖼] to check your settings.

Command: *rr*

18. Save the rendering as you did previously. Compare it to previous renderings. Notice the changes? Look at the reflective surfaces of the wood objects (table, lamp base, picture frames).

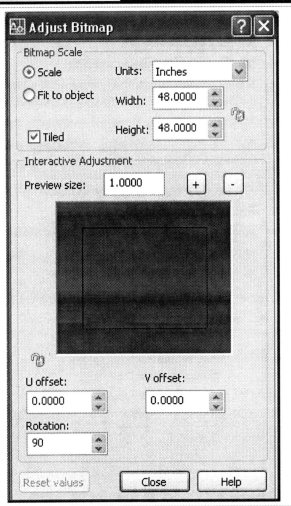

289

19. Make the following changes to the floor (the carpet material):
- Set the **Shininess** to 50.
- Set the **Refractive** index to 1.200.
- We've changed our minds about using carpet; let's use tile. Pick the **Finish** button in the **Diffuse map** frame and pick the *Finishes.Flooring.VCT.Diamonds.jpg* image file.
- Do the same for the **Bump map** (use the same image file).
- Pick the **Adjust scale/tiling, offset, and rotation** button in the **Diffuse map** frame and make the **Width** and **Height** of the tiled image 48 (the drawing's scale factor).

20. Make the following changes to the walls (the stucco material):
- Set the **Shininess** to 35.
- Select the image file *Finishes.Plaster.Stucco.Medium.White.jpg* for use as a **Bump map**.
- Pick the **Adjust scale/tiling, offset, and rotation** button in the **Diffuse map** frame and set the **Bitmap Scale** to **Fit to object**.

21. Make the following changes to the windows (the clear glass material):
- Set the **Opacity** to 15.

22. Render the drawing .

      Command: *rr*

How's it look now (see the image below)?

23. Save the drawing , but don't exit.

What's that? It doesn't look real yet? Something's still missing? Well, aren't you particular! What's missing (you are the intuitive one!) is *light*! And that's the topic of our next section!

11.4   Lights

> Then God said, "Let there be light," and there was light. God saw how
> good the light was. ... - the first day.
>
> Genesis 1:3

Perhaps we can better understand the importance of light when we consider that it was the first thing He created.

AutoCAD provides five types of lighting. These include Ambient Light (aka Default Lighting) – and three that you define and control – **Point Light, Spotlight,** and **Distant Light**. Then it tackles the sun!

- **Ambient Light** lights all surfaces with equal intensity. AutoCAD has two distant sources which light the visible surfaces of a 3D model.

- A **Point Light** works like a light bulb. It spreads rays in all directions from a single source. It dissipates as it moves away from the source, and it casts shadows.

- A **Spotlight** works like a **Point Light**, except that it can be pointed in a single direction.

- A **Distant Light** is an even light coming from a distant location.

- The **Sun Light** works much like a distant light except that you can define its location in terms of geography, calendar and time of day.

You can use any combination of one, two, three, or all types of light in your rendering (except **Ambient Light** – *which AutoCAD turns off when another light is active*).

11.4.1   The Three Basic Lights – Point, Spot, and Distant

You can work with lights on the command line or using the Lights control panel. The command line looks like this:

> **Command:** *light*
>
> **Enter light type [Point/Spot/Distant] <Spot>:** *[tell AutoCAD what kind of light you want – your choice will determine the prompts that follow]*
>
> **Specify source location <0,0,0>:** *[locate your light]*
>
> **Specify target location <0,0,-10>:** *[at what is your light pointing]*
>
> **Enter an option to change**
> **[Name/Intensity/Status/Hotspot/Falloff/shadoW/Attenuation/Color/eXit] <eXit>:** *[manage your light's properties]*

We'll use the command line to look at all our options.

- The first prompt asks for the type of light you want to create. Your choice determines the prompts that follow.

  o Selecting the default option – **Spot** – (or picking **Create a spot light** button on the Light control panel) presents the options shown above.

  o Selecting **Point** (or picking the **Create a point light** button on the Light control panel) prompts like this:

  > **Specify source location <0,0,0>:** *[locate your light]*
  >
  > **Enter an option to change**
  > **[Name/Intensity/Status/shadoW/Attenuation/Color/eXit] <eXit>:** *[manage your light's properties]*

o Selecting **Distant** (or picking the **Create a distant light** button 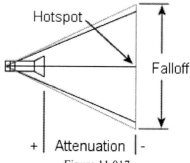 on the Light control panel) prompts like this:

> **Specify light direction FROM <0,0,0> or [Vector]:** *[as this light will be a distance away from your drawing area, locate it by direction rather than a specific point]*
>
> **Specify light direction TO <1,1,1>:** *[the second prompt can be confusing – the easy way to understand this one is simply to pick a point in the direction you want your light to shine]*
>
> **Enter an option to change [Name/Intensity/Status/shadoW/Color/eXit] <eXit>:** *[manage your light's properties]*

o The various lights have several options to manage their properties. These properties options, of course, are also available on the Properties palette when you edit the light. Let's look at each option. (Refer to Figure 11.017.)

- **Name** – Give the light a specific name to make it easy to identify from a list of lights. Prompts for a light name.

- **Intensity** – Sets the intensity (brightness) of the light. Your system's resources determine the maximum setting.

- **Status** – Turns the light on or off. You can change this setting in the Properties palette for the specific light.

Figure 11.017

- **Hotspot** – The hotspot is the focal angle of a spotlight – in other words, it's the center of the spotlight's cone.

- **Falloff** – Falloff determines the actual size of the focal point of the spotlight. You'll determine this by angle (from 0° to 160°). The default is 45°, but the falloff angle must be greater than the hotspot angle.

- **Shadow** – Do you want your light to cast shadows? **Shadows** includes on or off options as well as **Sharp** (hard edges) or **Soft** (soft edges) options.

- **Attenuation** –**Attenuation** refers to how light dissipates over distance. You'll be prompted with three options:

  ∴ **None** means that distant objects will reflect as much light from this point light as closer objects reflect.

  ∴ **Inverse Linear** is normal reflectivity. In other words, an object twice as far away as another object will reflect half the light the closer one reflects. This is the default setting and appropriate for most situations.

  ∴ **Inverse Square** is similar to **Inverse Linear** but works with squared numbers. That is, in our previous example, the distant object will reflect one-quarter the light that the closer one reflected.

> The OpenGL video driver doesn't support attenuation at the time of this writing. Enter *3dconfig* at the command prompt and pick the **View Tune Log** button.

- **Color** – The Color option uses standard AutoCAD procedures to allow you to control the color of the light you're creating.

Let's see what we can do with these lights before we tackle the sun!

Do This: 11.4.1.1	Basic Lighting

    I.   Be sure you're still in the *rendering project.dwg* file in the C:\Steps3D\Lesson11 folder.

   II.   Change the **Opacity** of the **Blue Glass** material to 0. (What we had worked fine for a lamp with no light in it. We're going to put a light in it now.)

  III.   Follow these steps.

11.4.1.1: BASIC LIGHTING

1. Let's start with a simple spot light. Enter the command sequence below. Alternately, you can pick the **Create new spot light** button on the Light control panel.

> **Command:** *light*
> **Enter light type [Point/Spot/Distant] <Spot>:** *[enter]*

2. Specify the location indicated …

> **Specify source location <0,0,0>:** *20'6,10'6,3'*

3. … and the target location (about the center of Barbara's picture).

> **Specify target location <0,0,-10>:** *20'6,16'6,5'6*

4. **Name** the light something convenient.

> **Enter an option to change [Name/Intensity/Status/Hotspot/Falloff/shadoW/Attenuation/Color/eXit] <eXit>:** *n*
> **Enter light name <Spotlight1>:** *Spot*

5. Lower the **Intensity** a bit so we don't outshine our picture.

> **Enter an option to change [Name/Intensity/Status/Hotspot/Falloff/shadoW/Attenuation/Color/eXit] <eXit>:** *i*
> **Enter intensity (0.00 - max float) <1.0000>:** *.5*

6. Set the **Hotspot** and **Falloff** to spotlight just the one photograph.

> **Enter an option to change [Name/Intensity/Status/Hotspot/Falloff/shadoW/Attenuation/Color/eXit] <eXit>:** *h*
> **Enter hotspot angle (0.00-160.00) <3'-9">:** *30*
> **Enter an option to change [Name/Intensity/Status/Hotspot/Falloff/shadoW/Attenuation/Color/eXit] <eXit>:** *f*
> **Enter falloff angle (0.00-160.00) <160>:** *50*

7. Complete the command.

> **Enter an option to change [Name/Intensity/Status/Hotspot/Falloff/shadoW/Attenuation/Color/eXit] <eXit>:** *[enter]*

Notice that AutoCAD places a spotlight glyph at your spotlight's location.

8. Render the drawing .

> **Command:** *rr*

Notice that AutoCAD eliminates the ambient (default) lighting in favor of the user-defined light.

9. Save the drawing , but don't exit.

> **Command:** *qsave*

10. Let's create a couple point lights – one for the lamp and a ceiling light. Enter the sequence below. Alternately, you can pick the **Create new point light** button on the Light control panel.

> **Command:** *light*
>
> **Enter light type [Point/Spot/Distant] <Spot>:** *p*

11. Locate the first light (the lamp) at the center of the lamp's globe.

> **Specify source location <0,0,0>:** *cen*

12. **Name** the light something convenient.

> **Enter an option to change [Name/Intensity/Status/shadoW/Attenuation/Color/ eXit] <eXit>:***n*
>
> **Enter light name <Pointlight1>:** *lamp*

13. Change the light's color to blue. (I used AutoCAD's index color 5.)

> **Enter an option to change [Name/Intensity/Status/shadoW/Attenuation/Color/eXit] <eXit>:** *C*
>
> **Enter true color (R,G,B) or enter an option [Index color/Hsl/colorBook] <0,0,0>:** *i*
>
> **Enter color name or number (1-255):** *5*

14. We'll accept the other defaults. Complete the command.

> **Enter an option to change [Name/Intensity/Status/shadoW/Attenuation/Color/eXit] <eXit>:** *[enter]*

AutoCAD has placed a point light glyph in the center of the lamp's globe.

15. Create a ceiling light (also a point light) at the coordinates indicated. (Accept the other defaults.)

> **Specify source location <0,0,0>:** *19'10,2',7'11*

16. Turn the spotlight off. (Select the spotlight glyph and use the Properties palette.)

17. Render the drawing .
Command: *rr*

Notice (below) the shadows. What has blue tints from the blue point light? Notice the double shadows where both lights have shone. Notice the reflections on the table and in the windows. Save the rendering and compare it with earlier efforts.

18. Change to the Perspective *View*. (Be sure the **ceiling** layer thaws.)
Command: *view*

19. Render the drawing again .
Command: *rr*

This is more of an inside look. Notice the shadows outside – as though it's night.

20. Save the drawing , but don't exit.
Command: *qsave*

Did I leave you in the dark? Of course not, now you can create light!

But we've left out the most import light – the sun. Let's look at that one next.

11.4.2	The Sun

Despite its size, the sun is the easiest light to manage!

You'll use two simple tools – the Geographic Locator (Figure 11.018) and the Sun Properties palette (Figure 11.019).

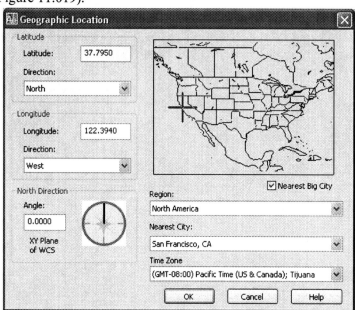

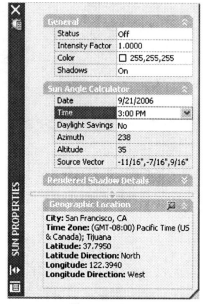

Figure 11.018   Figure 11.019

Yes, you can complicate the Geographic Location procedure by trying to figure out the longitude and latitude of your house/plant/etc. But why not make it simple and just tell AutoCAD where you are? We'll locate our dining room in our next exercise.

Once you've located your objects, set the time of day and date using the **Sun Angle Calculator** on the Sun Properties palette. (You can even tell it to use that bane of spring – Daylight Savings time!) Then turn the sun "on" and tell it to cast shadows in the **General** section of the same palette.

Com'n; let's do it!

Do This: 11.4.2.1	Controlling the Sun

    I. Be sure you're still in the *rendering project.dwg* file in the C:\Steps3D\Lesson11 folder.

    II. Follow these steps.

11.4.2.1: CONTROLLING THE SUN

1. Begin by opening the Geographic Location dialog box (Figure 11.018). You can enter the command on the command line, or you can pick the **Geographic Location** button ⊙ on the Light control panel.

        Command: *geographiclocation*

2. We'll do this the easy way. Select **North America** in the **Region** control box, and **Houston, TX** in the **Nearest City** control box as indicated. Too much work? Pick a point near the red + on the map. AutoCAD will do the rest if you have a check in the **Nearest Big City** check box.

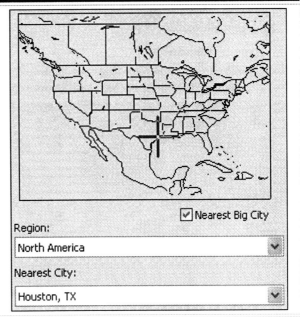

3. Now we'll tell AutoCAD about the orientation of our room – set the North Direction to 180°. Notice that this is a nautical direction – not AutoCAD default NSEW directions.

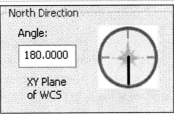

4. Pick the **OK** button [OK] to complete the procedure. You may get a message box telling you that it's a good idea to double check AutoCAD's time zone calculations. Pick the **OK** button again to close the box.

5. Open the Sun Properties palette. You can enter the command shown or pick the **Edit the sun** button [▣] on the Light control panel.

Command: *sunproperties*

6. On the **General** tab, turn the **Status** of the sun **On**.

Using the **Sun Angle Calculator**, enter the date and time indicated.

7. Save the drawing [💾], but don't exit.

Command: *qsave*

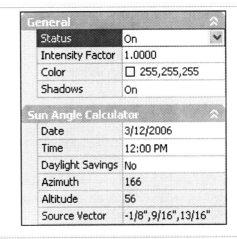

297

8. Render the drawing .

Command: *rr*

You'll notice some additional shadows coming from sunlight filtering through the windows. You should also be able to see the outside fence a little better.

We've almost finished!

11.5   Some Final Touches – Fog and Background

In our "real" world, nothing is perfectly clear – from politics to religion to that stuff that flows from our kitchen faucets. Despite a photographer's best efforts to cut through it, pictures reflect the "haze" that permeates our environment robbing it of the clarity for which we long.

In its efforts to recreate reality, AutoCAD has even provided for the haze!

Use the ***RenderEnvironment*** command to help you de-clarify your efforts. Alternately, of course, you can use the **Render**

Environment button 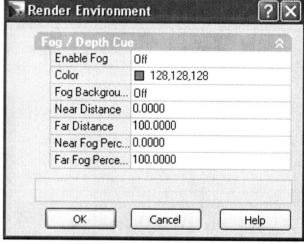 on the Render control panel. AutoCAD assists with a tool panel (Figure 11.020).

Figure 11.020

You'll find a single tab with which to work – **Fog/Depth Cue**. To keep it simple, think of Fog and Depth Cue as essentially the same thing. (They're actually opposite extremes of "haze"; fog is a white haze while depth cue is a black haze.) Here you can fog (tint) the objects being rendered as well as the background of the rendering.

- The **Enable Fog** toggle controls whether or not the objects in the drawing will be tinted according to the **Color** defined in the option below. When **Fog Background** is also toggled on, the entire image will be tinted.

- The **Color** option provides AutoCAD's standard color selection methods. In this case, you'll define the tint of the haze in your drawing.

298

- The **Near distance** and **Far distance** options provide values AutoCAD uses to determine where to begin and end the fog. Values are percentages of the distance from the camera to the back working plane.
- The last options provide percentage values AutoCAD uses to determine how much fog to place at the **Near** and **Far Distance** points.

You'll find the other aspect of the Rendering Environment – Background – accessible through the *View* command. We discussed this is Lesson 4 of our basic text, but we'll set up our drawing with a gradient background to refresh your memory.

Let's finish our dining room.

Do This: 11.5.1	Making It "Real"

I. Be sure you're still in the *rendering project.dwg* file in the C:\Steps3D\Lesson11 folder.

II. Follow these steps.

11.5.1: MAKING IT "REAL"

1. We'll start by setting up our background. Enter the *View* command [icon].

   Command: *v*

2. Select the **Perspective** view as a starting point, then select the **New** button

   [New...]

3. In the **Background** frame, put a check in the box next to **Override default background**. AutoCAD will open the Background dialog box (see Step 4).

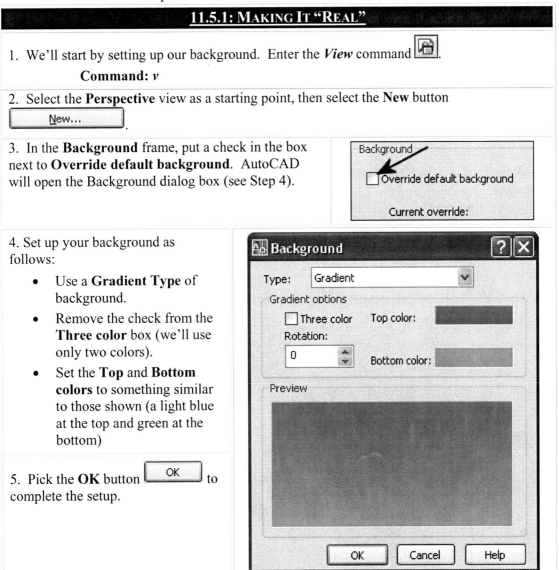

4. Set up your background as follows:

   - Use a **Gradient Type** of background.
   - Remove the check from the **Three color** box (we'll use only two colors).
   - Set the **Top** and **Bottom colors** to something similar to those shown (a light blue at the top and green at the bottom)

5. Pick the **OK** button [OK] to complete the setup.

6. Back in the New View dialog box, name your new view *Background*.

View name:	Background

7. Close the New View dialog box [OK].

7. Set the **Background** view current [Set Current], and close the View Manager [OK]. Notice the change? Don't let the odd colors bother you. It'll look nice once we've finished.

8. Now let's set up the fog. Enter the *RenderEnvironment* command 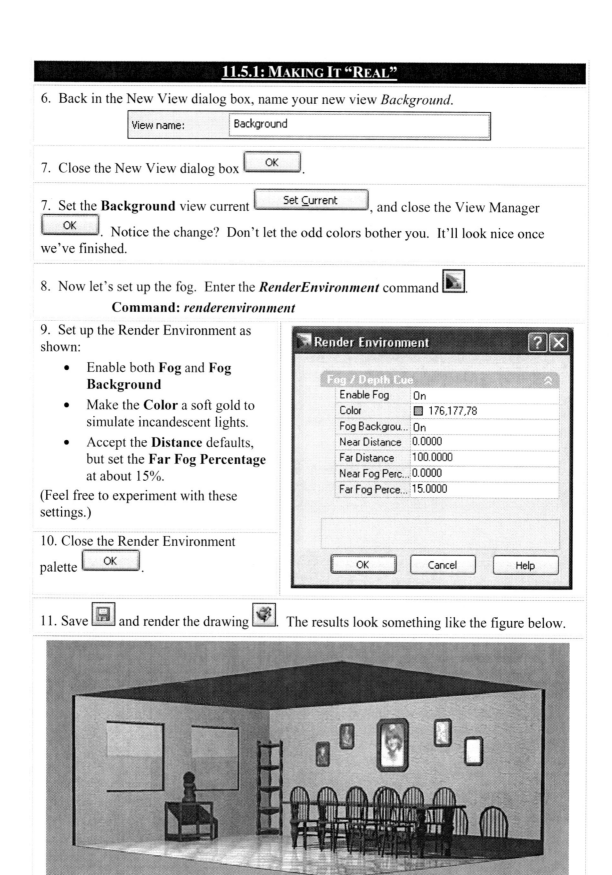.

   Command: *renderenvironment*

9. Set up the Render Environment as shown:

   - Enable both **Fog** and **Fog Background**
   - Make the **Color** a soft gold to simulate incandescent lights.
   - Accept the **Distance** defaults, but set the **Far Fog Percentage** at about 15%.

   (Feel free to experiment with these settings.)

   Render Environment

   Fog / Depth Cue

Enable Fog	On
Color	☐ 176,177,78
Fog Backgrou...	On
Near Distance	0.0000
Far Distance	100.0000
Near Fog Perc...	0.0000
Far Fog Perce...	15.0000

   [OK] [Cancel] [Help]

10. Close the Render Environment palette [OK].

11. Save 🖫 and render the drawing 🎨. The results look something like the figure below.

12. Save the rendering and compare it with earlier efforts. What do you think?

Use the rendered image in your client presentations, or include them as image inserts to show the final product in your drawings. Clients are always impressed by these efforts!

Just a couple quick notes about the transition from AutoCAD 2006 and earlier releases to AutoCAD 2007:

- R2006 and earlier releases used a single distance light as a default; R2007 uses two. You can control how many lights you use with the **DefaultLightingType** system variable. A setting of **0** means to use the older method; a setting of **1** tells AutoCAD to use the newer, two-light default.

- R2006 and earlier releases use a different type of lighting. Use the *ConvertToLights* command to convert older release lights to the 2007 format. The command isn't perfect; you may need to adjust some of the settings. But it's the best AutoCAD has to offer at this time.

11.6 The Animated Walk-Through

Okay, it's not like you need to be sold on AutoCAD any further, right? Well, this section might be considered the part of the commercial where a hyper-announcer demands that you "WAIT! Don't order yet!"

Once your new home (or plant or part etc.) has been built, you still demand that final walk-through before signing the papers. Well, now you can give your client that final walk-through before he buys the first nail!

We'll examine two approaches – the Manual Approach and the Super-Terrific-Automatic-Realistic (Star) Approach. (Okay, I just made that up, but you'll see that it really is the Star in AutoCAD's crown!)

You'll want to remember a couple things before we look at AutoCAD's animation.

- First, AutoCAD utilizes a very basic form of animation designed to allow simple walk (or fly) throughs. You won't be able to open and close doors and have a hummingbird fly past. If you want that sort of thing, invest in one of the true animation packages available on the market today (Lightwave, 3D Studio, Maya, Poser, etc). Most will have at least some ability to use AutoCAD drawings (or to translate them into something they can use).

- Second, to create a nice, rendered animation takes time – buckets of it! It also takes a healthy investment in system resources. I'll let you know how long it takes me to create the animations we'll be doing in our exercises. FYI: I'm using an HP Pavilion D4100Y with a GEForce 6800 graphics card (256Mb), 2Gb of RAM, and an Intel P4 processor with a speed of 3GHz. I'm using Hardware Acceleration as well. (To use Hardware Acceleration, follow this path: enter *3dconfig* at the command line, pick the **Manual Tune** button, and place a check next to **Enable hardware acceleration** in the **Hardware settings** frame.) You can figure your approximate time by how much faster or slower your system is than mine.

11.6.1 The Manual Approach – 3DWalk and 3DFly

What's the difference between *3DWalk* and *3DFly*? You walk on the ground; you fly in the air. (It's really that simple.) Use *3DWalk* to do a "walk-through" and *3DFly* to do a "fly-by". Settings and tools are shared.

Begin by setting up the walk-through or fly-by with the *WalkFlySettings* command. Alternately, you can use the

Walk and Fly settings button 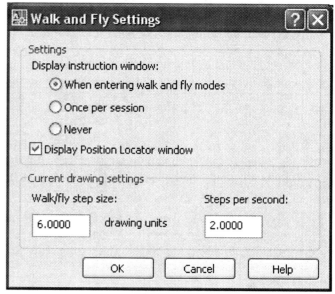 on the 3D Navigate control panel to open the Walk and Fly Settings dialog box (Figure 11.021).

- Two **Settings** can save your sanity.
  - ○ The two boxes in the **Current drawing settings** frame control how large the steps are you'll take. The default settings mean you'll be taking 6" steps every two seconds. These small steps allow you time to view, but really cost you in terms of

Figure 11.021

system resources and the size of the animation file you may want to create.
  - ○ The instruction window, by default, appears every time you enter the *3DWalk* or *3DFly* command. It tells you how to walk (or fly) through the drawing. Once you've learned to walk (so to speak) turn the window off so it doesn't become an irritant. To keep it simple, use these tools to walk/fly:

TOOL	ACTION	TOOL	ACTION
Up Arrow or **W**	Move forward	Right Arrow or **D**	Move Right
Down Arrow or **S**	Move backward	Drag Mouse	Look around or Turn
Left Arrow or **A**	Move Left	**F**	Fly mode / Walk mode toggle
Tab	Reopens the instruction window		

  - ○ **Display Position Locator window**, when checked, tells AutoCAD to display the Position Locator (Figure 11.022 – next page) while in the *3DWalk* or *3DFly* command. This tool makes the manual procedure a lot easier – but you have to remember that easy tends toward making a designer think he can make it longer. Unfortunately, *easier doesn't mean faster!*
    - ▪ Use the three buttons across the top of the Position Locator to Zoom in or out on the display window, or to move the locator. Note that you don't have to use the **Move** button here to move the locator.
    - ▪ The display window below the buttons provides a very dynamic method of creating a walk-through.

302

∴ Pick on the indicator's green lines to move it about on the drawing. (Your cursor will become a "pan" hand.

∴ Pick on the green "ball" at the wide end of the indicator and drag it to adjust the target of your camera.

∴ Pick on the red ball at the pointed end of the indicator and drag it to adjust the camera itself.

- The **General** tab below the display allows you to adjust some of the particulars of the display – mostly position and target colors on the indicator. You can even make the indicator blink in the display. (I don't recommend this for the high-strung among my readers.) More importantly, it allows you to adjust the **Preview visual style**. Set this back to **3D Wireframe** to speed things up a bit. (You don't need realistic in this window.) If you insist on a higher resolution, you can ease the image by increasing the **Preview transparency**.

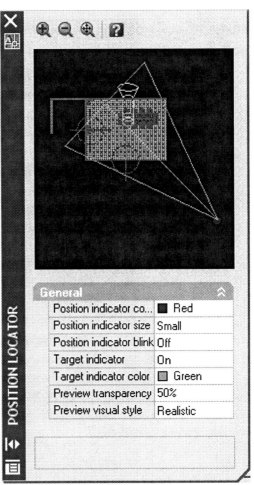

Figure 11.022

Once you've set up your 3D Walk (Fly) tools, you might want to consider recording your walk-through. After all, unless your client is at your elbow, you'll need to provide him access to the results.

Multimedia Controls

Use the standard multimedia controls provided on the 3D Navigation control panel to manage your recording. (From the left, these are: **Play, Record, Pause, Save Animation**.)

During the recording, you can pause and preview what you've done with the **Pause** and **Play** buttons. AutoCAD will display the preview in a window (Figure 11.023). Notice that the same multimedia buttons are available in the preview window, so you can see your walk through as you record it. You can also adjust your position in the preview using the slider rod, and you can adjust how you view the preview. (You'll find the visual styles you've already studied in the control box.)

You'll find animations created using AutoCAD defaults to be somewhat disappointing. Use the Animation Settings dialog box (Figure 11.024 – next page) to help spruce them up a bit. (Access the dialog box with the **Animation Settings**

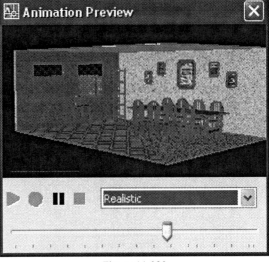

Figure 11.023

button 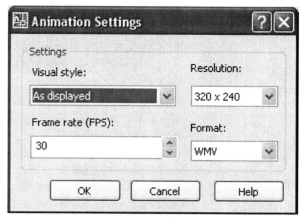 on the 3D Navigate control panel.)

Here you can adjust:

- The **Visual style** you'll use to create your animation – notice that you can use a rendered style.

- **Resolution** – higher makes a better picture but takes longer.

- **Frame rate** – again, higher makes a better picture but takes longer.

- The **Format** you'll save the file in (choose one that you know your client can use).

  o WMV – popular windows format; plays in the Media Player that comes with Windows.

Figure 11.024

  o MPG – good for web play, small size, also plays in the Windows Media Player.

  o AVI – older file type, much larger, also plays in the Windows Media Player.

  o MOV – Quicktime movie, player is downloadable and free, works on both IBM compatibles and Mac computers.

Let's create a simple walk-through before we look at the Super-Terrific-Automatic-Realistic (Star) Approach. (I suppose I could just call that the "other" way, but let's go with the Automatic approach to sound more professional.)

Do This: 11.6.1.1	A Simple Walk-Through

I. Be sure you're still in the *rendering project.dwg* file in the C:\Steps3D\Lesson11 folder.

II. Set the **Perspective** view current. (You must be in a perspective view to create a 3D walk-through or a 3D fly-by.)

III. Use the **Light Glyphs** toggle ▓ on the Lights control panel to hide the glyphs for this procedure.

IV. Follow these steps.

11.6.1.1: MAKING IT "REAL"

1. First, we'll do some set up. Open the Walk and Fly Settings dialog box 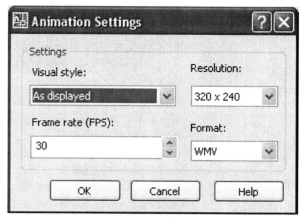 (Figure 11.021). (You'll find the button under the **Walk** flyout on the 3D Navigate control panel.)

   Command: *walkflysettings*

2. Create the setup shown.

   - Don't display the instruction window.
   - Set your **step size** to something closer to normal.
   - Accept the other defaults.

3. Close the Walk and Fly Settings dialog box [OK].

4. Open the Animation Settings dialog box .

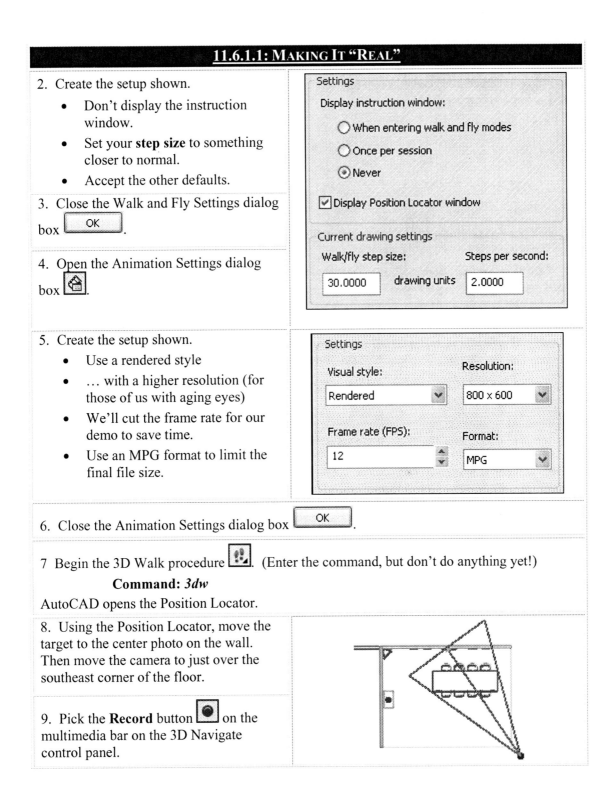

5. Create the setup shown.

   - Use a rendered style
   - … with a higher resolution (for those of us with aging eyes)
   - We'll cut the frame rate for our demo to save time.
   - Use an MPG format to limit the final file size.

6. Close the Animation Settings dialog box [OK].

7 Begin the 3D Walk procedure . (Enter the command, but don't do anything yet!)

   Command: *3dw*

AutoCAD opens the Position Locator.

8. Using the Position Locator, move the target to the center photo on the wall. Then move the camera to just over the southeast corner of the floor.

9. Pick the **Record** button on the multimedia bar on the 3D Navigate control panel.

305

10. Using the Position Locator, move the camera to the other southern corner of the room.	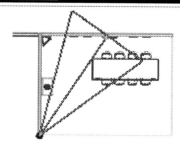

11. Pick the **Pause** button ⏸ on the multimedia bar on the 3D Navigate control panel.

12. Now pick the **Play** button ▶ and watch your animation. Experiment with the different visual styles during the preview.

13. You can save ⏹ the animation if you wish, but don't do it unless you have some time. (It took ~35 minutes on my system.) I've included the animation file as *First Animation* in the C:\Steps\Lesson\Steps3D\Lesson11 folder if you'd like to view it.

14. Use the ESCAPE key to close the procedure. Zoom previous to restore the drawing to its original view.

15. View the animation using Windows Media Player to get a better understanding of what you can do. There, you'll see the rendered animation. (It looks a lot better than the preview!)

Of course, you could have used arrow keys to establish a more interesting path, but you'll find a much easier approach when you create an animation using the automatic process we'll discuss next. Personally, I find it more versatile as well.

11.6.2	**The Automatic Approach – Motion Path Animation**

When you use the automatic approach – Motion Path Animations – you can create the path you wish your camera and/or target to follow. Then you just let AutoCAD handle the repositioning.

Access the Motion Path Animations dialog box (Figure 11.025) with the *AniPath* command or by selecting Motion Path Animations from the View pull down menu. The dialog box contains everything you'll need for this effort.

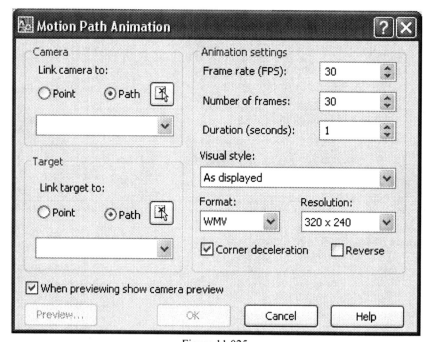

Figure 11.025

306

- Define your camera's location (**Point**) or **Path** in the **Camera** frame. Tell AutoCAD which you want to use for the camera with the radio buttons, then use the **Select Path / Pick Point** button to return to the drawing for your selection. A path can be a line, arc, elliptical arc, circle, polyline, 3D polyline, or spline. Once you've made your selection, AutoCAD will ask you to name the point or path. It then places the name in the control box for later selection if you need it again.

- You'll do the same thing for the **Target** that you did for the camera. Both can have paths if you wish the animation to move that way. Both cannot, however, have points. (Forgive the pun, but what would be the point? Nothing would move!)

- **Animation Settings** work together. Enter values into any two of the three numbered control boxes (**Frame rate**, **Number of frames**, and **Duration** of animation) and AutoCAD will fill out the third. You'll also set the **Visual Style** or rendering option here, as well as the **Format** of the file you wish to create and the **Resolution** of the animation. A check next to **Corner deceleration** slows the camera at the ends of the animation, while a check next to **Reverse** reverses the animation.

> Movies run at 24 frames per second (FPS); computer animations typically run at about 30 FPS. A frame rate of 12 isn't unusual, especially for web animations, but they can appear choppy. You can experiment with different rates to determine what works best for you, but be aware that experimenting with animation can be an absorbing and time-consuming task.

- With a check next to **When previewing show camera preview**, AutoCAD shows the same Animation Preview window (Figure 11.023) you saw in our last exercise as it creates the animation for you.

Once you've filled out the Motion Path Animation settings, pick the **OK** button to begin creating the animation.

> On my system, AutoCAD took just over an hour to complete the animation sequence in the following exercise. If you haven't that much time, read over the exercise and view the results (the *MP Animation.mpg* file in the C:\Steps3D\Lesson11 folder).

Do This: 11.6.2.1	Motion Path Animation

   I. Be sure you're still in the *rendering project.dwg* file in the C:\Steps3D\Lesson11 folder.
   II. Be sure the **Perspective** view is still current and that light glyphs are still toggled off.
   III. Thaw the **animation path** layer. The object you see is a spline I created to speed up the exercise. Normally, you'll create your own path.
   IV. Follow these steps.

11.6.2.1: MOTION PATH ANIMATION

1. Begin the command.

   Command: *anipath*

2. Create the setup shown in the following figure.
   - Select the spline for the **Camera Path** and accept the default name.
   - Your target should the center of the large photograph on the wall. Use OSNAPs! (You don't want to spend the time to create an animation to find it focused on the wrong target!)
   - Give it a reasonable frame rate for your animation. (For a client, you might want to

307

set the FPS at 24 – 30, but that isn't necessary for our movie.)

- Set the **Duration** to 10 seconds. (Any longer and you'd be here all day!)
- Use the **Presentation** rendering for a really nice show.
- Use the same 320 x 240 **Resolution**. It creates a smaller movie but doesn't take as long as larger imaging.
- Create an MPG to save on the size of the final movie.
- Finally, Use **Corner deceleration** to avoid sharp starts and stops.

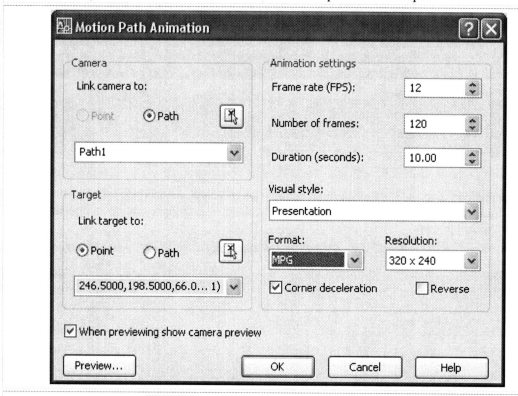

3. Begin the animation [OK]. (Call it, *My MP Animation* and save it to the C:\Steps3D\Lesson11 folder.) If you checked **When previewing show camera preview**, you can watch AutoCAD creating your animation. (Relax, this is going to take awhile.)

4. View your animation using Windows Media Player. (Let the video loop several times while you study your results.) Pay particular attention to the smoothness of the video (controlled by the **FPS** setting), the detail (**Visual Style**), and the size of the video on your screen (**Resolution**). Notice the wood grain pattern in the picture frame and table, and the reflection of the light on the photo and table top. These are the result of careful material controls. Finally, notice the difference when the camera moves outside and you see the photo through the window.

11.7	A Final Word

Well, I have to leave you here. We've come a long way together and you're ready to go out and make your fortune (sniffle), so I suppose I should leave you with some words of wisdom and some thoughts on where to go from here.

AutoCAD serves as a backbone – almost an operating system – for several other programs. These include many industry-specific applications, such as *Architectural Desktop*, *Mechanical Desktop*, and a host of third-party applications. You can continue your training into any of those.

If you wish to continue with the animation side of things, I highly recommend NewTek's *Lightwave*. It's hard to get better bang for your design bucks. Autodesk has a cool package it calls *Viz* (or *3D Studio Viz*), which is really cool and serves as a healthy start toward *3D Studio Max*. Use *Max* or *Lightwave* for your cartooning efforts. (I've found the support personnel for *Lightwave* to stand head-and-shoulders above those for Max.) Curious Labs makes an animation package – *Poser* – for those on a budget. I've been very pleased with it as a tool for creating cartoons for some of my other books.

Oh, yes; final words of wisdom. I've racked my brain and can't come up with anything better than the immortal words of Dr. Sidney Freedman (MASH psychiatrist). So, from an old piper to all you kids out there looking to get ahead in the world, here's my advice: *pull down your pants and slide on the ice.*

11.8   What Have We Learned?

Items covered in this lesson include:

- *Rendering commands and techniques*
    - *Assigning materials*
    - *Adding lights*
    - *Rendering*
    - *Creating animations*
- *Commands*
    - **Render**
    - **Materials**
    - **MaterialAttach**
    - **Light**
    - **GeographicLocation**
    - **SunProperties**
    - **RenderEnvironment**
    - **RPref**
    - **3DWalk**
    - **3DFly**
    - **WalkFlySettings**
    - **AniPath**

You've accomplished a great deal with the completion of Lesson 11. In this lesson, you've conquered the bridge between CAD operation and art. This is as far as AutoCAD goes toward the creation of design imagery. (Beyond this, you'll have to get some tools and build the objects!)

Let's tackle some final exercises before we say goodbye.

11.9   Exercises

1. Open the *emerald11.dwg* file in the C:\Steps3D\Lesson11 folder. My rendering appears here.

    1.1. Assign materials to the emerald and tabletop. (I used **Green Glass** and **Mirrored Glass**. I changed the transparency of the glass to a value of **0.5**.)

    1.2. Assign a background. (I used a two-color gradient.)

    1.3. Place a light(s). (I used a single-point light located at coordinates **18,4,9**.)

    1.4. Render the drawing.

    1.5. Repeat Steps 1.1 to 1.4 using a different set of assignments.

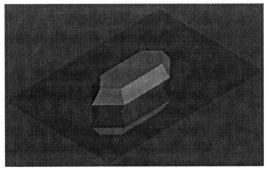
Emerald

2. Open the *caster11.dwg* file in the C:\Steps3D\Lesson11 folder. My rendering appears here.
   2.1. Assign materials to the objects. I used
       2.1.1. Copper (bearings)
       2.1.2. Concrete (flooring)
       2.1.3. Plastic (wheel)
       2.1.4. Steel (axle, spindle, bearing case)
   2.2. Place a light(s). (I used a single-point light with an intensity of **2** located at coordinates **0,-10,4**.)
   2.3. Render the drawing.
   2.4. Repeat Steps 2.1 through 2.3 using a different set of assignments.

Caster

3. Open the *pipe11.dwg* file in the C:\Steps3D\Lesson11 folder. My rendering appears here.
   3.1. Assign materials to the objects. I used colored plastic templates for the following materials:
       3.1.1. Steel (tank and nozzle)
       3.1.2. Copper (large pipe and fittings)
       3.1.3. Concrete (model platform)
       3.1.4. Steel (pipe rack)

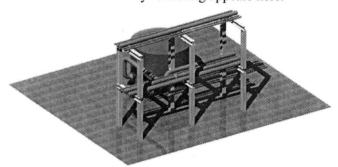

Pipe Model

   3.2. Place a light(s). (I used the sun. The unit is located in a plant in New Orleans. The graphic was created at 3:00 P.M. in late September.)
   3.3. Render the drawing.

4. Open the *train11.dwg* file in the C:\Steps3D\Lesson11 folder. My rendering appears here.
   4.1. Assign materials to objects. I used:
       4.1.1. Urethane (front of train)
       4.1.2. Urethane (cab, base, top of cattle guard)
       4.1.3. Urethane (wheels, smokestack, bell)
       4.1.4. Stucco (backdrop)
       4.1.5. Urethane (water tank, undercarriage, base of cattle guard, flag)
       4.1.6. Hickory (bell frame, box, flagpole)
   4.2. Assign a background. (I used a solid green background.)
   4.3. Place a light(s). (I used a single spotlight located at 0,-60,0, and a target location of **4,1,4.5**. Sun light intensity is **0.5**.)
   4.4. Render the drawing.

Train

You have quite a variety of exercises from which to choose in this lesson. Your next assignment is to return to any of the exercises you've completed in the text, assign materials, graphics, and lights, as you deem necessary and then render the drawings. Following are several exercises you can do. (If you haven't completed these drawings, they're available in the C:\Steps3D\Lesson11 folder.)

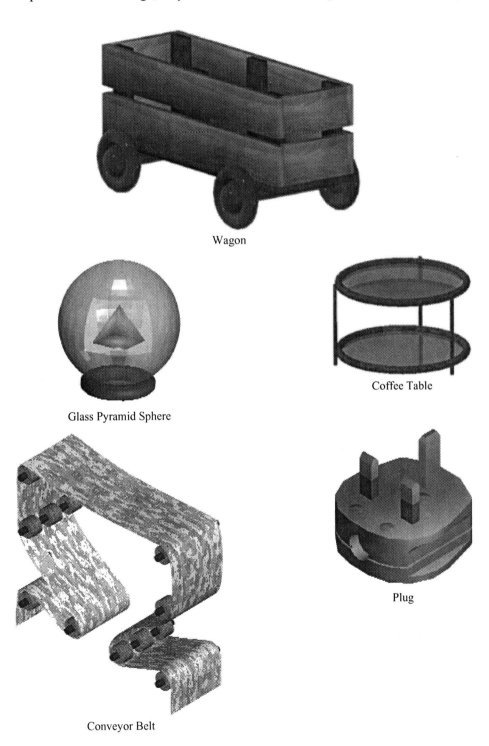

Wagon

Glass Pyramid Sphere

Coffee Table

Plug

Conveyor Belt

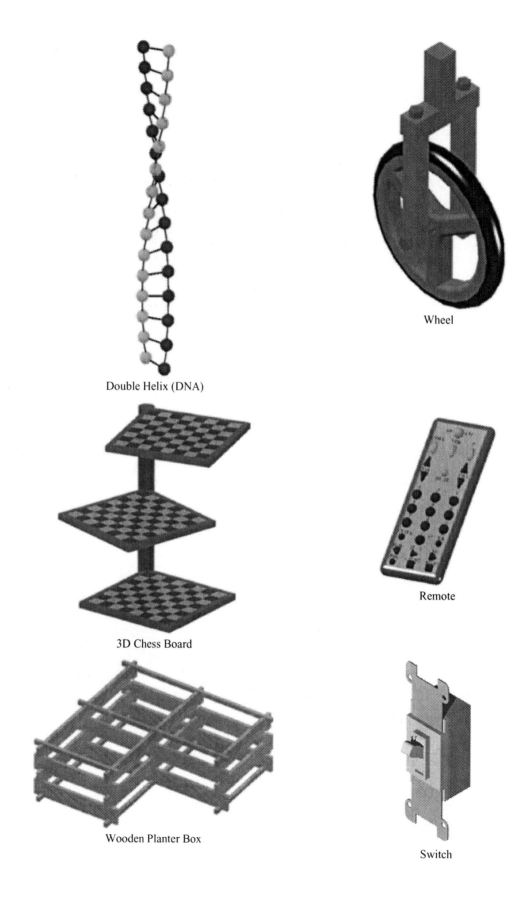

Double Helix (DNA)

Wheel

3D Chess Board

Remote

Wooden Planter Box

Switch

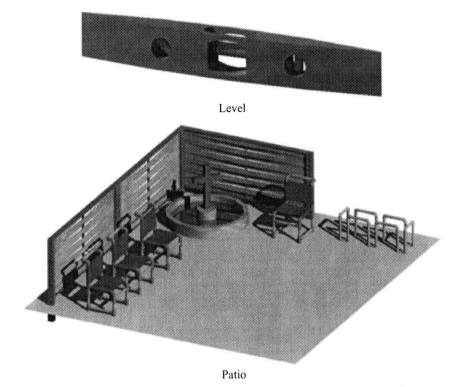

Level

Patio

18. Using other objects you've created in Lessons 4 through 11, redesign the patio scene. Some suggestions follow:

    18.1.   Replace the fountain with the planter box.

    18.2.   Place planters in the planter box.

    18.3.   Add a sidewalk or some decking.

19. Using other objects you've created, redesign the room we created in our rendering project. Some suggestions follow:

    19.1.   Replace the corner shelf with the standing lamp (Lesson 4).

    19.2.   Put the 3D chess set on the table.

    19.3.   Change the pictures on the wall.

11.10	For Web-Based Review Questions, visit: http://www.uneedcad.com/Files/06R11-3D.pdf

3D AutoCAD 2007: One Step at a Time

Appendix – A: Drawing Scales

SCALE (= 1')	SCALE FACTOR	DIMENSIONS OF DRAWING WHEN FINAL PLOT SIZE IS:				
		8½"x11"	11"x17"	17"x22"	22"x34"	24"x36"
1/16"	192	136'x176'	176'x272'	272'x352'	352'x544'	384'x576'
3/32"	128	90'8x117'4	117'4x181'4	181'4x234'8	234'8x362'8	256'x384'
1/8"	96	68'x88'	88'x136'	136'x176'	176'x272'	192'x288'
3/16"	64	45'4x58'8	58'8x90'8	90'8x117'4	117'4x181'4	128'x192'
¼"	48	34'x44'	44'x68'	68'x88'	88'x136'	96'x144'
3/8"	32	22'8x29'4	29'4x45'4	45'4x58'8	58'8x90'8	64'x96'
½"	24	17'x22'	22'x34'	34'x44'	44'x68'	48'x72'
¾"	16	11'4x14'8	14'8x22'8	22'8x29'4	29'4x45'4	32'x48'
1"	12	8'x6'11	11'x17'	17'x22'	22'x34'	24'x36'
1½"	8	5'8x7'4	7'4x11'4	11'4x14'8	14'8x22'8	16'x24'
3"	4	34"x44"	3'8x5'8	8'x6'11	7'4x11'4	8'x12'
(1" =)						
10'	120	85'x110'	110'x170'	170'x220'	220'x340'	240'x360'
20'	240	170'x220'	220'x340'	340'x440'	440'x680'	480'x720'
25'	300	212'6x275'	275'x425'	425'x550'	550'x850'	600'x900'
30'	360	255'x330'	330'x510'	510'x660'	660'x1020'	720'x1080'
40'	480	340'x440'	440'x680'	680'x880'	880'x1360'	960'x1440'
50'	600	425'x550'	550'x850'	850'x1100'	1100'x1700'	1200'x1800'
60'	720	510'x660'	660'x1020'	1020'x1320'	1320'x2040'	1440'x2160'
80'	960	680'x880'	880'x1360'	1360'x1760'	1760'x2720'	1920'x2880'
100'	1200	850'x1100'	1100'x1700'	1700'x2200'	2200'x3400'	2400'x3600'
200'	2400	1700'x2200'	2200'x3400'	3400'x4400'	4400'x6800'	4800'x7200'

Appendix – B: Project Drawings

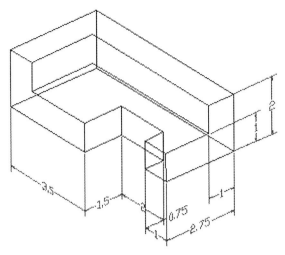

Figure B-1w

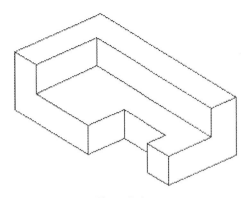

Figure B-1su

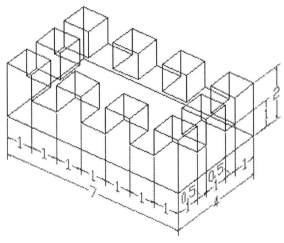

Figure B-2w

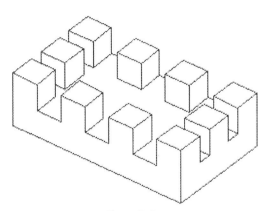

Figure B-2su

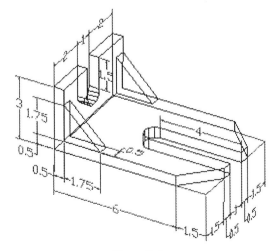

Figure B-3w

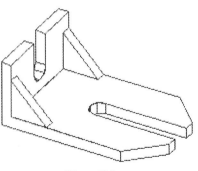

Figure B-3su

315

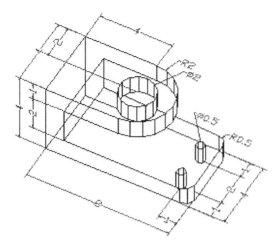

Figure B-4w

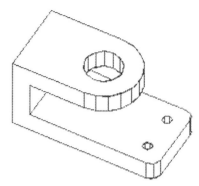

Figure B-4su

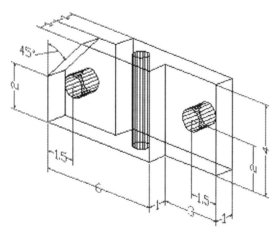

Figure B-5w

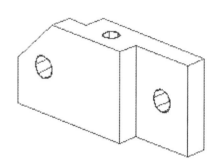

Figure B-5su

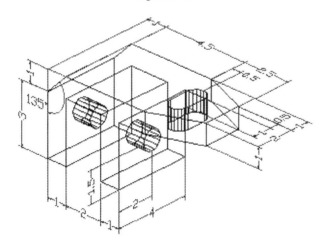

Figure B-6w

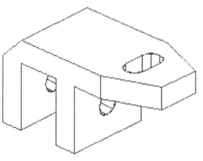

Figure B-6su

316

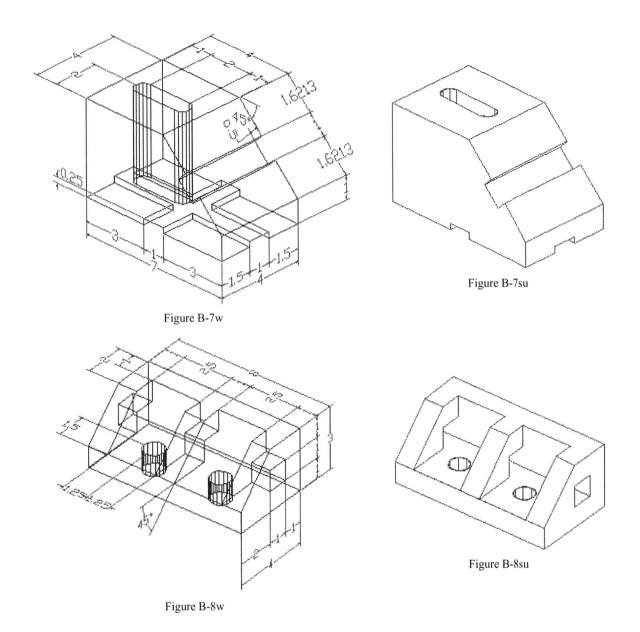

Figure B-7su

Figure B-7w

Figure B-8su

Figure B-8w

[Note: Appendix C has been replaced with web addresses for chapter review questions and their answers.]

Appendix – D: Additional Projects

Here are two drawings that might challenge you.
1. The pieces for Aloysius' Cabin can be found in C:\Steps3D\Lesson\Cabin. They include:

    1.1. *longlog.dwg*

    1.2. *medlog.dwg*

    1.3. *shortlog.dwg*

    1.4. *longhalflog.dwg*

    1.5. *medhalflog.dwg*

    1.6. *roof.dwg*

    1.7. *gable.dwg*

    1.8. *HS Logo.bmp*

2. The bookshelves are 7'-6" square x 11½" deep, with a ½" plywood back inserted into rabbets on the sides. Use your own spacing for the internal shelves.

3. Search the web for additional projects. Try to draw some of them. I used keywords like "3D render" and "solid model" and found these:

    3.1. http://www.blackline.com/drafting/drawings/buildings.htm [This is a good site to see some dwf files.]

    3.2. http://www.pleione.com/pithouse/ [This site has some cool renderings.]

    3.3. http://www.gsmmedia.com/cad/renderings.html [Fair renderings.]

    3.4. http://www.3drender.com/ [renderings from the technical director at Pixar – not necessarily AutoCAD, but most of these things can be done in AutoCAD]

    3.5. http://www.cadalyst.net/ [leading industry mag]

    3.6. http://www.sonic.net/~odin/sfsu/autocad_level_3d_examples.htm

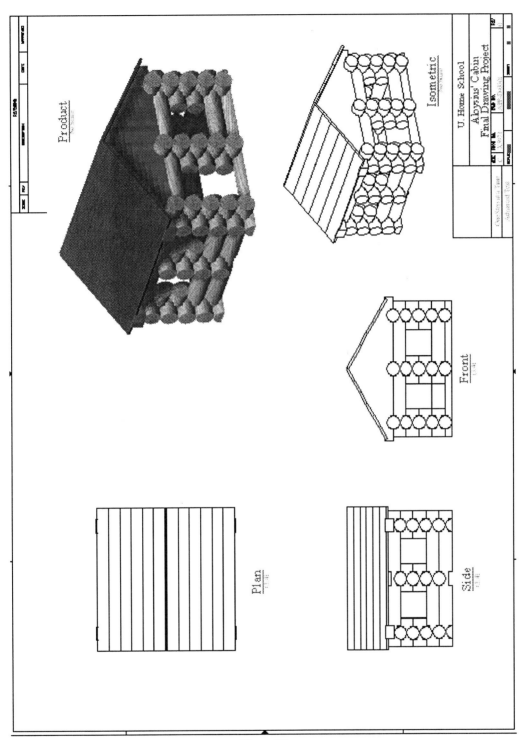

Figure D1

Figure D2

Printed in the United States
97894LV00004B/8/A

9 780976 588887